THE BEST OF
MALAYSIAN COOKING

MRS LEONG YEE SOO

Times Books International
Singapore • Kuala Lumpur

All photographs by Yim Chee Peng except those on pages 31, 35, 69, 119, 125, 139, 143, 149, 153, 156, 159, 171, 191, 205, 233 and 239 which are by Mun Dan Wong.

First published in 1991
Reprinted 1992, 1994, 1996, 2000

© 1991 TIMES EDITIONS PTE LTD
© 2000 TIMES MEDIA PRIVATE LIMITED

Published by Times Books International
an imprint of Times Media Private Limited

Times Centre, 1 New Industrial Road
Singapore 536196
Fax: (65) 2854871 Tel: (65) 2848844
E-mail: te@corp.tpl.com.sg
Online bookstore: http://www.timesone.com.sg/te

Times Subang
Lot 46, Subang Hi-Tech Industrial Park
Batu Tiga, 40000 Shah Alam
Selangor Darul Ehsan, Malaysia
Fax & Tel: (603) 7363517
E-mail: cchong@tpg.com.my

Printed by Times Offset (M) Sdn Bhd, Malaysia

ISBN 981 204 261 X

Foreword

Mrs Leong Yee Soo belonged to the generation of Straits 'nonyas' to whom good cuisine is an article of faith and a personal challenge.

Having spent the major part of her life in thinking, talking, experimenting and teaching food preparation, Mrs Leong felt that she could contribute nothing better to society than to pass on the results of her research and experience. She did regret that the fine art of cooking is fast dying out with women taking up jobs and with instant foods, frozen dinners, snack bars and take-aways so much in evidence.

Realising the role of woman in this nuclear age, Mrs Leong planned her meals with a keen eye on the cost and quality of ingredients, time in preparation, calorie content, food value, etc. She also summoned to her aid modern kitchen equiptment and had so simplified her procedure that dabbling in the kitchen can be a source of fun.

The recipes will speak for themselves. There are household staples that have fortified the Oriental home for generations, meals for large and small groups, young and old, in and out of doors, titbits, snatched meals and feasts for special occasions.

I would recommend this book of tested recipes for every kitchen shelf, for not only is wholesome food conducive to health and happiness, but, like "mother's cooking", it will be affectionately remembered and will go a long way towards fostering goodwill and happy relationships.

Mrs Goh Kok Kee
J.P., M.B.E.

Author's Acknowledgements

My sincere thanks go to Mrs. Rosa Lee, Mrs. Dorothy Norris, Miss Marie Choo, and Miss Patricia Lim who, by their co-operation and inspiring ideas, have made this book possible.

My thanks are due also to Mrs. Dinah Sharif, Miss Iris Kng, Miss Chau Mei Po, Mrs. Irene Oei, and Miss Monica Funk who gave up so much of their precious time in helping me type the recipes.

I would also like to thank all those who have been so helpful in the preparation and arrangement of the food and cakes for the photography sessions.

CONTENTS

Foreword 1
Acknowledgements 1
Culinary Terms 6
Helpful Hints 7

Hawker Favourites
Char Kway Teow 12
Fried Spring Chicken 12
Hae Mee 14
Ju Her Eng Chye 15
Kon Loh Mee 15
Laksa Lemak 16
Laksa Penang 17
Loh Kai Yik 18
Loh Mee 19
Mee Goreng 20
Mee Rebus 21
Mee Siam 22
Murtabak 24
Ngoh Hiang 24
Otak-Otak Panggang 25
Otak-Otak Puteh 25
Poh Pia 26
Satay Chelop 27
Satay 28
Yong Tau Fu 30

Nonya Specialities
Assam Gulai 34
Ayam Buah Keluak 34
Ayam Goreng Assam 36
Ayam Kleo 36
Ayam Merah 38
Ayam Risa Risa 38
Ayam Sioh 39
Ayam Tempra 39
Babi Assam 40
Babi Chin 40
Babi Pong Tay 42
Buah Paya Masak Titek 42
Bak Wan Kepiting 43
Chap Chye Masak Titek 44
Goreng Ikan Terubok 44
Hati Babi Bungkus 45
Ikan Masak Assam Pekat 45
Itek Tim 46
Kari Ayam 46

Pong Tauhu 47
Satay Babi 47
Sayor Nanka Masak Lemak 48
Tauhu Masak Titek 49
Udang Kuah Pedas Nanas 49

Porridge and Rice
Kai Chok 52
Chicken Rice 53
Flavoured Chicken Rice 54
Fried Rice 54
Nasi Kuning 54
Nasi Lemak Kuning 55
Nasi Briani Ayam 56
Nasi Pilau 58
Nasi Ulam 58
Pineapple Rice 59
Steamed Glutinous Rice 59

Noodles
Birthday Noodles, Nonya Style 62
Crispy Noodles with Prawns 63
Beef Kway Teow 64
Fried Noodles 64
Hokien Mee 65
Kai See Ho Fun 66
Nonya Mahmee 67
Teochew Kway Teow 67

Claypot Dishes
Beef Shin With Mixed Vegetables 70
Braised Beef Brisket 70
Chicken 71
Fish Head 71
Seafood 72
Tofu and Crab Meat 73
Tofu with Pork and Prawns 73

Soups
Bak Kut Teh 76
Chicken and Corn 76
Chicken Macaroni 77
Hot and Sour 77
Shark's Fin Soup 78
Sop Kambing 78
Soto Ayam 79
Thom Yam Soup 79

Pork and Mutton
Barbecued Spareribs 82

Braised Pork with Crunchy Black Fungus 82
Braised Pork in Soya Sauce 83
Buns for Braised Pork 83
Roast Pork Strips (Char Siew) 84
Sweet and Sour Pork Ribs 84
Braised Mutton Ribs 85
Mutton in Tomato Curry 85

Beef
Beef Curry 88
Dry Beef Curry 88
Beef Brisket 89
Beef Braised in Dark Soya Sauce 89
Beef with Celery 90
Chinese Beef Steak 90
Fillet Steak 92
Ox Tail Stew 92

Poultry
Abalone Chicken 96
Braised Ginger Chicken 96
Chicken Almond Curry 97
Chicken Coconut Curry 97
Chicken Bon Bon 98
Chicken Curry Devil 99
Chicken fried with Dried Red Chillies 99
Chicken in the Basket 100
Lemon Curried Chicken 101
Paper-Wrapped Chicken 101
Roast Turkey with Mince Pork and
    Rice Filling 102
Salt-Baked Chicken 102
Seven-Minute Crispy Chicken 104
Steamed Stuffed Duck 104
Stew 105
Turmeric Chicken 105

Seafood
Braised Grouper with Black Soya
    Bean Sauce 108
Baked Crabs 108
Crabs in Spicy Soya Bean Paste 109
Crabs in Tomato Chilli Sauce 109
Dry Fish Curry 110
Fish Head Curry 111
Ikan Masak Kuah Lada 111
Rendang Ikan 112
Steamed Pomfret 112
Chilli Prawns 114
Glassy Prawns 114
Prawns in Soya Sauce 114
Sweet Sour Prawns 115
Tempura Prawns 115

Crayfish Mornay 116
Chilli Cuttlefish 116
Stuffed Cuttlefish Soup 117
Spicy Cockles 117

Starters and Salads
Chinese Rojak 120
Indian Rojak 120, 121
Cold Dish Salad 122
Gado Gado 123
Nonya Salad 123
Shredded Duck and Fruit Salad 124
Yue Sung 124

Vegetarian Greens
Bean Sprouts fried with Crispy
    Salted Fish 128
Cauliflower and Long Beans in
    Creamy Sauce 128
Chinese Mustard with Abalone 129
Chop Suey 129
Egg Plant with Pork and Prawns 130
Egg Plant in Spicy Sauce 130
Loh Hon Chye 131
Long Beans with Minced Meat 131
Mustard with Crab Meat Sauce 132
Rebong Masak Lemak 132
Vegetarian Spring Rolls 133
Vegetarian Beehoon 134
Vegetarian Curry 134

Special Combinations
Kuey Chap 138
Nasi Lemak 138, 140, 141
Nasi Padang 142, 144
Nasi Lontong 146, 147
Nasi Minyak 148, 150, 151
Taiwan Porridge 152, 154, 155
Roti Jala 156

Dim Sum
Bak Pow 160
Char Siew Pow 160
Fried Wan Tan 161
Har Kow 161
Hum Sui Kok 162
Kee Chang 162
Prawn Fritters 163
Kueh Chang Babi 164
Siew Mai 166
Steamed Beef Balls 166
Stuffed Mushrooms 167
Yam Puff 167
Tan Tart 168

Savoury Snacks

Beef Curry Puffs	172
Bun Susi	173
Cheese Straws	174
Chee Cheong Fun	174
Cheesey Beef Patties	175
Chwee Kuey	175
Kueh Pie Tee	176
Lemper Ayam	177
Minced Pork and Prawn Toast	178
Morokoo	178
Prawn Sambal Sandwiches	178
Rissoles	179
Pork Rolls	180
Spicy Prawn Rolls	180
Soon Kuey	181
Steamed Fish and Milk Sauce Sandwiches	181

Sambals, Pickles and Sauces

Chilli Sauce — Hot	184
Chilli Sauce — Sweet	184
Chilli Garam Paste	185
Dried Chilli Paste	185
Garam Assam Paste	185
Luak Chye	186
Rempah Sambal Udang	186
Salt Fish Sambal	187
Sambal Belimbing	187
Sambal Tempe Udang	188
Sambal Tumis	188
Sambal Lengkong	189
Sambal Udang Kering Goreng	189

Nonya Kueh

Apom Berkuah	192
Abok-Abok Sago	193
Kueh Bangket	193
Kueh Bengka Ambon	194
Kueh Bengka Ubi Kayu	194
Kueh Bolu	195
Savory Kueh Bolu	195
Kueh Dadar	196
Kueh Khoo	197
Kueh Ko Chee	198
Kueh Ko Swee	198
Kueh Lapis Batavia	199
Kueh Lapis Almond	200
Kueh Lapis Beras	200
Kueh Lompang	201
Kueh Pulot Bengka	201
Kueh Lopis	202
Kueh Pisang	202

Kueh Sarlat	203
Kueh Talam Pandan	204
Jemput-Jemput	204
Onde Onde	206
Pulot Panggang	206
Pulot Tarpay	207
Pulot Tartar	208
Sar-sargon	209
Seray-kaya	209

Desserts

Agar-Agar Cordial	212
Agar-Agar Delight	212
Agar-Agar Talam	213
Au Nee	213
Almond Creme	214
Almond Jelly	214
Bubor Terigu	214
Bubor Cha Cha	215
Chendol	216
Green Beans with Pearl Sago	217
Groundnut Creme	217
Kueh Kuria	218
Lek-Tow-Suan	218
Lotus Seed Fluff	219
Len-Chee-Suan	219
Lotus Seed Paste Mooncakes	220
Mock Pomegranate	222
Pearl Sago with Mixed Fruit	223
Red Beans with Coconut Creme Topping	223
Sago Pudding	224
Sweet Red Bean and Lotus Seed Soup	224
Sweet Lotus Seeds and Dried Longan Soup	225

Cakes

Banana Cake	228
Butter Cake	228
Cheesecake	229
No Bake Lemon Cheesecake	229
Chocolate Chiffon Cake	230
Coffee Walnut Cake	230
Fruit Cake	231
Ginger Cake	231
Lemon Sponge Cake	232
Pandan Chiffon Cake	232
Pound Cake	234
Rose Marie Cake	234
Semolina Cake	234
Sponge Sandwich	235
Super Light Sponge Sandwich	235

Sultana Cake   236
Swiss Roll   236
Walnut Cake   236
White Christmas   237

Biscuits, Cookies and Pastries
Special Almond Biscuits   240
Almond Raisin Rock Cookies   240
Cat's Tongues   241
Cheese Cookies   241
Chocolate Eclairs/Cream Puffs   242
Chocolate Butter Icing   242
Custard Tartlets   243
Fruit Scones   243
Melting Moments   243
Pineapple-Shaped Tarts   244
Pineapple 'Open' Tarts   246
Sponge Fingers   246
Spritches Butter Biscuits   247
Sujee Biscuits   247
Sweet Corn Fritters   247

List of Some Ingredients   249
Kitchen Equipment   250
Index   251

Weights & Measures

American measuring spoons are used in this book. All measures are level except when stated. British measuring spoons are slightly bigger in capacity. Use a standard measuring jug for fluid measurement.

Metric equivalents are approximate.

Mass		
1 oz	—	30 g
2 oz	—	55 g
3 oz	—	85 g
4 oz	—	115 g
5 oz	—	140 g
6 oz	—	170 g
7 oz	—	200 g
8 oz	—	225 g
9 oz	—	255 g
10 oz	—	285 g
11 oz	—	310 g
12 oz	—	340 g
13 oz	—	370 g
14 oz	—	395 g
15 oz	—	425 g
16 oz (1 lb)	—	455 g
2 lb	—	905 g
3 lb	—	1.4 kg
4 lb	—	1.8 kg

Capacity		
1 fl oz	—	30 ml
4 fl oz	—	115 ml
8 fl oz	—	225 ml
16 fl oz	—	455 ml

Temperature		
°F	Gas Regulo	°C
225	1	105
250	2	120
275	3	135
300	4	150
325	5	165
350	6	175
375	7	190
400	8	205
425	9	220
450	10	230

Pre-heat oven 15 minutes before use.

Culinary Terms

Bake:
To cook in dry heat, usually in an oven.

Barbecue:
To roast or broil whole such as a pig or fowl, usually on a revolving frame over coals. To cook slices of marinated meat over a coal fire.

Baste:
To pour melted fat, dripping or sauce over roasting food in order to moisten.

Beat:
A quick regular motion that lifts a mixture over and over to make it smooth and to introduce air.

Blanch:
(i) Whiten, i.e., cover with cold water, bring to the boil, strain and remove skins as for almonds.
(ii) To pour boiling water over food then drain and rinse with cold water.

Blend:
Mix to a smooth paste with a little cold or hot liquid.

Boil:
To cook rapidly in liquid over very high heat till bubbles rise continually.

Braise:
To cook meat in fat, then simmer in a covered saucepan or dish with a small amount of water till tender.

Caramelize:
To heat dry sugar or foods containing sugar till light brown.

Dredge:
To sprinkle with flour or sugar.

Fold in:
To mix cake mixture by lifting a part of the batter from the bottom through the rest of the mixture without releasing air bubbles.

Garnish:
To decorate savoury food with sprigs of parsley, sliced lemon wedges, cooked or uncooked vegetables, shallots, grated yolk of egg and cheese, etc.

Glaze:
To brush over pastries, bread, etc. with a liquid such as eggs, milk or water and sugar to improve the appearance.

Grill:
To cook by direct heat on a grill iron or under a red hot grill; used for small tender pieces of meat, fish, etc.

Knead:
To mix by hand or electric dough hook. To press, fold and stretch. Usually applied to dough.

Marinate:
To give flavour to meats, salads, etc. by soaking in a sauce.

Mince:
To chop very finely.

Par-boil:
To boil raw food until partially cooked as for carrots, cauliflower, cabbage, etc.

Roast:
To cook with a little fat in a hot oven. Fat from the baking tin is used to baste the meat or poultry, from time to time.

Score:
To cut very lightly or to mark with lines before cooking. Applied to roast pork, fish, egg plant.

Simmer:
To cook just below boiling point. Small bubbles rise occasionally to the surface of the liquid.

Stew:
To cook slowly until tender in just sufficient liquid to cover the food. A stew may be cooked in a covered saucepan or casserole, on a hot plate or in the oven.

Helpful Hints

Seasoning:

The salt used in these recipes is local fine salt and not the fine table salt. Fine table salt is used mostly in Western cakes where it can be sifted together with the flour. As table salt is finer, it is more saltish than the local fine salt. So measure less salt if you use fine table salt. Use your discretion when seasoning with salt, sugar, chilli, or tamarind; season to your own taste. There is no hard and fast rule for seasoning food. However, for cakes, one must be precise and follow the recipe to get the best results. Msg in recipes refers to monosodium glutamate. As a substitute, chicken stock may be used. Use 1 chicken cube for 1 teaspoon msg.

Oil and fats:

To get the best results, when cooking Chinese dishes especially, use an equal portion of both lard and oil. It gives the dish a special fragrance. In recipes where it is specified that lard is preferable to oil, use lard in order to get its distinct flavour.

For deep-frying, always use cither refined deodorised coconut oil, palm cooking oil or corn oil. Do not use olive oil.

Substitutes:

The purplish variety of onion is a good substitute for shallots. If fresh ginger, lemon grass and galangal are not easily available, use the powdered form. It is always advisable to use powdered turmeric. Almonds, cashew nuts, Brazil nuts or macadamia nuts can be used if candlenuts are not available.

Thickening:

Thickening for Chinese dishes means to thicken the gravy so as to coat the food rather than have the gravy running over the serving plate. Corn flour in the recipes refers to tapioca flour sold in the local markets. It is also known as sago flour (refined quality, and not the type used to starch clothes).

Selecting meat, poultry and seafood:

Pork:
Pork should be pink, the fat very white, and the skin thin.

Beef:
Choose meat that is light red and the cross-grain smooth and fine. The same applies to mutton. Do not buy dark-coloured meat with fat that is yellow.

Chicken:
Fresh local chickens have a much better taste and flavour than frozen ones. Frozen chicken is more suitable for roasting, frying or grilling. When buying a local chicken, select one with a white, smooth skin. The tip of the breastbone should be soft and pliable when pressed with the thumb.

Duck:
Select as for chicken. The smaller ones are mostly used for soups and the larger ducks for roasting or braising.

Fish:
When buying fish, first of all make sure that the flesh is firm to the touch. The eyes should be shiny, the gills blood-red and the scales silvery white. Squeezing lemon juice over fish will whiten it and keep it firm when boiling or steaming.

Mix tamarind, salt and some sugar to marinate fish for ½ hour before cooking curries or tamarind dishes.

Prawns:
Fresh prawns are firm to the touch, with shiny shells. The head is attached fast to the body. Avoid buying prawns with heads loosely hanging on.

Cuttlefish:
When cuttlefish is very fresh, the body is well-rounded, firm and shiny. The head is stuck fast to the body and the ink pouch in the stomach is firmly attached.

To fry shallots:

Slice shallots thinly and dip in salt water for a while. Rinse and drain well. Scatter sliced shallots on to absorbent paper to dry or roll up in a tea towel for ½ hour. Heat oil for deep-frying till smoking hot. Add the sliced shallots and stir-fry over high heat till shallots turn light brown. Reduce the heat and keep stirring all the time until the shallots are light golden brown. Remove at once with a wire sieve to drain the oil and scatter on to absorbent paper to cool. Keep in a clean, dry bottle immediately. The shallots keep crisp for months in an airtight bottle.

To fry pounded garlic:

Pound garlic or use an electric mincer to mince the garlic. Place garlic in a wire sieve and immerse in salt water. Drain. Use a thin piece of muslin to squeeze out the water. Heat an iron wok (kuali). Heat oil for deep-frying till smoking hot. Put the garlic in the wok and stir-fry till it turns light brown. Reduce the heat to very low and keep stirring till garlic is light golden brown. Remove at once with a wire sieve and scatter on to absorbent paper. Cool and store as for crispy shallots.

Note:
The crispy shallots and garlic do not retain so much oil when the heat is increased just before removing from wok.

To cook rice:

Wash rice till water runs clear. Use 55 ml (2 fl oz) of water for each 30 g (1 oz) of rice. For 455 g (16 oz) of rice, use between 795-910 ml (28-32 fl oz) water, depending on the quality of the rice. Boil the rice till the water evaporates, leaving steam holes when dry. Reduce heat to low and cook for a further ½ hour. 455 g (16 oz) of rice is sufficient for 8 servings.

To cook meat:

Pork chops should be cooked in moderate heat in a very hot pan or grilled under a hot grill. This will seal in the meat juices. Brown on both sides, turning over twice; lower to medium heat till done, about 15-20 minutes. Cut off the rind and snip the fat in two or three places to prevent bacon from curling during frying.

Fillet steak is the best and most tender of meat cuts; next comes sirloin, scotch, porterhouse, rump and minute steak. Marinating a steak before cooking not only gives it a better flavour but also helps to make it tender. Minute steak, however, is best grilled or fried without marinating.

To cook vegetables:

1. To fry leafy vegetables, separate the leaves from the stalk. The stalks should be placed in the pan together with any other ingredients and cooked first. Stir-fry for a minute or so before adding the leaves.

2. (a) To boil and blanch vegetables, boil a sauce-pan of water over very high heat. When the water is boiling, add some salt, sugar and a tablespoonful of oil.

   (b) Add the stalks, cook for ½ minute and then add the leaves. Cook for another ½ minute. Use a wire ladle to remove the vegetables and drain in a colander.

   (c) Rinse under a running tap and drain well before use.

   (d) Vegetables like long beans and cabbage should be cooked for 5-7 minutes only, to retain their sweetness and crispness.

   (e) When boiling bean sprouts it is important to place them in boiling water for 1 minute. Do not add any oil. Remove and drain with a wire ladle. Transfer to a basin of cold water and soak for 10 minutes or till cold. Spread thinly in a colander till ready for use. The bean sprouts will then keep without 'souring'.

Frying:

1. The pan should be very hot before you pour in the oil; but do not make the oil smoking hot. To get the best results when frying vegetables:-

   (a) Use an iron wok (kuali) as it can take and retain extreme heat, which is most important.

   (b) Add the oil to a smoking hot wok. This prevents food from sticking to the bottom. But overheated fat or oil turns bitter and loses its fine flavour.

2. (a) For deep-frying, the oil must be smoky, that is, when a faint haze of smoke rises from the oil. It is then ready for frying.

   (b) When deep-frying in large quantities, put enough food in the pan and keep the oil boiling all the time.

   (c) Bring the fat back to smoking hot each time you put in food to be fried.

   (d) When frying large pieces of meat or a whole chicken, the heat must be very high for the first 5 minutes to seal in the juices, then lower for the rest of the cooking time so as to give the meat or chicken a nice golden colour as well as to let it be cooked right through.

3. (a) After frying food that is coated with flour or breadcrumbs [this also seals in the meat juices], filter the oil through a wire sieve lined thinly with cotton wool. The oil will come clean of sediments.

   (b) Add more fresh oil to the strained oil for future use.

4. Oil that has been used to deep-fry fish and prawns should be kept separately for future use, i.e., for cooking fish and prawns only.

5. You may clarify hot oil by squeezing some lemon juice on to it but remember to turn off the heat first. Strain and store for future use.

6. Butter will not take intense heat when frying; so put in some oil before the butter.

7. Dust food with seasoned flour before coating with or dipping in batter for frying.

The coconut:

Coconut referred to in all recipes is fresh coconut unless specified. Coconut is used mainly for its rich milky juice so necessary for Asian dishes like curries, sambals and cakes.

Grated white coconut is coconut that is grated after the brown skin has been removed. This form is required for certain nonya kueh.

Use a piece of muslin to squeeze small handfuls of grated coconut so as to get more milk. No 1 milk is got by squeezing the grated coconut without adding water. When water is added to the grated coconut after the first squeeze, the milky liquid extracted is called No 2 milk.

Lemon grass:

Lemon grass gives a pleasant fragrance to cooked dishes. Use lemon rind as a substitute only when this is not available. The fragrance comes from the end of the stalk, about 7 cm (3 in) from the root end. The green outer layer is usually taken off before use. To "bruise" lemon grass, bash with the flat surface of a cleaver or chopper.

Candlenuts:

If unavailable, use almonds, cashew nuts, Brazil nuts or macadamia nuts. Their nutty flavour is the nearest to the candlenut.

Turmeric:

Fresh turmeric is usually used for 'nonya' dishes for its flavour and colour. Oriental dishes, especially curries, need dry turmeric or turmeric powder.

Lard:

The oil extracted from pork fat after it has been fried is called lard. Dice the pork fat before frying. Do not overburn the cubes otherwise the oil extracted will be dark and bitter. Unlike butter or margarine, lard can take intense heat without burning so it is most suitable for food that has to be cooked over high heat.

Screw pine leaves:

These give a special fragrance. There is no substitute. Before tying into a knot, tear lengthwise to get the strongest fragrance.

Hawker Favourites

Char Kway Teow

Fried Spring Chicken

Hae Mee

Ju Her Eng Chye

Kon Loh Mee

Laksa Lemak

Laksa Penang

Loh Kai Yik

Loh Mee

Mee Goreng

Mee Rebus

Mee Siam

Murtabak

Ngoh Hiang

Otak-Otak Panggang

Otak-Otak Puteh

Poh Pia

Satay Chelop

Satay

Yong Tau Fu

Hae Mee

CHAR KWAY TEOW
(FRIED RICE NOODLES)

INGREDIENTS

6 tablespoons water
1 teaspoon salt } A
½ teaspoon msg

Lard for frying
2 teaspoons pounded garlic
310 g (11 oz) bean sprouts, washed and drained
310 g (11 oz) flat rice noodles (kway teow)
2 tablespoons dark soya sauce
4 eggs
Chilli sauce (see recipe)
1 pair of Chinese sausages, sliced thinly and fried
115 g (4 oz) cockles, shelled
55 g (2 oz) chives, cut into 5 cm (2 in) lengths
1–2 tablespoons sweet thick black sauce

METHOD

1. Mix **A** in a bowl.
2. Heat large wok till smoking hot. Put in 4 tablespoons lard and fry garlic till light brown. Add bean sprouts and rice noodles. Sprinkle **A** mixture and dark soya sauce and stir-fry for ½ minute.
3. Push rice noodle mixture to one side of wok. Add 4 tablespoons lard and scramble eggs.
4. Stir in scrambled eggs and mix well with noodles.
5. Pour in chilli sauce, according to taste.
6. Add sausages, and stir-fry for another minute, adding some lard to sides of wok.
7. Leave space in centre of noodles to put in cockles. Cover cockles with mixture, add chives and sweet thick black sauce. Toss for ½ minute and serve on a large serving plate.

Note:
Fry rice noodles in two parts if wok is not large enough. Fry over a very high heat to keep the bean sprouts crunchy.

Lard is preferable to groundnut oil.

Chilli Sauce:
285 g (10 oz) liquidized chilli
340 ml (12 fl oz) water
1½ tablespoons salt
1 tablespoon sugar } A
1 teaspoon msg
1 teaspoon pepper

1 tablespoon lard
1 tablespoon chopped garlic
¾ teaspoon shrimp paste, crumbled

METHOD

1. Heat lard in a small saucepan and fry garlic and shrimp paste till brown.
2. Add **A** and bring to boil.
3. Boil gently for further 5 minutes.
4. Cool and use as required.

Note:
Cool the chilli sauce before pouring it into a plastic container to store in the freezer.

FRIED SPRING CHICKEN

INGREDIENTS

115 g (4 oz) sugar
55 ml (2 fl oz) dark soya sauce
55 ml (2 fl oz) light soya sauce
2 tablespoons wine or sherry
6 cloves
2 tablespoons honey
1 teaspoon msg } A
1 teaspoon salt
1 teaspoon five-spice powder
2.5 cm (1 in) piece cinnamon bark
1 teaspoon sesame oil

4 spring chickens, whole, each weighing 455 g (1 lb)
Oil for deep-frying

METHOD

1. Mix **A** in a deep saucepan to marinate the chickens for 2 hours.
2. Drain the chickens.
3. Boil marinade for 10 minutes. Put in chickens and boil in 570 ml (20 fl oz) water for another 7 minutes.
4. Drain chickens in a colander.
5. Heat oil in wok till smoky hot. Deep-fry two chickens for 2 minutes. Lower the heat a little and fry till golden brown (about 7–10 minutes).
6. Repeat process with the other two chickens.

Char Kway Teow

HAE MEE
(PRAWN MEE SOUP)

INGREDIENTS

625 g (22 oz) medium-sized prawns
170 g (6 oz) pork fat
  2 tablespoons oil

  4.5 litres (8 pints) water
625 g (22 oz) pork ribs, cut into pieces
  1 pig's tail, cut into pieces
310 g (11 oz) lean pork
  2 teaspoons salt
  2 teaspoons sugar   **A**
  2 teaspoons msg
  1 tablespoon peppercorns
  2 tablespoons light soya sauce
  2 teaspoons dark soya sauce

  1 tablespoon crispy shallots★
455 g (16 oz) bean sprouts
310 g (11 oz) water convolvulus, cut into long
    pieces
625 g (22 oz) fresh yellow noodles
310 g (11 oz) rice vermicelli, scalded

METHOD

1. Wash and drain prawns. Remove heads and keep aside.

2. Cut pork fat into small cubes and fry in pan till brown. Remove to a bowl.

3. Stir-fry prawn heads with 2 tablespoons oil for five minutes till colour turns red. Set aside in a bowl, for soup.

4. Cook unshelled prawns for 2 minutes in basin with 4.5 litres water. Remove prawns, shell and slice into halves, lengthwise.

5. Return prawn shells to saucepan, add **A** and prawn heads. Cook over a very high heat for 10 minutes. Reduce heat to low and let soup simmer for 1–1½ hours.

6. Strain soup. Return pork ribs and tail to soup.

7. Slice lean pork and set aside.

Garnish:
55 g (2 oz) crispy shallots
    Lard
    Crispy cubed pork fat
    Pepper
  5 red chillies, sliced thinly
  5 green chillies, sliced thinly
    Light soya sauce

To serve:
1. Boil a saucepan of water.

2. Dip a handful of bean sprouts, water convolvulus, noodles, and rice vermicelli in the boiling water, using a wire-mesh ladle. Drain and place in bowl.

3. Add boiling soup and a few pieces of pork ribs, tail, sliced lean pork and sliced prawns to each bowl.

4. Garnish with crispy shallots, lard-oil and crispy fat cubes. Sprinkle with pepper. Serve with sliced chillies and light soya sauce.

Note:
Only very fresh prawns make a sweet soup.
★For crispy shallots, see "Helpful Hints".

(12 servings)

JU HER ENG CHYE
(CUTTLEFISH SALAD)

INGREDIENTS

225 g (8 oz) processed cuttlefish
55 g (2 oz) processed jellyfish
6 pieces fried soya bean cakes
285 g (10 oz) young water convolvulus
2 tablespoons toasted sesame seeds

Sauce Ingredients:
(*Mix together*)
4-6 tablespoons chilli sauce
3 tablespoons Hoisin sauce
1 tablespoon lime juice
1 tablespoon peanut oil
½ teaspoon sesame oil

METHOD

1. Cut cuttlefish into thick slices.

2. Cut processed jellyfish into thin slices.

3. Toast fried soya bean cakes till crispy. Cut into pieces.

4. Blanch water convolvulus for 10 seconds in boiling water with 1 teaspoon each of salt and sugar and 1 tablespoon oil.

5. Scoop out with a wire mesh ladle and drain well. Place on large plate. Arrange cuttlefish, jellyfish shreds and soya bean pieces over vegetables. Sprinkle toasted sesame seeds and pour the chilli sauce mixture over. Serve.

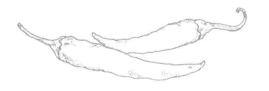

KON LOH MEE
(NOODLES WITH CHAR SIEW)

INGREDIENTS

115 g (4 oz) anchovies 680 ml(24 fl oz) water 2 cloves garlic, lightly bashed ½ thumb-sized piece ginger, lightly bashed	**A**

2–3 tablespoons chilli sauce 1 tablespoon peanut oil ¼ teaspoon msg 1 tablespoon light soya sauce 1 teaspoon oyster sauce ½ teaspoon sesame oil 4-6 tablespoons stock	*sauce mixture for one serving*

225 g (8 oz) Chinese mustard greens
1 teaspoon salt
1 teaspoon sugar
8 bundles fresh egg noodles
225 g (8 oz) roast pork strips, sliced finely

METHOD

1. Boil **A** for 1 hour. Strain and keep stock in a bowl.

2. Wash mustard greens, cut into short lengths and blanch in saucepan together with the salt and sugar. Using a wire sieve, remove and immerse in cold water for 5 minutes. Drain.

3. Bring a large saucepan of water to the boil over high heat. Loosen a bundle of noodles and put it into the boiling water. Stir with a wooden chopstick for 1 minute, then scoop it out with a wire-mesh ladle. Immerse in a large basin of cold water for ½ minute. Repeat boiling process for another ¼ minute. Remove and drain.

4. Stir noodles in a bowl of prepared sauce mixture.

5. Transfer to a serving plate, garnish with mustard greens and slices of roast pork. Serve hot. Repeat process with other servings.

(8 servings)

LAKSA LEMAK

INGREDIENTS

1 thumb-sized piece turmeric
½ teacup galangal, sliced
20 dried chillies
5 red chillies
6 candlenuts
2 tablespoons shrimp paste
225 g (8 oz) shallots
1 tablespoon coriander powder or seeds

A

55 g (2 oz) dried prawns, pounded
1 tablespoon sugar
2 tablespoons salt

B

1.2 kg (2½ lb) grated coconut
1 teaspoon salt
1 teaspoon sugar
445 g (1 lb) fresh prawns, for garnishing
225 ml (8 fl oz) oil
2 stalks lemon grass, bruised
625 g (22 oz) bean sprouts, boiled and drained
1.2 kg (2½ lb) fresh rice vermicelli

METHOD

1. Grind **A** to a fine paste.
2. Squeeze coconut for No. 1 milk. Add 2.7 litres (5 pints) water to coconut and extract No. 2 milk. Set aside.
3. Boil 455 ml (16 fl oz) water with 1 teaspoon salt and 1 teaspoon sugar. Add fresh prawns and cook for about 5–7 minutes.
4. Remove prawns, shell and slice lengthwise. Set aside for garnishing.
5. Return shells to saucepan. Boil for 10 minutes. Strain liquid for stock.
6. Heat oil in aluminium wok. Fry paste (Method 1) and lemon grass till fragrant and the oil comes to the surface.
7. Add No. 2 milk and prawn stock and bring to the boil. Add **B**. Boil for 10 minutes over low heat.
8. Reduce the heat to simmering point. Add No. 1 milk, setting aside 2 tablespoonfuls for the chilli paste. Stir gravy for a minute then remove from heat. Continue stirring to prevent curdling.

CHILLI PASTE:

55 g (2 oz) dried chillies
5 red chillies
1 teaspoon shrimp paste

A

2 teaspoons sugar
1 teaspoon salt
2 tablespoons No. 1 milk

B

2 tablespoons oil
1–2 tablespoons water

METHOD

1. Grind **A** to a fine paste.
2. Heat pan till hot. Heat oil and fry paste till well done and oil comes through.
3. Add 1–2 tablespoons water, stir-fry with **B**.
4. Remove to a bowl.

GARNISH:
Cooked prawns, shelled and sliced lengthwise
8 fish cakes, fried and sliced into thin strips
3 skinned cucumbers, sliced lengthwise (remove soft centre)
55 g (2 oz) polygonum (daun kesom), cut finely

To serve the rice vermicelli:
Place some bean sprouts and rice vermicelli in several bowls. Add hot gravy and garnish with prawns, fish cake, cucumber, polygonum, and chilli paste.

Note:
Transparent bean vermicelli can also be added to the rice vermicelli.

(10 servings)

LAKSA PENANG

INGREDIENTS

455 g (16 oz) shallots
10 stalks lemon grass, thinly sliced   A
1 thumb-sized piece turmeric
30-40 pieces dried chillies or 4 tablespoons
    chilli paste
1 tablespoon shrimp paste
1 clove garlic

8 slices dried tamarind
30 stalks polygonum (daun kesom)   B
2 stalks phaeomaria (bunga kantan) cut
    into halves
6 heaped tablespoons sugar
2 tablespoons salt

170 g (6 oz) tamarind
4.5 l (10 pt) water
1.2 kg (2½ lb) wolf-herring (Ikan Parang)
2.4 kg (5 lb) fresh coarse rice vermicelli
6 tablespoons prawn paste, mixed with ¾ cup
    warm water

METHOD

1. Soak tamarind in 455 ml (16 fl oz) water; squeeze and sieve into an enamel saucepan. Repeat process three times with the rest of the water.
2. Grind **A** to a fine paste.
3. Bring tamarind water to the boil with **A** and **B**.
4. Boil for 10 minutes; add the fish and let gravy simmer for 15 minutes till fish is cooked.
5. Remove fish to a plate to cool; remove all bones. Place flaked fish meat in a bowl and set aside.
6. Let the tamarind gravy simmer for 1 hour. Remove the polygonum and phaeomaria.
7. Return the flaked fish to the gravy and bring back to boil.

GARNISH:
1 pineapple, diced
905 g (2 lb) cucumber, thinly shredded without skin
    and centre
55 g (2 oz) mint leaves
225 g (8 oz) onions, cut into small cubes
15 green chillies, sliced
12 red chillies, sliced
115 g (4 oz) preserved leeks, sliced thinly

To serve:
1. Bring a saucepan of water to a rapid boil. Scald the rice vermicelli and drain in a colander.
2. Place a small handful of scalded rice vermicelli in a medium-sized bowl; pour hot tamarind gravy and some fish over it. Top with garnish, and 1 teaspoon of the thinned prawn paste. Serve.

Note:
Only very fresh fish is suitable for this dish. Dried coarse rice vermicelli can be substituted for fresh. Boil rice vermicelli till soft but not soggy; about 15 minutes. Rinse in cold water and drain.

LOH KAI YIK
(COMBINATION HOT POT)

INGREDIENTS

6 pieces salted bean curd in oil, mashed
4 tablespoons preserved soya beans,
   pounded

4 tablespoons sugar
2 tablespoons ginger juice

8 tablespoons sweet red sauce

A

½ tablespoon salt
2 tablespoons light soya sauce
1 teaspoon msg

B

565 g (20 oz) water convolvulus
 20 dried bean curd cakes
  6 tablespoons lard or oil
  8 slices ginger
  3 tablespoons pounded garlic
455 g (1 lb) chicken wings
455 g (1 lb) lean streaky pork
455 g (1 lb) pig's skin, cleaned and cut into 10 cm
   (4 in) squares
455 g (1 lb) pig's small intestines
  2 large treated cuttlefish, cut into quarters

METHOD

1. Wash and blanch water convolvulus. Drain and knot each strand.

2. Scald the dried bean curd cakes. Drain and squeeze lightly to remove the oil.

3. Heat lard in wok and fry ginger slices and garlic till light brown. Add **A** and half of the sweet red sauce. Stir-fry over moderate heat till sugar dissolves.

4. Add **B** to 225 ml (8 fl oz) of water. Bring to the boil.

5. Add chicken wings, streaky pork, pig's skin and small intestines. Cook for 20 minutes.

6. Remove chicken wings to a dish.

7. Add another 225 ml (8 fl oz) water and the remaining sweet red sauce.

8. Put in the water convolvulus, dried bean curd cakes and cuttlefish. Boil gently for 5 minutes. Remove to a dish.

9. Let gravy simmer till pork, pig's skin and small intestines are tender. Add hot water to gravy if necessary.

10. Return the chicken wings, water convolvulus, dried bean curd cakes and cuttlefish to the gravy. Let simmer until ready to serve. Put chilli sauce and sweet red sauce in separate saucers to serve with Loh Kai Yik.

Note:
Buy cuttlefish that has been soaked in alkaline water from any market. Pork and chicken livers can be added to this dish.

LOH MEE

INGREDIENTS

250 g (9 oz) small grey prawns, shelled and deveined
200 g (7 oz) squids, cut into thin rings (remove ink bags)
250 g (9 oz) Spanish mackerel (tenggiri papan) cut into thick small pieces
200 g (7 oz) fresh oysters (optional) **A**

1 tablespoon light soya sauce
1 teaspoon sugar *seasoning*
1 teaspoon ginger juice

600 g (21 oz) fresh flat yellow noodles
400 g (14 oz) bean sprouts, washed and drained
200 g (7 oz) Chinese mustard (chye sim), cut into short lengths
½ teaspoon chopped garlic
½ thumb-sized piece ginger, thinly sliced
3 tablespoons plain flour
600 ml (21 fl oz) prawn stock

3 tablespoons oyster sauce
2 tablespoons top quality Thai sauce
1 tablespoon dark soya sauce
1 teaspoon sesame oil **B**
½ teaspoon pepper
1 teaspoon chicken stock granules

Garnish:
3 sprigs coriander leaf (wan swee) cut in short lengths
2 red chillies, seeded, sliced thinly lengthwise
6 tablespoons crispy shallots

METHOD

1. Wash and drain prawn shells and fry with 2 tablespoons oil. Add 1 litre water, bring to boil in wok till stock is reduced by one-third.

2. Marinate **A** in seasoning for ½ hour.

3. Heat 4 tablespoons oil in wok. Fry garlic and sliced ginger till light brown. Add the flour; stir for ½ minute, pour in ½ of prawn stock and **B** and bring to boil. Pour in remaining stock with the seasoned **A** ingredients, cover pan and bring to boil.

4. Remove prawns and fish to one side of pan, put in the chye sim and bean sprouts to cook for ½ minute over high heat, then add in the noodles and cook for approximately 1 minute. Remove noodles to a large serving plate. Spoon gravy over and garnish. Serve hot.

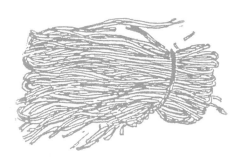

MEE GORENG
(FRIED NOODLES — INDIAN-STYLE)

INGREDIENTS

2–3 tablespoons tomato sauce
1–2 tablespoons light soya sauce
4 green chillies, sliced
4 red chillies, sliced
4 small potatoes; boiled, skinned and cut
   into wedges   **A**

Oil for frying
1 onion, sliced finely
2 tomatoes, cut into wedges
225 g (8 oz) Chinese cabbage cut into 5 cm (2 in)
   lengths
455 g (16 oz) bean sprouts
340 g (12 oz) fresh yellow noodles
4 eggs
   Light soya sauce
2 tablespoons crispy shallots*
6 small local limes, halved

METHOD

1. Heat iron wok till smoky. Put in 2 tablespoons oil, and fry onion slices till soft and transparent.
2. Lightly toss in tomatoes and Chinese cabbage.
3. Add bean sprouts and noodles and stir for 1 minute.
4. Toss in **A** and mix well.
5. Push noodles to one side of wok. Add 2 tablespoons oil and scramble eggs (two at a time) with a sprinkling of light soya sauce. Mix egg and noodles thoroughly.
6. Add paste for noodles (see below) according to taste. Stir mixture over a very high heat for 1 minute. Remove to serving plate.
7. Garnish with crispy shallots, and local limes.

PASTE FOR NOODLES:
225 g (8 oz) onions
55 g (2 oz) dried chillies
4 cloves garlic   **A**
1 tablespoon shrimp paste

1 tablespoon sugar
1 teaspoon salt   **B**
1 teaspoon msg

340 ml (12 fl oz) oil
55 g (2 oz) dried anchovies

METHOD

1. Grind **A** till fine.
2. Heat 115 ml (4 fl oz) oil in pan; fry anchovies over a moderate heat till crisp. Drain and pound coarsely.
3. In a clean pan, heat remaining oil. Stir in **A** (Method 1) and fry till fragrant and oil comes through. Add **B**. Lower the heat; add the pounded anchovies. Cook for 2–3 minutes, remove to a bowl. Use as required. Store the remainder in a freezer.

Note:
Fry noodles over a very high heat to keep the bean sprouts crunchy and to prevent the noodles from being soggy. Fry in two parts if the wok is not large enough.
*For crispy shallots, see "Helpful Hints".

(8 servings)

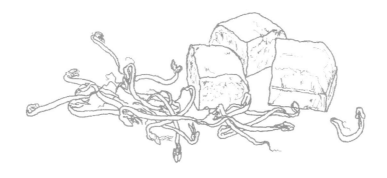

MEE REBUS
(BRAISED NOODLES — MALAY STYLE)

INGREDIENTS

18 slices galangal
4 cloves garlic
115 g (4 oz) shallots
14–20 dried chillies
½ thumb-sized piece turmeric
1 teaspoon shrimp paste

A

115 g (4 oz) preserved soya beans, pounded
1 teaspoon msg
1–1½ tablespoons salt
2 tablespoons sugar

B

115 g (4 oz) boiled sweet potatoes, mashed
finely
2 tablespoons flour
2 tablespoons cornflour
225 ml (8 fl oz) water

C

1 chicken cube
225 g (½ lb) beef shin, cut into small pieces
225 g (½ lb) small prawns, shelled
115 ml (4 fl oz) oil
680 g (1½ lb) fresh yellow noodles
565 g (1¼ lb) bean sprouts, washed and picked

METHOD

1. Grind **A** to a paste.
2. Boil beef shin and chicken cube in 680 ml (1½ pints) water over a low heat till meat is tender.
3. Fry prawn shells with 1 tablespoon oil for 1 minute. Remove.
4. Bring 900 ml (2 pints) water to boiling point. Add fried shells and let water boil for further 7 minutes. Strain and set aside the stock for gravy.
5. Heat the rest of the oil in wok and fry **A** (Method 1) till it smells fragrant (5–7 minutes). Add **B**. Stir and remove paste.
6. Place the prawns, prawn stock, beef shin and the fried paste in a saucepan. Bring to the boil.
7. Thicken 225 ml (8 fl oz) of this gravy with **C**. Pour it back gradually into the saucepan and stir. Let gravy simmer for 10 minutes.

GARNISH :
8 sprigs Chinese celery, cut into small pieces
4 soya bean cakes, diced and fried
10 green chillies, sliced
6 red chillies, sliced
55 g (2 oz) crispy shallots
12–14 local limes, halved
6 hard-boiled eggs, sliced

To prepare and serve noodles:
1. Scald a handful of noodles and some bean sprouts in boiling water.
2. Using a wire-mesh ladle, drain noodles and bean sprouts and place on plate.
3. Spoon gravy, prawns, and beef over noodles. Garnish. Serve hot.

(10 servings)

MEE SIAM

INGREDIENTS

RICE VERMICELLI:

225 g (8 oz) shallots
50–60 dried chillies
2 tablespoons shrimp paste **A**

400 ml (14 fl oz) water
1 tablespoon salt
3 tablespoons sugar **B**
1 teaspoon msg

340 ml (12 fl oz) oil
3 tablespoons dried prawns, pounded finely
1.2 kg (2½ lb) bean sprouts, washed and drained
625 g (1½ lb) rice vermicelli, soaked in a saucepan of boiling water for ½ minute and drained

METHOD

1. Pound **A** to a fine paste.
2. Heat oil in wok and fry dried prawns for 1 minute. Add paste (**A**) and fry till fragrant and oil comes through. Set aside 3 tablespoonfuls of this fried paste and some oil for the gravy.
3. Add **B** in wok and simmer.
4. Add the bean sprouts and stir-fry for 1 minute. Push bean sprouts to one side of the wok. Add rice vermicelli and stir-fry over a high heat, using a pair of chopsticks. Continue stirring till gravy is absorbed.
5. Mix bean sprouts and rice vermicelli thoroughly. Reduce heat, stir and cook till rice vermicelli is dry and fluffy. Remove to cool on a large tray.

GRAVY:

8 tablespoons preserved soya beans, pounded finely
6 tablespoons sugar
2 onions, sliced thinly **A**
2 walnut-sized tamarind with 225 ml (8 fl oz) water, squeezed and strained
1.8 litres (4 pints) water

METHOD

1. Mix **A** in saucepan. Stir and bring to boil. Let simmer for ¾ hour.
2. Add 3 tablespoons fried paste and oil. (Rice vermicelli, Step 2). Boil for 5 minutes. Remove from heat. Serve hot.

SPICY PASTE (SAMBAL):

40 g dried chillies or 10 tablespoons chilli paste
1 teaspoon shrimp paste
8 tablespoons oil
1 onion, chopped finely
1 teaspoon salt
2 tablespoons sugar
1 tablespoon tamarind with 125 ml (4 fl oz) water, squeezed and strained

1. Grind dried chillies with shrimp paste till very fine.
2. Heat oil in wok and fry chopped onion till soft and slightly brown. Add chilli paste (Step 1) and fry over a moderate heat till fragrant and oil comes through.
3. Add salt, sugar, and half of the tamarind water. Stir-fry for 1 minute, add the rest of the tamarind water and cook for another 2 minutes, stirring all the time. Remove to a bowl. Serve with the rice vermicelli.

GARNISH:

12 hard-boiled eggs, cut into wedges or sliced
4 big soya bean cakes, diced and fried
625 g (1 lb 6 oz) medium-sized prawns (shelled and deveined), fried and halved lengthwise
115 g (4 oz) chives cut into 2.5 cm (1 in) lengths
310 g (11 oz) local limes, cut into halves

To serve:

Place rice vermicelli on a large serving plate or on individual dinner plates.

Garnish and serve with the gravy and the spicy paste.

(12 servings)

Mee Siam

MURTABAK
(MEAT CREPES)

INGREDIENTS

455 g (1 lb) plain flour
½ teaspoon pepper ⎤
¾ teaspoon baking powder   **A**
¾ teaspoon fine salt ⎦

  Ghee
4 eggs

METHOD

1. Sift **A** together into a bowl. Add 340 ml (12 fl oz) water, to form a smooth dough. Leave overnight in a covered bowl.

2. Divide dough into 4 equal portions. Roll out thinly on an oiled marble top or formica table top, and spread liberally with ghee. Fold and shape into balls. Cover with a damp cloth. Set aside for ½ hour.

3. Roll out each ball into a thin rectangle. Spread filling in centre of dough. Pat lightly beaten egg over meat. Fold dough over meat to form a rectangle or square and fry in hot ghee till brown on both sides. Serve hot.

FILLING:

605 g (20 oz) minced mutton or veal ⎤
¼ teaspoon turmeric powder
½ teaspoon msg   **A**
½ teaspoon salt ⎦

605 g (20 oz) onions, diced ⎤
¼ teaspoon turmeric powder
¼ teaspoon salt   **B**
½ teaspoon msg ⎦

  2 heaped tablespoons roasted
    coriander seeds
  2 level tablespoons aniseed   **C** *pounded finely*
20 cardamoms, seeded ⎦

METHOD

1. Fry **A** in a little oil. Remove from pan.

2. Fry **B** in 2 tablespoons oil for 2 minutes. Add **A** and **C**. Mix well and season to taste. Cool on a plate.

NGOH HIANG
(MEAT ROLLS)

INGREDIENTS

1 teaspoon salt ⎤
2 teaspoons sugar
1 teaspoon msg
2 teaspoons light soya sauce
1 teaspoon dark soya sauce
1 teaspoon pepper   **A**
1 tablespoon lard or oil
1 tablespoon flour
1 rounded teaspoon five-spice powder ⎦

455 g (1 lb) minced pork ⎤
225 g (½ lb) prawns; shelled, deveined, and
    chopped coarsely   **B**
1 onion, chopped finely ⎦

  2 dried bean curd wrappers
  2 small eggs
170 g (6 oz) steamed crab meat
Oil for deep-frying

METHOD

1. Cut bean curd wrappers into rectangles, 15 cm × 18 cm (6 in × 7 in).

2. Beat eggs lightly. Add **A**. Mix well.

3. Mix **B** in a large basin. Add the egg mixture and mix thoroughly. Add the steamed crab meat. Mix well.

4. Place a small heap of mixture on each of the wrappers. Roll as for sausages, dampen the open ends with a little flour mixed with water and seal. Steam the rolls for 10 minutes. Cool.

5. Deep-fry rolls in hot fat. Cool before cutting. Serve with cucumber slices.

OTAK OTAK PANGGANG
(SPICY FISH GRILLED IN BANANA LEAVES)

INGREDIENTS

2 onions, weighing 225 g (8 oz) 30 slices galangal (weighing approx. 85 g or 3 oz) 5 candlenuts 25 dried chillies 1 tablespoon shrimp paste 1 thumb-sized piece turmeric	**A**

1.2 kg (2 lb 11 oz) Spanish mackerel
680 g (24 oz) grated coconut (extract 285 ml (10 fl oz) No. 1 milk)
  2 eggs

3 tablespoons sugar 2 tablespoons salt 1 teaspoon msg 3 tablespoons oil 2 teaspoons roasted coriander	**B**

2 lime leaves, sliced very finely
4 turmeric leaves, sliced very finely
26 banana leaves (22 cm × 20 cm or 10 in × 8 in), washed and scalded

METHOD

1. Grind **A** to a fine paste.

2. Bone and fillet the fish. Use a spoon to scrape half of the meat into a bowl. Slice the other half thinly.

3. Pound or mince the scraped fish meat till smooth. Add 170 ml (6 fl oz) water and a pinch of salt. Beat mixture manually till it forms a sticky paste.

4. Add the No. 1 milk. Beat till well-blended. Add the eggs, **A** and **B** and beat till well-blended. Add the sliced fish, lime leaves and turmeric leaves. Mix well into the fish mixture.

5. Place 2 tablespoonfuls of fish mixture in the middle of each banana leaf. Fasten the two ends of the leaf with a stapler or a sharp toothpick.

6. Pre-heat grill. When very hot, place wrapped fish in grill pan, 8 cm (3 in) from the hot grill, for 7–10 minutes on each side.

OTAK OTAK PUTEH
(BAKED FISH PASTE WITH RICH COCONUT CREAM)

INGREDIENTS

¾ tablespoon salt 1½ teaspoons msg 1 teaspoon sugar 1 teaspoon tapioca flour Dash of pepper 1 teaspoon galangal juice	**A**

225 g (8 oz) grated coconut, white
570 g (19 oz) fish meat
  2 egg whites, lightly beaten
40 pieces banana leaves (20 × 25 cm)

METHOD

1. Add 4 tablespoons water to coconut and squeeze for milk. Set aside.

2. Stir **A** into coconut milk till dissolved. Set aside.

3. Blend fish meat and coconut mixture in electric food processor to make a fine paste.

4. Remove paste to a large basin and gradually add the egg white. Beat till stiff.

5. Place banana leaf on table. Wet hands and pat spoonful of paste into longish, flat shape on leaf. Fold longer ends of banana leaf over to cover paste. Pin ends with tooth picks. Repeat with remaining paste.

6. Fry packets in iron pan or place under a hot grill until cooked (7–8 minutes).

Note:
To get a fine texture for this dish, use Ikan Parang (Wolf Herring)

POH PIA
(FRESH SPRING ROLLS)

INGREDIENTS

Filling:

905 g (2 lb) streaky pork | **A**
A pinch of salt

8 tablespoons preserved soya beans,
   pounded
1–1½ tablespoons salt | **B**
8 tablespoons sugar
2 teaspoons msg

455 g (1 lb) small prawns
225 ml (8 fl oz) lard or oil
8 tablespoons pounded garlic (about 30 cloves)

1.8 kg (4 lb) Chinese turnip, shredded
1.8 kg (4 lb) boiled, tender, bamboo shoots,
   shredded
12 soya bean cakes cut into thin strips and fried

METHOD

To cook filling:

1. Boil **A** with 1 litre (32 fl oz) water for ¾ hour. Remove pork and slice into fine strips. Set aside 455 ml (16 fl oz) of the stock.

2. Shell and devein prawns. Pound prawn shells; add 1 litre water. Strain and set aside liquid.

3. Heat lard in wok and fry garlic till light brown. Add **B**. Stir-fry for 1 minute. Pour in the prawn liquid (Method 2) and bring to boil.

4. Add turnip to cook, then add bamboo shoots and pork stock (Method 1). Boil for ½ hour over moderate heat.

5. Lower heat, add fried soya bean strips and sliced pork. Cook for 1½ hours, stirring occasionally. Add the prawns and cook for a further 10 minutes.

6. Remove filling to an aluminium saucepan. Simmer until ready to serve.

White Skins:

625 g (22 oz) white skins, large, obtainable at markets.

Note:
Keep white skins covered with a damp cloth before serving.

Egg Skins:

285 g (10 oz) flour
A pinch of salt | **A**
3 tablespoons cornflour

10 eggs
680–740 ml (24–26 fl oz) water
85 ml (3 fl oz) oil

To make egg skins:

1. Sieve **A** into a basin.

2. Beat eggs lightly in a bowl. Add water and oil.

3. Add egg mixture to flour and mix evenly.

4. Grease a well-heated omelette pan. Pour enough batter to spread over base of pan thinly, as for a pancake. Cook pancake till sides curl slightly. Turn pancake over on to a flat surface. Repeat process until batter is used up. Pile egg skins on a plate.

Garnish:

8 eggs
A pinch of salt | **A**
3 tablespoons oil

455 g (1 lb) small prawns, shelled and
   deveined | **B**
A pinch of salt

905 g (2 lb) cucumber, shredded thinly and with centre and skin removed
905 g (2 lb) bean sprouts; picked, washed and scalded
8 bundles of fine Chinese parsley (roots removed), washed and drained
455 g (1 lb) green lettuce, washed and drained
225 g (½ lb) steamed crab meat
2 pairs Chinese sausages, fried and sliced thinly
285 g (10 oz) sweet, thick black sauce
30 cloves garlic, pounded to a fine paste
30 cloves garlic, pounded and fried till crisp
455 g (1 lb) red chillies, pounded to a fine paste

METHOD

1. Beat **A**. Grease pan lightly. Fry egg mixture as for omelette. Fold and slice very thinly. (Grease pan only once.)

2. Fry **B**. Slice prawns lengthwise.

To serve Poh Pia:

1. Place small heaps of cucumber, bean sprouts, Chinese parsley, and lettuce on serving plate.

2. Arrange crab meat, prawns, egg and sausages on separate plate.

3. Place the sweet, thick black sauce, garlic, fried garlic, and pounded chillies in small separate bowls.

4. Arrange the white skins and the egg skins on two separate plates.

5. Place the filling in a deep large bowl.

To roll:

1. Place a white or egg skin on a plate and spread ingredients in this order — a little sweet, thick black sauce, pounded chillies, and pounded garlic.

2. Add a piece of lettuce, a few strands of bean sprouts, shredded cucumber, and a spoonful of filling.

SATAY CHELOP
(STEAMBOAT SATAY)

INGREDIENTS

Gravy:

10 candlenuts	
140 g (5 oz) shallots	
6 cloves garlic	
4 stalks lemon grass, sliced	**A**
4 slices galangal	
30 dried chillies	
1 tablespoon shrimp paste	

625 g (22 oz) roasted peanuts, pounded finely	
900 ml (32 fl oz) water	**B**

225 ml (8 fl oz) oil

115 g (4 oz) sugar	**C**
1 tablespoon salt	

METHOD

1. Grind **A** to a paste.

2. Boil **B** over a low heat for 20 minutes.

3. Heat oil in wok. Fry paste (Method 1) in heated oil till fragrant and oil comes to surface. Add fried paste to peanut sauce. Add **C**, stir and let simmer for 10 minutes. Set aside gravy.

3. Garnish with a few slices of Chinese sausages, egg, prawn, and crab meat. Add a little Chinese parsley, sprinkle a bit of crispy garlic and fold into a neat roll.

4. Cut and serve.

Note:
1. *You need to grease the omelette pan only once as the mixture has sufficient oil.*
2. *Dip shredded Chinese turnip in water to remove the starch. Drain in a colander before cooking.*
3. *Drain gravy from filling before serving.*

(12–15 servings)

INGREDIENTS

225 g (8 oz) pork chop meat, sliced thinly	
225 g (8 oz) cockles	
225 g (8 oz) shelled prawns, halved lengthwise	**A**
225 g (8 oz) pork liver, sliced thinly	
1 treated cuttlefish (obtainable at wet markets)	

685 g (1½ lb) water convolvulus	**B**
455 g (1 lb) bean sprouts, picked	

225 g (8 oz) rice vermicelli

METHOD

1. Scald rice vermicelli for 2 minutes. Drain in colander.

2. Thread **A** on to wooden skewers or satay sticks.

3. Scald **B**. Drain in colander.

4. Add 225 ml (8 fl oz) of peanut gravy to 900 ml (32 fl oz) boiling water in a small saucepan. Let simmer to cook the skewered ingredients.

To serve:
Place small servings of water convolvulus, bean sprouts, and rice vermicelli on a plate. Place the skewered ingredients in the saucepan, letting them simmer till done. Remove cooked food from skewers to the plate of rice vermicelli. Add thick gravy and serve.

(10 servings)

SATAY
(BARBECUED BEEF WITH PEANUT SAUCE)

INGREDIENTS

Meat preparation:
10 shallots
2 cloves garlic
¼ thumb-sized piece turmeric or
　½ teaspoon turmeric powder
4 stalks lemon grass, sliced
2 slices galangal　　　　　　　　**A**

2 tablespoons coriander seeds
2 teaspoons cumin　　　　　　　**B**

1 teaspoon dark soya sauce
1 teaspoon salt
4–5 tablespoons sugar
4 tablespoons oil　　　　　　　　**C**

455 g (1 lb) beef, chilled and cut into
　thin pieces

METHOD

1. Pound **A** to a smooth paste.

2. Fry **B** over low heat for 5 minutes, till fragrant. Pound to a fine powder while still hot.

3. Mix **C** in a bowl and add to pounded paste (Method 1).

4. Rub paste mixture into the beef. Sprinkle the coriander and cumin powder over the beef and mix thoroughly. Marinate beef for 1 hour. Thread seasoned meat on to satay sticks or fine metal skewers. Grill over charcoal fire or under hot grill. Baste with oil and water mixture to keep beef moist.

Peanut Sauce:
15 shallots
8 cloves garlic
2 stalks lemon grass, thinly sliced
20–30 dried chillies, deseeded, or 4–5
　tablespoons chilli paste
4 thin slices galangal　　　　　　**A**

2 tablespoons salt
8–10 tablespoons sugar
4 tablespoons lime juice or 4 tablespoons
　thick tamarind water　　　　　　**B**

455 g (16 oz) freshly roasted ground peanuts
225 ml (8 fl oz) oil

METHOD

1. Pound **A** to a fine paste.

2. Boil pounded peanuts with 900 ml (32 fl oz) water over low heat till thick. Stir constantly for about ½ hour. Set aside.

3. Heat oil in wok and fry pounded paste (Method 1) till fragrant and oil seeps through the paste.

4. Add paste to peanut mixture. Add **B**. Boil sauce over a low heat for 5–7 minutes till sugar is dissolved, stirring constantly. Cool peanut sauce and serve separately with barbecued beef and garnish.

Garnish:
2 cucumbers, cut into wedges
2 onions, cut into wedges

Note:
If lemon grass is not available, use 1 teaspoon grated lemon rind.

Satay

YONG TAU FU

INGREDIENTS

(*available at market stalls selling fish balls*)
  20 pieces stuffed triangular white bean curd
  10 slices stuffed bitter gourd
  60 fish balls
  30 pieces stuffed fried spongy bean curd triangles
  30 pieces stuffed fried spongy bean curd cubes
  10 stuffed green chillies
  10 stuffed red chillies

  ½ cup oil
  4 stalks spring onions, chopped coarsely
900 g (2 lb) rice vermicelli
900 g (2 lb) water convolvulus

METHOD

1. Heat ½ cup oil in iron wok. Fry the white bean curd till light brown on all sides. Remove to large tray.

2. Remove rest of oil from wok leaving about 2 tablespoonfuls. Fry bitter gourd over low heat (2 minutes on each side) then add ¼ cup water. Cover wok and cook for 5 minutes. Remove.

3. Cook rice vermicelli for 2–3 minutes in saucepan of boiling water. Remove to a basin of cold water and drain immediately in a colander.

4. Add 1 teaspoon each of salt, sugar and oil to a saucepan of water and bring to a rapid boil. Add water convolvulus and boil rapidly for ½ minute. Pour into a colander and immerse in cold water for 15 minutes. Drain and set aside.

5. Bring soup to the boil. Cook fish balls and remove to a bowl. Add bean curd pieces and boil for 5 minutes; remove to a tray. Boil the green and red chillies with 1 teaspooon oil for 2 minutes. Remove.

Soup:
3.6 litres (7 pints) water
  1 thumb-sized piece ginger, bashed
  6 cloves garlic, lightly bashed
170 g (6 oz) anchovies, washed and drained
  1 chicken cube

Seasoning:
1–2 teaspoons salt
  2 teaspoons msg
  1 teaspoon sugar

To make soup:
Put some ingredients in a saucepan and bring to the boil togetherr with seasoning. Boil over moderate heat for 1½ hours. Strain and set aside.

To serve:
Bring soup to a boil and boil gently over low heat till ready to serve. Into medium sized bowls put a little rice vermicelli, some water convolvulus and a few pieces each of the *yong tau fu*, fish balls, chilli and bitter gourd. Add boiling soup, garnish with a little spring onion and serve hot with chilli sauce and sweet red sauce.

***Note*:**
Yong tau fu *can also be served 'dry' with the soup served in a separate bowl. Sprinkle toasted sesame seeds over each serving and add chilli sauce and sweet red sauce to taste.*

(10 servings)

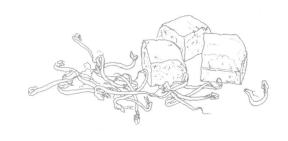

Yong Tau Fu

Nonya Specialities

Assam Gulai
Ayam Buah Keluak
Ayam Goreng Assam
Ayam Kleo
Ayam Merah
Ayam Risa Risa
Ayam Sioh
Ayam Tempra
Babi Assam
Babi Chin
Babi Pong Tay
Buah Paya Masak Titek
Bak Wan Kepiting
Chap Chye Masak Titek
Goreng Ikan Terubok
Hati Babi Bungkus
Ikan Masak Assam Pekat
Itek Tim
Kari Ayam
Pong Tauhu
Satay Babi
Sayor Nanka Masak Lemak
Tauhu Masak Titek
Udang Kuah Pedas Nanas

Udang Kuah Pedas Nanas

ASSAM GULAI
(FISH IN SPICY TAMARIND JUICE)

INGREDIENTS

2 dried tamarind slices
1 tablespoon sugar   **A**
A pinch of salt
Water

3 stalks lemon grass, thinly sliced
½ thumb-sized piece turmeric
20 dried chillies or 2–3 tablespoons
   chilli paste   **B**
20 shallots
2 cloves garlic
1 tablespoon shrimp paste

2 tablespoons sugar
2 teaspoons salt
½ teaspoon msg   **C**
2 stalks phaeomaria (bunga kantan),
   halved lengthwise

1–1½ tablespoons tamarind with 900 ml (2 pints)
water, squeezed and strained

310 g (11 oz) lady's fingers
625 g (22 oz) prawns or fish head, trimmed and
washed

METHOD

1. Cut away the stems of the lady's fingers before halving them.

2. Boil **A** in a saucepan. Put in the lady's fingers and boil till tender (10–15 minutes). Drain and set aside.

3. Grind **B** to a fine paste.

4. Heat 115 ml (4 fl oz) oil in wok and fry paste till oil bubbles through; stir constantly.

5. Stir in **C** and some of the tamarind water.

6. Cook for 1 minute, then add the rest of the tamarind water and bring to boil. Cook for further 2 minutes. Do not cover wok.

7. Put in the prawns or fish head and cook till done. Finally, add the lady's fingers.

Note:
To choose young and tender lady's fingers, bend the ends to see if they snap easily. Those that do not break easily are tough and stringy.

AYAM BUAH KELUAK
(CHICKEN IN BLACK NUT CURRY)

INGREDIENTS

30 Indonesian black nuts
   Pinch of salt
½ teaspoon sugar
1 chicken, 1.4 kg (3 lb), cut into pieces
1 teaspoon salt
1 teaspoon msg
340 g (12 oz) *garam assam* paste*, thawed

570 g (20 oz) pork ribs, cut into pieces

85 g (3 oz) tamarind soaked in 170 ml
   (6 fl oz) water, squeezed and strained
1–1½ level teaspoons salt   **A**
1 teaspoon msg
905 ml (32 fl oz) water

METHOD

1. Soak nuts in cold water for ½ hour. Brush nuts to remove sandy particles. Crack where nut is smooth and remove meat. Add a pinch of salt and ½ teaspoon sugar and pound together to form a firm, smooth paste, then refill shells.

2. Season chicken with 1 teaspoon salt and 1 teaspoon msg and leave for ½ hour.

3. Place the thawed *garam assam* paste in an enamel pan with **A** and bring to the boil over high heat. Add pork ribs and boil for 5 minutes. Reduce heat to moderate and cook for ½ hour. Add the nuts and then the chicken and continue cooking for another ½ hour or till chicken is tender, stirring occasionally.

4. Serve with white rice.

*See page 185.

Ayam Buah Keluak

AYAM GORENG ASSAM
(FRIED TAMARIND CHICKEN)

INGREDIENTS

Marinade Ingredients:

3 tablespoons tamarind pulp (light coloured)	
1½ teaspoons salt	
3 teaspoons fine sugar	
1 teaspoon msg, optional	**A**
1 teaspoon pepper	
2 teaspoons light soya sauce	
8 tablespoons water	

1.2 kg (2½ lb) whole chicken, cut into 4 pieces
Oil for deep frying

METHOD

1. Combine **A** in a bowl. Stir till well mixed.
2. Wash chicken pieces and wipe with kitchen towel till very dry.
3. Prick chicken with fork to allow marinade to soak in. Leave to marinate for ¾ hour.
4. Heat an aluminium kuali till hot. Pour in approximately 570 ml (20 fl oz) of oil and heat till very hot. Add chicken pieces, bring down heat to moderate and fry till light brown, dry and crispy on both sides. Turn heat to low if chicken browns too quickly.

Note:
To prevent chicken being greasy, keep oil at boiling point.

AYAM KLEO
(CHICKEN IN RICH SPICY GRAVY)

INGREDIENTS

1.2 kg (2½ lb) chicken, cut into 4 pieces
625 g (22 oz) grated coconut with 435 ml (14 fl oz) water, squeezed and strained

4 dried chillies	
2 red chillies	
1 stalk lemon grass, thinly sliced	
6 candlenuts	
1 thumb-sized piece ginger	**A**
¼ thumb-sized piece turmeric	
3 cloves garlic	
15 shallots	

1 teaspoon salt	
1 teaspoon msg	**B**
2 tablespoons water	

1 teaspoon salt	
½ teaspoon msg	
1 slice dried tamarind	**C**
5 lime leaves	
2 stalks lemon grass, lightly bashed	

METHOD

1. Grind **A** to a fine paste.
2. Marinate the chicken in **B** and 2 tablespoonfuls of the paste for ½ hour.
3. Set grill to hot. Grill the marinated chicken till brown on both sides (10 minutes for each side).
4. Mix the rest of the paste with the coconut milk and **C**, in a saucepan. Put in the chicken and mix well. Cook over a moderate heat for 15 minutes. Reduce heat and let chicken simmer till tender. Cook until the gravy is thick and oil comes up to the surface.

Ayam Kleo

AYAM MERAH
(CHICKEN IN RED SPICY SAUCE)

INGREDIENTS

10 daun limau purot
2 stalks lemon grass, bashed   **A**

10 candlenuts
¼ thumb-sized piece ginger
2 tablespoons chilli powder
10 red chillies, seeded
10 red chilli padi   **B**   *ground to a fine paste*
1 clove garlic
1 teaspoon shrimp paste
55 g (2 oz) shallots

1.2 kg (2½ lb) chicken, cut into big pieces
455 g (1 lb) grated coconut
4 tablespoons oil
30 g (1 oz) tamarind, squeezed in 115 ml (4 fl oz) water, strained

METHOD

1. Marinate chicken with 1 tablespoon sugar and 1 teaspoon each of salt and msg for ½ hour.

2. Squeeze coconut for No. 1 milk; set aside. Add 285 ml (10 fl oz) water to squeezed coconut and squeeze again for No. 2 milk. Set aside.

3. Grease a roasting pan with 2 tablespoons oil. Rub chicken pieces with another 2 tablespoons oil and roast chicken in a hot oven till lightly brown. Repeat for other side. Remove from oven and set aside.

4. Heat an aluminium pan. Combine No. 2 milk, **A** and **B**, and boil over medium heat for 10 minutes, adding 1 tablespoon salt and ½ teaspoon msg.

5. Add roasted chicken, pan juices and tamarind water. Boil for another 10 minutes.

6. Pour in No. 1 milk, reduce heat to low and simmer uncovered for 10–12 minutes or till chicken is tender. Remove from heat. Serve hot or cold.

AYAM RISA RISA
(CHICKEN IN SPICY COCONUT SAUCE)

INGREDIENTS

1.6 kg (3½ lb) chicken, cut into big pieces
455 g (1 lb) grated coconut, white
155 ml (6 fl oz) oil

6 cloves garlic
½ thumb-sized piece ginger
6 slices galangal
2 stalks lemon grass
½ thumb-sized piece turmeric or ½ teaspoon turmeric powder   **A**   *ground to a fine paste*
20 dried chillies or 2–3 tablespoons chilli powder

4 daun limau purot, sliced thinly
10 candlenuts, pounded finely
2 tablespoons lime or lemon juice
115 g (4 oz) shallots, sliced thinly and fried till light brown

METHOD

1. Season chicken pieces with 1 teaspoon each of salt, sugar and msg. Set aside.

2. Squeeze coconut for approximately 230 ml (8 fl oz) No. 1 milk. Add 170 ml (6 fl oz) water to same coconut and squeeze again for No. 2 milk.

3. Heat an aluminium saucepan with 115 ml oil to fry **A** with the daun limau purot till fragrant and oil seeps through. Add candlenut paste and stir-fry for ½ minute. Put in chicken pieces, 1 teaspoon each of salt and msg, 2 teaspoons sugar and No. 2 milk. Cook over moderately high heat for 10 minutes; stir to prevent burning.

4. Add ½ of No. 1 milk and lime juice. Stir and cook uncovered over moderate heat for 10 minutes or till chicken is tender and gravy begins to thicken. Reduce heat to low, add in remaining No. 1 milk and allow to simmer for another 5 minutes till gravy is thick, moist and oily. Stir in fried shallots. Remove from heat. Serve hot or cold.

AYAM SIOH
(CHICKEN IN THICK SPICY
TAMARIND JUICE)

INGREDIENTS

3 tablespoons coriander powder, roasted   ⎤
10 tablespoons sugar
1 tablespoon salt
2 tablespoons dark soya sauce   **A**
1 heaped teaspoon pepper
170 g (6 oz) shallots, pounded finely   ⎦

1.6 kg (3½ lb) chicken, quartered
2 tablespoons salt
225 g (8 oz) tamarind
    Oil

METHOD

1. Wash chicken in water mixed with salt. Drain.

2. Soak tamarind in 340 ml (12 fl oz) water and squeeze into deep bowl. Strain and add **A**. Stir well.

3. Add chicken pieces. Cover and leave to marinate overnight or at least for 10 hours.

4. Transfer chicken and marinade to heavy-bottomed aluminium saucepan and cook for 20 minutes over moderate heat.

5. Reduce heat to low and cook for another 20–30 minutes or till chicken is very tender. Remove from heat and cool before frying chicken pieces in oil. Serve hot or cold.

AYAM TEMPRA
(SPICY CHICKEN)

INGREDIENTS

1 teaspoon salt   ⎤ **A**
1 teaspoon msg   ⎦

1 tablespoon dark soya sauce   ⎤
1 tablespoon sugar
½ teaspoon salt
½ teaspoon msg   **B**
2 teaspoons lime juice
225 ml (8 fl oz) water   ⎦

905 g (2 lb) chicken, cut into pieces
8 green chillies
6 red chillies
5 tablespoons oil
225 g (8 oz) onions, cut into rings

METHOD

1. Marinate the chicken in **A** for ½ hour.

2. Slice the chillies slantwise, thickly.

3. Mix **B** in bowl.

4. Heat iron wok. When very hot, heat 4 tablespoons oil and fry onions and chillies for ½ minute.

5. Add the marinated chicken and stir-fry over high heat till cooked (7 minutes). Add **B** (Method 3) and cook for another 5 minutes.

6. Lower the heat, cover wok and cook gently for 20 minutes or till chicken is tender.

7. Remove lid, add the last tablespoon of oil, stir well and serve hot or cold.

BABI ASSAM
(PORK BRAISED IN TAMARIND SAUCE)

INGREDIENTS

4 candlenuts
90 g (3 oz) shallots   **A** *pounded finely*
1 tablespoon shrimp paste

Seasoning:
½ teaspoon salt
1 chicken cube   **B**
2 tablespoons sugar

4 tablespoons oil
2 tablespoons preserved salted soya beans, pounded

570 g (20 oz) belly pork, cut into thick strips
30 g (1 oz) tamarind, squeezed in 285 ml (10 fl oz) water, strained

8 green chillies, slit halfway lengthwise
6 red chillies, slit halfway lengthwise

METHOD

1. Heat oil in kuali and fry **A** till fragrant and light brown. Add salted preserved soya bean paste, seasoning (**B**) and stir over low heat for short while.

2. Put in pork with ⅓ of tamarind juice. When pork begins to change colour add in red and green chillies and the remaining tamarind juice. Bring to boil, reduce heat and simmer till pork is tender (approx. ¾– 1 hour). While cooking, add a little water if gravy is too thick. Serve hot.

BABI CHIN
(BRAISED PORK IN DARK SOYA SAUCE)

INGREDIENTS

115 g (4 oz) shallots, pounded coarsely
30 g (1 oz) garlic, pounded coarsely   **A**
1 thumb-sized piece cinnamon bark

Seasoning:
2 tablespoons sugar
1 teaspoon salt   **B**
2 teaspoons dark soya sauce

1.4 kg (3 lb) shoulder pork (with skin)
2 lengths sugarcane, 30 cm long

1 tablespoon coriander powder
3 tablespoons preserved salted soya beans, pounded finely

85 g (3 oz) Chinese mushrooms
455 g (1 lb) boiled bamboo shoots, cut into thick wedges

METHOD

1. Wash and cut meat into 4 cm (1½ in.) cubes.

2. Remove skin of sugarcane, cut into two lengthwise and cut again into 8 cm (3 in.) lengths.

3. Heat oil in non-stick wok. Fry **A** till brown, add preserved salted soya beans, coriander powder and seasoning (**B**). Stir-fry for 2 minutes, add 425 ml (15 fl oz) water and sugarcane and bring to boil.

4. Increase heat to high and put in pork pieces. Cook till sauce is almost dry, stirring occasionally. Add in another 425 ml water and stir till gravy starts to boil. Keep boiling for 5 minutes.

5. Put in the mushrooms and bamboo shoots. Reduce heat to low, cover pan and allow to simmer till pork is tender. Stir from time to time to prevent burning. Add a little water if gravy becomes too thick while cooking. Serve hot.

Babi Chin

BABI PONG TAY
(STEWED PORK)

INGREDIENTS

115 g (4 oz) shallots, pounded coarsely
4 pieces garlic, pounded coarsely   **A**
8 cm (3 in) piece cinnamon bark

2 tablespoons preserved soya beans,
  pounded
1 tablespoon sugar   **B**
1 teaspoon salt
1 teaspoon dark soya sauce

625 g (1 lb 6 oz) pig's trotters
625 g (1 lb 6 oz) shoulder of pork
6 tablespoons cooking oil

METHOD

1. Cut meat into pieces.

2. Heat oil in wok and fry **A** till brown. Add **B** and stir-fry for ½ minute.

3. Put in meat. Add 150 ml (5 fl oz) water and cook over high heat, stirring occasionally till almost dry (½ hour).

4. Pour in 305 ml (11 fl oz) water and bring to a rapid boil for 5 minutes. Transfer the stewed pork to a heavy-bottomed aluminium saucepan, cover and let simmer for 1–1½ hours or till meat is tender. Serve hot or cold.

Note:
This is an ideal picnic dish eaten with French loaf. Add more hot water when meat is tender, for more gravy.

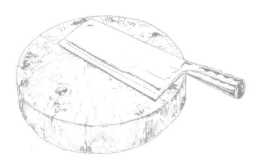

BUAH PAYA MASAK TITEK
(PAPAYA SOUP)

INGREDIENTS

3 candlenuts
1 tablespoon shrimp paste
85 g (3 oz) shallots
1 red chilli   **A**
1 tablespoon peppercorns or 1 tablespoon
  pepper powder

Seasoning:
1 teaspoon salt
2 teaspoons sugar   **B**
1 chicken cube

1 green papaya, approximately 905 g (2 lb)
340 g (12 oz) small fresh prawns
900 ml (30 fl oz) water
55 g (2 oz) dried prawns, pounded finely
225 g (8 oz) salt fish bones, cut into small pieces
1 handful basil leaves (daun kemangi)

METHOD

1. Grind **A** to a fine paste.

2. Skin papaya and cut into small pieces.

3. Shell fresh prawns and reserve shells. Rub prawns with a little salt and sugar; fry shells in 1 tablespoon oil, then pound and boil in 900 ml (30 fl oz) water for 5 minutes. Strain and keep prawn stock.

4. Combine dried prawns, paste **A**, salt fish bones and seasoning (**B**) in the stock. Bring to boil in an enamel saucepan. Put in papaya pieces and boil over moderately hot fire till tender. Add prawns and cook for 2–3 minutes. Remove from heat and serve hot.

To serve:
Dish papaya itek into a large bowl. Place basil leaves over and sprinkle a tablespoon of lard. Serve boiling hot.

BAK WAN KEPITING
(MINCED PORK WITH CRAB AND
BAMBOO SHOOT SOUP)

INGREDIENTS

1 tablespoon lard or oil
1 tablespoon chopped garlic, browned
1 teaspoon salt
Dash of pepper
1 teaspoon msg   **A**
1 egg
½ teaspoon sugar
1 tablespoon light soya sauce

115 g (4 oz) steamed crab meat
55 g (2 oz) boiled bamboo shoots,   **B**
    shredded very finely

455 g (1 lb) minced pork
115 g (4 oz) fish paste

Ingredients for soup:
2 tablespoons lard or oil
1 teaspoon garlic, chopped finely
250 g (9 oz) boiled bamboo shoots, thinly shredded
1 chicken cube
1 level teaspoon salt
1 teaspoon msg

METHOD

1. Mix minced pork, fish paste and **A** in large
   bowl. Add **B** and mix well. Set aside.

2. Heat 2 tablespoons lard in an aluminium
   saucepan. Fry 1 teaspoon garlic till lightly
   browned. Add finely shredded bamboo
   shoots and fry for short while. Pour in
   2.5 litres (5 pints) water and chicken cube
   and bring to boil.

3. Take spoonfuls of meat and form balls the
   size of walnuts. Bring soup to rapid boil
   and put in meatballs. When meatballs float
   to surface, test one to see if cooked. Dish
   into serving bowl and serve hot.

CHAP CHYE MASAK TITEK
(STEWED VEGETABLES, NONYA STYLE)

INGREDIENTS

120 g (4 oz) shallots
  4 candlenuts   *pound*
  1 red chilli   *together*
  2 tablespoons shrimp paste

250 g (9 oz) belly pork, to boil in 500 ml (17 fl oz) water
250 g (9 oz) medium-sized grey prawns
 30 g (1 oz) cloud ear fungus (bok nee), soaked in warm water
 60 g (2 oz) golden needles (kim chiam)
 30 g (1 oz) transparent vermicelli, soaked in boiling water
 60 g (2 oz) soya bean strips (foo chok)
  6 tablespoons oil
 10 sweet bean curd strips (thim chok)

  2 tablespoons preserved salted soya bean, pounded

600 g (21 oz) cabbage, cut into pieces
 60 g (2 oz) Chinese mushrooms, soaked in hot water

Seasoning:
1¼ teaspoons salt
 1 teaspoon msg
 2 teaspoons sugar

METHOD

1. Add ¼ teaspoon salt in 500 ml (17 fl oz) water and boil belly pork in it for 20 minutes. When done, cut into thin slices and set aside. Keep stock.

2. Shell prawns and devein. Pound shells finely, stir in 250 ml (9 fl oz) water and strain. Set aside.

3. Wash cloud ear fungus thoroughly to remove grit. Cut away rough patch at base and set aside.

4. Cut off hard tops of golden needles and wash in water; drain. Cut transparent vermicelli into short lengths. Soak soya bean strips in cold water for 10 minutes. Drain.

To cook stew:

1. Heat an iron or non-stick wok. Add oil and fry sweet bean curd strips over low heat till they blister and turn light brown. Remove immediately.

2. In the same pan, fry the paste over moderate heat till oil bubbles through and is fragrant. Add preserved bean paste and seasoning and stir fry for 2 minutes. Then add prawns and prawn stock and bring to boil. Put in cabbage, cook over high heat for 5 minutes, then pour in pork stock and remaining ingredients. Continue cooking for another 15–20 minutes or till cabbage is tender. Serve hot.

GORENG IKAN TERUBOK
(FISH IN SCREW PINE LEAVES)

INGREDIENTS

905 g (2 lb) herring, whole or cut into two pieces
  1 teaspoon salt
  6 screw pine leaves
225 ml (8 fl oz) oil

METHOD

1. Wash the fish, rub it with the salt and leave to marinate for ½ hour.

2. Wrap the screw pine leaves round the fish.

3. Heat oil in an iron wok and fry fish till crisp and brown on both sides.

4. Remove the screw pine leaves and place the fish on a plate. Pour the hot oil over and serve hot.

Note:
Do not scale the fish. The fish should be fried over a moderately high heat so that it is thoroughly cooked and the scales are crisp. Sprinkle some water whilst frying before covering the pan. The steam from the water will hasten the cooking.

HATI BABI BUNGKUS
(MEAT AND LIVER BALLS)

INGREDIENTS

3 tablespoons sugar
1 teaspoon salt
2 tablespoons dark soya sauce
2 tablespoons vinegar ⟩ **A**

4 tablespoons oil
15 shallots, pounded very finely

310 g (11 oz) minced pork
310 g (11 oz) pork liver, boiled, and diced very finely
2 teaspoons pepper
2 tablespoons roasted coriander powder
455 g (1 lb) pork membrane, cleaned and cut into 15 cm (6 in) squares

METHOD

1. Heat oil in pan and fry pounded shallots till light brown. Reduce the heat to low.

2. Add **A**. Stir-fry for ½ minute. Remove pan from heat.

3. Mix minced pork and liver with fried ingredients. Sprinkle pepper and coriander powder. Knead well to mix thoroughly.

4. Form walnut-size balls from meat mixture. Place on tray.

5. Wrap each meat ball tightly with a small piece of pork membrane. Overlap the membrane two or three times to prevent the meat from bursting out of the wrapper while being fried.

To fry meat balls:
1. Heat a flat-bottomed frying pan, half-filled with oil.

2. Fry meat balls (sealed end downwards) over moderate heat till brown.

Note:
1. Boil liver till it is half-cooked. It will then bind with the minced meat and not crumble easily.

2. Do not buy pig's membrane that has been kept overnight.

3. Wash membrane with water and remove all dirt and bristle.

4. Squeeze membrane lightly to drain excess water.

IKAN MASAK ASSAM PEKAT
(FISH IN TAMARIND JUICE)

INGREDIENTS

Thumb-sized piece fresh turmeric or 1 teaspoon turmeric powder
2 tablespoons shrimp paste
8 shallots, weighing approximately 55 g (2 oz) ⟩ **A**

1 teaspoon sugar
½ teaspoon salt
Walnut-sized piece tamarind, seeded
½ cup water ⟩ **B**

625 g (1 lb 5 oz) spotted Spanish mackerel

Seasoning:
6 tablespoons sugar
1½ teaspoons salt

6 red chillies, slit lengthwise
6 green chillies, slit lengthwise
1 teaspoon lard or oil

METHOD

1. Grind or blend **A** to a very fine paste.

2. Scale and wash fish. Remove bones and cut fish into 2.5 cm (1 in) cubes.

3. Marinate fish with **B** for ½ hour. Drain in a colander.

4. Pour tamarind juice into an enamel saucepan and boil gently for 15 minutes with the seasoning and **A**.

5. Put fish, red and green chillies into the saucepan and cook for 5–7 minutes or till fish is cooked.

6. Stir in the lard and remove from heat. Serve hot or cold.

ITEK TIM
(SALTED CHINESE MUSTARD DUCK SOUP)

INGREDIENTS

4 dried tamarind slices
2 thick slices ginger   **A**
4 salted plums

625 g (1½ lb) pig's foreleg, cut into pieces
½ tablespoon brandy
2 teaspoons salt   **B**
1 teaspoon msg

565 g (20 oz) preserved salted Chinese mustard
1 duck, cut into four pieces
1 tablespoon brandy

METHOD

1. Cut the salted mustard into big pieces and soak in water for ½ hour. Drain.
2. Season the duck with brandy.
3. Boil 3.6 litres (7 pints) water. Add the duck, salted mustard and **A**. When the water re-boils, add **B**.
4. Let the soup boil rapidly for 10 minutes. Lower the heat and let simmer till the meat is tender (about 1–1½ hours).

Note:
You may add four tomatoes (quartered) during the last 10 minutes of cooking time.

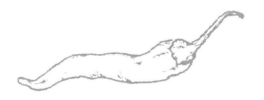

KARI AYAM
(CHICKEN CURRY)

INGREDIENTS

85 g (3 oz) shallots
3 cloves garlic
½ thumb-sized piece ginger, thinly sliced   **A**
1 teaspoon shrimp paste

1 chicken approx. 1.6 kg (3½ lb), cut into pieces
455 g (1 lb) grated coconut (white)

1 sprig curry leaves
5 tablespoons corn oil or refined oil
55 g (2 oz) curry powder for cooking
30 g (1 oz) curry powder for marinating chicken

METHOD

1. Season chicken pieces with 1 level teaspoon each of salt, sugar and msg and the curry powder for ½ hour.
2. Squeeze coconut for first milk. Set aside, add 570 ml (20 fl oz) water to coconut and squeeze for second milk. Set aside.
3. Grind **A** to a rough paste. Heat oil in an aluminium wok. Fry paste till oil bubbles through, and mixture turns light brown.
4. Add in the curry powder, curry leaves with ½ of the first milk. Stir till oil bubbles through and turns reddish. Add in the rest of the first milk, and bring to the boil, continually stirring to prevent burning at bottom.
5. Put in seasoned chicken pieces and stir well with the paste **A** mixture. Cook over moderate heat stirring occasionally.
6. Reduce heat to low, put lid on saucepan and simmer for 20 to 25 minutes or till chicken is tender. Add in some of the second milk to get desired thickness for the gravy — thinner gravy if eaten with bread and thicker gravy for rice. Simmer again for 5 to 7 minutes. Remove from heat. Serve hot or cold.

PONG TAUHU
(BEAN CURD WITH MEAT BALL SOUP)

INGREDIENTS

625 g (1 lb 6 oz) prawns   **A**
4 small soya bean cakes

1 tablespoon salt
1 teaspoon msg
1 egg
1 teaspoon dark soya sauce   **B**
4 tablespoons oil
1 tablespoon fried crispy garlic
1 teaspoon pepper

1 tablespoon preserved brown
   soya beans, pounded   **C**
1 teaspoon sugar

1–1½ teaspoons salt   **D**
1 teaspoon msg

625 g (1 lb 6 oz) young bamboo shoots, boiled
310 g (11 oz) streaky pork
625 g (1 lb 6 oz) minced pork
2 tablespoons finely chopped spring onions
1 teaspoon pounded garlic

METHOD

1. Shell and devein prawns. Wash, drain and fry the shells. Pound the fried shells and mix with 1.4 litres (48 fl oz) water. Strain and set aside prawn stock.

2. Mince **A** together to fine mixture.

3. Cut bamboo shoots into fine strips.

4. Boil streaky pork with 900 ml (32 fl oz) water. Cut into fine strips. Set aside pork stock.

5. Mix **B** in bowl. Add **A**, minced pork and spring onions. Grease hands and roll mixture into walnut-sized balls. Place the meat balls on a tray.

6. Heat 2 tablespoons lard or oil and fry garlic till light brown. Add **C**. Stir-fry for 1 minute. Add bamboo shoots and stir. Add prawn and pork stock. Season soup with **D**. Boil for 15 minutes.

7. Add meat balls and pork strips to boiling soup. Boil gently till meat balls float to the surface. Keep boiling for 5–7 minutes. Remove from the heat.

SATAY BABI
(GRILLED OR FRIED SPICY PORK SLICES)

INGREDIENTS

4 stalks lemon grass, thinly sliced
4 red chillies, seeded
10 dried chillies, seeded   **A**
4 candlenuts
1 teaspoon shrimp paste
15 shallots

1 teaspoon salt
½ teaspoon msg
½ teaspoon pepper   **B**
2 teaspoons sugar
3 tablespoons oil

225 g (8 oz) grated coconut
680 g (1 lb 8 oz) pork, cut into 1½ cm (½ in) thick slices
85 ml (3 fl oz) oil

METHOD

1. Extract No. 1 milk from coconut.

2. Grind **A** to a fine paste.

3. Mix with **B** and No. 1 milk to season pork. Marinate for 1 hour.

4. Thread the meat on to wooden or metal skewers. Brush with oil and place under a pre-heated hot grill until cooked.

Peanut sauce and garnish:
Please see page 28.

Pineapple sauce:
1 small ripe pineapple

1. Cut skin off pineapple and ensure "eyes" are removed.

2. Scrape into a bowl leaving out the hard core.

3. Drain off excess juice and serve the pulp on top of peanut sauce, or separately.

Note
The marinated meat can also be fried over a high heat in an iron wok (kuali) till almost dry and the oil comes through. Chicken can be used instead of pork.

SAYOR NANKA MASAK LEMAK

(JACKFRUIT AND CHICKEN IN RICH SPICY COCONUT GRAVY)

INGREDIENTS

115 g (4 oz) shallots or onions
  2 cloves garlic
  2 candlenuts
  6 pieces galangal, sliced thinly   **A**
  1 stalk lemon grass, sliced thinly
10 dried chillies
  1 teaspoon shrimp paste
¼ thumb-sized piece ginger
½ thumb-sized piece turmeric or
  ¾ teaspoon turmeric powder

680 g (1½ lb) young jackfruit
  1 tablespoon salt
565 g (20 oz) grated coconut, white
  1 tablespoon coriander seeds, roasted and pounded finely
  4 tablespoons oil
680 g (1½ lb) small whole chicken, cut into small pieces

Seasoning:
 2 teaspoons sugar
 2 teaspoons salt
 1 teaspoon msg
½ teaspoon pepper

 1 turmeric leaf
 6 daun limau purot

METHOD

1. Cut the jackfruit into small pieces. Put in a saucepan with enough water to cover the jackfruit. Boil with 1 tablespoon salt for 20–25 minutes or till jackfruit is tender. Drain jackfruit in a colander and set aside.

2. Squeeze coconut for No. 1 milk. Set aside. Add 565 ml (20 fl oz) water to coconut and squeeze for No. 2 milk. Set aside.

3. Roast the coriander seeds in a frying pan till fragrant. Pound till fine while still hot. Set aside.

4. Heat 4 tablespoons oil in wok and fry the paste **A** over moderate heat for 2 minutes. Add roasted coriander, chicken pieces, seasoning and ¼ of No. 1 milk. Keep stirring for 2 minutes until oil appears on surface and mixture is fragrant.

5. Add in turmeric leaf and daun limau purot. Then add No. 2 milk and jackfruit. Cook over moderate heat for ½ hour or till chicken is tender.

6. Pour in the remaining No. 1 milk. Stir well, reduce heat and simmer for 5–7 minutes. Remove from heat. Serve hot or cold.

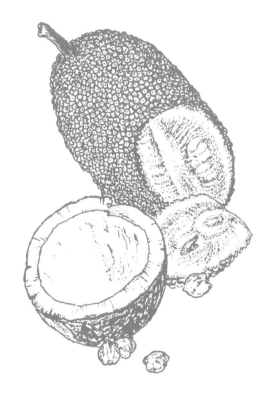

TAUHU MASAK TITEK
(SPICY SOFT BEAN CURD AND SALT FISH SOUP)

INGREDIENTS

455 g (1 lb) minced pork
455 g (1 lb) fresh prawns, minced
½ teaspoon salt
½ teaspoon sugar   **A**
½ teaspoon msg
1 teaspoon light soya sauce
Dash of pepper
1 tablespoon lard or oil

Ingredients for spicy paste:
55 g (2 oz) shallots
4 candlenuts
1 fresh red chilli, seeded   **B** *Ground finely*
1 tablespoon shrimp paste
¼ teaspoon pepper

1 piece soft bean curd, cut into 24 pieces
115 g (4 oz) Penang salt fish bones, cut into pieces

Seasoning for stock:
1 teaspoon salt
1 teaspoon msg or 1 chicken cube

4 stalks Chinese celery, chopped

METHOD

1. Wash salt fish bones and drain.
2. Wash and drain prawn shells; fry in 1 tablespoon oil till cooked. Boil shells in 905 ml (2 pints) water for 10 minutes adding stock seasoning. Set aside stock after straining.
3. Mix **A** in a large bowl and blend well by hand. Make small candlenut-sized balls and set aside.
4. Heat 3 tablespoons of oil in an aluminium saucepan till very hot. Fry spicy paste **B** till fragrant. Pour in prawn stock, salt fish bones and bring to boil. Put meat balls in to cook till well done. Add soft bean curd pieces, cook for 10 minutes and remove from heat.
5. Remove to serving bowl and garnish with Chinese celery.

UDANG KUAH PEDAS NANAS
(PRAWNS IN PINEAPPLE GRAVY)

INGREDIENTS

14 slices galangal
½ thumb-sized piece turmeric
115 g (4 oz) shallots   **A**
3 red chillies
1 tablespoon shrimp paste

900 ml (32 fl oz) water
1 tablespoon salt
1 tablespoon sugar   **B**
1 pineapple, cut into thin pieces
2 dried tamarind slices

625 g (1 lb 6 oz) king prawns, washed and trimmed
Sprigs of basil leaves

METHOD

1. Pound **A** in the given order to a fine paste.
2. Transfer the paste to an enamel saucepan. Add **B** and mix well. Boil over a moderate heat for 10 minutes.
3. Add the prawns, cook uncovered for 2 minutes. Remove from heat. Garnish with basil leaves. Serve hot.

Note:
The gravy can be boiled first. Add the prawns to cook just before serving so that the prawns will be sweet and more tasty.

Porridge and Rice

Kai Chok

Chicken Rice

Flavoured Chicken Rice

Fried Rice

Nasi Kuning

Nasi Lemak Kuning

Nasi Briani Ayam

Nasi Pilau

Nasi Ulam

Pineapple Rice

Steamed Glutinous Rice

Kai Chok

KAI CHOK

(CHICKEN CONGEE — HONG KONG STYLE)

INGREDIENTS

2.8 litres (6 pints) water
  1 teaspoon salt
  1 teaspoon msg   **A**
  2 tablespoons peppercorn

795 g (1¾ lb) chicken
  1 tablespoon light soya sauce
  1 teaspoon sesame oil
170 g (6 oz) No. 1 Thai fragrant rice
1.7 litres (4 pints) water
  ½ teaspoon salt
  1 tablespoon oil

  3 tablespoons glutinous rice powder | *thickening*
225 ml (8 fl oz) water

  1 oz young ginger, shredded very finely
  2 stalks spring onions, cut finely | *garnishing*
  Dash of pepper
  Chinese crullers, sliced

METHOD

1. Boil **A** in a saucepan. Add chicken and boil rapidly for 5 minutes, reduce heat, cover pan and simmer chicken for 30 minutes.

2. Remove chicken and immerse in a basin of cold water for 5 minutes. Debone chicken and set aside. Put bones back in saucepan to simmer with the chicken stock for 1½ hours.

3. Strain chicken stock into another saucepan adding boiling water, if necessary, so that it measures 2.2 litres (4 pints).

4. Cut chicken meat into small cubes and mix with 1 tablespoon light soya sauce and 1 teaspoon sesame oil. Put in a bowl, cover and set aside.

5. While chicken is being cooked, boil rice with the salt and oil in a fairly large saucepan till porridge is thick and smooth, stirring occasionally to prevent burning.

6. Pour in the chicken stock, stir till well blended and bring to boil. Mix thickening and pour gradually into the porridge, stirring all the time. Simmer for 5 minutes before serving.

To serve:
Put some chicken into individual bowls, add the boiling porridge and garnish with shredded ginger, spring onions and a dash of pepper. Top with Chinese crullers and serve hot.

Note
Pressure cooker can also be used to cook the porridge.

Cooking time depends on each brand, approximate time 20–30 minutes. Remove the lid of cooker to check if porridge is smooth. Add some hot water if porridge is too thick. Cover lid and cook for further 5–7 minutes.

To make Chee Yiok Chok *(pork congee), use instant seasoned minced pork instead of chicken and put in to boil with the congee. Sliced liver can be added if desired.*

(10 servings)

INSTANT SEASONED MINCED PORK

INGREDIENTS

1 teaspoon sugar
1 teaspoon sesame oil
1 teaspoon light soya sauce   **A**
1 teaspoon msg
1 tablespoon corn flour

455 g (1 lb) minced pork
  3 tablespoons *twa tow chye* (salted radish), finely chopped

METHOD

1. Place minced pork and *twa tow chye* in a large bowl.

2. Mix **A** with the minced pork and stir by hand till well blended.

Note:
Pack meat mixture into plastic bag if storing in freezer.
To use frozen meat, chop off one chunk and leave to thaw before putting into soup. Form into balls while cold and set aside. Return rest of meat to freezer immediately.

CHICKEN RICE

INGREDIENTS

CHICKEN:
6–8 cloves garlic, bashed lightly
  2 thumb-sized pieces ginger, bashed lightly | **A**
  4 stalks spring onions, tied into a knot

1.6 kg (3½ lb) whole chicken

GARNISH:
2 cucumbers, sliced
4 tomatoes, sliced
2 sprigs Chinese parsley, cut into pieces

METHOD

To boil the chicken:
1. Wash chicken and rub some salt over it. Stuff chicken with **A**.
2. Boil 2.1 litres (4 pints) water with 1 teaspoon salt rapidly over high heat.
3. Add chicken, leaving saucepan uncovered. When water re-boils, cook for further 2 minutes then reduce the heat to very low, cover and let simmer for 25–30 minutes. (Do not remove lid throughout cooking time).
4. Set aside 995 ml (35 fl oz) chicken stock for the rice. Remove chicken immediately to immerse in a basin of cold water for 5 minutes.
5. Transfer chicken to a large plate and brush it immediately with oil. Remove stuffing.
6. Allow chicken to cool before cutting it into pieces. Arrange on a serving plate.
7. Garnish. Serve with chilli sauce and ginger sauce.

RICE:
625 g (22 oz) Thai No. 1 rice
115 ml (4 fl oz) lard or oil
995 ml (35 fl oz) chicken stock (Method 4)
  2 teaspoons salt
  1 teaspoon msg
  6 screw pine leaves, tied into a knot

1. Wash rice until water runs clear. Drain.
2. Heat pan. Fry rice in heated lard for 2 minutes. Put the chicken stock, salt and msg in a saucepan. Add the fried rice and screw pine leaves. Boil over moderate heat till all the stock is absorbed.
3. Reduce heat to low and cook for a further 15 minutes. Rake rice with a fork and serve hot.

GINGER SAUCE:
55 ml (2 fl oz) chicken stock |
½ teaspoon salt |
½ teaspoon msg | **A**
½ teaspoon sugar |

2 thumb-sized pieces ginger

1. Slice ginger thinly and pound till fine.
2. Mix **A** in a bowl and add the pounded ginger.

CHILLI SAUCE:
10-12 red chillies
  ½ teaspoon salt
  55 ml (2 fl oz) warm water
  2-3 tablespoons lime juice

1. Scald chillies. Remove stems and pound chillies coarsely with ½ teaspoon salt.
2. Remove to a bowl and mix with warm water and lime juice.

Note:
When cooking 625 g–1.2 kg (22-43 oz) rice, use an electric rice cooker. When rice is cooked, wipe water from under the lid of cooker to prevent rice getting soggy.

(8 servings)

FLAVOURED CHICKEN RICE

INGREDIENTS

1 teaspoon salt
1 teaspoon msg   **A**
1 teaspoon dark soya sauce

1 thumb-sized piece of ginger,
   shredded finely
3 cloves garlic, thinly sliced   **B**
4 shallots, thinly sliced

2 tablespoons light soya sauce
1 teaspoon dark soya sauce
1 teaspoon msg
1 teaspoon salt   **C**
1 tablespoon sesame oil
1 chicken cube, mashed
¼ teaspoon pepper

905 g (2 lb) deboned chicken, cut into pieces

115 ml (4 fl oz) lard or oil

4 dried Chinese mushrooms, soaked and sliced
   thinly
625 g (22 oz) No. 1 Thai rice, washed and drained

935 ml (33 fl oz) boiling water
2 pairs Chinese sausages, fried and cut into 4 cm
   (1½ in) pieces
Chinese parsley

METHOD

1. Marinate the chicken in **A** for ½ hour.

2. Heat 2 tablespoons oil in hot pan and fry chicken till brown on all sides. Set aside.

3. Heat lard in wok and fry **B** till light brown. Add the mushrooms and stir-fry for 1 minute. Add the rice and fry till oil is absorbed.

4. Mix **C** in a bowl. Add to rice together with 935 ml (33 fl oz) boiling water. Cook till rice is quite dry.

5. Place the fried sausages and the fried chicken pieces on the rice. Allow to cook for ½ hour over a low heat. Serve hot.

FRIED RICE

INGREDIENTS

6 tablespoons water
1 teaspoon salt
1 teaspoon msg   **A**
1 tablespoon light soya sauce
¼ teaspoon pepper

4 tablespoons lard or oil
4 eggs, lightly beaten with a pinch of salt
2 tablespoons chopped onions
85 g (3 oz) small shelled prawns
455 g (16 oz) cold cooked rice
115 g (¼ lb) roast pork, diced
4 tablespoons chopped spring onions

METHOD

1. Heat 2 tablespoons lard in wok and scramble beaten eggs. Remove and set aside.

2. Heat rest of the lard and fry onions till transparent. Stir-fry prawns, followed by rice.

3. Mix **A** in a bowl and add to the rice, stir-frying all ingredients.

4. Add the scrambled eggs and roast pork. Continue to stir-fry over a high heat. Finally add the spring onions. Serve fried rice hot, in a large dish.

NASI KUNING
(YELLOW RICE)

INGREDIENTS

625 g (22 oz) briani rice
  2 tablespoons oil

1 teaspoon pounded ginger 4 cloves garlic 6 shallots, thinly sliced	**A**

8 cm (3 in) piece cinnamon bark 8 cardamons, lightly bashed 8 cloves	**B**

115 g (4 oz) ghee or butter
½ teaspoon turmeric powder
  blended with 1 tablespoon
  lime juice
	C

995 ml (35 fl oz) boiling water

1 teaspoon msg 1 rounded teaspoon salt 1 chicken cube 55 g (2 oz) almonds, chopped 115 g (4 oz) sultanas	**D**

METHOD

1. Wash the rice and drain it in a colander.
2. Heat an iron wok (kuali). Heat the oil and brown **A** in the given order.
3. Add **B** and stir-fry. Add **C**.
4. Add the rice and stir-fry till the oil is absorbed.
5. Remove the rice to a saucepan or an electric rice cooker. Pour in the boiling water and season with **D**. Boil with the lid on over a moderate heat till the rice has absorbed all the water. Reduce the heat to low and cook for about 15 minutes. Spoon the cooked rice on to a large platter. Garnish with a sprinkling of fried almonds and sultanas.

To fry the almonds and sultanas:
1. Place 3 tablespoons oil in a heated pan to stir-fry the chopped almonds till light brown, over a low heat. Drain on absorbent paper. Store in a bottle.
2. In the same oil, fry the sultanas for 2 minutes. Drain and cool on absorbent paper.

NASI LEMAK KUNING
(SPICY YELLOW RICE)

INGREDIENTS

30 g (1 oz) SANTAN instant coconut cream
  powder
1½ teaspoons salt
  1 cube chicken stock
  6 tablespoons oil
  2 stalks lemon grass, bashed
100 g (3 oz) shallots/onions, thinly sliced
  1 thumb-sized cinnamon stick
500 g (18 oz) long grain rice
1½ level teaspoons turmeric powder
  1 tablespoon lime juice
  4 screw pine leaves, tied into a knot

METHOD

1. Dissolve SANTAN powder in 720 mls (25 fl oz) water and strain into a saucepan. Stir in salt and chicken stock. Allow to heat over very low fire till mixture comes to a boil. Set aside.
2. Heat oil in the wok, fry lemon grass till fragrant and light brown. Add in cinnamon and shallots/onions, continue to stir fry till brown. Pour in rice, turmeric powder, lime juice and stir till evenly mixed. Remove from heat.
3. Transfer rice mixture into the rice cooker and pour in the hot SANTAN mixture and screw pine leaves. Leave rice to cook till dry and grainy.
4. Wipe steam from underlid to prevent rice from getting wet and soggy.
5. Transfer rice onto a large serving plate. Garnish with sliced egg omelette, fine chilli strips and crispy shallots.

One 30 g packet of SANTAN powder is equivalent to 1 lb white grated coconut.

NASI BRIANI AYAM

(GHEE RICE WITH MILD SPICY CHICKEN)

INGREDIENTS

1 thumb-sized piece ginger
3 cloves garlic   **A**
4 green chillies

1 handful mint leaves
2 stalks coriander with roots, rinsed
2 tomatoes, cut in eighths   **B**
2 tablespoons tomato puree

Seasoning:
2 teaspoons salt
2 teaspoons msg
1 teaspoon sugar

1.6 (3½ lb) chicken quartered
225 g (8 oz) ghee or 112 g (4 oz) butter with 112 ml (4 fl oz) oil
1 teaspoon dry chilli powder mixed to a paste with water
1 level teaspoon garam masala (see recipe)
170 ml (6 fl oz) evaporated milk mixed with 1 tablespoon lemon juice and 112 ml (4 fl oz) water
285 g (10 oz) shallots, thinly sliced

METHOD

1. Marinate chicken pieces with 1 level tablespoon salt and 1 teaspoon msg for 1 hour.

2. Heat a large saucepan with half of the ghee. Fry the shallots till golden brown. Set aside.

3. Fry **A** till fragrant. Add chilli paste and garam masala, then add in **B**, seasoning and ½ of the milk mixture. Stir-fry till oil bubbles through.

4. Put in chicken pieces, fried shallots, remaining milk and oil. Cook over high heat for 10 minutes.

5. Reduce heat to low and cook gently till chicken is tender. Drain chicken, keeping oil to cook the briani rice.

To Cook Rice :
1 teaspoon chopped ginger
1 tablespoon chopped garlic   **C**
4 shallots, thinly sliced

5 cm (2 in) cinnamon bark
8 cardamoms, lightly bashed   **D**
6 cloves

600 g (21 oz) Basmati (long grain) rice, washed and drained
55 g (2 oz) ghee

Seasoning:
1 teaspoon msg or 1 chicken cube
1½ teaspoons salt
1.1 litres (40 fl oz) boiling water

Colouring for Rice :
Mix 1 teaspoon yellow food colouring with ¼ teaspoon Rose essence and 4 tablespoons water.

1. Heat wok with 55 g (2 oz) ghee to fry **C** till lightly browned, add in **D** and stir-fry for ½ minute. Add in the remaining oil and the rice. Stir in pan till oil is absorbed into rice.

2. Pour in the boiling water and the seasoning. Cook rice in an electric rice-cooker till dry and fluffy. Do not stir while cooking.

3. Remove lid and sprinkle the yellow colouring mixture over rice. Continue to cook for another 10 minutes. Remove from heat. Loosen rice, mixing colours evenly. Serve hot with chicken.

GARAM MASALA
(GROUND MIXED SPICES)

115 g (4 oz) coriander seeds, washed and dried
55 g (2 oz) cumin seeds, washed and dried
2 tablespoons black pepper
1 tablespoon white pepper
3 teaspoons cardamom seeds
30 g (1 oz) cinnamon bark, broken into small pieces
2 teaspoons cloves
3 nutmegs

1. Spread the ingredients in a large aluminium tray. Heat under a warm grill till fragrant and very lightly browned — do not allow to darken. Grind mixture, while still warm, in a coffee grinder till very fine. Keep in an air-tight bottle and store in fridge.

Nasi Briani Ayam

NASI PILAU
(BUTTERED RICE WITH ROAST CHICKEN)

INGREDIENTS

Seasoning:

1 teaspoon salt
1 teaspoon msg
1 teaspoon pepper
1 teaspoon brandy   **A**
1 teaspoon sugar
1 tablespoon ginger juice
1 tablespoon light soya sauce

625 g (22 oz) No. 1 Thai rice   **B**
1 litre (32 fl oz) water

1.4 kg (3 lb) chicken, whole
170 g (6 oz) butter
115 ml (4 fl oz) water

1 handful raisins, fried
30 almonds, sliced and fried
6 slices cooked ham, cut into pieces and rolled
A few lettuce leaves
1 cucumber, sliced

METHOD

1. Mix **A** in a bowl.
2. Marinate chicken, both inside and out, using 1 tablespoon of the seasoning. Leave for an hour.
3. Heat roasting pan. Grease chicken with half of the butter and place it in heated pan. Add water to the leftover marinade, mix well and pour into the roasting pan. Roast chicken for ½ hour till brown. Reduce the heat to moderate and continue roasting till the chicken is cooked (¾–1 hour).
4. Debone and cut the chicken into serving portions. Set aside. Leave the juices in the pan.
5. Cook **B** in a rice cooker.
6. Rake rice with a fork, add the rest of the butter, pan juices and mix well.
7. Dish the rice onto a large serving plate. Scatter the raisins and almonds over it. Arrange the chicken and rolled ham on top. Decorate border of the dish with lettuce and cucumber.

NASI ULAM

INGREDIENTS

455 g (1 lb) small prawns, shelled
225 g (½ lb) wolf herring (ikan parang), remove centre bone
170 g (6 oz) grated coconut, white
55 g (2 oz) long beans
1 cucumber
905 g (2 lb) cooked rice (cooled)
1 tablespoon light soya sauce
6 lime leaves, sliced very thinly
2 turmeric leaves, sliced very thinly
55 g (2 oz) dried shrimps, optional
Cooking oil
Salt

METHOD

1. Fry prawns with a pinch of salt.
2. Season fish with salt and fry with oil till cooked. Break fish into small pieces and place under grill for 10 minutes or till dry.
3. Add a pinch of salt to the coconut and fry in an iron wok over low heat till light brown, stirring all the time. Cool.
4. Scald and cut long beans into very fine pieces.
5. Skin cucumber, remove soft centre and cut into tiny cubes.

To serve:
1. Place the cooled rice in a large bowl.
2. Sprinkle ½ teaspoon fine salt and 1 tablespoon light soya sauce, and mix well.
3. Add the prepared ingredients, together with the lime leaves, turmeric leaves and dried shrimps. Stir with two wooden spoons till well mixed. Serve cold.

(8 servings)

PINEAPPLE RICE

INGREDIENTS

55 g (2 oz) shallots or onions, sliced finely
2 cloves garlic, sliced finely **A**
2 cm (¾ in) cinnamon stick

1 teaspoon curry powder
¾ teaspoon turmeric powder
1 teaspoon msg or 1 chicken cube, crushed **B**
2 level teaspoons salt
1 tablespoon lemon juice

3 tablespoons oil
55 g (2 oz) dried prawns, pounded coarsely
55 g (2 oz) ham, cut into small squares
225 g (8 oz) pineapple cubes (from can)
2 tablespoons butter

560 g fragrant (20 oz) Thai rice, washed and
   drained
170 ml (6 fl oz) pineapple juice (from can)
   Boiling water
4 pandan leaves, knotted

METHOD

1. Pour 3 tablespoons oil in a heated wok. When hot, fry dried prawns and ham till brown. Remove to a plate. In the same wok, fry pineapple cubes for 5 minutes till light brown. Remove to a plate.

2. Add butter to wok and fry **A** till light brown. Add **B** and stir. Put rice in and keep stirring till oil is absorbed. Pour in pineapple juice and stir for 1 minute.

3. Transfer rice into an electric rice cooker. Add enough boiling water and pandan leaves. When rice is cooked, allow rice to rest in cooker to dry for ½ hour. Loosen rice with fork and reheat briefly. Serve hot in cut-out pineapple.

STEAMED GLUTINOUS RICE

INGREDIENTS

1 piece dried streaky pork★
6 dried Chinese mushrooms, soaked **A**
2 pairs Chinese sausages

1 teaspoon ginger
1 teaspoon garlic **B**

310 g (11 oz) pork bones
680 ml (24 fl oz) water
¼ teaspoon salt **C**
1 teaspoon peppercorns

2 teaspoons dark soya sauce
1 teaspoon msg **D**
1 teaspoon sesame oil

4 tablespoons lard
10 shallots, thinly sliced
625 g (22 oz) glutinous rice, washed, soaked overnight and drained

METHOD

1. Dice **A** and chop **B**.

2. Boil **C** and let it simmer gently until the stock is reduced by half (approximately 1 hour). Strain.

3. Heat lard in wok and fry chopped ingredients and shallots till brown. Add diced ingredients and stir-fry for 1 minute. Add the glutinous rice and mix it thoroughly with the fried mixture. Pour in the stock. Season with **D** and stir-fry for a moment.

4. Reduce heat to very low. Cover wok and cook for a further 5 minutes till the stock is absorbed.

5. Remove cooked glutinous rice and press it down firmly into small bowls. Place the bowls in a steamer and steam for 20 minutes. Serve hot.

★This is the seasoned, dried variety imported from China.

Noodles

Birthday Noodles, Nonya Style

Crispy Noodles with Prawns

Beef Kway Teow

Fried Noodles

Hokien Mee

Kai See Ho Fun

Nonya Mahmee

Teochew Kway Teow

Birthday Noodles, Nonya Style

BIRTHDAY NOODLES NONYA STYLE

INGREDIENTS

285 g (10 oz) belly pork
285 g (10 oz) small prawns, shelled and deveined
  (keep shells)
285 g (10 oz) big prawns, shelled and deveined
  (keep shells), minced finely
175 g (6 oz) fish paste (available from wet markets)
  1 tablespoon tapioca flour
2–3 drops red food colouring
225 g (8 oz) fine rice vermicelli (mee suah)*
  1 litre (32 fl oz) oil
  5 tablespoons lard
  1 tablespoon pounded garlic
  1 tablespoon preserved soya bean paste, pounded

Garnish:
30 g (1 oz) coriander leaves, cut into short lengths
30 g (1 oz) spring onions, cut into 1 cm (½ in.)
  lengths
 3 tablespoons crispy shallots

METHOD

1. Boil belly pork with 1 teaspoon msg in 1 litre (32 fl oz) water. Keep stock.

2. Marinate whole prawns with ¼ teaspoon each of salt and sugar. Set aside.

3. Fry all the prawn shells in 2 tablespoons oil till well cooked. Put shells in a saucepan, add 1 litre water and boil for 20 minutes. Strain stock and set aside.

4. Put minced prawns in a large bowl. Add fish paste and sprinkle in ¾ teaspoon fine salt, 1 teaspoon msg, 1 tablespoon tapioca flour and 2–3 drops red food colouring. Rub paste with palm of hand in a circular motion for 2 minutes. Sprinkle 3 tablespoons water and rub again till paste becomes sticky. Take fistfuls and throw against side of bowl (10–15 times) to smoothen paste.

5. Take fistfuls of paste to squeeze through thumb and first finger to make balls, then leave in cold water for 30 minutes.

6. Slice belly pork thinly and cut into thin strips. Pour prawn and pork stock into saucepan and bring to a boil. Drop in the prawn-and-fish balls till they rise to the surface. Scoop out and keep stock.

To cook noodles:

1. Loosen fine rice vermicelli for deep frying. Heat 1 litre oil in a wok till hot. Oil is ready when a piece of noodle put in for testing rises to the surface. Fry each skein of noodles separately till light brown, turning once. Set aside.

2. Heat lard in a hot aluminium or iron wok and fry garlic till light brown. Add 1 tablespoon sugar and preserved soya bean paste. Stir-fry till oil seeps through. Add 2 cups of reserved stock, whole prawns, shredded pork and prawn-and-fish balls. Cook for 2 minutes and scoop out prawns, pork and prawn-and-fish balls, leaving gravy.

3. Pour in remaining stock and bring to a boil. Reduce heat to low, put in fried vermicelli and stir well with chopsticks. Season to taste after vermicelli softens in gravy.

4. Dish vermicelli onto a large serving plate. Return the prawns, pork and prawn-and-fish balls to boil gently. When ready, pour over vermicelli. Sprinkle with pepper and garnish. Serve immediately.

Note:
This is a traditional nonya dish served only on birthdays.
Instead of making tiny prawn-and-fish balls, the mixture can be made into square patties and boiled in the prawn stock. When cooled, cut into small cubes.

*The best fine rice vermicelli is made in China. They are available in boxes and are packed in skeins tied with red strings. No seasoning is added to the gravy because the vermicelli is quite salty. Season gravy to taste only after vermicelli has been introduced.

See Page 123 for Nonya Salad to complement Noodles.

CRISPY NOODLES WITH PRAWNS

INGREDIENTS

605 g (21 oz) big prawns
 ¼ teaspoon msg
 1 teaspoon ginger
 1 chicken cube
 2 tablespoons oil
 1 packet dry egg noodles (200 g)
   Oil for deep frying
 4 tablespoons lard
 6 slices ginger
 1 teaspoon pounded garlic
 4 dry Chinese mushrooms, soaked and sliced
285 g (10 oz) Chinese mustard greens, cut into 3 cm
   (1½ in) lengths
455 ml (16 fl oz) chicken stock, or 455 ml hot water
   with 1 chicken cube for gravy

Seasoning:
 1 tablespoon light soya sauce
 1 tablespoon oyster sauce
 ½ teaspoon sugar   **A** *mixed in a bowl*
 1 teaspoon msg
 ¼ teaspoon salt
 ½ teaspoon sesame oil

 2 tablespoons corn flour   **B** *thickening*
 4 tablespoons water

METHOD

Shell prawns leaving tails; devein and marinate
with ¼ teaspoon msg and 1 teaspoon ginger.

To prepare crispy noodles:
1. Bring 565 ml (20 fl oz) water to boil with
   one chicken cube and 2 tablespoons oil. Put
   in noodles and cook till noodles separate
   and become soft (approximately 3–4 minutes). Immerse noodles in cold water and
   drain immediately in a steel colander. Allow
   to cool and dry for ½ hour before frying.
2. When wok is heated, pour in oil. When
   very hot, put in the noodles, a little each
   time and fry till crispy and light brown.
   Scoop out with wire ladle onto absorbent
   paper. Keep the noodles warm.

3. Heat 3 tablespoons lard in wok and fry ginger and garlic till light brown. Add
   mushrooms and mustard stalks and stir-fry
   for a short while. Add mustard leaves,
   chicken stock and seasoning and bring to
   boil.
4. Arrange prawns over the leaves, cover pan
   and cook over high heat for 2 minutes. Remove lid, gradually add in thickening, stirring constantly. Lower heat and when gravy
   boils, add last tablespoon of lard.
5. Transfer crispy noodles to a serving plate
   and immediately pour sauce over. Serve
   hot.

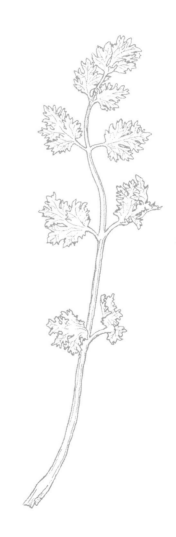

BEEF KWAY TEOW

INGREDIENTS

455 g (1 lb) beef tripe, scalded
455 g (1 lb) beef ribs
905 g (2 lb) beef shin or brisket, whole
1 tablespoon salt
1 teaspoon msg
1 teaspoon dark soya sauce   **A**
1 teaspoon peppercorns
4 cloves
2 thick slices galangal
1 tablespoon grated palm sugar

1 tablespoon Bovril (optional)
565 g (20 oz) bean sprouts
905 g (2 lb) flat rice noodles
115 g (4 oz) salted Chinese mustard, cut into thin pieces
6 sprigs Chinese celery, cut into pieces

METHOD

1. Bring 2.7 litres (5 pints) water to a rapid boil in saucepan. Add **A**. Boil rapidly for 20 minutes.

2. Reduce heat and let simmer till meat and tripe are tender. Add Bovril to taste.

3. Remove tripe and meat from the soup and cut into small pieces.

To serve:
Boil water to scald bean sprouts. Drain. Immerse noodles in the boiling water for a moment and drain. Place a small handful of bean sprouts and noodles in a bowl, add some meat and tripe. Add boiling soup and garnish with salted Chinese mustard and Chinese celery. Serve hot with chilli sauce and pounded galangal.

Note:
Remove meat when tender and leave tripe to simmer till soft.
For pounded galangal, skin two thumb-sized pieces. Slice thinly and pound till fine.

(15 servings)

FRIED NOODLES

INGREDIENTS

1 packet dried egg noodles
1 chicken cube   **A**
1 tablespoon lard

1 tablespoon oyster sauce
½ teaspoon salt
2 tablespoons light soya sauce
1 teaspoon sesame oil   **B**
½ teaspoon pepper
1 teaspoon msg
½ teaspoon sugar
115 ml (4 fl oz) hot water

225 g (8 oz) lettuce, cut into strips
2–3 chillies, seeded and cut into long thin   **C**
strips

6 eggs, lightly beaten with a pinch of salt
1 teaspoon pounded garlic
112 g (¼ lb) small, cooked prawns, shelled
455 g (16 oz) bean sprouts, washed and picked
225 g (½ lb) roast pork, shredded finely

METHOD

1. Boil 900 ml (32 fl oz) water in a saucepan. Add **A**. Boil for 5–7 minutes or till noodles separate. Immerse in cold water. Drain in a colander.

2. Heat a little oil and scramble eggs in heated wok. Remove to a dish.

3. In the same wok, add 2 tablespoons lard. Fry garlic till light brown. Add prawns and stir-fry for ½ minute.

4. Add bean sprouts, noodles, eggs and roast pork.

5. Toss mixture in wok. Mix **B** in a bowl, then pour over and around the noodle mixture. Stir-fry and cook for 2 minutes.

6. Remove noodles to a large serving plate. Garnish with **C** and serve.

HOKIEN MEE

INGREDIENTS

455 ml (16 fl oz) water
  1 teaspoon salt   **A**
  2 teaspoons msg

  4 eggs
625 g (22 oz) bean sprouts, picked and washed
625 g (22 oz) fresh yellow noodles
  2 teaspoons pounded garlic   **B**
  2 tablespoons light soya sauce
  55 g (2 oz) chives, cut into 3 cm lengths

  4 limes, halved   **C**
  4 red chillies, sliced thinly

310 g (11 oz) medium size prawns
310 g (11 oz) cuttlefish (remove the centre bone and ink bag)
310 g (11 oz) streaky pork
  Lard for frying

METHOD

To make the stock:
1. Remove prawn heads. Wash and drain. Fry heads in 1 tablespoon oil for 1 minute. Remove from pan and pound. Mix with 225 ml water. Strain and set liquid aside.

2. Boil **A** in saucepan.

3. Put in cuttlefish to boil for 2 minutes. Remove and cut cylindrically. Set aside.

4. Cook prawns in the same stock. Remove and shell, leaving tails on. Set aside.

5. Cook streaky pork in stock till done (about 15 minutes). Set aside to cool. Slice pork into thin strips. Set aside.

6. Pour the prawn liquid (Method 1) into the stock and continue boiling till liquid is reduced to 455 ml (16 fl oz). Strain.

To fry the noodles:
1. Halve **B** and the cooked prawns, pork and cuttlefish to fry in two separate lots.

2. Heat a large iron wok. When very hot, heat 2 tablespoons lard to fry one lot. Add eggs to scramble, then add bean sprouts and noodles. Add 1 tablespoonful of stock to noodles, stir-fry and cover.

3. Remove lid, put prawns, pork and cuttlefish over noodle mixture. Cover and cook for a further 2 minutes. Remove lid and stir-fry noodle mixture evenly over a high heat for a short while.

4. Push aside noodle mixture. Add another 2 tablespoons lard to fry the garlic till light brown. Add light soya sauce and a ladleful of stock. Stir in noodle mixture and mix evenly.

5. Lastly, add chives and stir. Remove to a plate, garnish with **C** and serve hot.

6. Repeat process with the other half of the ingredients.

Note
Use lard to fry as it gives a better flavour and aroma than ordinary cooking oil. Frying should be done over a high heat throughout to prevent the noodles from becoming soggy and to keep the bean sprouts crunchy.

(6 servings)

KAI SEE HO FUN
(FLAT RICE NOODLES WITH BRAISED CHICKEN)

INGREDIENTS

55 g (2 oz) ginger, lightly bashed
6 cloves garlic, lightly bashed
3 stalks spring onion, tied into a knot } **A**

Lard or oil for frying

Seasoning:
1 teaspoon msg
4 tablespoons light soya sauce
1 teaspoon dark soya sauce
1 teaspoon sesame oil
½ teaspoon pepper
½–1 teaspoon salt
455 ml (16 fl oz) water } **B**

Thickening:
1½ tablespoons corn flour
115 ml (4 fl oz) water
1 tablespoon lard
1 teaspoon sesame oil } **C** *mixed in a bowl*

1.14 kg (2½ lb) chicken
1 tablespoon pounded rock sugar
455 g (1 lb) Chinese mustard greens, cut into 5 cm (2 in) lengths
1 tablespoon sugar
1 teaspoon salt
1 tablespoon oil
905 g (2 lb) flat rice noodles
8 tablespoons crispy shallots★ (optional)

METHOD

To braise chicken:

1. Wash chicken and season both inside and outside with salt. Drain. Stuff chicken with **A**.

2. Heat 4 tablespoons lard or oil in an iron wok. Add pounded rock sugar and fry till sugar turns light brown. Pour in the seasoning **B**, stir and bring to the boil.

3. Put in chicken, increase heat to high, spoon gravy all over chicken and cook till chicken is nicely browned. Boil for 15 minutes. Reduce heat to medium, cover pan and simmer for 30–40 minutes or till chicken is well done. Add a little water if necessary during cooking. Remove chicken to cool.

4. Remove stuffing, debone and reserve bones and set aside meat.

5. Pour gravy into a saucepan. Add 830 ml (30 fl oz) hot water, and chicken bones and simmer for 1 hour. Stir in the thickening **C**, cook for 1 minute and remove from heat.

6. Bring 2.3 litres (80 fl oz) water to the boil. Put in the vegetable stalks to boil for ½ minute. Add the leaves, sprinkle 1 tablespoon sugar, 1 teaspoon salt and 1 tablespoon oil into saucepan. Stir and continue boiling over high heat for another ½ minute. Drain in a colander. Place colander in an enamel basin and put under running water till vegetable is well cooled. Drain and set aside till ready to serve.

To serve flat rice noodles:

1. Cut chicken into bite-sized pieces.

2. Heat gravy till almost boiling point.

3. Divide noodles into 8 portions.

4. Bring 3.4 litres (7 pints) water in a saucepan to a rapid boil. Put one portion of the noodles into the saucepan and boil for 10 seconds only. Scoop and drain noodles with a wire mesh ladle and remove to a bowl. Sprinkle 1 teaspoon of light soya sauce and a few drops of sesame oil. Stir with chopsticks and remove to a plate.

5. Place some vegetables and a few pieces of chicken over noodles, pour hot gravy over and serve. Repeat process for the other seven portions.

Note:
Garnish with crispy shallots just before serving.

Choose the broad and smooth, very white and light-textured noodles for this recipe.

★See "Helpful Hints".

NONYA MAHMEE

INGREDIENTS

1 tablespoon preserved soya beans, pounded
½ teaspoon salt
1 teaspoon msg   **A**
½ teaspoon pepper
1 teaspoon sugar

170 g (6 oz) water convolvulus, cut into short
    lengths
625 g (22 oz) bean sprouts, washed and pick-   **B**
    ed
625 g (22 oz) fresh yellow noodles

1 cucumber, without skin and centre,
    shredded very finely into 4 cm lengths
2 eggs, fried into thin omelettes and finely
    shredded
3 tablespoons fried crispy shallots   **C**
3 red chillies, slit, seeded and shredded as
    for cucumber
Dash of pepper
1 bundle coriander leaves

170 g (6 oz) streaky pork

310 g (11 oz) small prawns
  4 tablespoons lard or oil
  1 tablespoon pounded garlic

METHOD

1. Boil the streaky pork in 455 ml (16 fl oz)
   water and ¼ teaspoon salt for 20 minutes.
   Set aside the stock and cut the boiled pork
   into thin strips.

2. Shell the prawns. Wash and drain shells in
   colander and pound coarsely, adding 455 ml
   (16 fl oz) water. Stir and strain liquid into a
   bowl.

3. Heat lard in wok and fry pounded garlic till
   light brown. Add and stir-fry **A** for
   1 minute.

4. Pour in the prawn liquid and pork stock
   and bring to the boil. Add prawns and
   streaky pork. Cook for 1 minute.

5. Add **B** to the boiled mixture. Stir-fry for
   2–3 minutes over high heat to cook the noodles.

6. Dish on to a large plate and garnish with **C**.
   Serve hot.

TEOCHEW KWAY TEOW
(FLAT RICE NOODLES IN SOUP)

INGREDIENTS

Seasoning: (A)
½ teaspoon sugar, ¼ teaspoon salt, 1 teaspoon light
soya sauce

3.4 litres (6 pints) water
1½ tablespoons salt
  2 teaspoons msg   **B**
  1 tablespoon peppercorns
605 g (21 oz) pork bones

Cooked prawns
Cooked fish balls
4 fish cakes, fried and sliced thinly   *garnishing*
4 tablespoons *tung chye*
Chinese celery
Spring onions

605 g (21 oz) medium-sized prawns
 40 small fish balls
115 g (4 oz) minced pork, mixed with 4 tablespoons
    water and ½ teaspoon msg
605 g (21 oz) flat rice noodles
605 g (21 oz) bean sprouts, wash and picked
  4 cloves garlic, chopped and fried to a light
    brown with 8 tablespoons lard or oil
  8 fresh red chillies, sliced thinly and mixed with
    8 tablespoons fish soya sauce

METHOD

1. Shell prawns leaving the tail unshelled. Slit
   prawns half-way lengthwise and remove
   dark veins. Season with **A**.

2. Bring **B** to a fast boil in a saucepan for
   ½ hour. Remove froth as it floats to the
   surface. Add another 455 ml (16 fl oz) water
   and bring it to the boil again over high
   heat. Remove froth as it rises and continue
   boiling for 1 hour over moderate heat. Add
   prawn shells and continue boiling for
   another hour.

3. Strain stock into a saucepan. Cook prawns.
   Set aside. Put in fish balls.

4. Scoop out fish balls as they rise.

5. Dish a portion of noodles and bean sprouts
   (blanched) into a bowl, add soup, garlic oil,
   top with garnishing and serve with chillies.

Claypot Dishes

Beef Shin With Mixed Vegetables

Braised Beef Brisket

Chicken

Fish Head

Seafood

Tofu and Crab Meat

Tofu with Pork and Prawns

Fish Head in Clay Pot

BEEF SHIN WITH MIXED VEGETABLES

INGREDIENTS

455 g (1 lb) beef shin, sliced thickly
55 g (2 oz) golden needles (kim chiam)
55 g (2 oz) cloud ear fungus (wan yee)
10 slices young ginger
2 cloves garlic, sliced
4 pieces Chinese mushrooms, soaked and sliced thinly
1 carrot, parboiled and flower cut
55 g (2 oz) canned bamboo shoots, flower cut
10 dried red dates, pips removed and soaked
2 soya bean strips (tow kee), cut into small pieces
1 can asparagus tips
55 g (2 oz) spring onion, cut into 4 cm (1½ in) lengths

Seasoning A:
½ teaspoon bicarbonate of soda
2 teaspoons light soya sauce
2 tablespoons oil
1 tablespoon peppercorns

Seasoning B:
(Mix together)
2 teaspoons sugar
½ teaspoon salt
1 teaspoon msg
1 crumbled chicken stock cube
1 teaspoon sesame oil

Thickening:
Mix together 2 tablespoons tapioca flour with 3 tablespoons water

METHOD

1. Stir-fry beef with 2 tablespoons oil over high heat till beef changes colour; add in 455 ml (16 fl oz) boiling water and seasoning **A**. Cook over low heat till beef is tender. Drain beef and keep stock.
2. Cut off hard tips of golden needles and tie each piece into a knot.
3. Soak cloud ear fungus in boiling water for 5 minutes. Rub well in cold water to remove sandy particles and cut off hard tips.
4. Heat an iron wok, add in 3 tablespoons lard or oil to fry the sliced ginger, garlic and mushrooms till lightly browned. Add in the carrots, bamboo shoots, red dates and tow kee. Stir-fry for 1 minute. Add seasoning **B**, beef stock and bring to the boil.
5. Transfer cooked mixture to a large clay pot, place beef shin and asparagus over and return to heat to cook for 20 minutes over moderate heat. Add spring onions.
6. Add thickening, stir well to thicken and stir in 1 tablespoon lard. Serve hot.

BRAISED BEEF BRISKET

INGREDIENTS

680 g (1½ lb) beef brisket, cut into thick slices

570 ml (20 fl oz) water 2 tablespoons dark soya sauce 2 tablespoons light soya sauce 1 teaspoon msg 1 teaspoon sugar 2 teaspoons vinegar 1 teaspoon pepper	**A** *mixed in a bowl*
2 tablespoons oil	
3 cloves garlic, bashed 2 segments star anise 4 shallots, bashed 4 slices ginger 2 thick slices galangal 2 stalks lemon grass, bashed	**B**

455 g (1 lb) lettuce, cut into big pieces

METHOD

1. Marinate beef in **A** for ½ hour.
2. Heat oil in clay pot till very hot. Add **B** and stir-fry for 2 minutes. Add the beef and marinade and bring to the boil over high heat. Boil for 10 minutes. Reduce heat, cover and simmer for 1½–2 hours or till beef is tender. Arrange lettuce on a serving plate and add beef just before serving.

CHICKEN

INGREDIENTS

905 g (2 lb) chicken, cut into 4 pieces

½ teaspoon salt
1 teaspoon sugar   **A**
½ teaspoon pepper

Oil
2 tablespoons lard

2 cloves garlic, bashed
4 slices ginger   **B**
4 shallots, bashed

55 g (2 oz) boiled bamboo shoots
55 g (2 oz) sliced carrots
170 g (6 oz) canned button mushrooms   **C**
6 Chinese mushrooms
225 g (½ lb) long Chinese cabbage

905 ml (1½ pints) water
1 chicken cube
2 tablespoons light soya sauce
1 teaspoon dark soya sauce
½ teaspoon sesame oil   **D**
1 tablespoon oyster sauce
1 tablespoon A1 sauce
¼ teaspoon pepper
1 teaspoon msg
½ teaspoon sugar

1 level tablespoon corn flour   **E**
4 tablespoons water

METHOD

1. Season chicken with **A** and set aside for ½ hour.

2. Heat oil in pan to brown chicken on all sides. Remove to a dish.

3. Heat lard in a fairly large clay pot. Brown **B**. Add **C** and stir-fry for 2 minutes over high heat. Pour in **D** and bring to the boil. Put chicken in pot, cover and cook over a high heat for 10 minutes. Reduce heat and simmer for 30 minutes or till chicken is tender. Remove lid. Stir in **E** and serve.

FISH HEAD

INGREDIENTS

1 large threadfin fish head, cut into big pieces
1 tablespoon ginger juice
1 tablespoon light soya sauce
1 soft soya bean cake, cut into pieces
2 tablespoons oil
3 tablespoons lard
4 slices ginger
4 cloves garlic, lightly bashed

55 g (2 oz) boiled bamboo shoots, cut into slices
55 g (2 oz) sliced carrots   **A**
4 Chinese mushrooms, soaked and cut into pieces
225 g (½ lb) long Chinese cabbage

905 ml (1½ pints) water with 1 chicken cube for stock
½ teaspoon salt   **B**
½ teaspoon sugar   *mixed together*
1 teaspoon msg
3 teaspoons light soya sauce
1 tablespoon oyster sauce
Dash of pepper

115 g (4 oz) roast pork, cut into small pieces
2 stalks spring onions, cut into short lengths

METHOD

1. Season fish head with ginger juice and light soya sauce and set aside for ½ hour.

2. Fry soya bean cake in a non-stick wok with 2 tablespoons oil till lightly browned. Remove to a plate.

3. Heat 1 tablespoon lard and brown the fish head on all sides. Set aside. Pour in the rest of the lard; brown the ginger and garlic. Add **A**, stir-fry for 2 minutes, add **B** and bring to the boil. Transfer to a clay pot. Add the roast pork, fish head and the fried soya bean cake. Cover and cook over moderate heat for 20 minutes. Add the spring onions and serve hot.

SEAFOOD

INGREDIENTS

Stock:
455 g (1 lb) pork bones or chicken pieces
　1 tablespoon peppercorns
　1 soft soya bean cake, cut into pieces
　2 tablespoons oil
170 g (6 oz) threadfin
170 g (6 oz) medium-sized prawns
　　Oil
　1 cup boiling water

½ teaspoon msg
¼ teaspoon salt
1 teaspoon ginger juice   **A**
1 tablespoon oil

　2 tablespoons lard
　1 clove garlic, chopped
　4 slices ginger
4–6 Chinese mushrooms, or
　　10–12 button mushrooms
　55 g (2 oz) canned bamboo shoots, sliced
225 g (8 oz) pak choy, cut into pieces
　½ carrot, cut into small pieces

Seasoning:
　1 teaspoon salt
　1 teaspoon msg
½ teaspoon sugar
　1 tablespoon oyster sauce
　1 chicken cube

20 fish balls
　Few slices of canned abalone (optional)
　2 stalks spring onions, cut into short lengths

METHOD

1. Boil pork bones or chicken with 1.7 litres (3 pints) water and 1 tablespoon peppercorns for 2 hours till stock is reduced by one-third.

2. Lightly brown the soya bean cake in a non-stick pan with 2 tablespoons oil. Set aside.

3. Slice the threadfin fairly thickly. Shell prawns leaving tail unshelled. Slit back of prawns and remove dark veins. Wash shells and fry them in a little oil till they turn colour and smell fragrant. Pour in 1 cup boiling water and simmer for ½ hour. Strain and keep stock.

4. Season fish and prawns with **A**.

5. Heat 2 tablespoons lard or oil in a large clay pot. Fry the ginger and garlic till light brown. Fry the mushrooms and the rest of the vegetables for 2 minutes over a high heat. Add the prawn and chicken or pork stock and seasoning; bring it to a fast boil for 5 minutes. Cover and continue boiling for 15 minutes over a moderate heat.

6. When vegetables are tender, add the prawns, soya bean cake, fish and fish balls. Continue to simmer for 5–7 minutes or till prawns and fish are cooked. Add more boiling water to clay pot if stock evaporates too much. Lastly add abalone. Garnish with short lengths of spring onions before serving.

TOFU AND CRAB MEAT

INGREDIENTS

115 g (4 oz) crab meat from 1.2 kg (42 oz) crabs
1 chicken breast, minced finely
1 teaspoon light soya sauce
115 ml (4 fl oz) water

225 g (½ lb) chicken and 1 chicken cube for stock   A
1 tablespoon peppercorns
½ teaspoon salt
1 teaspoon msg

1 soft soya bean cake

Seasoning:
1 teaspoon salt, 1 teaspoon msg, dash of pepper,
2 tablespoons light soya sauce

1 small can creamed corn
2 eggs, lightly beaten

Thickening:
1½ tablespoons corn flour
55 ml (2 fl oz) water

2 tablespoons finely cut spring onions
1 tablespoon lard (optional)

METHOD

1. Steam crabs whole, for 20 minutes. Remove and immerse in cold water. Drain. Remove meat and keep in refrigerator.

2. Combine minced chicken with 1 teaspoon light soya sauce and 115 ml water. Set aside.

3. Boil **A** in a clay pot over moderately high heat for ½ hour. Reduce heat and simmer for 1½ hours. Strain.

4. Chop soya bean cake into very fine pieces. Set aside.

5. Return stock to clay pot, add seasoning and bring it to the boil. Mix ½ cup stock with the minced chicken and add together with soya bean cake. Stir and bring to the boil. Add the corn, crab meat and beaten egg. Stir in the thickening. Add the tablespoon of lard and sprinkle spring onions.

TOFU WITH PORK AND PRAWNS

INGREDIENTS

1 soft soya bean cake, 10 cm × 10 cm × 3 cm (4 in × 4 in × 1¼ in), cut into small squares
Oil
15 medium-sized prawns
2 tablespoons oil or lard
2 cloves garlic, bashed
3 shallots, bashed
3 slices ginger

55 g (2 oz) boiled bamboo shoots, sliced into thin pieces
15 button mushrooms   A
4 dried mushrooms, soaked and quartered
1 or 2 fresh cuttlefish, cleaned and sliced

285 g (10 oz) *peck chye*, white longish type
55–85 g (2–3 oz) roast pork

710 ml (25 fl oz) boiling water
1 chicken cube
2 teaspoons light soya sauce   B
1 teaspoon oyster sauce
1 teaspoon msg
½ teaspoon sesame oil

1 teaspoon tapioca flour
3 tablespoons water

2 stalks spring onions cut into 3.5 cm lengths

METHOD

1. Soak soya bean cake in salted water for 10 minutes and drain. Heat an iron wok, add ½ cup oil and fry soya bean cake. Remove and set aside.

2. Remove shells from prawns. Heat clay pot and put in 2 tablespoons oil to fry the garlic, shallots and ginger till lightly browned. Add **A**, stir-fry over high heat for a minute, add the *peck chye* and roast pork and stir-fry for another minute.

3. Add **B**, bring to the boil and boil over moderately high heat for 5 minutes.

4. Add soya bean cake and prawns to cook for a while. Add thickening, and lastly the spring onions. Serve hot.

Soups

Bak Kut Teh
Chicken and Corn
Chicken Macaroni
Hot and Sour
Shark's Fin Soup
Sop Kambing
Soto Ayam
Thom Yam Soup

Thom Yam Soup

BAK KUT TEH
(SPICY SPARERIB CONSOMME)

INGREDIENTS

625 g (1 lb 6 oz) pork sparerib, cut into small pieces

½ teaspoon pepper
½ teaspoon salt | **A**

3 tablespoons lard
1 tablespoon sugar

2 cloves garlic, bashed
1 teaspoon preserved brown soya beans, | **B**
  pounded

2 segments star anise
2.5 cm (1 in) piece cinnamon bark
1 teaspoon peppercorns
1 teaspoon salt | **C**
1 teaspoon msg
1 teaspoon dark soya sauce
1.4 litres (3 pints) boiling water

1 tablespoon crispy shallots*
  Crispy Chinese crullers, sliced

METHOD

1. Marinate sparerib in **A** for ½ hour.
2. Heat pan till very hot. Add 2 tablespoons lard and fry sparerib till well-browned. Remove to a dish.
3. In a clean pan, heat 1 tablespoon lard and caramelize the sugar till light brown. Add **B**. Stir-fry for ½ minute, then add the fried sparerib and **C**.
4. Let the consomme boil rapidly for 10 minutes, reduce the heat and let simmer for a further 1½–1¾ hours or till the meat is tender. Remove excess oil from the surface before serving.
5. Serve hot with cruller slices.

*See "Helpful Hints".

CHICKEN AND CORN

INGREDIENTS

1.2 kg (2½ lb) chicken

1.4 litres (3 pints) water
1 teaspoon salt | **A**
1 teaspoon peppercorns

2 eggs, beaten with 2 tablespoons water
½ teaspoon salt | **B**
1 teaspoon msg
1 teaspoon light soya sauce

1 big can of creamed corn

4 tablespoons cornflour
1 tablespoon plain flour | **C**
115 ml (4 fl oz) water

METHOD

1. Cut the chicken into large pieces.
2. Mince the chicken breast and mix with 4 tablespoons water. Set aside.
3. Boil **A** in a saucepan. Add the cut chicken pieces, and let soup simmer for 1½ hours. Boil until three-quarters of the soup is left. Strain into another saucepan.
4. Add 225 ml (8 fl oz) soup to the minced chicken. Mix well.
5. Bring the rest of the soup to the boil rapidly. Add **B**, stirring slowly till the egg mixture floats to the top. Add the corn and the minced chicken and bring to the boil. Reduce heat, blend **C** in a bowl and stir it in gradually.
6. Remove from the heat and serve in large bowl.

CHICKEN MACARONI

INGREDIENTS

1 teaspoon salt
1.2 kg (2½ lb) chicken, whole

3.7 litres (8 pints) water   ┐
1 tablespoon peppercorns
2 teaspoons salt   **A**
2 teaspoons msg
1 teaspoon sugar   ┘

2 tablespoons light soya sauce ┐
1 teaspoon msg   **B**
½ teaspoon sesame oil   ┘

225 g (8 oz) macaroni, boiled and drained

4 tablespoons crispy shallots* ┐
1 bunch coriander leaves
1 cup croutons   **C**
Dash of pepper   ┘

METHOD

1. Rub 1 teaspoon salt over chicken. Marinate for ½ hour.
2. Boil **A**.
3. Put in the chicken and bring to rapid boil for 5 minutes. Cover the saucepan and let simmer for 40 minutes.
4. Remove and immerse chicken in cold water for 10 minutes. Debone the chicken and return the bones to the soup. Let soup simmer for 2 hours till it is reduced by one-third. Strain into another saucepan.
5. Shred or dice the chicken.
6. Mix **B** in a bowl. Add 4 tablespoons soup. Add the chicken and mix well.

To serve:
Place the macaroni in a large bowl and arrange the chicken on top. Add boiling soup and garnish with **C**.

See "Helpful Hints".

HOT AND SOUR

INGREDIENTS

115 g (4 oz) pork fillet, shredded
1 tablespoon tapioca flour
905 g (2 lbs) chicken, quartered
1 teaspoon peppercorns

4 dried Chinese mushrooms, soaked, shredded ┐
1 small carrot, parboiled, shredded thinly
115 g (4 oz) bamboo shoots, shredded thinly **A**
55 g (2 oz) ham, shredded thinly ┘

Seasoning:
1 teaspoon salt
1 teaspoon msg
1 tablespoon light soya sauce
2 tablespoons Thai fish sauce
1 teaspoon sugar
2 tablespoons vinegar
2 tablespoons tapioca flour in 1 cup water

55 g (2 oz) cooked crab meat
2 eggs beaten with 2 tablespoons water
1 tablespoon lard
½ teaspoon sesame oil
2 tablespoons spring onions, chopped coarsely

METHOD

1. Marinate shredded pork with a pinch each of salt, msg, sugar and 1 tablespoon tapioca flour with 1 tablespoon water. Set aside.
2. To make stock, boil chicken in 1.5 litres (3 pints) water with 1 teaspoon peppercorns and ½ teaspoon salt. Boil rapidly for 10 minutes, removing froth as it rises. Add 1 cup cold water and continue boiling over moderate heat, uncovered, till stock is reduced by half. Strain stock. Take chicken drumsticks only and shred into thick pieces. Set aside.
3. Bring chicken stock in a saucepan to a boil. Add **A** and pork and boil for 3 minutes. Pour in seasoning gradually and stir till stock reboils. Add crab meat. Pour in slowly the beaten eggs, lard and sesame oil and stir gently. Add chicken meat and remove from heat as soon as it comes to a boil. Pour into a large soup bowl, sprinkle with spring onions and dust with pepper. Serve hot.

SHARK'S FIN SOUP

INGREDIENTS

905 g (2 lb) small chicken, cut into
    four pieces   **A**
1.4 litres (2½ pints) water
1 teaspoon peppercorns

1 tablespoon oyster sauce
1 tablespoon light soya sauce
1 teaspoon msg   **B**
1 teaspoon sherry or wine
Dash of pepper

225 g (½ lb) steamed crab meat
115 g (¼ lb) prepared softened shark's fins   **C**
    (already soaked in alkaline water)

2 eggs, beaten with 2 tablespoons water

5 tablespoons cornflour   **D**
55 ml (2 fl oz) water

2 tablespoons lard

METHOD

1. Boil **A**. Simmer till stock is reduced by one-third (1–1½ hours). Strain into another saucepan. Return chicken stock to the boil.
2. Mix **B** in a bowl. Add to the stock with **C**. Bring to the boil. Add beaten eggs, stirring gently till they rise to the surface.
3. Blend **D** and pour gradually into the soup, stirring all the time to prevent curdling. Lastly, stir in the lard. Serve hot.

Note:
You can buy softened shark's fins at certain supermarkets.

SOP KAMBING
(MUTTON SOUP)

INGREDIENTS

285 g (10 oz) shallots
55 g (2 oz) garlic   **A**
115 g (4 oz) ginger
½ piece nutmeg

2 teaspoons pepper
1 teaspoon turmeric powder
1 teaspoon cumin powder   **B**
2 tablespoons coriander powder

2 pairs sheep's trotters, cut into short lengths
1.8 kg (4 lb) mutton ribs, cut into pieces

3.6 litres (7 pints) water
10 cm (4 in) piece cinnamon bark
20 cardamom seeds, bashed   **C**
1 cluster star anise

2 tablespoons salt
1–2 teaspoons msg
½ teaspoon bicarbonate of soda

6 tablespoons plain flour
2 tablespoons quick cooking oats, pounded finely   **D**
225 ml (8 fl oz) water

½ cup crispy shallots
15 sprigs Chinese celery, cut into pieces   **E**

METHOD

1. Pound **A** to a fine paste. Add **B** and mix thoroughly in a large bowl. Marinate ribs in mixture for ½ hour.
2. Boil **C**. Add the marinated ribs and season with salt and msg. Boil rapidly for 20 minutes. Reduce the heat and let simmer for 1½–2 hours or till the meat is tender.
3. Boil the trotters in a small saucepan with 455 ml (16 fl oz) soup and the bicarbonate of soda. Let simmer till trotters are tender.
4. Pour the soup and trotters back into the saucepan of ribs. Mix and bring to the boil.
5. Blend **D** in a bowl and pour gradually into the soup. Stir till well-blended.
6. Let simmer until ready to serve. Serve hot.
7. Serve in individual soup bowls and garnish with **E**.

SOTO AYAM
(INDONESIAN CHICKEN SOUP)

INGREDIENTS

1.2 kg (2½ lb) chicken, whole, including liver and
    gizzard
1 teaspoon salt
1 tablespoon oil

8 shallots, chopped coarsely
2 cloves garlic, bashed
1 teaspoon peppercorns
½ thumb-sized piece fresh turmeric   **A**
4 candlenuts, lightly bashed
1 thumb-sized piece ginger, lightly bashed
3 stalks lemon grass, bruised

2–3 teaspoons salt
2 teaspoons msg   **B**
3.5 litres (7 pints) water

1–2 tablespoons chilli padi, pounded finely
4 tablespoons dark soya sauce   **C**
1 teaspoon sugar

4 hard-boiled eggs, shelled and diced
225 g (8 oz) boiled potatoes, diced
30 g (1 oz) bean vermicelli, soaked in hot water

4 sprigs Chinese celery, cut into pieces
2 stalks spring onions, cut into pieces
½ cup crispy shallots   **D**
8 local lemons, cut into wedges

METHOD

1. Wash the chicken and rub in 1 teaspoon
   salt. Set aside.

2. Heat oil in a pan and fry **A** over a high heat
   for ½ minute. Set aside.

3. Boil **B** in a saucepan. Put in **A**, the chicken,
   liver and gizzard.

4. Cover the pan and let simmer for ¾ hour.
   Remove the chicken, liver and gizzard to a
   basin of cold water for 10 minutes to cool.

5. Debone chicken. Dice and put the meat
   aside. Return bones to the stock. Boil gently for 1½ hours. Strain stock and leave to
   simmer till ready to serve.

6. Mix **C** together in a bowl.

To serve:
Place a little of the diced ingredients and the
bean vermicelli in individual soup bowls. Add
boiling soup and garnish with **D**. Add **C** sauce
with a squeeze of local lemon to taste. Serve
hot.

THOM YAM SOUP
(HOT SOUP, THAI-STYLE)

INGREDIENTS

500 g (17 oz) medium-sized prawns
400 g (14 oz) fish meat, cut into cubes
200 g (7 oz) cuttlefish, cleaned and cut into small
    pieces
2 blue-flower crabs, cleaned and cut into small
    pieces
1 small can sliced button mushrooms

Ingredients for Stock:
3 stalks lemon grass, cut into thick slices,
    slantwise
3 green chillies, each cut into two
10 green chilli padi, bashed lightly
10 red chilli padi, bashed lightly
2 stalks coriander, washed and left whole
1 onion or 6 shallots, sliced thinly
6–8 tablespoons green lime juice (from limau nipis)
8 daun limau purot

Seasoning:
2–3 tablespoons Thai soya sauce
1 tablespoon sugar
1 tablespoon msg

METHOD

1. Cut whiskers from prawns and soak in
   2 tablespoons sugar, rinse before cooking.

2. Marinate fish meat in 1 tablespoon Thai
   soya sauce.

3. Marinate cuttlefish with 1 tablespoon sugar.

4. Combine ingredients for stock in an enamel
   saucepan with 855 ml (2 pints) water and
   bring to the boil. Boil gently for
   10 minutes. Put in the crabs, prawns, fish
   and cook till stock boils. Boil for 2–
   3 minutes, lastly add in the seasoning,
   sliced mushrooms and the cuttlefish, boil
   for ½ a minute and remove from heat.
   Serve immediately.

Pork and Mutton

Barbecued Spareribs

Braised Pork with Crunchy Black Fungus

Braised Pork in Soya Sauce, Buns for Braised Pork

Roast Pork Strips (Char Siew)

Sweet and Sour Pork Ribs

Braised Mutton Ribs

Mutton in Tomato Curry

Braised Pork with Crunchy Black Fungus

BARBECUED SPARERIBS

INGREDIENTS

2 tablespoons tomato sauce
2 tablespoons sugar
1 tablespoon sweet chilli sauce
1 tablespoon sherry or brandy   A
2 tablespoons light soya sauce
½ tablespoon lime juice
1 tablespoon msg
1 teaspoon pepper

905 g (2 lb) pork spareribs, cut into pieces
4 tablespoons lard
4 cucumbers, sliced

METHOD

1. Mix **A** in a bowl.

2. Wash sparerib pieces. Drain and dry with a tea towel.

3. Marinate spareribs in **A** (Method 1) for 4 hours. Thread the pieces on to skewers. (Set aside marinade in a bowl for basting.)

4. Line baking tray or grill pan with foil to collect the juices and dripping for basting.

5. Heat grill or oven, 230°C (450°F) or Regulo 9–10. When very hot, brush sparerib pieces with lard. Grill or bake for 10 minutes. Turn over once to brown the other side. Reduce the heat to 150°C (300°F) or Regulo 4 and cook for another 15–20 minutes. Mix the dripping with the marinade. Baste and grill till well done. Serve hot or cold with cucumber slices.

BRAISED PORK WITH CRUNCHY BLACK FUNGUS

INGREDIENTS

1.6 kg (3½ lb) pork belly
30 g (1 oz) black fungus (mok yee)
2 eggs lightly beaten
5 tablespoons plain flour
6 cloves garlic, cut into 2–3 pieces
3 pieces salted preserved bean curds (mashed)

Seasoning:
2 tablespoons light soya sauce
2 tablespoons dark soya sauce
2 tablespoons sugar
½ teaspoon pepper
2 level teaspoons five-spice powder

METHOD

1. Wash and cut pork into 4 cm (1½ in) squares; drain.

2. Soak black fungus in boiling water for 20 minutes. Remove the gritty hard bits.

3. Place pork pieces in a large mixing bowl, add in beaten eggs, seasoning mixture and rub into the pork. Add in the flour and mix well. Leave to marinate for half an hour.

4. Heat oil for deep frying. Put in one-quarter of the pork pieces to fry till pork turns golden brown. Scoop pork to a heavy bottom saucepan. Leave oil in pan to be really heated before frying each batch of the seasoned pork.

5. In a clean wok, heat 3 tablespoons oil. Fry garlic, add mashed bean curd, stir for a moment then put in 4 tablespoons water to cook for 1 minute. Add in 24 fl oz water and allow to boil.

6. Pour the gravy sauce over the pork in saucepan. Sprinkle 2 teaspoons sugar and 2 teaspoons dark soy sauce, add the black fungus and cook over moderately high heat for 10 minutes. Reduce heat, and simmer for ¾–1 hour or till pork is tender. Add hot water if gravy evaporates before pork becomes tender. Serve hot.

BRAISED PORK IN SOYA SAUCE

INGREDIENTS

1 tablespoon dark soya sauce 1 teaspoon honey ½ teaspoon five-spice powder	**A**

2 tablespoons lard

2 cloves garlic, pounded finely 4 shallots, pounded finely 3 segments star anise 1 tablespoon sugar	**B**

2 tablespoons dark soya sauce 1 teaspoon msg 1 teaspoon salt	**C**

905 g (2 lb) pork, with skin and some fat
225 ml (8 fl oz) water

METHOD

1. Marinate the whole piece of pork in **A** for ½ hour.
2. Heat lard in an aluminium wok, then fry **B** till light brown.
3. Reduce heat to moderate. Add the marinated pork and cook till brown on all sides. Add **C** and half of the water. Cover and cook for 10 minutes.
4. Remove lid, turn pork over and continue boiling gently till sauce is thick and oily.
5. Add rest of the water and bring to the boil, stirring constantly to prevent the sauce from sticking to bottom of wok.
6. Remove meat and sauce to a heavy-bottomed saucepan. Cover and let simmer till meat is tender (1–1¼ hours). Add a little water if sauce thickens before meat is tender. Leave to cool. Slice pork and add hot sauce. Serve hot with buns.

BUNS FOR BRAISED PORK

INGREDIENTS

1½ tablespoons fresh yeast 1 teaspoon sugar 2 tablespoons lukewarm water ½ tablespoon salt 3 tablespoons lard or oil	**A**

8 tablespoons castor sugar 225 ml (8 fl oz) lukewarm water	**B**

565 g (20 oz) flour, slightly warmed under a low grill
Small pieces of greaseproof paper
Flour for dusting

METHOD

1. Dissolve **A** in a bowl and let stand for 5 minutes.
2. Place flour in a mixing bowl. Pour yeast mixture **A** in centre. Add **B** (dissolved in a bowl).
3. Stir flour gradually to form a smooth dough.
4. Knead dough on a floured board (or use an electric dough hook) till smooth and glossy. Dough should not stick to hands or bowl. Place dough in a greased bowl. Cover with a damp cloth and leave dough to rise in a warm place till double its bulk.
5. Turn dough on to a floured board. Divide it into four portions. Roll each portion and cut it into equal pieces (each the size of a hen's egg).
6. Flatten each piece with a rolling pin and shape into a flat ball, 0.5 cm thick × 7 cm diameter. Brush half of each lightly with oil. Fold into two and place on a piece of greaseproof paper.
7. Space buns apart on trays. Cover with a dry cloth and leave to rise in a warm place for 15–20 minutes.
8. Steam buns over rapidly boiling water for 7–10 minutes.

ROAST PORK STRIPS
(CHAR SIEW)

INGREDIENTS

1 tablespoon salt
7 tablespoons sugar
1 tablespoon light soya sauce   A
1 tablespoon sherry or wine
2 tablespoons msg
  Orange food colouring
4 tablespoons water

905 g (2 lb) pork, cut into thick strips
3 tablespoons lard

METHOD

1. Mix **A** in a bowl to marinate pork for 6–8 hours.
2. Thread pork on to skewers. Brush lard over pork.
3. Pre-heat grill till very hot. Grease rack with lard. Grill pork on both sides till brown. Reduce heat and cook the pork till well done. Baste pork from time to time while grilling.

Note:
Line grill pan with foil to collect the dripping for basting. Serve with sliced cucumber.

SWEET AND SOUR PORK RIBS

Marinade:
¼ teaspoon salt
¼ teaspoon sugar
1 teaspoon msg
1 teaspoon ginger juice   A
2 teaspoons light soya sauce
1 small egg, beaten with 1 tablespoon cornflour

455 g (1 lb) tender pork ribs, cut into 3 cm (1 in) pieces
  Salt water
115 g (4 oz) cornflour
  Oil for deep-frying

METHOD

1. Wash pork ribs in salt water and drain.
2. Mix **A** in a bowl. Marinate ribs for ½ hour.
3. Roll the marinated ribs in cornflour. Leave to stand for 10 minutes.
4. Deep-fry ribs and drain.
5. Arrange on a serving dish to serve with sweet and sour sauce.

Sauce:
170 ml (6 fl oz) water   A
  1 tablespoon cornflour

¼ teaspoon salt
¼ teaspoon msg
3 tablespoons sugar
5 tablespoons tomato ketchup   B
1 teaspoon sesame oil
1 teaspoon soya sauce
3 tablespoons vinegar

2 Chinese mushrooms, soaked and shredded
1 onion, quartered   C
2 small tomatoes, quartered
2 red chillies, seeded and sliced thickly

1 cucumber
2 tablespoons lard
2 stalks spring onions, cut into 5 cm (2 in) lengths

METHOD

1. Skin the cucumber and cut it lengthwise into quarters. Remove the soft centre and cut into fairly thick pieces, slantwise.
2. Blend **A** and **B** in separate bowls.
3. Pour lard in a hot pan and stir-fry **C** for a minute over a high heat. Lower the heat. Add **A** and **B** (Method 2) and stir mixture till it boils.
4. Add the cucumber and spring onions. Remove from heat.
5. Pour sauce over the fried ribs just before serving. Serve hot.

Note:
Green peppers and pineapple can also be added to this dish. Put them in to cook with the other vegetables.

BRAISED MUTTON RIBS

INGREDIENTS

1 tablespoon wine or sherry
1 tablespoon light soya sauce
2 teaspoons dark soya sauce   **A**
2 teaspoons sugar

1 tablespoon oyster sauce
1 teaspoon sugar
2 teaspoons msg   **B**
1 tablespoon dark soya sauce
1 tablespoon light soya sauce

1 tablespoon cornflour
4 tablespoons water   **C**
1 teaspoon lard

565 g (1¼ lb) mutton ribs, cut into pieces
Oil
2 tablespoons lard

170 g (6 oz) boiled tender bamboo shoots, cut into wedges
170 g (6 oz) young tender ginger, cut into wedges   **D**
10 Chinese mushrooms, with stems removed, soaked in hot water and drained before use

1 tablespoon wine or sherry

METHOD

1. Marinate ribs for ½ hour in **A**.

2. Mix **B** and **C** in separate bowls.

3. Deep-fry ribs in hot smoking oil for 3 minutes. Remove and immerse fried ribs in a basin of ice-cold water. Discard the flakes of floating fat and place ribs in a dish.

4. Heat wok (kuali). When very hot, add the lard and stir-fry **D** for 1 minute. Add the ribs. Sprinkle the wine and stir-fry for another minute.

5. Pour in **B** (Method 2) and 225 ml (8 fl oz) water. Cook over a low heat till ribs are tender and gravy is thick and almost dry. Remove ribs to a dish.

6. Add **C** (Method 2), stir-fry and return ribs to cook for ½ minute. Place on a plate and serve immediately.

MUTTON IN TOMATO CURRY

INGREDIENTS

2 tablespoons ginger juice
1 teaspoon salt
1 teaspoon msg
2 tablespoons curry powder   **A**
4 tablespoons water
1 tablespoon oil

2 cloves garlic, thinly sliced
10 cardamoms, bashed   **B**
8 cloves
1 thumb-sized piece cinnamon bark

1 teaspoon salt
1 teaspoon msg   **C**
2 teaspoons sugar

905 g (2 lb) mutton chops, cut into pieces
4 tablespoons ghee or 2 tablespoons butter and 2 tablespoons oil
2 onions, thinly sliced
2 tablespoons tomato ketchup
2 tablespoons tomato purée
6 tablespoons curry powder, mixed to a paste with 8 tablespoons water
2 teaspoons lime juice
1 small can evaporated milk

METHOD

1. Marinate chops in **A** for ½ hour.

2. Heat wok. Add ghee to brown **B**. Add sliced onions and fry till fragrant (5 minutes). Stir in the tomato ketchup and purée.

3. Add curry paste and fry over a moderate heat till oil seeps through. Add 225 ml (8 fl oz) water and **C** and stir-fry for 5 minutes. Add the lime juice.

4. Add marinated chops, half of the evaporated milk, and another 225 ml water. Cook over a high heat for 15 minutes, stirring occasionally. Let meat simmer till tender (about ¾ hour).

5. Add the remaining evaporated milk, stir and continue simmering for another 10 minutes. Serve hot.

Beef

Beef Curry

Dry Beef Curry

Beef Brisket

Beef Braised in Dark Soya Sauce

Beef with Celery

Chinese Beef Steak

Fillet Steak

Ox Tail Stew

Dry Beef Curry

BEEF CURRY

INGREDIENTS

1 thumb-sized piece ginger
2 green chillies   **A**
4 cloves garlic

8 tablespoons curry powder
225 ml (8 fl oz) water   **B**
2 onions, thinly sliced

20 shallots, thinly sliced
5 cloves
6 cardamoms, bashed   **C**
1 thumb-sized piece cinnamon bark

1 teaspoon salt
1 teaspoon msg
905 g (2 lb) beef (rump steak), cut into pieces
4 tablespoons ghee or oil
115 g (4 oz) grated coconut with 455 ml (16 fl oz) water, squeezed and strained

1 teaspoon salt
1 teaspoon msg
4 sprigs mint leaves, picked   **D**
2 sprigs Chinese parsley, cut finely
4 tomatoes, quartered

METHOD

1. Pound **A** finely. Add salt and msg and marinate beef for ½ hour.

2. Mix **B** in a bowl.

3. Heat ghee in wok and fry **C** till light brown. Add the marinated beef, stir-fry for 5 minutes, then add 285 ml (10 fl oz) water. Boil gently till meat is tender, adding more water if necessary. Cook till almost dry.

4. Add **B** (Method 2), stir-fry over a low heat for 5 minutes with one-third of the coconut milk. Add **D** and the rest of the coconut milk. Let curry simmer for 15 minutes, stirring occasionally.

5. Remove from heat. Serve hot or cold.

Note:
New potatoes can be added to the curry. Add them to cook with the mint, Chinese parsley and tomatoes.

DRY BEEF CURRY

INGREDIENTS

285 g (10 oz) grated coconut
455 g (1 lb) beef (rump steak) cut into thick slices

1 clove garlic, pounded finely
4 slices ginger, pounded finely
½ teaspoon salt
1 teaspoon msg   **A**
1 teaspoon sugar
1 tablespoon curry powder

55 ml (2 fl oz) oil
55 g (2 oz) shallots or onions, thinly sliced
2 tablespoons tomato sauce
3 tablespoons curry powder mixed to a paste with a little water

Seasoning:
¾–1 teaspoon salt
1 teaspoon sugar
1 teaspoon msg

METHOD

1. Squeeze grated coconut for No. 1 milk. Set aside. Add 455 ml (16 fl oz) water to the grated coconut and squeeze for No. 2 milk. Set aside.

2. Season beef with **A** and leave for ½ hour.

3. Heat oil in non-stick saucepan or heavy-bottomed aluminium saucepan. When hot, fry the sliced shallots till lightly browned. Add the seasoned beef and fry till beef changes colour. Add tomato sauce and stir for a short while. Add ½ of the No. 2 milk, cover pan and cook over moderate heat for ¾ hour, stirring occasionally.

4. Mix the curry powder paste with the No. 1 milk and the rest of the No. 2 milk. Pour into saucepan, add seasoning and simmer till meat becomes tender and gravy starts to thicken (about ½–¾ hour). Add a few spoonfuls of water if mixture becomes dry before meat is tender.

BEEF BRISKET

INGREDIENTS

1 tablespoon ginger juice
2 tablespoons light soya sauce
3 tablespoons dark soya sauce **A**
1 teaspoon pepper
1 teaspoon msg

1 tablespoon sugar
½ teaspoon msg
¼ teaspoon salt **B**
1½–2 tablespoons vinegar

1 tablespoon cornflour **C**
3 tablespoons water

1 tablespoon sugar **D**
6 slices ginger

8 cloves garlic, lightly bashed **E**
10 shallots, cut into halves

2 segments star anise
1 stalk lemon grass, bruised **F**
2.5 cm (1 in) piece cinnamon bark

905 g (2 lb) beef brisket, cut into pieces
2 tablespoons lard or oil

METHOD

1. Marinate beef in **A** for 1 hour.

2. Mix **B** and **C** in separate bowls.

3. Heat lard in a hot saucepan to brown **D**. Add **E** and fry for 1 minute. Add **F**, marinated beef and **B** (Method 2). Stir-fry and cook over a high heat for 10 minutes. Add 285 ml (10 fl oz) water, and let it boil for 10 minutes.

4. Transfer dish to an earthen clay pot. Bring back to heat and simmer till meat is tender, (about 1½–2 hours).

5. Thicken gravy with **C** (Method 2) and stir well.

To serve:
Place whole pieces of lettuce on a large serving plate. Arrange beef on lettuce and serve hot.

BEEF BRAISED IN DARK SOYA SAUCE

INGREDIENTS

1 tablespoon dark soya sauce
1½ tablespoons sugar **A**
1 tablespoon oil

2 tablespoons lard or oil

2 slices ginger
1 clove garlic, sliced thinly
1 onion, sliced thinly
1 tablespoon sugar **B**
5 cm (2 in) piece cinnamon bark
2 segments star anise

½ teaspoon salt
1 tablespoon sugar
1 teaspoon msg **C**
2 tablespoons dark soya sauce
1 teaspoon peppercorns

905 g (2 lb) rump steak

METHOD

1. Marinate beef in **A** for 1 hour.

2. Heat lard in a heavy-bottomed saucepan. Brown **B**. Add the marinated beef. Increase heat; brown beef on all sides to seal in the juices. Add **C** and 115 ml (4 fl oz) water. Cook for 10 minutes. Add another 115 ml water and boil for another 10 minutes.

3. Reduce heat, cover pan and simmer till beef is tender (about 1½–2 hours), turning beef over once in the pan. Add more water if necessary.

Note:
When beef is tender, remove the lid and increase heat to high to thicken the sauce. Cool for a while before slicing the beef. Heat gravy and pour over meat before serving.

BEEF WITH CELERY

INGREDIENTS

Marinade:

1 tablespoon light soya sauce
1 teaspoon dark soya sauce
1 teaspoon msg   **A**
1 teaspoon sugar
1 teaspoon vinegar
1 egg white, beaten lightly

Gravy:

3 teaspoons tapioca or cornflour
6 tablespoons water
1 tablespoon light soya sauce   **B** *mixed in bowl*
1 tablespoon sherry
1 tablespoon oyster sauce

455 g (1 lb) fillet or rump steak
6 stalks celery
6 slices ginger
1 tablespoon chopped garlic
2 stalks spring onions, cut into 2½ cm (1 in) lengths

METHOD

1. Slice meat into 2½ cm (1 in) strips. Let beef stand in marinade **A** for 1 hour.

2. Cut celery diagonally and boil rapidly in salted water for ½ minute. Drain and rinse in cold water. Set aside.

3. Heat wok. Add 2 tablespoons oil and when hot, cook the beef in two portions. Remove and set aside.

4. In a clean pan, heat 2 tablespoons of oil till very hot. Fry celery for ½ minute, push to one side of pan and stir-fry ginger and garlic till light golden brown. Bring back celery and fried beef into pan. Stir in gravy **B** and add to meat mixture. Add spring onions and stir till well combined. Serve hot.

CHINESE BEEF STEAK

INGREDIENTS

1 teaspoon light soya sauce
1 teaspoon dark soya sauce
1 teaspoon sherry or brandy
½ teaspoon oyster sauce
1 teaspoon msg
½ teaspoon pepper   **A**
¼ teaspoon bicarbonate of soda
½ teaspoon sesame oil
1 teaspoon ginger juice
2 tablespoons oil
1 egg white, beaten

½ tablespoon cornflour   **B**
1 tablespoon water

225 g (8 oz) bean sprouts; picked, washed and drained
½ teaspoon pounded garlic, fried   **C**
A pinch of salt
1 teaspoon sugar

225 g (8 oz) fillet or Scotch steak, thinly sliced
4 tablespoons lard
2 sprigs spring onions, cut into 5 cm (2 in) lengths

METHOD

1. Mix **A** in a bowl and marinate beef for 1 hour.

2. Mix **B** in a bowl for the thickening.

3. Heat 2 tablespoons lard in heated wok and stir-fry **C** for 15 seconds. Remove to a serving plate.

4. Place the other 2 tablespoons lard in wok. Stir-fry the marinated beef slices over a high heat for 1 minute. Add spring onions, stir-fry and add thickening. Mix well. Add to fried bean sprouts. Serve immediately.

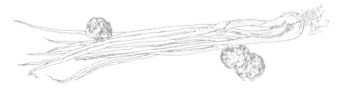

Beef with Celery

FILLET STEAK

INGREDIENTS

1 teaspoon dark soya sauce
½ teaspoon msg
½ teaspoon sugar
½ teaspoon bicarbonate of soda   **A**
1 teaspoon light soya sauce
1 teaspoon sherry *or* brandy
1 teaspoon cornflour
2 tablespoons oil

1 teaspoon light soya sauce
1 teaspoon oyster sauce
½ teaspoon sugar
½ teaspoon msg   **B**
¼ teaspoon salt
1 teaspoon sesame oil
1 teaspoon sherry

2 tablespoons cornflour   **C**
3 tablespoons water

4 slices ginger
1 teaspoon chopped garlic
115 g (4 oz) snow peas or French beans   **D**
1 green pepper, cut into small squares

225 g (½ lb) beef fillet, sliced into bite-sized pieces
225 ml (8 fl oz) oil
3 tablespoons lard
115 g (4 oz) canned button mushrooms, cut into halves
115 g (4 oz) canned straw mushrooms, cut into halves
2 stalks spring onions, cut into 5 cm (2 in) lengths

METHOD

1. Marinate beef in **A** for ½ hour.

2. Mix **B** and **C** in separate bowls.

3. Heat an iron wok till smoking hot. Heat oil for deep-frying. Add the marinated beef, stir-fry for ½ minute and remove to a plate.

4. Heat 2 tablespoons lard in a clean wok and stir-fry **D** over a high heat. Remove to a plate.

5. Add mushrooms and stir-fry for ½ minute. Add fried mixed vegetables, fried beef, spring onions, **B**, and **C**. Stir in the last tablespoon of lard, and mix well. Serve.

OX TAIL STEW

INGREDIENTS

1 teaspoon salt
½ teaspoon sugar
1 teaspoon msg
1 level teaspoon pepper   **A**
1 teaspoon dark soya sauce
1 tablespoon plain flour

340 g (12 oz) cabbage, cut into pieces
1 carrot, cut into wedges
340 g (12 oz) new potatoes, boiled and skinned   **B**
7.5 cm (3 in) piece cinnamon bark
340 g (12 oz) onions, small, whole or halved

¼ nutmeg   *to put in a*
4 cloves   **C** *muslin*
1 tablespoon peppercorns   *bag*

1 teaspoon msg
1 beef cube
½–1 teaspoon salt
1 teaspoon Bisto gravy powder, optional
2 teaspoons light soya sauce   **D**
1 teaspoon sugar
1 teaspoon dark soya sauce
1 teaspoon bicarbonate of soda

1 kg (2.2 lb) ox tail, chopped. Remove all fat.
1 beef cube
2 tablespoons oil
1 tablespoon butter
55 g (2 oz) thinly sliced shallots or onions
225 g (8 oz) French beans, sliced
115 g (4 oz) tomatoes, quartered
1 tablespoon plain flour mixed with 55 ml (2 fl oz) water, for thickening

METHOD

1. Season ox tail with **A** and leave for ½ hour.

2. Bring 1.4 litres (48 fl oz) water and the beef cube to a fast boil in a saucepan. Add **B** and bring to the boil over high heat for about 10 minutes.

3. Heat oil and butter and fry the sliced onions. Add seasoned ox tail and fry. Add stock, **C**, and **D**, bring to the boil and simmer for 2–2½ hours till meat is tender.

4. Bring vegetables to the boil again with French beans and tomatoes and cook for a further 20 minutes.

5. Add thickening. Serve hot.

Ox Tail Stew

Poultry

Abalone Chicken

Braised Ginger Chicken

Chicken Almond Curry

Chicken Coconut Curry

Chicken Bon Bon

Chicken Curry Devil

Chicken fried with Dried Red Chillies

Chicken in the Basket

Lemon Curried Chicken

Paper-Wrapped Chicken

Roast Turkey with Mince Pork and Rice Filling

Salt-Baked Chicken

Seven-Minute Crispy Chicken

Steamed Stuffed Duck

Stew

Turmeric Chicken

Chicken Curry

ABALONE CHICKEN

INGREDIENTS

6 pieces garlic, lightly bashed
4 stalks spring onion, tied into a knot   **A**
55 g (2 oz) ginger, lightly bashed

115 g (4 oz) abalone liquid
¼ teaspoon salt
½ teaspoon msg
½ teaspoon sugar   **B** *mixed in a bowl*
1 teaspoon sesame oil
1 teaspoon sherry
   Chicken stock (from Method 2)

Thickening:
1 tablespoon cornflour   **C**
2 tablespoons water

1 chicken, 1.14 kg (2½ lb)
1 teaspoon salt
   Green lettuce and tomato for garnishing
1 can abalone, 455 g (16 oz), cut into slices (reserve liquid)
1 tablespoon lard

METHOD

1. Wash chicken well and rub 1 teaspoon salt all over the skin of chicken. Stuff chicken with **A** and leave for ½ hour.

2. Place chicken on an enamel plate. Pour 3 tablespoons boiling water over chicken. Bring a large saucepan of water to a rapid boil. Place a metal steaming rack in saucepan and steam chicken till cooked (30–45 minutes). Cut into pieces when chicken is cool. Reserve stock for gravy.

3. Place lettuce on a large serving plate, arrange the sliced abalone on top and then the chicken.

4. Boil **B** in a saucepan, stir in **C** and allow to boil. Add the lard, stir and pour over chicken and abalone. Garnish with sliced tomato. Serve immediately.

BRAISED GINGER CHICKEN

INGREDIENTS

8 slices ginger   **A**
1 tablespoon sugar

4 tablespoons dark soya sauce
1 tablespoon sugar   **B**
½ teaspoon salt
1 teaspoon msg

455 g (1 lb) chicken wings
6 chicken livers   **C**
6 chicken gizzards
6 chicken drumsticks

2 tablespoons oil
3 tablespoons lard
½ teaspoon sesame oil

METHOD

1. Preheat wok. When very hot, heat the oil to fry **A**. Add 2 tablespoons lard.

2. Pour in **B** together with 115 ml (4 fl oz) water. Add **C**. Stir and cook for 10 minutes, covered. Remove the livers to a dish. Leave the rest to simmer for ½ hour, covered.

3. Remove the chicken wings to a dish. Pour in another 115 ml water and let the chicken drumsticks and gizzards continue to simmer till tender. Add the remaining tablespoonful of lard and sesame oil.

To serve:
Slice the cooked liver and gizzard. Serve hot or cold.

CHICKEN ALMOND CURRY

INGREDIENTS

8 cloves garlic, sliced thinly
¼ thumb-sized piece turmeric or ¾ teaspoon turmeric powder
2 teaspoons salt
1 teaspoon msg

A

8 cashew nuts
8 almonds
3 candlenuts
1 heaped tablespoon cumin seeds or cumin powder
½ cup water

B *blended to a fine paste*

285 g (10 oz) grated coconut, white
115 ml (4 fl oz) water
Oil for deep frying
285 g (10 oz) shallots, sliced thinly
4 tablespoons ghee or 2 tablespoons each of oil and butter
10 dried chillies, soaked and blended to a fine paste
1 sprig curry leaf

1.6 kg (3½ lb) whole chicken, cut into pieces

METHOD

1. Squeeze grated coconut with 115 ml (4 fl oz) water for milk. Set aside.

2. Heat oil for deep frying. When very hot, fry sliced shallots till light golden brown. Remove to absorbent paper to drain. Divide into two equal parts.

3. Combine **A** with half the coconut milk and rub into chicken pieces to marinate for ¾ hour.

4. Heat ghee in wok. Fry the dried chilli paste and curry leaf till oil turns red.

5. Add chicken and one part crispy shallots and cook over moderate heat. Transfer chicken to a heavy-bottomed aluminium saucepan. Cook for 20 minutes.

6. Remove lid, mix **B** with remaining coconut milk and pour in pan. Stir, reduce heat to low and simmer till chicken is tender.

CHICKEN COCONUT CURRY

INGREDIENTS

6 candlenuts
55 g (2 oz) shallots/onions
6 cloves garlic
5 red chillies
½ thumb-sized ginger
30 dried chillies
6 thin slices galangal
½ teaspoon turmeric powder

A *ground finely*

Seasoning:
2 teaspoons sugar
1 teaspoon salt
½ cube chicken stock

B

60 g (2 oz) SANTAN instant coconut cream powder*
1.6 kg chicken, cut into pieces
4 fragrant lime leaves, sliced thinly
2 tablespoons lime juice**
3 tablespoons crispy shallots/onions

METHOD

1. Dissolve SANTAN in 455 ml (16 fl oz) water. Strain.

2. Marinate the chicken with 1 level tablespoon salt and 1 teaspoon sugar.

3. Heat 115 ml (4 fl oz) oil in a hot pan. Fry **A** till oil seeps through and smells fragrant. Add 4 spoonfuls of SANTAN milk while frying.

4. Put in chicken pieces, **B**, fragrant lime leaves and half of the SANTAN milk. Stir and cook over moderate heat for 10 minutes.

5. Pour in remaining SANTAN milk, lime juice and allow to simmer for about 15 minutes. Lastly, add in crispy shallots, stir and remove from heat.

Equivalent to 2 lb white grated coconut.
**The lime juice can be replaced with 2 pieces of dried tamarind.*

CHICKEN BON BON
(SHREDDED CHICKEN AND MIXED
VEGETABLE SALAD)

INGREDIENTS

1 chicken breast, steamed
115 g (4 oz) treated jellyfish (available at wet markets)
2 tablespoons sesame seeds, toasted
1 cucumber
1 cup shredded lettuce

Ingredients for Sauce:
¼ teaspoon fine salt
2½ tablespoons fine sugar
1½ teaspoons vinegar
4 tablespoons mustard powder
1 tablespoon chilli sauce
1½ tablespoons Lea and Perrins Sauce
2 teaspoons sesame oil
115 ml (4 fl oz) evaporated milk
115 g (4 oz) roasted ground peanuts or chunky peanut butter

well blended

METHOD

1. Rub chicken breast with ½ teaspoon each of salt and msg for ½ hour. Then steam for ½ hour or till chicken is cooked. Leave to cool and shred into long pieces. Set aside.
2. Shred the jellyfish thinly and set aside.
3. Skin cucumber, cut into 3 and shred thinly leaving out soft centre.

To serve chicken bon bon:
Put shredded lettuce and cucumber on large serving plate. Place jellyfish over cucumber, then put the shredded chicken over and sprinkle the sesame seeds. Pour the sauce over just before serving.

CHICKEN CURRY DEVIL

INGREDIENTS

1 teaspoon salt
1 teaspoon msg   **A**
1 teaspoon pepper

115 g (4 oz) shallots or onions
4 cloves garlic
55 g (2 oz) ginger, sliced   **B**
1 stalk lemon grass, sliced   *ground to a fine paste*
10 fresh red chillies
8 dried chillies, soaked in warm water

1½ teaspoons powdered mustard or
   1 tablespoon prepared mustard
1 tablespoon sugar
1 teaspoon salt   **C**
1 teaspoon msg
2 tablespoons sugar
2 tablespoons vinegar

1.4 kg (3 lb) chicken, cut into pieces
285 g (10 oz) grated coconut
115 ml (4 fl oz) oil

METHOD

1. Season chicken with **A**.

2. Squeeze coconut in small handfuls through a piece of muslin for No. 1 milk, to obtain approximately 140 ml (5 fl oz). Add 225 ml water to the coconut. Squeeze for No. 2 milk and set aside in another bowl.

3. Grind **B** (or use an electric blender) to a fine paste.

4. Heat oil in wok and fry paste over moderate heat till oil bubbles through and paste is fragrant, adding a few tablespoons of No. 2 milk while frying. Add **C** and the rest of the No. 2 milk, stir till gravy starts to boil, add the chicken and cook over moderate heat for 10 minutes.

5. Add No. 1 milk, stir well, reduce heat to low, cover pan and simmer for 15–20 minutes or till chicken is tender.

CHICKEN FRIED WITH DRIED RED CHILLIES

INGREDIENTS

1 tablespoon honey
2 teaspoons light soya sauce   **A**
1 teaspoon msg
1 teaspoon pepper

1 teaspoon sugar
½ teaspoon msg
2 teaspoons oyster sauce
1 teaspoon dark soya sauce
1 teaspoon light soya sauce   **B**
1 tablespoon vinegar
1 teaspoon Lea and Perrins sauce
1 teaspoon rice wine or sherry

1 tablespoon cornflour   **C** *blended*
6 tablespoons water

455 g (1 lb) chicken meat, cut into bite-sized pieces
20–30 dried chillies, remove stems
285 ml (10 fl oz) oil
3 cloves garlic
1 teaspoon ginger, chopped
2 teaspoons spicy soya bean paste* (page 109)

METHOD

1. Marinate chicken in **A** for ½ hour.

2. Cut dried chillies into big pieces, diagonally across, and remove the seeds. Dip the chillies in cold water and drain immediately in a colander. Set aside.

3. Heat oil in iron wok. When hot, fry chillies till dark brown. Scoop out with perforated ladle and drain. In the same pan, heat oil till smoking hot, and fry chicken till it changes colour. Remove and drain.

4. Remove all oil, except 4 tablespoons, from wok. Fry the garlic and ginger till light brown. Add the spicy soya bean paste, stir, and add chillies, **B** and **C**. Stir till mixture comes to the boil. Add the chicken, toss in pan and remove to a serving plate. Serve immediately.

Note:
It is preferable to use broad, thick dried chillies for this recipe.

CHICKEN IN THE BASKET

Yam Baskets (a pair of perforated ladles for making yam baskets is required):

565 g (20 oz) yam
    4 tablespoons cornflour for dusting
    Oil for deep-frying

METHOD

1. Skin the yam. Do not wash the yam or it will become slimy and difficult to handle. Cut yam into thin strips, about 0.5 cm broad and 18 cm (7 in) long.

2. Place yam strips on a tray and dust with cornflour to keep the strips separated.

3. Put a towel in a bowl. Place a perforated ladle on the towel. Level the yam sticks then spread them, level edge upwards, around the sides of the ladle to form a basket.

4. Fill half a medium-sized saucepan with oil and heat till smoking hot.

5. Press the other ladle lightly over the yam basket and gently dip the sandwiched yam basket into the hot oil to fry for two minutes.

6. Reduce the heat a little to fry till the yam is cooked and turns light brown (about 5–6 minutes). Remove the ladles when the yam basket slips out of the lower ladle. Place on absorbent paper.

7. Make as many baskets as possible, until all the yam strips are used up.

8. Strain the oil to fry the chicken.

Filling:

1 teaspoon bicarbonate of soda	
1 teaspoon msg	
1 teaspoon sugar	
½ teaspoon salt	**A**
2 teaspoons light soya sauce	
2 tablespoons cornflour	
3 tablespoons water	
2 tablespoons oil	

3 Chinese mushrooms	
85 g (3 oz) bamboo shoots	**B**
1 large green pepper	
1 large tomato	

1 teaspoon salt	
1 teaspoon msg	
1 teaspoon sugar	
2 teaspoons light soya sauce	
1 teaspoon sesame oil	**C**
1 teaspoon sherry or brandy	
1 tablespoon oyster sauce	
Dash of pepper	

1 tablespoon cornflour	**D**
4 tablespoons water	

340 g (12 oz) chicken shreds
  2 tablespoons lard
  4 red chillies, seeded and sliced thinly
  2 stalks spring onions, cut into 5 cm (2 in) lengths
115 g (4 oz) lettuce, shredded

METHOD

1. Blend **A** in a bowl and marinate the chicken shreds for 1 hour.

2. Heat the strained hot oil in a clean iron wok till smoking hot. Add the seasoned chicken shreds and deep-fry for 1 minute. Use a perforated ladle to lift chicken shreds on to a plate.

3. Slice **B** thinly into strips.

4. Heat the lard in a clean saucepan. Stir-fry the sliced vegetables and red chillies over high heat.

5. Reduce heat and add the fried chicken shreds. Mix **C** in a bowl, add and stir well.

6. Blend **D** in a bowl and add to sauce in pan. Stir well till sauce thickens.

7. Add the spring onions, stir and remove to a dish.

To serve:
Spread shredded lettuce on a large serving plate. Fill baskets with chicken filling and place on top of the lettuce. Serve hot.

Note:
Oil for frying the yam baskets must be sizzling hot. Test it by putting in a strip of yam. If the yam strip sizzles and floats up immediately, the oil is ready for use. Do not wait for the yam to brown in the oil. Fried yam baskets can be stored in an airtight container for 2–3 weeks.

LEMON CURRIED CHICKEN

INGREDIENTS

12 shallots 6 candlenuts 4 stalks lemon grass, thinly sliced 1 teaspoon shrimp paste	**A**

1 tablespoon sugar 1–1½ teaspoons salt 1 teaspoon msg 1 tablespoon curry powder	**B**

4 tablespoons lemon juice 1 tablespoon tamarind with 115 ml (4 fl oz) water, squeezed and strained	**C**

455 g (16 oz) grated coconut
1.8 kg (4 lb) chicken, cut into pieces
4 tablespoons oil
15–20 pounded dried chillies or 4 tablespoons chilli paste
1 stalk lemon grass, bashed lightly
2 lime leaves

METHOD

1. Grind **A** to a fine paste.
2. Squeeze grated coconut for No. 1 milk. Add 170 ml (6 fl oz) water to coconut and squeeze again for No. 2 milk.
3. Mix half of the No. 1 milk with **B** and marinate chicken for ½ hour.
4. Heat aluminium wok. When very hot, heat oil and fry chilli paste over low heat till oil bubbles through. Add the rest of the No. 1 milk, stir-fry for 1 minute, then add Paste **A** (Method 1) and lemon grass. Fry till fragrant.
5. Add the marinated chicken and **C**. Lower heat and stir-fry till chicken is cooked. Add No. 2 milk and bring to the boil.
6. Reduce heat to low. Add the lime leaves and simmer in a covered pan till chicken is tender (½–¾ hour). Add more water if necessary.

PAPER-WRAPPED CHICKEN

INGREDIENTS

1 tablespoon cornflour 2 tablespoons water	**A**

1 teaspoon salt 1 teaspoon msg 1 teaspoon sugar 2 teaspoons sesame oil ¼ teaspoon pepper 1 tablespoon light soya sauce 1 tablespoon ginger juice 3 tablespoons lard or oil 1 tablespoon brandy or sherry	**B**

Cellophane or 'glass' paper
1.4 kg (3 lb) chicken, cut into pieces
Oil for deep-frying

METHOD

1. Cut the cellophane or 'glass' paper into 20 cm (8 in) squares.
2. Blend **A** in a bowl. Add **B**, stir well and pour over the chicken. Marinate chicken for 2 hours.
3. Wrap up a few pieces of chicken in each piece of cellophane paper and staple the edges.
4. Heat oil. Fry paper-wrapped chicken till light brown. Lift chicken onto a wire sieve to drain.
5. Serve hot, leaving wrappers on.

ROAST TURKEY WITH MINCE PORK AND RICE FILLING

INGREDIENTS

1 tablespoon fine salt
1 teaspoon pepper
1 teaspoon honey
1 teaspoon soya sauce **A**

Filling:
  2 slices bacon, chopped roughly
 55 g (2 oz) butter
 55 g (2 oz) chopped onions
340 g (12 oz) roughly minced pork
  3 cups cooked rice
  1 chicken cube, crushed in 4 tablespoons boiling water

 ½ cup roughly chopped Chinese parsley
 ¾ cup sultanas
 ½ cup blanched almonds, browned and chopped coarsely **B**
120 g (4 oz) spam *or* ham

  One 3½–4 kg (7½–8½ lb) turkey
 2 tablespoons sherry
 3 tablespoons butter, softened

METHOD

1. Thaw and wash turkey. Pat dry, inside and out, with cloth. Rub inside with 2 tablespoons sherry, 1 teaspoon salt and ½ teaspoon pepper. Brush the turkey with butter and rub all over with **A**. Set aside for ½ hour.

To make filling:
2. Fry bacon in a dry frying pan till oil runs out and bacon turns crisp. Remove to a plate. Heat butter and fry onions in the same pan till onions become soft. Increase heat to high, add minced pork to stir-fry till pork changes colour. Put in rice and stir for a moment. Stir in chicken cube stock. Add **B** and mix till well combined.

To prepare and roast turkey:
3. Fill turkey, but not too tightly as filling will expand on cooking. Secure cavity to prevent filling from spilling. Brush again with butter. Cross end of drumstick and secure with string.

4. Place turkey on a rack over a baking tray lined with foil to catch drippings. Bake in a preheated oven (220°C or 425°F) for about 2½–3 hours. Reduce heat after turkey turns light brown and continue baking till golden brown.

5. Baste turkey with drippings regularly. Use foil to cover parts that brown too quickly before turkey is cooked.

6. Allow turkey to cool for 15–20 minutes before carving.

SALT-BAKED CHICKEN

INGREDIENTS

½ teaspoon fine salt
1 teaspoon msg
¼ teaspoon five-spice powder **A**

1 teaspoon salt
1 teaspoon sherry
1 teaspoon oil **B**

1 young tender chicken (905 g or 2 lb)
3.6 kg (8 lb) coarse salt

METHOD

1. Clean and wash chicken, both outside and inside. Cut off the neck and legs. Wipe dry.

2. Rub **A** on the inside of chicken. Rub **B** all over surface of chicken and set aside for 1 hour.

To cook chicken:
1. Wrap up chicken with 2 large white paper napkins.

2. Line a shallow baking tin with tin foil. Fill with salt and heat in oven till salt becomes very hot. Alternatively, fry salt in an old wok till very hot and immediately pour half into large Chinese clay pot. Put the chicken in the middle of the pot and pour in the rest of the salt over the chicken.

3. Place clay pot over low heat on stove and cook for 1 hour or till chicken is well done. Serve hot.

Roast Turkey

SEVEN-MINUTE CRISPY CHICKEN

INGREDIENTS

2 tablespoons light soya sauce
4 tablespoons water
1 tablespoon sugar
1 tablespoon ginger juice
1 teaspoon sherry
1 teaspoon msg
¾ teaspoon salt
½ teaspoon cinnamon powder   **A**

115 g (4 oz) self-raising flour
¼ teaspoon salt
¼ teaspoon msg
¼ teaspoon pepper   **B**

0.8 kg (1½–1¾ lb) spring chicken, whole
    Oil for deep-frying
1 cucumber, sliced

METHOD

1. Cut chicken open from the breast downwards.
2. Turn over and crack backbone and thigh bones with blunt edge of a chopper.
3. Mix **A** in a bowl and marinate the chicken for 1 hour.
4. Sift **B** together to coat the chicken.
5. Heat oil in wok and deep-fry chicken for 1 minute on each side over high heat. Lower the heat. Fry for another 5 minutes. Turn chicken over once to brown. Lift chicken to drain.
6. Cool for a while before cutting it into pieces. Arrange on a serving dish and garnish with cucumber slices. Serve hot.

STEAMED STUFFED DUCK

INGREDIENTS

2 slices ginger
2 cloves garlic, bashed   **A**

½ teaspoon salt
1 teaspoon msg
2 teaspoons light soya sauce
1 teaspoon brandy
4 tablespoons pearl barley, soaked in water
  and drained
55 g (2 oz) lotus seeds, boiled and drained
55 g (2 oz) gingko nuts, shelled and skinned   **B**

1.8 kg (4 lb) duck, whole
    Salt water
2 tablespoons ginger juice
2 tablespoons lard or oil
4 Chinese mushrooms, soaked in hot water and sliced thinly
225 g (½ lb) pork, chopped coarsely
    Liver and gizzard, diced

METHOD

1. Wash duck thoroughly with salt water. Wipe dry. Rub ginger juice over the whole duck, including the inside.
2. Heat lard or oil in heated wok and stir-fry **A** till brown. Add mushrooms and stir-fry for 1 minute. Add the chopped pork, stir-fry for 2 minutes then add the diced liver and gizzard. Cook for 5 minutes.
3. Remove fried mixture to a saucepan. Add **B**. Pour in 680 ml (24 fl oz) boiling water and let simmer for ½ hour. Remove the meat mixture and keep gravy aside.
4. Stuff duck with meat mixture. Place duck in large bowl and pour gravy over. Steam over rapidly boiling water for 3 hours or till duck is tender. Serve hot.

Note:
Add boiling water to the steamer if necessary. Keep the water boiling all the time.

STEW

INGREDIENTS

1 tablespoon light soya sauce
1 teaspoon msg
1 teaspoon sugar   **A**
1 teaspoon salt
1 teaspoon pepper

10 new potatoes, skinned
1 teaspoon peppercorns
1 carrot, cut into wedges   **B**
2 onions, cut into quarters
1 chicken cube
455 ml (16 fl oz) water

10 shallots, pounded coarsely   **C**
1 thumb-sized piece cinnamon bark

1 teaspoon dark soya sauce
1 teaspoon msg
¾ teaspoon salt   **D**
2 tablespoons flour
4 tablespoons water

1.2 kg (2½ lb) chicken, cut into pieces
2 tablespoons oil
3 tablespoons butter or margarine
8 tomatoes, cut into halves

METHOD

1. Marinate the chicken in **A** for ½ hour.
2. Boil **B** in a saucepan for 10 minutes.
3. Heat the oil in a frying pan and brown **C**. Remove to a plate.
4. In the same pan, add the butter and fry the marinated chicken till brown on all sides.
5. Mix **D** in a bowl and add to pan together with **B** (Method 2) and **C** (Method 3).
6. Stir and let simmer till chicken is tender, (20 minutes). Add the tomatoes and cook for 5 minutes. Remove from heat. Serve hot or cold.

TURMERIC CHICKEN

INGREDIENTS

1 tablespoon coriander powder
2½ tablespoons cumin powder
1 teaspoon pepper powder
½ teaspoon cinnamon powder   **A** *mixed in a bowl*
1 tablespoon turmeric powder
1 tablespoon curry powder

170 g (6 oz) onions
2 cloves garlic   **B** *ground to a fine paste*
½ thumb-sized piece ginger

1.6 kg (3½ lb) chicken, cut into big pieces
6 tablespoons natural yogurt
170 ml (6 fl oz) evaporated milk
2 stalks coriander, with roots intact

Seasoning:
2 tablespoons lemon juice
1½ tablespoons sugar
1½ teaspoons salt
1 teaspoon msg

200 g (7 oz) ghee or 140 g (5 oz) butter and 55 ml (2 fl oz) oil

METHOD

1. Marinate chicken pieces for ¾ hour with yogurt, 1½ teaspoons salt, 1 teaspoon each of sugar, msg and pepper.
2. Mix evaporated milk, 225 ml (8 fl oz) water, **A** and seasoning in large bowl. Add in chicken and mix well. Set aside.
3. Heat a heavy bottomed saucepan or aluminium wok. Heat ghee and fry **B** over medium heat till oil comes through and is fragrant. Add in chicken mixture, stir and cook over moderate heat for 15 minutes. Stir occasionally to prevent burning. Reduce heat to low, add coriander leaves and stalk. Cover pan to simmer for another 15–20 minutes or till chicken is tender and gravy is rather thick.
4. Add another 225 ml (8 fl oz) water. Stir and continue cooking for 2 minutes. Remove from heat.

Note:
If a thick gravy is preferred, omit Method (4).

Seafood

Braised Grouper with Black Soya Bean Sauce

Baked Crabs

Crabs in Spicy Soya Bean Paste

Crabs in Tomato Chilli Sauce

Dry Fish Curry

Fish Head Curry

Ikan Masak Kuah Lada

Rendang Ikan

Steamed Pomfret

Chilli Prawns

Glassy Prawns

Prawns in Soya Sauce

Sweet Sour Prawns

Tempura Prawns

Crayfish Mornay

Chilli Cuttlefish

Stuffed Cuttlefish Soup

Spicy Cockles

Crabs in Tomato Chilli Sauce

BRAISED GROUPER WITH BLACK SOYA BEAN SAUCE

INGREDIENTS

2 teaspoons light soya sauce
½–1 teaspoon msg
2 teaspoons sugar   **A** *mixed in a bowl*
1–2 teaspoons vinegar
½ teaspoon sesame oil
½ teaspoon cornflour

1 grouper, approximately 680 g (1½ lb)
1 teaspoon salt
½ teaspoon pepper
  Oil for frying fish
3 tablespoons lard
6 slices ginger
1 teaspoon pounded garlic
3–4 tablespoons black soya beans, pounded to a paste
285 ml (10 fl oz) chicken stock or 285 ml (10 fl oz) water with ½ chicken cube

1 red chilli   *seeded and cut into thin strips*
1 green chilli

3 stalks spring onions, cut into 4 cm (1½ in) lengths

METHOD

1. Scale and clean fish. Cut slits on both sides of fish. Rub in salt and pepper including inside of fish. Leave for ½ hour.

2. Heat iron wok. Put in enough oil to pan-fry fish and heat till very hot. Fry fish to a crisp golden brown on both sides. Remove fish to a serving plate.

3. Drain oil from pan, heat 2 tablespoons of the lard and fry the ginger and garlic till light brown. Add soya bean paste, **A** and chicken stock and stir-fry for short while. Lastly, add the red and green chillies and spring onions. Put fish in and cook for 1 minute adding extra tablespoon lard. Remove to a serving plate. Serve hot.

BAKED CRABS

INGREDIENTS

1 teaspoon salt
1 teaspoon msg
½ teaspoon pepper
2 tablespoons lard   **A**
1 teaspoon dark soya sauce
1 teaspoon light soya sauce
1 egg, beaten

225 g (½ lb) minced pork, with some fat
225 g (½ lb) prawns, shelled, deveined and chopped finely   **B**
2 tablespoons breadcrumbs, soaked in 2 tablespoons water

8 medium-sized fresh crabs, whole
  Flour for dusting
1 egg, breaten
  Breadcrumbs

METHOD

1. Steam the crabs, whole, over rapidly boiling water for 20 minutes. Do not remove lid while steaming. Cool. Remove meat and set aside the shells for stuffing.

2. Mix **A** in a bowl.

3. Add **B** and mix thoroughly. Add the crab meat and mix lightly.

4. Dust crab shells with flour. Fill the shells with the crab meat mixture and grill or bake in a pre-heated oven at 190°C (375°F) or Regulo 7 till cooked, (about ½–¾ hour).

5. Remove baked crabs from oven. Brush with beaten egg and sprinkle on breadcrumbs. Return to oven for another 5–7 minutes. Serve hot or cold.

CRABS IN SPICY SOYA BEAN PASTE

INGREDIENTS

8 shallots
4 cloves garlic
2 red chillies, seeded
4 slices ginger

A *ground to a paste*

3 large crabs weighing approximately 1.8 kg (4 lb)
4 tablespoons lard or oil
2 tablespoons spicy salted soya bean paste (*see recipe below*)

1 cup water, 225 ml (8 fl oz)
1 tablespoon sugar
1 teaspoon vinegar
1 teaspoon msg
¼ teaspoon salt
2 tablespoons light soya sauce

gravy sauce

1 large egg, lightly beaten
3 stalks spring onions, cut into 3 cm (1½ in) lengths
2 tablespoons lard

METHOD

1. Clean crabs and cut into 4 pieces. Cut off claws and crack them lightly.

2. Heat a pan, add lard and fry **A** till fragrant, stirring frequently. Add salted bean paste; fry for ½ minute. Pour in gravy sauce and bring it to boil. Put in crabs, stir well and cook for 10–15 minutes or till crabs are well done.

3. Add more water if gravy is too dry, pour in the beaten egg, add spring onions and lard, stir in pan for a moment and remove crabs to a serving dish.

SPICY SOYA BEAN PASTE

115 g (4 oz) preserved soya beans (brown)
2 tablespoons plum paste
4 tablespoons hot chilli sauce
2 teaspoons sesame oil

Combine all ingredients in a bowl and blend well.

CRABS IN TOMATO CHILLI SAUCE

INGREDIENTS

1 tablespoon chilli sauce
2 tablespoons light soya sauce
¼ teaspoon salt
1 tablespoon sugar
½ teaspoon msg
2 tablespoons vinegar
8 tablespoons tomato ketchup
1 teaspoon sesame oil

A

340 ml (12 fl oz) water

4 cloves garlic
10 shallots
½ thumb-sized piece ginger

B

2 tablespoons cornflour
4 tablespoons water

C

6 tablespoons lard

1.5 kg (3¼ lb) crabs, cleaned and cut into pieces
1 egg, beaten

METHOD

1. Mix **A** in a bowl for the sauce.

2. Pound **B** to a fine paste.

3. Blend **C** in a separate bowl for the thickening.

4. Heat 6 tablespoons lard in wok and fry paste till fragrant. Add crabs and one-third of the sauce. Stir-fry for 2 minutes over a high heat.

5. Add the rest of the sauce; stir and cover wok for 10 minutes. (Do not remove the lid.)

6. Pour in thickening and stir well. Add beaten egg, mix thoroughly with the chillied crabs and remove to a serving plate. Serve at once.

DRY FISH CURRY

INGREDIENTS

1½ teaspoons turmeric powder
1½ teaspoons dried chilli powder
1 tablespoon cumin powder   **A**
1 tablespoon cinnamon powder
1 teaspoon aniseed powder
1 teaspoon black pepper powder

455 g (1 lb) coconut
680 g (24 oz) Spanish mackerel

Marinade:
2 tablespoons fish sauce
1 teaspoon pepper
1 tablespoon lime juice
1 tablespoon sugar

115 ml (4 fl oz) oil for frying fish
3 tablespoons oil for frying paste
55 g (2 oz) onions, sliced thinly
½ thumb-sized piece ginger, shredded thinly
1 teaspoon rempah tumis (*see recipe*)
2 sprigs curry leaves
2 cloves garlic, chopped finely
55 g (2 oz) shallots, pounded coarsely
2 ripe tomatoes, peeled and sliced thickly

Seasoning:
1 teaspoon salt
1 teaspoon sugar
1 teaspoon msg

METHOD

1. Squeeze coconut with 225 ml (8 fl oz) water to extract milk. Set aside.

2. Wash and cut fish into pieces. Soak in marinade for 20 minutes. Drain fish and fry till lightly browned on both sides. Remove and set aside.

3. Heat 3 tablespoons oil in an aluminium wok. Fry sliced onions till soft; add ginger, rempah tumis and curry leaves. Fry till ginger turns light brown. Stir in garlic, fry for 1 minute; add shallots and stir-fry till light brown.

4. Add **A** with ½ cup coconut milk. Stir for ½ minute and add 115 ml (4 fl oz) water and tomatoes. Simmer for 5 minutes, stirring constantly to prevent burning.

5. Pour in remaining milk and seasoning. Cook over low heat till it reaches a boil. Put in fish and continue cooking till gravy is thick. Remove from heat. Serve hot or cold.

Note:
*Cut Spanish mackerel into pieces 2.5 cm (1 in) thick. Then cut each piece into four. Ingredients **A** may be substituted with 4 tablespoons curry powder and 1 teaspoon turmeric powder.*

REMPAH TUMIS

INGREDIENTS

55 g (2 oz) cumin seeds
55 g (2 oz) cinnamon bark
55 g (2 oz) fenugreek
55 g (2 oz) split black beans
30 g (1 oz) poppy seeds

METHOD

1. Wash cumin seeds and cinnamon bark. Drain. Dry in sun or under a warm grill for 35–45 minutes till ingredients are heated through and smell fragrant.

2. Mix everything together. Keep in a bottle and store in refrigerator.

Curry leaves give this dish a delightful aroma. Use 1–2 sprigs.

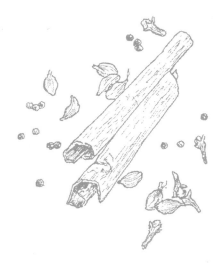

FISH HEAD CURRY

INGREDIENTS

1–2 teaspoons salt
2–3 teaspoons sugar
1 teaspoon msg
3 tomatoes, quartered } **A**
55 g (2 oz) tamarind with 225 ml (8 fl oz)
    water, squeezed and strained
2 sprigs curry leaves

6 red chillies
8 green chillies
5 tablespoons oil
1 tablespoon mixed curry seeds for fish curry★
½ thumb-sized piece ginger, thinly shredded
2 cloves garlic, sliced thinly
2 onions, sliced thinly
4 tablespoons curry powder, mixed into a paste
    with 225 ml (8 fl oz) water
225 g (8 oz) grated coconut, squeezed with 225 ml
    (8 fl oz) water
225 g (8 oz) tender lady's fingers
625 g (1 lb 6 oz) fish head

METHOD

1. Slit the chillies half-way, lengthwise.

2. Heat oil in wok and fry curry seeds and ginger till light brown. Add garlic and stir-fry for ½ minute. Add sliced onion and fry till soft and transparent. Add curry paste and 115 ml of the coconut milk. Stir-fry till oil comes through.

3. Add **A** and continue to cook over a low heat. Add remaining coconut milk. Let simmer for 5 minutes.

4. Add lady's fingers, fish head and sliced chillies, cover pan and let simmer till cooked.

★See "Helpful Hints".

Note:
You can add 3–4 dried tamarind slices for a sharp, sourish taste.

IKAN MASAK KUAH LADA
(FISH IN MILD SPICY PASTE)

INGREDIENTS

½ thumb-sized piece turmeric
10 slices galangal
2 stalks lemon grass, sliced
4 candlenuts
1 tablespoon shrimp paste } **A**
1 red chilli
12 shallots
1 clove garlic
2 teaspoons pepper

½ teaspoon salt
½ teaspoon msg } **B**
455 ml (16 fl oz) water

3 green egg plants
Salt water
625 g (1 lb 6 oz) Spanish mackerel or ray fish
Sugar and salt for seasoning
5 tablespoons oil
1 walnut-sized tamarind with 225 ml (8 fl oz)
    water, squeezed and strained

METHOD

1. Grind **A** to a fine paste.

2. Cut the egg plants into 6 cm (2½ in) lengths. Halve each piece lengthwise and score the cut surface. Soak in salt water until needed.

3. Wash and cut the fish. Season with 1 teaspoon salt and 1 teaspoon sugar. Set aside.

4. Heat an aluminium wok. Heat oil and stir-fry paste (Method 1) over a moderate heat till fragrant. Add the tamarind juice, 2 tablespoonfuls at a time.

5. Add **B** and boil for 5 minutes. Add the egg plants. Cover wok and cook for 5 minutes. Add the fish and cook till fish is done.

RENDANG IKAN
(FISH IN RICH COCONUT SAUCE)

INGREDIENTS

455 g (1 lb) Spotted Spanish Mackerel (Tenggiri Papan), cut into pieces
455 g (1 lb) grated coconut, white
2 teaspoons curry powder

115 g (4 oz) shallots
1 stalk lemon grass
½ thumb-sized piece galangal
6 red chillies, seeded
4 slices ginger
1 teaspoon shrimp paste
1 clove garlic
½ thumb-sized piece fresh turmeric or
  ½ teaspoon turmeric powder
4 daun limau purot

ground to a fine paste

1 walnut-sized piece tamarind mixed with 115 ml (4 fl oz) water, strained
1 slice dry tamarind

METHOD

1. Marinate fish pieces with 1 teaspoon sugar, ¾ teaspoon salt and 1 tablespoon tamarind with 2 tablespoons water, for 20 minutes.

2. Squeeze coconut for No. 1 milk, set aside. Add 225 ml water to coconut and squeeze for No. 2 milk. Set aside.

3. Heat wok. Add 4 tablespoons oil and when hot, fry curry powder and paste over moderate heat till oil bubbles through, adding 3 tablespoons No. 1 milk a spoonful at a time. Fry till paste is oily and fragrant.

4. Pour in No. 2 milk and tamarind juice and bring to a boil. Add slice of tamarind, fish, 2 teaspoons sugar and 1 teaspoon each of salt and msg to cook over moderate heat for 7–8 minutes. Reduce heat to low. Pour in the remaining No. 1 milk, stir well and simmer for 5 minutes uncovered. Remove from heat. Serve hot or cold.

STEAMED POMFRET

INGREDIENTS

2 teaspoons light soya sauce
1 teaspoon msg
½ teaspoon sugar
½ teaspoon sesame oil
¼ teaspoon fine salt
225 ml (8 fl oz) chicken stock

A

1 tablespoon *kiam chye*, finely shredded
1 stalk Chinese parsley, cut
2 red chillies, cut into strips
2 stalks spring onions, cut into 5 cm (2 in) lengths

B

2 dried mushrooms, soaked in hot water
1 pomfret, 455–680 g (1–1½ lb)
Salt
10 thin slices ginger
2 tablespoons lard
1 tablespoon pork fat, finely shredded

METHOD

1. Mix **A** in a bowl for the sauce.

2. Slice mushrooms into strips.

3. Clean fish and make two shallow slits on each side. Season with salt.

4. Arrange half of the ginger slices and spread 1 tablespoonful of the lard on a plate. Place fish on top.

5. Spread the rest of the ginger, pork fat and mushroom strips over the fish.

6. Steam for 12–15 minutes over a very high heat or till cooked.

7. Boil the sauce in another pan. Stir in the other tablespoonful of lard.

8. Place the steamed fish on a hot serving dish and pour the cooked sauce over the fish. Garnish with **B** and serve while very hot.

Steamed Pomfret

CHILLI PRAWNS

INGREDIENTS

15 red chillies
1 teaspoon shrimp paste   **A**
¼ teaspoon salt

1 teaspoon sugar   **B**
1 tablespoon lime juice

6 tablespoons oil
625 g (22 oz) king prawns, trimmed
½ teaspoon salt
1 big onion sliced

METHOD

1. Pound **A** till fine.

2. Heat oil in wok. Fry prawns till cooked. Add salt and sliced onions.

3. Push to one side of the wok and fry the chilli paste (Method 1). Stir in the prawns and onions, add **B**, and fry for 1 minute. Remove to a serving plate.

GLASSY PRAWNS

INGREDIENTS

680 g (1½ lb) big prawns

1 tablespoon *pheng say* powder (available at Chinese medicine shops)
1 tablespoon bicarbonate of soda   **A**
225 g (8 oz) castor sugar

170 ml (6 fl oz) water
1 tablespoon cornflour
½ teaspoon sesame oil
2 teaspoons light soya sauce   *sauce mixed in a bowl*
1 teaspoon msg
½ teaspoon sugar
Pinch of salt
1 teaspoon oyster sauce

225 ml (8 fl oz) oil to deep fry prawns
2 tablespoons lard
1 teaspoon coarsely chopped ginger
2 cloves garlic, coarsely chopped
3 stalks spring onion, cut into 5 cm (2 in) lengths

PRAWNS IN SOYA SAUCE

INGREDIENTS

4 tablespoons light soya sauce
1 tablespoon sugar
1 teaspoon cornflour   **A**
2 tablespoons water

455 g (1 lb) prawns, fairly large
Salt water
8 tablespoons lard or oil
2 thumb-sized pieces ginger, shredded finely
¼ teaspoon salt
2 stalks spring onions, cut into short lengths

METHOD

1. Mix **A** in a bowl for the sauce.

2. Trim prawns and wash in salt water. Drain.

3. Heat the lard in an iron wok. When very hot, fry ginger till it turns brown. Add prawns, salt and stir-fry for ½ minute. Cover and cook for 5–7 minutes.

4. Remove lid, add **A**, stir well with the prawns and add the spring onions. Serve.

METHOD

1. Shell prawns, slit lengthwise from the head to the tail without cutting through the prawns. Remove dark veins.

2. Wash prawns and drain. Season with **A** and set aside for 4 hours or leave overnight in the refrigerator. Add water to cover 8 cm (3 in) above the prawns in a bowl.

3. Place bowl of prawns under a slow running tap for ½ hour, stirring at 5 minute intervals. Leave in colander to drain.

4. Pour oil in heated wok. When very hot, put in prawns. Cover pan with lid and cook over high heat for 2 minutes or till prawns turn transparent. Remove prawns to a bowl.

5. Remove oil from the wok, add lard, and stir fry ginger and garlic till light brown. Return prawns to pan, stir sauce and pour over prawns. Toss in pan till gravy boils and thickens. Remove to a serving plate. Garnish with spring onions and serve.

SWEET SOUR PRAWNS

INGREDIENTS

6 tablespoons tomato sauce
2 tablespoons sweet chilli sauce
1 teaspoon light soya sauce
¼ teaspoon pepper
½ teaspoon msg
1 teaspoon sugar
1 teaspoon vinegar
1 tablespoon cornflour mixed with
   3 tablespoons water

A *mixed in a bowl*

1 tablespoon lard

605 g (21 oz) medium-sized prawns
4 tablespoons castor sugar
4 tablespoons lard or oil
2 cloves garlic, finely chopped
1 tablespoon chopped ginger
6 tablespoons spring onion, chopped
6 tablespoons Chinese celery, cut into 0.5 cm (¼ in) pieces

METHOD

1. Shell prawns, slit lengthwise and devein. Wash and drain in a colander.

2. Place prawns in a bowl, season with 4 tablespoons castor sugar and leave for 1 hour. Wash prawns under a running tap for a minute to remove all the sugar and put in colander to drain.

3. Heat lard in wok till very hot. Fry the garlic and ginger till light brown. Add prawns and stir fry over high heat for 2 minutes or till prawns are cooked. Add chopped spring onions and celery and stir-fry for 1 minute.

4. Stir **A** and pour over prawns. Add the extra tablespoon of lard, mix well, and remove to a serving plate. Serve hot.

TEMPURA PRAWNS
(FRIED PRAWNS, JAPANESE-STYLE)

INGREDIENTS

¼ teaspoon salt
½ teaspoon brandy
½ teaspoon msg

A

85 g (3 oz) cauliflower
55 g (2 oz) green peppers

B

85 g (3 oz) self-raising flour

½ teaspoon salt
½ teaspoon sugar
½ teaspoon msg
½ teaspoon pepper
1 tablespoon oil
130 ml (4½ fl oz) water

C

225 g (½ lb) small prawns, shelled and deveined
55 g (2 oz) pork chop meat, sliced thinly
   Oil for deep-frying

METHOD

1. Marinate prawns and pork in **A** for 10 minutes.

2. Slice **B** thinly.

3. Place flour in a bowl. Stir **C** till well mixed and pour gradually into the flour. Mix well to form a smooth batter. Leave to stand for 20 minutes.

4. Add the marinated prawns, pork and **B** to batter. Mix well.

5. Heat oil. When very hot, fry battered ingredients till golden brown. Drain on a wire sieve and leave to cool on absorbent paper. Serve hot with sauce.

SAUCE:
4 tablespoons tomato ketchup
1 tablespoon sweet chilli sauce
1 teaspoon 'A1' brand sauce
1 teaspoon vinegar
1 teaspoon msg
1 teaspoon lime juice
4 tablespoons boiled water, cooled

1. Mix all the ingredients and serve in a separate bowl.

CRAYFISH MORNAY

INGREDIENTS

340 g (12 oz) cooked crayfish meat
55 g (2 oz) butter with 1 tablespoon oil
85 g (3 oz) onions, sliced
4 tablespoons celery, sliced thinly
2 heaped tablespoons flour
285 ml (10 fl oz) milk

Seasoning:
½ teaspoon sugar
¼ teaspoon salt
½ teaspoon pepper

2 egg whites, lightly beaten
115 g mozzarella cheese, coarsely grated

Topping:
½ cup dry breadcrumbs
140 g (5 oz) chopped salami
½ cup mozzarella cheese, coarsely grated

METHOD

1. Chop crayfish into big serving chunks.

2. Heat the butter and oil to fry onions and celery till soft and transparent. Add in the flour and stir for a moment.

3. Pour in the milk and stir well in pan. Reduce heat to low and add crayfish, seasoning and egg whites. Cook for a minute and then add the cheese. Stir and remove from heat.

4. Grease a deep oven-proof dish; dust with flour and pour in crayfish mixture. Spread on ½ of breadcrumbs, put in salami and remaining cheese and top with remaining breadcrumbs.

5. Bake in a moderate oven (121°C) for ½ hour. Serve hot.

CHILLI CUTTLEFISH

INGREDIENTS

15 red chillies ⎤ **A**
½ teaspoon shrimp paste ⎦

½ teaspoon salt ⎤
1 teaspoon sugar ⎟ **B**
½ teaspoon msg ⎟
1 teaspoon lime juice ⎦

455 g (1 lb) cuttlefish
6 tablespoons lard or oil
2 big onions, sliced thinly

METHOD

1. Pound **A** to a fine paste.

2. Remove ink bag and bone from cuttlefish. Wash, drain and cut cuttlefish into 2.5 cm (1 in) rings.

3. Heat iron wok. When very hot, heat 3 tablespoons lard. Fry cuttlefish over high heat for 5 minutes. Remove to a dish.

4. Heat the rest of the lard and fry the sliced onions over a high heat for 1 minute. Reduce heat, add the paste and **B** and stir-fry for another minute. Add cuttlefish and stir well with the paste. Serve hot or cold.

STUFFED CUTTLEFISH SOUP

INGREDIENTS

310 g (11 oz) small cuttlefish

310 g (11 oz) minced pork
225 g (½ lb) prawns; shelled, deveined and
    chopped
¼ teaspoon salt   **A**
½ teaspoon msg
¼ teaspoon cornflour

1 teaspoon salt
1 teaspoon msg   **B**
1 chicken cube

15 g (½ oz) vermicelli, soaked in hot water

2 sprigs Chinese celery
2 cloves chopped garlic, fried in oil   **C**
    Dash of pepper

METHOD

1. Remove head, ink bag and cartilage from each cuttlefish. Set aside the heads. Wash and clean the inside of the cuttlefish. Drain cuttlefish in a colander.

2. Mix **A** thoroughly to stuff three-quarters of each cuttlefish. Re-attach head. Shape little meat balls with the remaining meat.

3. Boil 680 ml (1½ pints) water in a saucepan. Add the stuffed cuttlefish and meat balls. Boil for 3 minutes. Season with **B**. Cut up the vermicelli and add to the soup. Garnish with **C** and serve in a large bowl.

Note:
When cleaning the cuttlefish, remove the brown outer skin from the body. In this way, the soup remains clear. Before stuffing meat into the cuttlefish, make a slit at the tail end of the cuttlefish. This will prevent the heat from pushing the meat out.

SPICY COCKLES

INGREDIENTS

10 shallots
6 dried chillies or 1 tablespoon chilli paste
1 teaspoon shrimp paste   **A**
1 candlenut
1 stalk lemon grass, sliced

115 ml (4 fl oz) water
1 teaspoon tamarind with 115 ml (4 fl oz)
    water, squeezed and strained
1 teaspoon sugar   **B**
1 teaspoon salt
½ teaspoon msg

310 g (11 oz) shelled cockles
5 tablespoons oil
1 stalk lemon grass, bruised
115 g (4 oz) grated coconut, squeezed with 115 ml
    (4 fl oz) water for milk

METHOD

1. Pound **A** to a fine paste.
2. Scald the cockles and drain in a colander.
3. Heat oil in very hot pan. Fry the paste and bruised lemon grass till fragrant.
4. Add **B**. Allow mixture to boil.
5. Add the cockles and coconut milk.
6. Cook for 1 minute and remove to a dish.

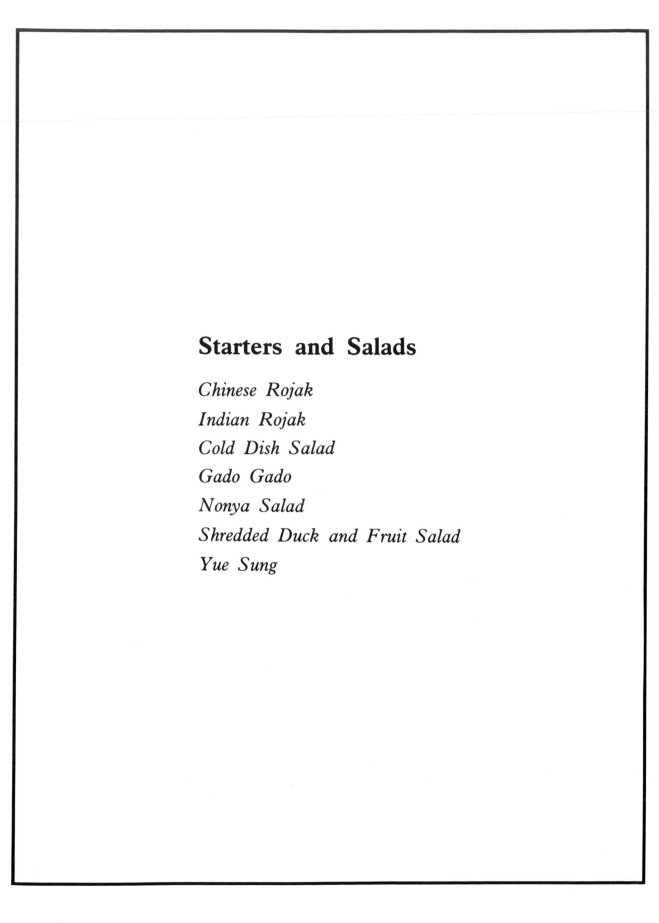

Starters and Salads

Chinese Rojak

Indian Rojak

Cold Dish Salad

Gado Gado

Nonya Salad

Shredded Duck and Fruit Salad

Yue Sung

Chinese Rojak

CHINESE ROJAK

INGREDIENTS

7–8 tablespoons sugar
1–1¼ teaspoons salt
2–4 tablespoons dried chilli paste
2–2½ tablespoons black prawn paste (hay ko) — **A**

170 g (6 oz) sliced cucumber
115 g (4 oz) beansprouts, blanched and drained
170 g (6 oz) sliced Chinese turnip
170 g (6 oz) sliced pineapple
115 g (4 oz) water convolvulus, blanched, drained and cut into 5 cm (2 in) lengths — **B**

1 tablespoon juice of local lime (*limau kesturi*)
1 walnut-sized knob of tamarind, soaked in 85 ml (3 fl oz) water and strained
225 g (8 oz) ground roasted peanuts
2 crispy Chinese crullers, sliced thickly
4 squares fried spongy bean curd, cut into pieces

METHOD

1. Put **A** into a large bowl and blend to a paste with the back of a wooden spoon. Add the lime juice and 4-5 tablespoons of the tamarind juice and stir.

2. Add peanuts with rest of the tamarind juice and stir well. Add **B** and stir with a wooden spoon. Just before serving, add the crispy Chinese crullers and fried spongy bean curd. Mix well.

Note:
Cuttlefish and jellyfish soaked in alkaline water can be purchased from local markets and included in the salad. Rinse, blanch, cut into thick strips and add with the other salad ingredients (Method 2).

INDIAN ROJAK

INGREDIENTS

225 g (8 oz) potatoes, boiled in jackets, peeled and quartered
8 eggs, hard boiled and quartered
5 big firm bean curd cakes, fried and cut into pieces
Coconut fingers*, sliced thickly
*Wardays***
Prawn fritters***
Spicy cuttlefish****
2 cucumbers, skinned and sliced
2 lettuce leaves, shredded

Sauce:
30–40 dried chillies
2 tablespoons chopped onions
1 clove garlic, chopped finely
1 teaspoon shrimp paste — **A**

4 tablespoons oil
400 g (14 oz) boiled sweet potatoes, mashed

Seasoning:
225–285 g (8–10 oz) sugar
1½–2 teaspoons salt
2 tablespoons vinegar
55 g (2 oz) tamarind soaked in 115 ml (4 fl oz) water and strained — **B**

30 g (1 oz) toasted sesame seeds, finely ground
30 g (1 oz) toasted sesame seeds

To make the sauce:

1. Grind or blend **A** to a fine paste.

2. Heat the oil in a pan and fry the paste over moderate heat till it is fragrant and oil bubbles through. Set aside.

3. Put mashed sweet potatoes in a heavy aluminium saucepan. Add 560 ml (1¼ pints) water in small amounts and stir till well-blended. Add **B** (seasoning), fried paste, and the ground sesame seeds. Boil gently for ½ hour to thicken, stirring occasionally to prevent sauce sticking to bottom of pan.

4. Remove from heat, add the rest of the sesame seeds, stir and cool.

★Coconut fingers

115 g (4 oz) plain flour
1 tablespoon dried prawns, pounded
½ teaspoon salt   **A**
1 teaspoon sugar
½ teaspoon msg
½ teaspoon pepper

30 g (1 oz) chickpea flour
115 g (4 oz) coarsely grated coconut, white
115 ml (4 fl oz) water

1. Put **A** in a bowl and stir till well mixed. Add chickpea flour and coconut and mix. Add water and knead lightly to make a soft dough.
2. Shape mixture into small 6.5 cm (2½ in) long rolls, tapering at both ends. Deep fry in hot oil for 5 minutes till golden brown and well cooked inside. Drain in a metal colander. Cool and set aside.

★★*Warday*

2 eggs
1 teaspoon sugar
¼ teaspoon salt
¼ teaspoon pepper   **A**
¼ teaspoon msg
85 ml (3 fl oz) water

¼ teaspoon bicarbonate soda
85 g (3 oz) chickpea flour
100 g (3½ oz) plain flour   **B**
3 tablespoons chopped onions

1. Put **A** in a bowl, beat lightly with a fork till well mixed.
2. Put **B** in a mixing bowl. Pour in the egg mixture and stir till batter is smooth and free of lumps.
3. Divide batter into two, setting aside one half to fry the prawn fritters.
4. Heat oil in an aluminium wok for deep frying. Spoon tablespoons of the remaining batter into the hot oil, allowing space for *warday* to expand. Fry over moderate heat till golden brown.
5. Drain in a colander and set aside.

★★★Prawn fritters

¼ teaspoon bicarbonate of soda
¼ teaspoon pepper   **A**
Pinch of salt
2 tablespoons self-raising flour

2 tablespoons water   **B**
½ *warday* batter

285 g (10 oz) small prawns, shelled and deveined

1. Put **A** in a bowl and mix well.
2. Add **B** and stir till batter is smooth. Coat prawns.
3. Fry fritters over moderately high heat till golden brown and set aside.

★★★★Spicy cuttlefish

1 tablespoon chilli powder
1 candlenut   **A** *ground to a fine paste*
4 shallots
1 teaspoon shrimp paste

115 g (4 oz) grated coconut
1 large cuttlefish (soaked in alkaline water)
6 tablespoons oil

1 teaspoon sugar
½ teaspoon msg   **B**
½ teaspoon pepper
½ teaspoon cumin powder

1. Squeeze coconut for No. 1 milk.
2. Cut cuttlefish into small pieces. Pat with kitchen towel to dry.
3. Heat oil in wok. When very hot, fry the cuttlefish a few at a time, for 1 minute. Remove to a bowl.
4. In the same wok, heat oil and fry **A** till oil bubbles through and smells fragrant. Add coconut milk and **B**, stir and continue cooking over moderate heat till dry.
5. Put in the fried cuttlefish, stir and cook over gentle heat.

To serve:
Put small amounts of each of the ingredients on individual plates, garnish with sliced cucumber and lettuce. Serve with sauce in separate small bowls.

COLD DISH SALAD

INGREDIENTS

1 tablespoon sugar	
¼ teaspoon salt	
4 tablespoons salad cream	
1 tablespoon sweet chilli sauce	**A**
½ teaspoon pepper	
1 teaspoon sesame oil	
3 tablespoons chunky peanut butter	

1 chicken breast, about 170–230 g (6–8 oz)
½ teaspoon salt
½ teaspoon msg
½ teaspoon sherry
1 tablespoon vinegar
1 tablespoon dry mustard
115 g (4 oz) lettuce, finely shredded
225 g (8 oz) shredded jellyfish, treated and seasoned*
2 stalks Chinese celery
2 tablespoons roasted sesame seeds

METHOD

1. Rub chicken with the salt, msg and sherry. Place on a small enamel plate in a steamer and steam for ½ hour. Leave to cool. Cut chicken in half lengthwise and then into thick shreds. Set aside.
2. Mix vinegar and mustard in a big bowl and add **A**. Mix well till sauce is smooth. Set aside.
3. Place the shredded lettuce on a large serving plate. Arrange jellyfish on the lettuce and spread the shredded chicken over it. Pour the sauce over and garnish with celery and sesame seeds. Chill for 1–2 hours. Serve as a cold starter to a Chinese meal.

To make alkaline water:
625 g (22 oz) white crystal balls, obtainable from local markets, finely pounded
680 ml (24 fl oz) boiling water

1. Place pounded alkaline crystal balls in a porcelain jar. Add boiling water and stir with a wooden spoon till crystal balls dissolve. Leave to stand overnight.
2. Strain alkaline water through fine muslin. Store the alkaline water in a bottle for future use. (Prepared alkaline water can be kept for almost a year.)

*To prepare jellyfish:
6 tablespoons alkaline water
1.7 litres (4 pints) cold water
605 g (20 oz) salted jellyfish

Seasoning:

3 teaspoons light soya sauce	
1 teaspoon sugar	
1½ teaspoons msg	*seasoning for 225 g jellyfish*
2 teaspoons peanut or corn oil	
1 teaspoon sesame oil	

1. Mix the alkaline water with the cold water in an enamel container and soak the jellyfish for 48 hours or till jellyfish swells and softens.
2. Wash in cold water and cut each into 2 or 4 pieces.
3. Bring a saucepan of water to a rapid boil. Blanch 2 or 3 pieces of jellyfish at a time in the boiling water. Scoop out immediately and soak in a basin of cold water. Bring water to a fast boil each time you add jellyfish. Drain jellyfish. Pat dry and shred thinly. Mix well with seasoning. Keep the rest in a container of water and store in the refrigerator for future use. (Prepared jellyfish can be stored in the refrigerator for at least 2–3 weeks if the water is changed every fourth day. Blanch in hot water and roll in dry tea towel before use.)

GADO-GADO
(INDONESIAN SALAD WITH PEANUT SAUCE)

INGREDIENTS

625 g (22 oz) bean sprouts
625 g (22 oz) cabbage, diced
625 g (22 oz) long beans, cut into 3.5 cm (1½ in) lengths
2.7 litres (6 pints) water
1 teaspoon salt
1 tablespoon sugar
4 stalks lettuce, cut into 2.5 cm (1 in) pieces
225 g (8 oz) potatoes, boiled, peeled and cut into pieces
6 soya bean cakes, fried and cut into pieces
3 packets fermented soya bean cake, fried and cut into pieces
10 hard-boiled eggs, sliced
Cucumber wedges

METHOD

1. Boil separately: bean sprouts (½ minute), cabbage (5 minutes) and long beans (5 minutes) in the water with 1 teaspoon salt and 1 tablespoon sugar.

2. Lift and drain. Soak bean sprouts immediately in a basin of cold water.

SAUCE:

680 g (24 oz) roasted groundnuts, pounded
1 litre (2 pints) water
10 tablespoons sugar
1½ tablespoons salt
} **A**

15 shallots
6 cloves garlic
1 tablespoon shrimp paste
20–30 dried chillies
} **B**

225 ml (8 fl oz) oil
6–8 tablespoons vinegar
½ cup crispy shallots

METHOD

1. Boil **A** for 10 minutes.
2. Grind **B** to a paste.
3. Heat oil in wok and fry paste till fragrant and oil comes through.

4. Add fried paste to the boiled groundnut sauce (Method 1). Stir, reduce the heat and let simmer for 10–15 minutes. Add vinegar to taste. Remove from heat. Set aside sauce to cool. Mix in half cup of the crispy shallots.

To serve:
Arrange the lettuce on a large serving plate. Place bean sprouts, cabbage, long beans, potatoes, soya bean cakes, and fermented soya bean cake on it. Garnish with sliced eggs and cucumber wedges. Serve with groundnut sauce separately.

NONYA SALAD

INGREDIENTS

1 lime leaf
¼ teaspoon salt
} **A**

2 or 3 red chillies
2 tablespoons toasted shrimp paste
} **B**

2–3 tablespoons vinegar
½–1 tablespoon sugar
1 teaspoon lime juice
} **C**

2 cucumbers
½ pineapple
4 tablespoons dried prawns, pounded

METHOD

1. Cut off the ends of each cucumber. Wash and dice cucumbers into 1 cm cubes (with skin).
2. Remove pineapple skin and dice pineapple into 1 cm cubes.
3. Pound **A** till fine. Add **B** and pound together till fine. Remove to a dish.
4. Add **C** to the shrimp paste mixture and stir till well mixed.

To mix the salad:
1. Place the cucumber and pineapple cubes in a large bowl. Add dried prawns and mix thoroughly by hand.
2. Add shrimp paste mixture, stir thoroughly, and serve.

SHREDDED DUCK AND FRUIT SALAD

INGREDIENTS

1 cup shredded green lettuce
1 cup shredded treated jellyfish
1 cup shredded cucumber
1 cup shredded honey-dew melon
1 cup shredded roast duck

Garnish:
¼ cup chopped walnuts
¼ cup ground roasted peanuts
3 tablespoons toasted sesame seeds

1. Place shredded ingredients in a large serving plate with green lettuce on the bottom and roast duck on top. Chill in refrigerator.
2. Before serving, sprinkle salad with walnuts, peanuts and sesame seeds. Pour sauce (see recipe below) over and serve.

Sauce:
4 tablespoons sour plum sauce (sung boey chew)
4 tablespoons apricot jam
1 tablespoon sweet chilli sauce
1 teaspoon vinegar
1 tablespoon peanut oil
1 teaspoon ginger wine (optional)
1 teaspoon sugar
½ teaspoon sesame oil

METHOD

1. Mix all ingredients in a small saucepan. Cook over low heat till heated through and well blended.
2. Strain mixture, cook and serve with cold salad.

YUE SUNG
(CANTONESE RAW FISH SALAD)

INGREDIENTS

455 g (1 lb) Chinese radish
115 g (4 oz) sweet potato
115 g (4 oz) carrot
55 g (2 oz) sweet crisp flakes (available in Chinatown confectionaries)
55–85 g (2–3 oz) roasted peanuts, coarsely ground
4 tablespoons sesame seeds, toasted
1 small segment pomelo
2 sprigs Chinese celery (short, dark green variety), cut leaves and tender stalks into short pieces
115 g (4 oz) preserved jellyfish, sliced thinly

30 g (1 oz) fresh young ginger
30 g (1 oz) preserved sweet ginger
30 g (1 oz) preserved sweet red ginger   *finely shredded*
2 fresh chillies, seeded
3 preserved, sweet and sour leeks
2 lime leaves
1 small piece preserved candied orange
55 g (2 oz) preserved candied winter melon

4–5 tablespoons corn oil
2 tablespoons lime juice
4 teaspoons castor sugar
¼ teaspoon five-spice powder   *seasoning*
½ teaspoon fine salt
¼ teaspoon pepper
3–4 tablespoons vinegar, set aside 1 tablespoon for fish

225 g (8 oz) thinly sliced wolf herring

METHOD

1. Skin radish, sweet potatoes and carrots. Soak in cold water for an hour and drain. Leave in a colander to air.
2. Grate sweet potatoes, immerse in water briefly, stir and strain immediately to drain well.
3. Grate carrot and radish and set aside. Do not immerse in water.

To serve:
Arrange all ingredients except fish, crispy flakes and seasoning on a large round tray. Place fish and flakes last with tablespoon of vinegar. Mix well with seasoning.

Yue Sung

Vegetarian Greens

Bean Sprouts fried with Crispy Salted Fish
Cauliflower and Long Beans in Creamy Sauce
Chinese Mustard with Abalone
Chop Suey
Egg Plant with Pork and Prawns
Egg Plant in Spicy Sauce
Loh Hon Chye
Long Beans with Minced Meat
Mustard with Crab Meat Sauce
Rebong Masak Lemak
Vegetarian Spring Rolls
Vegetarian Beehoon
Vegetarian Curry

Vegetarian Spring Rolls

BEAN SPROUTS FRIED WITH CRISPY SALTED FISH

INGREDIENTS

    30 g (1 oz) Penang salted fish
       Oil
     3 tablespoons lard
    ½ teaspoon pounded garlic
    285 g (10 oz) bean sprouts, picked, washed and
       drained
     2 stalks spring onions, cut into 4 cm (1½ in)
       lengths

Seasoning:
    ½ teaspoon salt
     1 teaspoon sugar
    ½ teaspoon msg
    ¼ teaspoon pepper

METHOD

1. Cut salted fish into thin strips, immerse in water and drain immediately. Heat oil in a small saucepan and fry salted fish over moderate heat till lightly browned and crispy. Drain on absorbent paper and leave to cool slightly. Keep in a bottle to keep it crisp.

2. Heat an iron wok. When very hot, heat 2 tablespoons lard and fry garlic till light brown, add bean sprouts, spring onions and seasoning. Sprinkle a little water and stir-fry for short while over high heat. Remove from heat and pour in the rest of the lard, stir and remove to a serving plate. Break crispy salt fish into fine pieces and place over bean sprouts before serving.

CAULIFLOWER AND LONG BEANS IN CREAMY SAUCE

INGREDIENTS

    115 g (4 oz) peas
    455 g (1 lb) cauliflower, cut into florets
    455 g (1 lb) long beans, cut into 7 cm (3 in) lengths
     1 carrot, sliced
     2 tablespoons each of butter and oil
     1 onion, thinly sliced
     1 clove garlic, finely chopped
     2 tablespoons plain flour

Seasoning:
     1 chicken cube, crushed
    ½ teaspoon turmeric powder
     1 teaspoon sugar
    ¼ teaspoon salt
       Dash of pepper
     2 teaspoons light soya sauce

    225 ml (8 fl oz) evaporated milk diluted in 225 ml
       (8 fl oz) water

METHOD

1. Blanch vegetables separately. Drain and set aside.

2. Heat butter and oil in wok. Fry onion and garlic till light brown. Add in flour and stir-fry for short while. Put in scalded vegetables and stir-fry over high heat for 1 minute.

3. Add seasoning with ½ of diluted milk into pan. Stir well, reduce heat to moderate and cook for 5–7 minutes. Pour in remaining milk and cook for another 5 minutes or till vegetables are tender.

CHINESE MUSTARD WITH ABALONE

INGREDIENTS

1 tablespoon oyster sauce
½ teaspoon sugar
½ teaspoon msg
Dash of pepper
½ teaspoon sesame oil   **A**
Abalone sauce from the can
1 teaspoon light soya sauce

1 tablespoon cornflour
4 tablespoons water   **B**

1 can 455 g (16 oz) abalone

285 g (10 oz) *poh chye* or Chinese mustard
1 teaspoon salt
1 tablespoon sugar
1 tablespoon oil
3 tablespoons lard
4 slices ginger
1 clove garlic, minced
2 slices cooked ham, cut into strips
1 tablespoon crispy shallots

METHOD

1. Slice abalone thinly and retain liquid.

2. Mix **A** in a bowl and set aside.

3. Wash Chinese mustard, drain and cut into 15 cm (6 in) lengths. Bring 1 litre (32 fl oz) water to a rapid boil with the salt, sugar and oil. Add Chinese mustard and boil over high heat for ¼ minute. Remove and immerse in a large bowl of cold water for 1 minute. Drain in colander and set aside.

4. In a hot iron wok, put in 2 tablespoons lard and fry the sliced ginger and minced garlic till lightly browned. Add **A** and bring to the boil gently. Add **B** and stir well. When gravy comes to a boil, place the Chinese mustard and sliced abalone separately in the pan. Cook till gravy starts to boil again. Boil for further 5 seconds, then add the remaining tablespoon of lard.

5. Remove the mustard to a serving plate and then arrange the abalone on top. Garnish with shredded ham and crispy shallots.

CHOP SUEY
(MIXED VEGETABLES)

INGREDIENTS

1 teaspoon light soya sauce
½ teaspoon msg
1 teaspoon ginger juice   **A**
Dash of pepper

85 g (3 oz) canned bamboo shoots
115 g (4 oz) French beans   **B**

1 teaspoon msg
½ teaspoon salt
½ teaspoon sugar
2 tablespoons light soya sauce
1 tablespoon oyster sauce   **C**
½ tablespoon dark soya sauce
½ tablespoon sesame oil
½ tablespoon sherry or wine

1 tablespoon cornflour
170 ml (6 fl oz) water   **D**

115 g (4 oz) pork fillet, sliced
115 g (4 oz) pork liver, sliced
6 red chillies, seeded
455 g (1 lb) prawns, shelled and deveined
1 onion, peeled and quartered
4 Chinese mushrooms, soaked in hot water and sliced
1 can button mushrooms

METHOD

1. Marinate pork and liver in **A** for 10 minutes.

2. Cut chillies into thick long strips.

3. Slice **B** thinly.

4. Heat a pan till very hot. Use 2 tablespoons lard, fry prawns for ½ minute. Remove. In the same pan, fry the following separately over a very high heat: onion, chillies, French beans and bamboo shoots. Remove to a dish.

5. Mix **C** in a bowl. Heat 2 tablespoons lard in a clean pan and fry the mushrooms, pork and liver for 2 minutes.

6. Add the fried ingredients and toss mixture in pan. Add **C**, stir for 1 minute. Blend **D** and add to pan. Stir-fry so that all ingredients are mixed thoroughly.

EGG PLANT WITH PORK AND PRAWNS

INGREDIENTS

3 teaspoons chopped garlic
1 teaspoon chopped ginger
1 tablespoon preserved salted soya beans, pounded   **A**
1 teaspoon chilli sauce

455 g (1 lb) egg plant (purple or green)
1 cup oil for frying
3 tablespoons lard or oil
4 dried Chinese mushrooms, sliced thinly
225 g (8 oz) minced pork
115 g (4 oz) shelled prawns, chopped coarsely

Seasoning:
½ teaspoon salt
½ teaspoon msg
2 teaspoons sugar
1 tablespoon Thai fish sauce   **B**
1 teaspoon sesame oil
2 teaspoons tapioca flour dissolved in
2 tablespoons water
¼ teaspoon pepper

METHOD

1. Remove stems and skin from egg plants. Cut into thick slices and soak in salt water. Drain before frying.

2. Heat 1 cup oil in an iron wok till very hot. Fry egg plant till lightly browned. Remove to a metal colander to drain oil.

3. Heat 3 tablespoons lard or oil in a heated wok. Fry **A** over moderate heat, till garlic and ginger brown. Add mushrooms and stir for 1 minute. Put in pork and prawns and stir fry for another minute before pouring in **B** (seasoning). Cook for 1 minute and add egg plant. Mix well and allow to simmer for 5 minutes. Serve.

EGG PLANT IN SPICY SAUCE

INGREDIENTS

6 fresh red chillies, seeded
20 dried chillies, seeded   **A**
1 teaspoon shrimp paste

½ teaspoon salt
1 level teaspoon sugar   **B**
½ teaspoon msg

6 green egg plants
4 tablespoons oil

METHOD

1. Remove stalks and cut egg plant into halves lengthwise. Soak in a bowl of slightly salted water.

2. Grind or blend **A** to a fine paste.

3. Heat the oil in a non-stick pan and fry the sliced egg plant lightly until cooked. Remove to a plate. Fry paste and **B** with remaining oil. Fry over low heat till oil bubbles through then add 2 tablespoons water. Stir for short while and pour over fried egg plant. Serve hot or cold.

Note:
Sprinkle water in pan, then cover while frying egg plant. This helps it cook right through quickly.

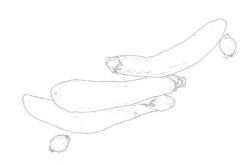

LOH HON CHYE
(MIXED VEGETABLES)

2 teaspoons sugar
1 tablespoon oil
½ teaspoon salt
½ teaspoon bicarbonate of soda **A**

2 teaspoons light soya sauce
1 teaspoon msg
½ teaspoon sesame oil **B**
1 teaspoon sugar
2 tablespoons oyster sauce

455 g (16 oz) green mustard, stalks only
115 g (4 oz) lard or oil
6 slices ginger
½ teaspoon pounded garlic
6–8 dried Chinese mushrooms, softened and quartered
115 g (4 oz) snow peas
½ can young corn, cut into halves
115 g (4 oz) sliced bamboo shoots
½ can button mushrooms, cut into halves
1 handful gingko nuts, boiled for ½ hour till softened
½ can mock abalone (obtainable from soya bean stalls at wet markets)
455 ml (16 fl oz) chicken stock or 455 ml boiling water with 1 chicken cube

1½ tablespoons tapioca flour or cornflour
4 tablespoons water **C**

METHOD

To boil green mustard:
1. Cut mustard stalks into big pieces, wash and drain. Boil 850 ml (30 fl oz) water in a saucepan. Put in stalks and **A**. Allow water to boil again over very high heat and cook for 3 minutes only.
2. Drain and immerse stalks in a large bowl of cold water for 2 minutes, drain in colander and keep in the refrigerator till ready for use.

To prepare *Loh Hon Chye*:
1. Heat 2 tablespoons lard in pre-heated wok and fry ginger and garlic till lightly browned. Stir-fry Chinese mushrooms and snow peas and remove.
2. Add another 2 tablespoons of lard and stir-fry the corn, bamboo shoots, button mushrooms, gingko nuts and mock abalone for ½ minute. Add in **B**, chicken stock and the rest of the ingredients and bring to the boil.
3. Lastly add the mustard stalks, cover pan and allow to boil. Remove lid, pour in **C** and stir well. Serve hot.

LONG BEANS WITH MINCED MEAT
(SICHUAN STYLE)

INGREDIENTS

2 teaspoons fine sugar
½ teaspoon msg
¼ teaspoon pepper
1 teaspoon oyster sauce **A** *mixed in a bowl*
½ teaspoon sesame oil
1 teaspoon sago flour
115 ml (4 fl oz) water

170 ml (6 fl oz) oil
225 g (8 oz) long beans, cut into 6 cm lengths

2 tablespoons lard or oil
3 cloves garlic, chopped coarsely
1½ tablespoons spicy soya bean paste*
115 g (4 oz) minced pork
55 g (2 oz) chopped prawn meat

METHOD

1. Heat iron wok. When very hot, add oil, and fry long beans till tender. Sprinkle a little water to avoid burning. Remove and drain.
2. Heat oil and fry garlic till very lightly browned. Add spicy soya bean paste, pork and prawns, and stir-fry till pork changes colour. Add **A**, then fried long beans. Continue cooking over low heat for 1–2 minutes. Remove and serve immediately.

*See page 109.

MUSTARD WITH CRAB MEAT SAUCE

INGREDIENTS

455 g (1 lb) crab (blue flowery or *kepiting batu*)
3 tablespoons dried prawns, pounded finely
6 tablespoons lard or oil
455 g (1 lb) green mustard stalks, cut into big pieces
1 can straw mushrooms, cut into halves
4 slices ginger
3 shallots, thinly sliced
2 level tablespoons plain flour (*for thickening*)
115 ml (4 fl oz) evaporated milk and 340 ml (12 fl oz) chicken stock

1 tablespoon light soya sauce ⎤
1 teaspoon msg |
1 teaspoon sugar |
  Dash of pepper ⎬ **A**
1 tablespoon oyster sauce |
½ teaspoon sesame oil ⎦

METHOD

1. Steam crabs over high heat for 20 minutes. Immerse in cold water for 1 minute. Clean and remove meat. Keep in refrigerator before use.

2. Fry dried prawns in oil till golden brown, drain and spread on a piece of absorbent paper. Keep prawns in a bottle till ready to use.

3. Pour 3 tablespoons lard in heated wok and stir-fry green mustard for short while. Remove to a bowl. In the same pan, add 1 tablespoon lard, stir-fry the straw mushrooms over high heat and remove.

4. Add the rest of the lard, fry ginger and shallots till lightly browned. Stir-fry the flour for short while till bubbly; reduce heat and pour in the milk mixture and **A**. Stir till well blended and bring to the boil. Put in green mustard and straw mushrooms, stir lightly and wait till gravy boils. Place crab meat over green mustard, cover pan with lid and simmer for 1 minute. Sprinkle the dried prawns over dish with a dash of pepper, and serve.

REBONG MASAK LEMAK
(BAMBOO SHOOTS IN SPICY COCONUT GRAVY)

INGREDIENTS

1 teaspoon peppercorns ⎤
2 teaspoons roasted coriander seeds |
14 slices galangal |
½ thumb-sized piece turmeric |
5 candlenuts ⎬ **A**
14 shallots |
1 clove garlic |
2 red chillies |
2 tablespoons shrimp paste ⎦

¾ tablespoon salt ⎤
1 teaspoon sugar ⎬ **B**
½ teaspoon msg ⎦

455 g (16 oz) boiled tender bamboo shoots, sliced thinly ⎤
905 g (2 lb) chicken, cut into pieces ⎬ **C**
340 g (12 oz) pork ribs, cut into pieces ⎦

455 g (16 oz) grated coconut

115 ml (4 fl oz) oil
2 stalks lemon grass

METHOD

1. Pound **A** together in the given order to a very fine paste.

2. Use a piece of muslin to squeeze coconut for No. 1 milk. Set aside.

3. Add 900 ml (32 fl oz) water to the grated coconut and squeeze again for No. 2 milk. Set aside.

4. In a very hot aluminium wok, heat oil. Stir-fry paste and bruised lemon grass over moderate heat, till oil bubbles through and paste is fragrant.

5. Add **B** and half of the No. 2 milk. When mixture boils, add **C**. Cook for 10 minutes, stirring occasionally.

6. Add remaining No. 2 milk, stir and cover. Cook over low heat for 20 minutes or till chicken is tender.

7. Finally, add No. 1 milk. Stir for 1 minute, remove from the heat.

VEGETARIAN SPRING ROLLS

INGREDIENTS

Seasoning:

1 teaspoon salt	
1 teaspoon sugar	**A**
1 teaspoon black soya sauce	

5 dried Chinese mushrooms
1 kg yambean (bangkuang)
1 carrot, approximately 115 g (4 oz)
10 sweet soya bean strips
6 tablespoons peanut oil
1 teaspoon shredded ginger
1 tablespoon preserved salted soya bean, pounded
　Oil for deep frying
1 tablespoon tapioca flour blended in 3 tablespoons
　water for thickening
1 small packet spring roll wrappers (50 pieces)

METHOD

1. Soak mushrooms in 225 ml (8 fl oz) hot water. Remove stalks and cut caps into thin slices. Reserve water for cooking.

2. Grate yambean using a coarse scraper. Rinse under cold water in a colander. Drain well. Using same scraper, grate carrot. Do not wash. Use scissors to cut the sweet soya bean strips into thin strips.

3. Heat 6 tablespoons peanut oil. Fry sweet bean strips till they blister and are slightly browned. Remove to a dish.

4. Reheat oil in pan. Saute 1 teaspoon ginger till light brown, adding preserved soya bean sauce to fry for short while. Add **A** (seasoning) and ½ of the water reserved. Stir till mixture boils, then put in the grated yambean and sweet soya bean curd strips. Cook for 10 minutes then add remaining water.

5. Put in carrots. Stir mixture and continue cooking till moist. Pour in thickening and stir well. Remove to a large plate to cool completely before making spring rolls.

To prepare spring rolls:

INGREDIENTS

2 tablespoons tapioca flour
2 tablespoons plain flour

METHOD

1. Mix 2 tablespoons each of tapioca flour and plain flour with 6 tablespoons water in a cup.

2. Scoop 2 tablespoons of filling on the lower half of the wrapper. Fold over to cover filling, fold sides, and roll wrapper to make spring roll. Seal with flour mixture. Repeat with remaining ingredients.

3. Heat oil for deep frying in an aluminium wok. Put in spring rolls a few at a time and fry till light brown. Remove to a steel colander to drain before putting on absorbent paper for a while. Serve hot with sweet chilli sauce.

VEGETARIAN BEEHOON

INGREDIENTS

225 g (8 oz) cabbage, thinly shredded
170 g (6 oz) french beans, cut diagonally   **A**
200 g (7 oz) carrots, grated

340 ml (12 fl oz) water
 1 level tablespoon salt
 2 tablespoons msg
 3 tablespoons sugar   **B**
 2 teaspoons dark soya sauce
 2 tablespoons light soya sauce
 1 teaspoon pepper
 2 teaspoons sesame oil

285 g (10 oz) rice vermicelli
170 ml (6 fl oz) peanut or corn oil
 Pinch of salt and sugar
 1 teaspoon each pounded garlic and ginger
 8 pieces sweet soya bean strips (tow kee), cut into thin slices
 6 dried Chinese mushrooms, soaked and thinly sliced
285 g (10 oz) prepared gluten (mock duck or mock abalone), thinly sliced
 4 tablespoons crispy shallots
 4 strips sweet soya bean strips, shredded, fried to a crisp
 4 tablespoons roasted sesame seeds

METHOD

1. Soak rice vermicelli in boiling water for 3 minutes. Drain and set aside for ½ hour.

2. In a heated iron wok, heat 2 tablespoons oil. Fry **A** separately for 1 minute each. Sprinkle water, a pinch of sugar and salt and a little oil for each vegetable. Set aside.

3. In the same wok, heat 4 tablespoons oil and fry garlic and ginger till light brown. Add sweet soya bean strips and Chinese mushrooms. Fry for 1 minute.

4. Add the sliced gluten and **B**. Allow to boil for 3 minutes.

5. Put in drained vermicelli and use fork to stir till gravy is absorbed. Add vegetables and stir well to mix evenly.

6. Garnish with crispy shallots and fried soya bean strips. Sprinkle with sesame seeds, pepper and sesame oil.

VEGETARIAN CURRY

INGREDIENTS

455 g (1 lb) cabbage, cut into bite-sized pieces
170 g (6 oz) long beans, cut into short lengths
 1 carrot, cut into bite-sized pieces
170 g (6 oz) cauliflower, cut into florets
170 g (6 oz) potatoes, cut into bite-sized pieces   **A**
115 g (4 oz) soya bean strips (foo chok)
 6 spongy fried soya bean cubes
 1 tin mock abalone, pour boiling water over and drain

455 g (1 lb) grated coconut
 6 tablespoons oil
115 g (4 oz) onions, sliced thinly
 2 cloves garlic, sliced thinly
 ½ thumb-sized piece ginger, sliced thinly
 1 tablespoon shrimp paste mixed in 4 tablespoons water
 4 tablespoons curry powder

Seasoning:
1 teaspoon salt
1 tablespoon sugar
1 teaspoon msg

METHOD

1. Squeeze coconut for No. 1 milk. Set aside. Add 570 ml (20 fl oz) water and squeeze for No. 2 milk. Set aside.

2. Heat oil in pan. Fry onions, garlic and ginger till lightly browned. Add shrimp paste and stir for a while.

3. Put in curry powder and ½ of No. 2 milk. Stir-fry till oil bubbles through. Add remaining No. 2 milk and bring to a boil. Put in all of **A** with seasoning and cook over moderate heat till vegetables are tender. Reduce heat to low, add No. 1 milk, stirring as you pour and cook for ½ minute. Remove from heat and serve.

Vegetarian Curry

Special Combinations
featuring dishes that are traditionally served together

Kuey Chap
Braised Belly Pork, Soya Bean Cakes and Eggs in Soya Sauce

Nasi Lemak
Crispy Anchovies with Sambal
Otak-Otak Rhio
Sambal Udang
Spicy Sambal Kangkong

Nasi Padang *(served with white rice)*
Beef Rendang
Cucumber Pickle
Sambal Telor
Spicy Fried Chicken

Nasi Lontong
Beef Serondeng
Sambal Goreng
Sayor Loday

Nasi Minyak
Achar
Dhal Char
Satay Ayam Panggang

Taiwan Porridge
Tow Yew Bak
Fried Anchovies and Groundnuts
Fried Salted Mustard
Steamed Minced Pork
Long Bean Omelette
Sweet and Spicy Fish
Threadfin fried with Soya Sauce and Pepper

Braised Belly Pork, Soya Bean Cakes and Eggs in Soya Sauce with Kuey Chap

BRAISED BELLY PORK, SOYA BEAN CAKES AND EGGS IN SOYA SAUCE

INGREDIENTS

4 large soya bean cakes, cut into small squares
2 tablespoons oil
2 tablespoons sugar
6 cloves garlic, lightly bashed

2 tablespoons light soya sauce
4 tablespoons dark soya sauce   **A**
225 ml (8 fl oz) boiling water
½ teaspoon salt

605 g (21 oz) belly pork, cut into pieces
10 hard-boiled eggs

METHOD

1. Immerse soya bean cakes in salted water for 5 minutes, drain and fry in a non-stick pan till lightly browned on all sides. Remove to a dish.

2. Heat a heavy-bottomed aluminium saucepan. Put in oil and sugar and leave till sugar turns a light golden brown. Add garlic, cook for a moment, add **A** and bring to the boil. Put in pork and cook briskly for about 20 minutes or till pork is well done.

3. Add eggs and leave to simmer for another ½ hour or till pork is tender. Add the fried soya bean cakes 10 minutes before the pork becomes tender and leave to simmer for 5 minutes. Serve hot.

Note:
Add small amounts of boiling water if gravy thickens before meat is tender.

Kuey Chap, a fatter smoother version of Kwayteow, can be bought from fresh noodle stalls at wet markets.

NASI LEMAK
(COCONUT MILK RICE)

INGREDIENTS

680 g (24 oz) No 1 Thai rice
625 g (22 oz) grated coconut, white
455 ml (16 fl oz) water
1½ teaspoons salt
6 screw pine leaves, tied into a knot

METHOD

1. Wash the rice and soak it in water for 2 hours. Drain before use.

2. Use a piece of muslin to squeeze 225 ml (8 fl oz) No. 1 milk from the grated coconut.

3. Add 455 ml water and squeeze for No. 2 milk. Measure, then add water to obtain 740 ml (26 fl oz) No. 2 milk.

4. Place rice in the rice cooker, stir in the No. 2 milk and the salt. Boil till rice is dry. Place the screw pine leaves on top and leave rice in the cooker for a further ½ hour.

5. Rake the rice with a fork, add the No. 1 milk and stir lightly to mix.

6. Leave the rice in the cooker to absorb the milk for another 20 minutes. Serve hot or cold.

Note:
Stir rice once or twice whilst boiling. Do not stir any more when the rice is dry. Stir again only when adding the No. 1 milk.

(10 servings)

Nasi Lemak

CRISPY ANCHOVIES WITH SAMBAL

INGREDIENTS

Sambal:

115 g (4 oz) dried chillies
1 clove garlic   **A**
115 g (4 oz) shallots *or* onions
55 g (2 oz) shrimp paste

170 g (6 oz) grated coconut
170 ml (6 fl oz) oil

4 level tablespoons sugar
¼ teaspoon salt
1 teaspoon msg   **B**
1 tablespoon tamarind, squeezed and
   strained with 4 tablespoons water

METHOD

1. Wash and soak dried chillies to soften. Grind or use electric blender to blend **A** to a fine paste.

2. Add 225 ml (8 fl oz) water to grated coconut and squeeze through muslin for milk.

3. Heat oil in aluminium wok and fry the chilli paste and one-third of the milk over moderate heat till oil bubbles through and smells fragrant.

4. Add **B**, stir and pour in the rest of the coconut milk. Lower heat and simmer for 2 minutes.

Anchovies:

1. Remove heads of 455 g (1 1b) medium sized anchovies. Wash and drain the anchovies.

2. Heat oil for deep frying till very hot. Put in the anchovies and fry over moderate heat to a light brown and to a crisp. Lower heat at the end of cooking time to prevent it from turning too dark. Remove anchovies to cool slightly on a paper towel and keep in container.

3. Mix in sambal when ready to serve.

OTAK-OTAK RHIO

INGREDIENTS

570 g (20 oz) grated coconut, white

85 g (3 oz) galangal, sliced
6 candlenuts
1 teaspoon shrimp paste   **A**
340 g (12 oz) shallots
30–40 g (1–1½ oz) dried chillies, cut into
   small pieces, soaked in warm water and
   drained

1.2 kg (2½ lb) spanish mackerel
Pinch of salt
6 tablespoons oil

4 teaspoons sugar
2 level teaspoons msg   *seasoning*
½ teaspoon pepper
2 level teaspoons salt

4 eggs
6 lime leaves, sliced finely
1 turmeric leaf, sliced finely
24 banana leaves (*daun pisang batu*), or heavy duty tin foil

METHOD

1. Squeeze grated coconut, without adding water, through a piece of muslin for No. 1 milk. Set aside.

2. Grind or use electric blender to blend **A** to a fine paste. Set aside.

3. Slit the fish right through lengthwise, and remove bones. Slice the meat from half the fish and set aside.

4. Pound or mince the other half of the fish until smooth, add a pinch of salt and 6 tablespoons of the coconut milk. Mix till well blended.

5. Heat an iron or aluminium wok and when hot, add 4 tablespoons oil and fry the paste over moderate heat till oil bubbles through and the paste is fragrant. Add seasoning and 12 tablespoons coconut milk, cooking over low heat till paste is almost dry. Stir frequently to prevent burning. Remove to a large plate to cool.

6. Into a large mixing bowl, put the minced fish, fried paste, eggs, sliced lime leaves, turmeric leaf and mix well. Lastly add the sliced fish and remaining oil. Stir lightly with a wooden spoon till well mixed. Cut 24 banana leaves into pieces, 21 cm × 22 cm (8 in × 8½ in).

7. Wash banana leaves and put into a saucepan of boiling water. Simmer for ½ minute to soften. Drain. Put 2–3 tablespoons of the fish mixture in the centre of each leaf, fold short ends of rectangle to cover mixture, then overlap left and right ends to form a neat square or oblong packet. Staple both ends of the leaf to seal before cooking.

To grill otak-otak:
Pre-heat grill and place the packets of otak-otak on a wire rack and grill for 5–7 minutes on each side. Leave to cool before serving.

To dry-fry otak-otak in an iron wok:
Heat an iron wok till hot. Place otak-otak side by side in the wok and cook over moderate heat for 5–6 minutes on each side. Serve cold.

Note:
Heavy duty tin foil is a good substitute for banana leaves.

SAMBAL UDANG
(PRAWNS IN HOT SPICY PASTE)

INGREDIENTS

605 g (21 oz) medium sized prawns, shelled and deveined
    Pinch of salt
½ teaspoon sugar
115 g (4 oz) frozen spicy paste, thawed (Page 186)
½ teaspoon salt
1 teaspoon sugar
½ teaspoon msg
1 teaspoon tamarind, mixed with 85 ml (3 fl oz) water and strained
115 g (4 oz) grated coconut squeezed to obtain 3 tablespoons No. 1 milk

METHOD

1. Season prawns with pinch of salt and ½ teaspoon sugar and set aside.

2. Heat an aluminium wok. Put in frozen spicy paste, and cook over low heat till oil bubbles through (½ minute).

3. Add the rest of the ingredients except the prawns and cook till mixture comes to the boil.

4. Add prawns and stir in pan till prawns are cooked, about 3–4 minutes. Serve hot or cold.

SPICY SAMBAL KANGKONG

INGREDIENTS

455 g (1 lb) water convolvulus (kangkong)
4 tablespoons lard or oil

3 fresh red chillies | *pounded to a fine paste*
1 tablespoon shrimp paste |

2 teaspoons sugar
    Pinch of salt
2 teaspoons pounded dried prawns

METHOD

1. Cut the water convolvulus into 7.5 cm (3 in) lengths, omitting the tough stalks and roots. Wash thoroughly and drain in a colander.

2. Heat an iron wok, put in 3 tablespoons oil to fry the chilli paste for half a minute. Add the water convolvulus, sugar, salt and dried prawns. Stir fry over high heat for 1 minute. Toss the water convolvulus in the wok to ensure that it is well cooked.

3. Add the remaining tablespoon of lard or oil, stir well and remove to a serving plate. Serve immediately.

BEEF RENDANG

INGREDIENTS

570 g (20 oz) coconut, white
605 g (21 oz) beef brisket or topside

1 teaspoon salt ½ teaspoon msg 2 teaspoons sugar 1½ teaspoons tamarind, remove seeds	**A**

1 turmeric leaf 2 lime leaves 1 stalk lemon grass, bashed 1 thick slice galangal	**B**

10 shallots 6 fresh red chillies 14 dried chillies 30 g (1 oz) ginger 1 stalk lemon grass 2 thin slices galangal 2 cloves garlic 2 tablespoons fried coconut	**C** *ground to a fine paste*

1–1½ tablespoons palm sugar 1 level teaspoon salt ½ teaspoon pepper ½ teaspoon msg 2 teaspoons dark soya sauce	**D**

2 tablespoons oil
170–225 ml (6–8 fl oz) boiling water

METHOD

1. Dry-fry 115 g of the coconut till dark brown. Cool.
2. Season beef with **A** and dry coconut and leave for 2 hours.
3. Squeeze remaining coconut for No. 1 milk. Set aside. Add 225 ml water and squeeze for No. 2 milk. Set aside.
4. Combine **B**, **C** and **D** in a saucepan. Add No. 2 milk and bring to the boil. Add meat and boil, uncovered, over moderately high heat for 1 hour, stirring occasionally to prevent burning.
5. Add No. 1 milk and stir well. Reduce heat, cover pan and cook for ¾–1 hour till gravy mixture turns oily and fragrant.

CUCUMBER PICKLE

INGREDIENTS

To boil vegetables:

225 ml (8 fl oz) vinegar 225 ml (8 fl oz) water 2 tablespoons sugar	**A**

55 g (2 oz) shallots, sliced thinly 30 g (1 oz) garlic, sliced thinly 1 thumb-sized piece ginger, sliced thinly	**B**

1.8 kg (4 lb) cucumber
2 tablespoons salt
305 g (11 oz) shallots (choose tiny ones)

1 thumb-sized piece turmeric 1 tablespoon shrimp paste	**C** *ground to a fine paste*

115 ml (4 fl oz) oil for frying paste
455 ml (16 fl oz) rice vinegar
225 ml (8 fl oz) water
Salt and sugar to taste
Toasted sesame seeds

METHOD

1. Wash cucumbers and quarter lengthwise. Remove cores and cut into 4 cm lengths. Then cut each piece into two, lengthwise. Rub with salt and leave overnight.
2. Rinse, squeeze lightly and dry. Place cucumber on a large bamboo tray to dry in the sun for 3–4 hours. Set aside.
3. Peel shallots and blanch in **A** for 1 minute. Drain well. Bring mixture to the boil again and blanch cucumber for 1 minute. Drain.
4. Fry **B** and **C** with oil over moderate heat till fragrant. Remove.
5. Put vinegar and water into an enamel saucepan and bring to a boil. Add salt and sugar to taste and boil over low heat for 5 minutes. Set aside and leave to cool completely.
6. Combine cucumber, shallots, **B** and **C** in a large bowl. Pour in the cooked vinegar.
7. Sprinkle with sesame seeds and store in bottles or porcelain jars for at least 2 days before serving.

Clockwise: Cucumber Pickle, Beef Rendang, Sambal Telor, Spicy Fried Chicken

SAMBAL TELOR

INGREDIENTS

10 hard-boiled eggs
140 g (5 oz) *chilli garam* paste*
  1 level teaspoon sugar
¼ teaspoon msg
   A pinch of salt
  4 tablespoons water
  4 tablespoons No. 1 milk
   Oil for frying

METHOD

1. Shell boiled eggs and soak in slightly salted water for 20 minutes. Dry eggs on a tray.

2. Deep-fry the eggs in hot smoking oil till light brown, stirring in pan till surface of eggs is slightly blistered all over. Remove to a plate.

3. Remove oil from pan and fry thawed paste over low heat till oil bubbles through. Add the rest of the ingredients, stir well for 1 minute and pour over eggs. Serve hot or cold.

*See page 185.

SPICY FRIED CHICKEN

INGREDIENTS

1.14 kg (2½ lb) chicken, cut into pieces

2 thick stalks lemon grass, lightly bashed 2 thick slices galangal, lightly bashed 2 pieces dried tamarind 1 teaspoon salt 1 teaspoon sugar 1 teaspoon msg	**A**
2 cloves garlic ½ thumb-sized piece turmeric 7 candlenuts 7 shallots	**B** *pounded roughly*

METHOD

1. Season chicken with **A** and **B** and leave for 1 hour. Place chicken in a saucepan, add 225 ml (8 fl oz) boiling water and boil, covered, for 15–20 minutes, over moderately high heat. Stir occasionally.

2. Remove pan from heat and remove chicken to a large plate. Reserve gravy.

3. Heat oil and fry chicken till golden brown. Place fried chicken on a large serving plate. Remove some oil from pan leaving 4 tablespoons. Remove lemon grass and galangal from marinade. Cook marinade in the oil till almost dry. Pour over chicken and serve.

Note:
Use a small saucepan to cook the chicken so that it is completely immersed in the water. Add more water if needed. Water should come up to 2.5 cm (1 inch) above the level of the meat.

Nasi Lontong and Sambal Goreng

BEEF SERONDENG
(BEEF WITH FRIED GRATED COCONUT)

INGREDIENTS

6 slices galangal
14 shallots
4 tablespoons coriander seeds
1 teaspoon cumin seeds   **A**
4 slices ginger
3 cloves garlic
2 slices turmeric
1 teaspoon pepper

565 g (20 oz) rump or Scotch steak, cut into pieces
6 tablespoons oil

1 tablespoon salt
5 tablespoons sugar
3 tablespoons grated palm sugar   **B**
55 g (2 oz) tamarind in 8 tablespoons water,
  squeezed and strained

565 g (20 oz) coconut, white, coarsely grated

METHOD

1. Pound **A** to a paste.
2. Let beef pieces simmer in 115 ml (4 fl oz) water and one-third of paste till tender and almost dry.
3. Heat 4 tablespoons oil, stir-fry remaining paste till fragrant. Add **B**, stir-fry for a minute and remove to a dish. Rub fried paste into the grated coconut.
4. Heat 2 tablespoons oil in a pan. Add the coconut mixture and the beef. Stir-fry over a low heat till moist and fragrant. Keep stirring constantly to prevent the coconut from burning.

NASI LONTONG
(COMPRESSED RICE CAKES)

INGREDIENTS

625 g (22 oz) No. 1 Thai rice

½ teaspoon salt
6 screw pine leaves, tied into a knot

METHOD

1. Wash and soak the rice overnight. Drain before use.
2. Wet two 10 cm × 20 cm (4 in × 8 in) cloth bags and fill each with half the rice. Stitch to seal the open end.
3. Boil 1.2 litres (2 pints) water in a heavy-bottomed aluminium saucepan. Add salt and screw pine leaves.
4. Place the cloth bags in the saucepan. The water should be 8 cm (3 in) above the bags. Add boiling water when necessary. Boil for 2 hours and remove.
5. Wrap the bags with a dry towel and place a bread board and a weight on top. Leave until the rice is firm and cold, at least 8–10 hours.
6. Unstitch the bags to remove the rice. Cut into long strips with a wet knife and again into thin squares, using a thick white thread.

(10 servings)

Note:
It is best to cook the rice in the evening and leave it pressed overnight.

Place an enamel plate in the saucepan before putting in the bag of rice to prevent it from sticking to the pan.

SAMBAL GORENG

INGREDIENTS

225 g (8 oz) beef liver, cubed
½ teaspoon salt
½ teaspoon msg
285 g (10 oz) grated coconut, white

Oil for frying

55 g shallots or onions, sliced thinly
4 slices garlic, sliced thinly — **A**
3 red chillies, seeded, sliced thinly

1 thick piece galangal, bashed (pounded finely)

1 teaspoon shrimp paste
6 dried chillies — **B** *pounded finely*

285 g (10 oz) small prawns, shelled and cleaned
2 large pieces soya bean cake, cut into small cubes, fried
2 packets *tempe*, cut into small pieces, fried

METHOD

1. Marinate beef liver with salt and msg.

2. Squeeze grated coconut for No. 1 milk. Set aside. Add 170 ml (6 fl oz) water and squeeze for No. 2 milk. Set aside.

3. Heat oil in an aluminium kuali. Fry **A** separately till light golden brown. Remove to a plate.

4. Pour oil from pan, leaving 3 tablespoons to fry liver for 5–6 minutes till liver is cooked. Remove to a plate.

5. In a clean pan, heat 2 tablespoons oil to fry bashed galangal for 1 minute. Add **B** and fry over moderate heat for another minute.

6. Add half of No. 1 milk and stir till it comes to a boil. Put in prawns, soya bean cake, liver and *tempe*. Cook over low heat for 2 minutes.

7. Pour in No. 2 milk and cook for 5 minutes then pour in No. 1 milk and fried ingredients **A**. Stir to mix well and simmer till gravy coats ingredients and is almost dry. Serve hot or cold.

SAYOR LODAY
(MIXED VEGETABLES IN SPICY COCONUT GRAVY)

INGREDIENTS

625 g (21 oz) grated coconut
6 soya bean cakes, cut into quarters and fried
310 g (11 oz) green egg-plants, cut into wedges and soaked in salt water. Drain before use.
Oil
2 cloves garlic, thinly sliced
8 shallots, thinly sliced
2 tablespoons chilli paste

115 g (4 oz) shallots
1 clove garlic
1½ tablespoons shrimp paste
½ thumb-sized piece turmeric — **A**
2 candlenuts
5 dried chillies or 1 tablespoon paste

625 g (21 oz) cabbage, cut into small pieces
625 g (21 oz) long beans, cut into short lengths
310 g (11 oz) Chinese turnip, cut into thick short strips — **B**
4 tablespoons dried prawns, pounded finely

1 tablespoon salt
3 tablespoons sugar — **C**
1 teaspoon msg

METHOD

1. Pound **A** to a fine paste.

2. Add 225 ml (8 fl oz) water to the grated coconut and squeeze for No. 1 milk.

3. Add another 2 litres (4 pints) water to the grated coconut and squeeze again for No. 2 milk. Pour into a saucepan. Add **A**, **B** and **C** and bring to the boil.

4. Boil gently for ½ hour, add the fried soya bean cakes and egg-plants and cook for another 5–7 minutes. Remove from heat.

5. Heat 6 tablespoons oil and fry the sliced garlic and shallots till light brown.

6. Add chilli paste and stir-fry for ½ minute. Pour in the No. 1 milk and keep stirring till it comes to a boil. Add boiled vegetables and stir for another 2–3 minutes.

ACHAR
(MIXED VEGETABLE PICKLE)

INGREDIENTS

3.8 kg (8¼ lb) cucumbers
140 g (5 oz) salt
20 green chillies
20 red chillies
1 teaspoon lime paste

310 g (11 oz) shallots   ⎤
55 g (2 oz) turmeric |
30–40 dried chillies or 6–8 tablespoons chilli   **A**
    paste |
5 red chillies   ⎦

570 ml (20 fl oz) oil
1 thumb-sized piece ginger, thinly shredded

570 ml (20 fl oz) rice vinegar ⎤
570 ml (20 fl oz) water   **B**
455 g (16 oz) sugar |
4 tablespoons salt   ⎦

900 ml (32 fl oz) water   ⎤
900 ml (32 fl oz) vinegar   **C**
2 tablespoons sugar |
2 tablespoon salt   ⎦

795 g (28 oz) cauliflower, cut into florets
2 carrots, peeled and cut into strips
935 g (2 lb) cabbage, cut into small pieces
455 g (1 lb) roasted peanuts, pounded
8 tablespoons roasted sesame seeds

METHOD

1. Wash the cucumbers and cut off the ends. Halve each cucumber lengthwise and cut into two or three pieces lengthwise. (Remove the seeds and soft centres.)

2. Cut again into 5 cm (2 in) lengths. Make a slit half-way down each piece.

3. Place the cucumber strips in a basin, sprinkle the salt, mix well and leave to season for 4–5 hours. Rinse, drain and squeeze in handfuls, using a piece of muslin. Set aside.

4. Slit the centre of the chillies to remove the seeds. Soak the chillies in a bowl of water with 1 teaspoon lime paste for 2–3 hours. Drain in a colander. (Do not wash after soaking in lime water.) Stuff chillies (see instructions.)

5. Pound **A** to a fine paste.

6. Heat oil in wok to fry the shredded ginger till light brown.

7. Add the paste (Method 5) and stir-fry till fragrant and oil comes up to the surface.

8. Add **B** and bring to the boil. Boil for a minute and remove to a bowl to cool completely.

9. Boil **C** rapidly and blanch the cucumbers, cauliflower, carrots and cabbage separately. Spread out to cool on large trays.

10. Heat an iron wok and stir-fry the vegetables separately for ½ minute with a little oil from the vinegar mixture. Spread on trays to cool.

To mix the pickle:
Place the fried vegetables, paste, pounded nuts, and sesame seeds in a large mixing bowl. Mix well and add the stuffed chillies. Leave overnight. Store in dry, clean bottles.

To stuff chillies:
5 candlenuts   ⎤
10 shallots   **A**
1 teaspoon shrimp paste ⎦

225 ml (8 fl oz) oil
¼ teaspoon salt
2 tablespoons sugar
225 g (½ lb) dried prawns, pounded finely

1 medium-sized green papaya, skinned, finely grated and dried in the sun [optional]

METHOD

1. Pound **A**.

2. Pour oil into a heated frying pan. Stir-fry the pounded paste till fragrant.

3. Stir in the salt and sugar.

4. Add the dried prawns and papaya and stir till well mixed. Fry for 5 minutes over a low heat. Cool on a tray before stuffing the chillies.

Note:
1. *Bring the vinegar water back to a rapid boil each time to blanch the vegetables. Spread the vegetables to cool to keep them crunchy.*

2. *Lime paste here refers to the white chalky edible lime that is used by betel-nut chewers. It can be bought from any Indian grocer. The crispness of the chillies can only be obtained by soaking them in the 'lime' water.*

Clockwise: Satay Ayam Panggang, Achar, Dhal Char, Nasi Minyak

DHAL CHAR
(MUTTON RIBS WITH VEGETABLES IN SPICY GRAVY)

INGREDIENTS

285 g (10 oz) mutton ribs, cut into small pieces

½ teaspoon salt
½ teaspoon pepper   **A**
½ teaspoon msg
1 teaspoon ginger juice

285 g (10 oz) grated coconut
170 g (6 oz) lentils, washed and soaked for ½ hour
6 tablespoons oil

½ thumb-sized piece ginger, thinly shredded
2 cloves garlic, thinly shredded   **B**
8 shallots or 1 small onion, thinly sliced

2 teaspoons curry powder
½ tablespoon cumin seeds   **C**
½ tablespoon aniseed

Seasoning for gravy:
1–1½ teaspoons salt
1 teaspoon msg
1 teaspoon sugar

115 g (4 oz) long beans, cut into 2.5 cm lengths
3 brinjals, cut into pieces
6 green chillies, slit halfway lengthwise
3 red chillies, slit halfway lengthwise
55 g (2 oz) onions, thinly sliced

5 cm (2 in) length cinnamon bark
2 segments star anise
10 cardamoms, lightly bashed   **D**
6 cloves
1 sprig curry leaves

1 tablespoon tamarind, mixed with
4 tablespoons water, strained

METHOD

1. Marinate ribs with ingredients **A** for ½ hour.
2. Squeeze coconut for No.1 milk in a bowl. Set aside. Add 340 ml (12 fl oz) water to coconut and squeeze for No. 2 milk. Set aside.
3. Boil mutton ribs with 340 ml (12 fl oz) water for 1–1½ hours or till tender. Add 225 ml (8 fl oz) water and the lentils and continue boiling over low heat till lentils are tender. Set aside.
4. Heat 3 tablespoons oil in wok and fry **B** till lightly browned, add **C** and stir for a moment only. Pour in the No. 2 milk and gravy seasoning and bring to the boil. Put in the long beans and cook for 5 minutes, then add the long beans, brinjals and the chillies and continue cooking over moderate heat till vegetables are tender. Set aside.
5. Heat 3 tablespoons oil and fry the sliced onions till lightly browned, add **D** and fry for ½ minute. Remove to a bowl.
6. Bring mutton ribs to the boil, add ingredients from Methods 4 and 5. Add No. 1 milk, and boil for 2 minutes. Lastly add the tamarind water, simmer for 5 minutes. Remove from heat.

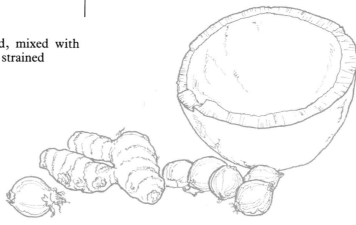

NASI MINYAK
(GHEE RICE)

INGREDIENTS

605 g (21 oz) briani rice
140 g (5 oz) white ghee

55 g (2 oz) onions, thinly sliced
1 cinnamon bark, 8 cm (3 in) long
6 cloves
15 cardamoms, lightly bashed   **A**

1 tablespoon chopped ginger
1 tablespoon chopped garlic

850 ml (30 fl oz) boiling water
4 drops rose essence
170 ml (6 fl oz) fresh milk
1½ teaspoons salt   **B**

2 tablespoons crispy shallots*

METHOD

1. Wash and drain rice.

2. Heat ghee in a non-stick or aluminium wok and fry **A** till onions turn light brown. Add ginger and garlic and stir-fry for 1 minute or until it turns light brown.

3. Add the rice; stir in pan for 1 minute, bring **B** to nearly boiling point in a saucepan and pour into pan to cook with the rice, then transfer to a rice cooker. Loosen rice when cooked and remove from heat. Sprinkle crispy shallots over rice. Serve hot.

See "Helpful Hints".

SATAY AYAM PANGGANG

INGREDIENTS

1 chicken, 1.14 kg (2½ lb)

55 g (2 oz) shallots or onions
1 teaspoon shrimp paste
10 dried chillies
2 fresh red chillies, seeded
3 stalks lemon grass, thinly sliced
4 slices galangal
1 candlenut   **A**

2 tablespoons sugar
1 level teaspoon salt
1 teaspoon msg
¼ teaspoon pepper
170 g (6 oz) grated coconut, squeezed for
85 ml (3 fl oz) No. 1 milk
½ teaspoon dark soya sauce
1 teaspoon lime juice
1 teaspoon coriander powder
1 tablespoon oil   **B**

4 lime leaves, thinly sliced
2 tablespoons oil with 1 tablespoon water for basting

METHOD

1. Cut chicken from the breast downwards. Use blunt end of cleaver or chopper and crack backbone and thigh bones to flatten.

2. Grind or blend **A** to a fine paste. Blend **B** to a paste in a bowl and mix well with the lime leaves and **A**.

3. With a fork, pierce chicken breast and thighs and rub the mixture all over the chicken. Leave to marinate for 1 hour.

4. Heat grill to high and grill chicken in pan till nicely browned on both sides. Baste with oil-and-water mixture to keep chicken moist. Remove from grill, cool for a while before cutting into pieces. Serve with sliced cucumber.

Note:
Line pan with tin foil to prevent the juices from burning. Pour juices over chicken before serving.

TOW YEW BAK
(STREAKY BELLY PORK IN SOYA SAUCE)

INGREDIENTS

455 g (1 lb) streaky belly pork
½ teaspoon salt
1 tablespoon dark soya sauce
2 tablespoons lard or oil
2 tablespoons sugar
2 pips star anise
2 cloves garlic, lightly bashed
2 tablespoons light soya sauce
½ teaspoon msg
230 ml (8 fl oz) boiling water

METHOD

1. Scrape pork skin of bristles; wash and drain. Rub salt and dark soya sauce into pork and leave for ½ hour.

2. Heat a heavy bottom aluminium saucepan with lard to fry sugar till light golden, add star anise and garlic, fry for 1 minute. Put in the pork, light soya sauce and msg and continue cooking for 2 minutes.

3. Turn pork over to cook the other side, pour in half of the boiling water and boil over moderately high heat for ½ hour. Add remaining water, cover saucepan and cook over low heat for ¾ hour or till pork is tender. Remove from heat.

To serve:
Lift pork onto a chopping board to cut into slices, place on a deep plate and pour gravy over.

FRIED ANCHOVIES AND GROUNDNUTS

INGREDIENTS

225 g (8 oz) groundnuts
225 g (8 oz) anchovies
Oil for frying

METHOD

1. Remove head of anchovies, wash, drain and leave in colander for ½ hour before frying.

2. Heat about 570 ml (20 fl oz) cooking oil and deep-fry the groundnuts over moderate heat till nuts turn light brown. Scoop out to drain on absorbent paper and leave to cool slightly. Keep in an airtight container till ready to serve.

3. Re-heat oil in pan till hot and fry the anchovies over moderate heat for 5–7 minutes. Reduce heat to low and continue frying, stirring frequently till anchovies are light brown and crispy. To test if anchovies are cooked and will remain crisp, put a few pieces on absorbent paper. Break fish when slightly cooled and test for crispness. If the centre is not crunchy, fry a few minutes more over very low heat. Drain fish in a metal colander and place on absorbent paper to cool. Keep in airtight container till ready to serve.

4. Combine anchovies and fried groundnuts on a plate and serve.

Taiwan Porridge

FRIED SALTED MUSTARD WITH MINCED PORK AND TOMATOES

INGREDIENTS

285 g (10 oz) salted mustard
4 tablespoons lard *or* oil
½ thumb-sized piece ginger, shredded finely
1 teaspoon pounded garlic
1 teaspoon preserved soya beans, pounded
170 g (6 oz) minced pork
2 teaspoons sugar
½ teaspoon msg
115 ml (4 fl oz) water
2 tomatoes, cut into wedges
½ chicken cube

METHOD

1. Slice mustard finely and soak in water for 5 minutes. Drain and squeeze hard. Set aside.

2. Heat 1 tablespoon oil in an iron wok and stir-fry the mustard till limp (3 to 4 minutes). Remove.

3. In the same pan, heat the rest of the oil and lightly brown the ginger and garlic. Add the preserved soya beans, minced pork, sugar, msg and half of the water and fry till fragrant. Put in the mustard, tomatoes, the rest of the water, and the chicken cube and cook over low heat for 20 minutes. Add a little water if gravy is greatly reduced. Remove to a dish. Serve hot or cold.

STEAMED MINCED PORK WITH PRESERVED BLACK BEANS AND PENANG SALTED FISH

INGREDIENTS

55 g (2 oz) Penang salted fish, cut into strips
285 g (10 oz) lean pork with a little fat, minced

4 tablespoons water	
½ teaspoon msg	
¼ teaspoon sugar	**A**
1 teaspoon oil	

2 tablespoons preserved black beans
½ thumb-sized piece ginger, cut into strips

METHOD

1. Soak salted fish for ½ minute. Drain.

2. Combine pork with **A**, add the black beans, ginger and mix well. Place meat mixture on a shallow enamel plate, put salted fish on top and steam for 10–15 minutes or till pork is well cooked.

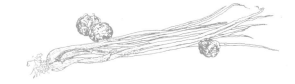

LONG BEAN OMELETTE

INGREDIENTS

115 g (4 oz) long beans, cut into very fine rounds
1 tablespoon oil
4 large eggs
55 g (2 oz) minced pork
55 g (2 oz) minced prawns
4 tablespoons chopped salted preserved radish
½ teaspoon msg
¼ teaspoon salt
Dash of pepper
Lard *or* oil

METHOD

1. Fry the long beans in a tablespoon of oil for ½ minute. Set aside.

2. Break eggs into a large bowl, beat lightly. Add the long beans and the rest of the ingredients and beat till well mixed.

3. Heat a frying pan and pour enough oil to fry the omelette till light golden brown on both sides. Serve hot or cold.

SWEET AND SPICY FISH

INGREDIENTS

455 g (1 lb) fish tail, Tenggiri or Snapper
1 teaspoon salt

3 cloves garlic, chopped finely
½ thumb-sized piece ginger, thinly sliced **A**

1 red chilli, seeded, sliced thinly
   lengthwise
2 sprigs coriander, cut into pieces **B**

150 ml fish sauce
1½ teaspoon tapioca or cornflour **C**

To cook fish sauce:
150 ml Best Quality Thai Fish Sauce
450 ml water
10 tablespoons sugar
5 tablespoons vinegar **D**
1 teaspoon salt
1 teaspoon dark soya sauce
8 tablespoons lemon juice

1 carrot, thinly shredded
8 cloves garlic, chopped coarsely
2 red chillies, seeded and coarsely **E**
   chopped

Boil **D** till sugar is dissolved. Add in **E**, boil for another minute. Remove to a large bowl to cool. Keep in a dry bottle to store in fridge for future use.

METHOD

1. Remove bone from fish, rub 1 teaspoon salt both sides and let stand for ½ hour.

2. Fry fish with 4 tablespoons oil in a non-stick wok till light golden brown on both sides. Remove to a serving plate. Keep warm.

3. In the same pan, put in **A**, stir-fry for ½ minute. Reduce heat, stir in **C** mixture, pour into pan and bring to boil. Pour sauce over fish and garnish with **B**. Serve hot.

Note:
Any type of fish fillet can be used, preferably the tail end.

THREADFIN FRIED WITH SOYA SAUCE AND PEPPER

INGREDIENTS

395 g (14 oz) threadfin

3 tablespoons dark soya sauce
2 tablespoons light soya sauce
1 tablespoon sugar **A**
½ teaspoon msg
½ teaspoon pepper

3 tablespoons oil and 3 tablespoons lard
4 tablespoons water

METHOD

1. Wash and drain threadfin.

2. Marinate fish in **A** for ½ hour.

3. Heat oil in a non-stick wok and fry the fish over moderate heat till brown. Reserve the marinade. Turn fish over, cover pan and cook till fish is done. Remove lid, pour in the marinade and the 4 tablespoons water and cook for ½ minute. Remove to a serving plate. Serve hot or cold.

CHICKEN CURRY

INGREDIENTS

1.6kg (3½ lb) chicken cut into pieces

10 cloves garlic
1 thumb-sized piece ginger
¼ thumb-sized piece turmeric
2 tablespoons curry powder mixed
  with 4 tablespoons water

A *pounded to a fine paste*

1 teaspoon salt
1 teaspoon msg
115 g (4 oz) grated coconut

1 heaped tablespoon cumin seeds *or*
¾ tablespoon cumin powder
1 heaped tablespoon poppy seeds
  (optional)
8 cashew nuts
8 almonds

B *ground to a fine paste*

115 ml (4 fl oz) oil
285 g (10 oz) shallots, thinly sliced
8–10 dried chillies, ground to a paste
1 stalk curry leaves

Seasoning:
¾–1 teaspoon salt
1 teaspoon msg

METHOD

1. Season chicken with **A**, salt, and msg and leave for ½ hour.
2. Add 225 ml (8 fl oz) water to coconut and squeeze milk into a bowl. Mix well with **B**.
3. Heat the oil in an aluminium wok and fry three-quarters of the sliced shallots till light golden brown. Lower heat, add chilli paste, curry leaves and fry till oil turns red.
4. Add the chicken, stir well, reduce heat to moderate and cook for ½ hour with lid on. Do not uncover whilst the chicken is cooking.
5. Remove the lid, add the rest of the sliced shallots, the seasoning and the milk mixture. Stir, bring to the boil, reduce heat and simmer for another 15–20 minutes or till chicken is tender.

ROTI JALA

INGREDIENTS

225 ml (8 fl oz) milk
  2 eggs
  Pinch of salt
1 tablespoon oil

A

115 g (4 oz) plain flour, sifted
Non-stick frying pan or electric skillet
Lacy pancake maker

METHOD

1. Combine **A** in a bowl and beat with fork till well blended.
2. Sift flour into a mixing bowl. Add egg mixture in centre of flour and stir till batter is smooth. Strain batter through a nylon sieve to remove lumps. Set aside for 15 minutes.
3. Lightly heat a non-stick frying pan or skillet. Grease lightly with oil and run the batter in a lacy pattern into the pan from the pancake maker. Cook for ½ minute or till batter changes colour. With a spatula, fold the pancake whilst still in pan.
4. Fry till all the batter is used up. Place the folded pancakes on top of one another and cover with a tea towel or tin foil to prevent drying. Serve hot or cold with Chicken Curry.

Chicken Curry and Roti Jala

Dim Sum

Bak Pow

Char Siew Pow

Fried Wan Tan

Har Kow

Hum Sui Kok

Kee Chang

Prawn Fritters

Kuey Chang Babi

Siew Mai

Steamed Beef Balls

Stuffed Mushrooms

Yam Puff

Tan Tart

Clockwise: Yam Puffs, Har Kow, Prawn Fritters, Fried Wan Tan

BAK POW
(MEAT BUNS)

INGREDIENTS

Filling:
1.2 kg (42 oz) pork, cut into thin pieces
  2 pairs Chinese sausages, cut into small
    pieces

Marinade:
  2 teaspoons dark soya sauce
  1 teaspoon light soya sauce
  2 teaspoons oyster sauce
  1 teaspoon pepper
1½ level teaspoons salt
  4 heaped teaspoons sugar
  1 teaspoon sesame oil
  4 tablespoons peanut butter
  3 tablespoons cornstarch *or* corn flour
  2 tablespoons lard
  2 teaspoons msg
  1 teaspoon coarsely chopped spring onions

METHOD

Place pork slices and Chinese sausages in a
bowl. Add the marinade and mix well and
allow to rest for 1 hour before filling.

Making The Bun:

INGREDIENTS

  2 tablespoons baking powder
455 g (1 lb) self-raising flour
  85 g (3 oz) castor sugar
200 ml (7 fl oz) hot water
  55 g (2 oz) lard

METHOD

1. Put flour in a bowl, make a well in the
   centre and put in the sugar.
2. Pour in the hot water and stir to dissolve
   the sugar.
3. Bring in half of the flour from the sides to
   mix with the sugar. Rub in the rest of the
   flour with the lard and mix till well
   blended. Leave to stand for 15 minutes.

CHAR SIEW POW
(STEAMED ROAST PORK BUNS)

INGREDIENTS

Filling:
285 g (10 oz) roast pork strips (*char siew*)
  2 tablespoons lard or oil
  2 cloves garlic, chopped finely
  55 g (2 oz) onions, chopped finely

  5 teaspoons sugar
  ½ teaspoon pepper
  1 teaspoon sesame oil   **A** *mixed together*
  1 teaspoon dark soya sauce
  1 teaspoon light soya sauce
115 ml (4 fl oz) water

  1 heaped tablespoon plain flour mixed with
    2 tablespoons oil

METHOD

1. Cut roast pork into very small cubes. Heat
   oil in frying pan to fry garlic till light
   brown, add chopped onions and cook till
   transparent. Pour in **A** and bring to boil
   over medium heat.
2. Put in the roast pork, stir for a moment and
   add flour and oil mixture. Mix well, cook
   for ½ minute and remove to a plate to cool.
   Chill in fridge before filling.

4. Divide dough into 3 parts and cut each into
   8 pieces, about the size of a small egg.
5. Roll each piece into a ball, press to flatten,
   place filling and seal by pleating the edge.
   Put bun on a square piece of grease-proof
   paper and leave for 10 minutes in a warm
   place. Steam over rapidly boiling water for
   10 minutes. Do not lift lid whilst steaming.
   Serve hot.

FRIED WAN TAN
(FRIED MEAT DUMPLINGS)

INGREDIENTS

½ teaspoon sesame oil
½ teaspoon salt
½ teaspoon sugar
 1 teaspoon light soya sauce **A**
 Dash of pepper
½ teaspoon msg
 1 tablespoon oil
½ egg yolk

170 g (6 oz) minced lean pork, with some fat
 55 g (2 oz) minced prawn meat
20–30 dumpling (*wan tan*) skins
 Oil for deep frying

METHOD

1. Put **A** in a bowl and stir well. Add minced pork and prawns and, using chopsticks, mix till well blended.

2. Place 1 teaspoon of meat mixture on one corner of skin, fold and roll to centre of skin. Wet the two ends, twist the folded meat and press the ends together to seal. Repeat with the rest of the meat. Place dumplings apart on a large tray to retain its shape.

3. Heat oil for deep frying in an aluminium wok or small saucepan. Put in as many dumplings as possible, leaving space for skin to expand whilst frying, and fry to a light golden colour. Scoop out gently with a large wire mesh ladle and drain on absorbent paper. Serve while hot and crunchy.

Note:
Dumpling skins are sold in different sizes in most markets. For fried dumplings, select the small thin skins.

HAR KOW
(STEAMED SHRIMP DUMPLINGS)

INGREDIENTS

Skin:
170 g (6 oz) non-glutinous flour
 1 teaspoon salt **A**
 1 teaspoon msg

170 ml (6 fl oz) boiling water
 30 ml (1 fl oz) cold water
 1 tablespoon lard

Pour boiling water over **A**, add cold water, lard and mix well in a bowl. Knead.

Filling:
 2 tablespoons lard
 55 g (2 oz) pork, finely minced
225 g (8 oz) prawn meat, cut into big pieces
 30 g (1 oz) boiled pork fat, chopped finely
½ teaspoon sugar
½ teaspoon msg
½ teaspoon sesame oil
¼ teaspoon pepper
 2 teaspoons light soya sauce
 1 tablespoon corn flour
 1 tablespoon ginger juice
 4 tablespoons finely chopped bamboo shoots
 1 teaspoon sherry

METHOD

1. Fry pork and prawn with lard for ½ minute. Remove to a bowl, add the rest of the ingredients, mix well and chill in refrigerator.

2. Roll dough into a thin log and cut into 35 pieces. Cover with damp cloth. Flatten each piece and spoon 1–1½ teaspoons filling in centre and fold. Seal by pleating from underside of dough to form a neat pouch.

3. Place on greased tin and steam over rapidly boiling water for 6–8 minutes. Serve hot.

HUM SUI KOK
(CHINESE CURRY PUFFS)

INGREDIENTS

Filling:
- 1 tablespoon oil
- 115 g (4 oz) lean pork, diced
- 115 g (4 oz) prawn meat, diced
- 55 g (2 oz) pork fat, boiled and diced
- 55 g (2 oz) roast pork, diced
- 2 tablespoons dried prawns, diced
- 8 water chestnuts, diced

Seasoning:

½ teaspoon salt	
1 teaspoon msg	
1½ teaspoons sugar	
2 teaspoons dark soya sauce	**A**
1 teaspoon sesame oil	
Dash of pepper	
115 ml (4 fl oz) water	

1 tablespoon oil blended with 1 tablespoon plain flour (thickening)

Heat 1 tablespoon oil and fry pork for ½ minute, add the prawns and the rest of the ingredients, and then the seasoning **A**. Cook till sauce is almost dry, add the thickening, stir well and remove to a dish to cool.

Pastry:
- 115 g (4 oz) non-glutinous flour
- 115 g (4 oz) castor sugar
- 255 g (9 oz) glutinous rice flour mixed with 225 ml (8 fl oz) water
- 115 g (4 oz) glutinous rice flour
- 115 g (4 oz) lard
- 55 g (2 oz) sesame seeds

METHOD

1. Mix 170 ml (6 oz) boiling water with the non-glutinous flour in a large basin, stir with chopstick, cover with cloth and leave for 5 minutes.

2. Knead the dough for 1 minute, add the sugar, the wet glutinous rice flour and knead well for 3 minutes. Add the glutinous rice flour and the fat and knead again till smooth.

3. Roll dough into a cylindrical shape, cut into equal parts — the size of a small egg — and set aside. Flatten each part into an oval, put filling in centre, fold and seal by pressing the edges of dough together. Brush dough lightly with water, roll in sesame seeds and deep fry in hot oil till light golden brown. Remove and leave to drain on absorbent paper. Serve hot.

Note:
Ground roasted groundnuts mixed with sugar and roasted sesame seeds, or grated coconut cooked with palm sugar can also be used for the filling.

KEE CHANG
(GLUTINOUS RICE DUMPLINGS)

INGREDIENTS

- 1.2 kg (42 oz) glutinous rice, remove transparent grains
- 1 teaspoon salt
- 4 tablespoons alkaline water*
- 60 bamboo leaves (fresh or dry), washed and drained
- 40–50 long strands of straw for tying (to be soaked overnight and tied together in equal lengths)

1 teaspoon salt	
1 teaspoon *pheng say* (available at Chinese medicine shops)	**A**

METHOD

1. Wash glutinous rice till water runs clear. Drain. Put the glutinous rice in a porcelain container, add 1 teaspoon salt and 2 tablespoons of alkaline water, mix well and add water to cover up to 2.5 cm (1 in) above level of glutinous rice. Soak overnight or for 12 hours at least.

2. Drain the glutinous rice in a colander. Transfer to an enamel or porcelain basin and pour in the rest of the alkaline water. Mix well by hand so that the alkaline water and the glutinous rice are evenly mixed. Set aside for ½ hour.

To wrap and boil the dumplings:

1. Take 1 broad long leaf or 2 narrow leaves and fold into a cone. Put in 3 tablespoons glutinous rice. Fold the leaf over the rice to form a triangular shape. Use straw to tie securely around the dumpling. Tie dumplings in groups of 20.

2. Fill half a large saucepan with water and bring it to a rapid boil over high heat.

3. Add **A**. Put in the dumplings and boil for 3–4 hours. To test whether dumplings are cooked, unwrap one after 3 hours, cut into half and see whether the glutinous rice is smooth to the touch. The number of hours in boiling depends on the size of the bundles of dumplings.

4. When dumplings are cooked, remove from saucepan, cut off protruding leaves and tie into neat bundles of 10. Leave to hang till cool. Remove leaves and cut dumplings into thin slices. Serve with screw pine flavoured syrup made by boiling sugar and water with screw pine leaves till fairly thick or with coarsely grated young coconut and palm sugar syrup.

To boil the syrup:

Grate the palm sugar, add sugar, water, screw pine leaves and boil in a saucepan for 10 minutes till syrup is fairly thick.

Note:
Add boiling water if water in saucepan evaporates. Boil over moderately high heat throughout.

When using dried bamboo leaves, soak them overnight in cold water, then boil in a basin or wok for 15 minutes. Drain. Adding pheng say *and salt to the boiling water prevents the leaves from sticking to the dumplings.*

Cool dumplings for at least 8–10 hours so that they will be firm before cutting into pieces to serve.

*See page 199.

PRAWN FRITTERS

INGREDIENTS

10 large prawns
  1 tablespoon ginger juice
  Pinch of salt
  Dash of pepper

70 g (2½ oz) self-raising flour
  1 teaspoon Bird's eye custard powder
  Pinch of salt   **A**
½ teaspoon bicarbonate of soda
70 ml (2½ fl oz) water
  1 tablespoon oil

1.14 litres (2 pints) oil for deep-frying
Cucumber
Tomatoes

METHOD

1. Shell prawns, leaving tail unshelled. Slit prawns halfway lengthwise and remove dark veins. Season with 1 tablespoon ginger juice, a pinch of salt and a dash of pepper. Set aside.

2. Combine **A** in a bowl and mix till well blended. Stand for 5 minutes.

3. Heat oil in an aluminium wok. Dip each prawn into batter and fry till light golden brown. Remove to absorbent paper to drain oil and place on a serving dish. Arrange cucumber and tomato slices around edge of plate and serve.

KUEH CHANG BABI
GLUTINOUS RICE DUMPLING

INGREDIENTS

2.1 kg (4.5 lb) glutinous rice
3 tablespoons salt
510 ml (18 fl oz) water
3 level teaspoons pepper
425 g (15 oz) lard
30–35 large screw pine leaves (8 cm × 55 cm)

Filling Ingredients:
1.2 kg (2.5 lb) lean pork
115 g (4 oz) pork fat
55 g (2 oz) dried Chinese mushrooms
225 g (8 oz) preserved sugared winter melon
200 ml (7 fl oz) lard or oil
55 g (2 oz) garlic, pounded finely
225 g (8 oz) shallots, pounded finely
1 rounded teaspoon salt
395 g (14 oz) sugar
2 tablespoons pepper
4 tablespoons dark soya sauce
6 tablespoons roasted ground coriander seeds

METHOD

To Prepare Rice:

1. Soak glutinous rice overnight. Drain and divide into three parts. Steam each part over rapidly boiling water for 20 minutes. Make steam holes before steaming.

2. Remove glutinous rice to a saucepan. Dissolve 1 tablespoon salt in 170 ml (6 fl oz) of water. Add 1 teaspoon pepper and pour around the steamed glutinous rice. Mix well. Cover for 10 minutes and mix lard evenly with rice. Keep warm in a saucepan with a tight fitting lid. Repeat with remaining glutinous rice.

To Prepare Filling:

3. Place the pork and pork fat in a saucepan. Pour in 850 ml (30 fl oz) water and bring to the boil. Boil over moderately high heat for 20 minutes then remove pork and fat. Cool, dice and set aside pork and fat. Continue boiling stock till it is reduced by half.

4. Soak Chinese mushrooms and cut into tiny cubes. Dice sugared melon.

5. Heat oil in wok and fry the pounded garlic and shallots adding pork, salt, sugar, pepper and dark soya sauce. Stir in pan till pork changes colour. Add stock, mushrooms, sugared melon and fat. Continue cooking over medium heat for ½ hour.

6. Now add the coriander powder and stir well. Reduce heat and simmer till filling is almost dry. Remove to a large bowl to cool. Keep overnight before filling.

To Wrap Dumplings:

7. Take 1 broad or two narrow screwpine leaves. Fold from the centre to form a cone. Take a fistful of glutinous rice and line the sides.

8. Put 2–3 tablespoons of pork filling over rice and cover neatly with more glutinous rice. Fold leaf over and tie tightly with raffia or string.

9. Tie dumplings in groups of ten and boil in rapidly boiling water for 3 to 3½ hours. Add 2 tablespoons of salt to the water.

Note:
Unwrap one dumpling to see if glutinous rice is cooked and smooth. Otherwise, continue boiling for another 30 to 45 minutes. Hang dumplings for 1 to 2 hours after cooking to drip dry, thus preventing sogginess.

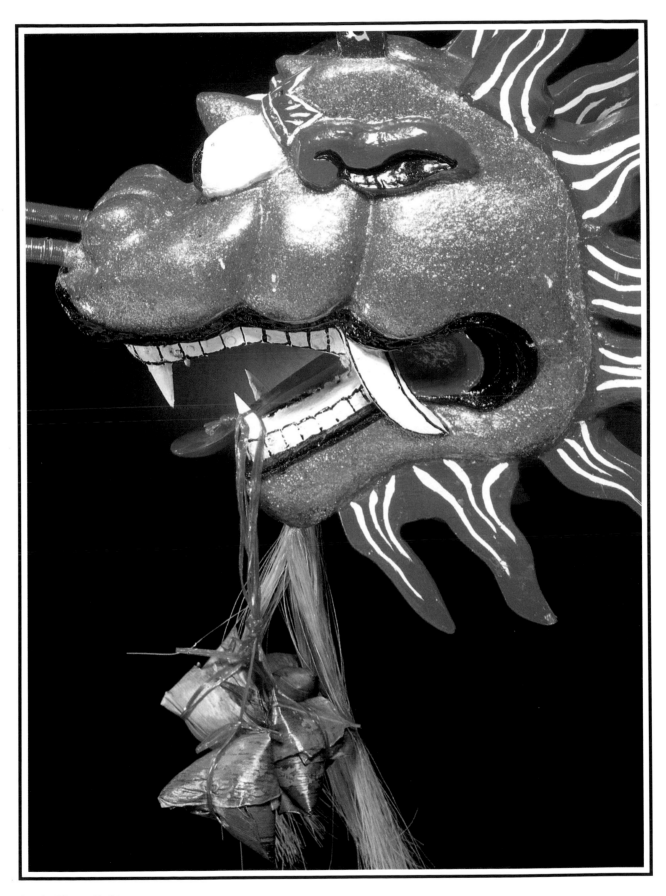

Kueh Chang Babi

SIEW MAI
(MEAT SAVOURIES)

INGREDIENTS

1 teaspoon msg	
1 teaspoon sherry	
2 tablespoons light soya sauce	
½ teaspoon salt	
1 teaspoon sugar	
½ teaspoon sesame oil	**A**
2 teaspoons cornflour	
1 tablespoon ginger juice	
1 small egg	
½ teaspoon pepper	
1 tablespoon chopped spring onions	

285 g (10 oz) minced pork	
225 g (½ lb) prawns, shelled, deveined and cut	
55 g (2 oz) boiled pork fat, finely cubed	**B**
4 tablespoons boiled bamboo shoots, chopped finely	

115 g (4 oz) square egg skins ('wan tan' skins), obtainable from local markets

METHOD

1. Mix **A** in a bowl. Add **B**. Mix well.
2. Cut off the four corners of the egg skins. Place a tablespoon of the meat mixture in the centre of each skin. Enclose filling with egg skin, so that the top filling is seen. Flatten base of each siew mai.

To steam:

Brush steamer rack with oil. Space siew mai on rack.

Steam over rapidly boiling water for 5–7 minutes or till cooked.

Serve hot with chilli sauce and mustard.

(Makes 30–40 'siew mai')

STEAMED BEEF BALLS

INGREDIENTS

115 ml (4 fl oz) water	
1½ tablespoons cornflour	**A**
1½ tablespoons water chestnut flour	

455 g (16 oz) topside beef, minced finely
1 teaspoon alkaline water*

½ teaspoon salt	
1½ teaspoons msg	
3 tablespoons sugar	**B**
1 teaspoon sesame oil	
Dash of pepper	

115 g (4 oz) pork fat, cut into very small squares	
4 sprigs Chinese parsley, chopped finely	**C**
½ teaspoon dried orange peel, chopped finely	

Pepper

METHOD

1. Blend **A** in a bowl.
2. Place minced beef and alkaline water in a mixing bowl and mix thoroughly by hand. Slap beef on to sides of bowl. Knead till it is sticky, about 10 minutes. Leave to stand for 2 hours.
3. Transfer beef paste to a large mixing bowl. Add **A** (Method 1) and **B**. Use palms of hands to rub and knead till beef is pasty and sticky, about 10 minutes.
4. Add **C** and dash of pepper. Mix well. Grease palms of hands. Roll mixture into balls (each the size of a small egg). Place beef balls on a greased plate.
5. Steam for 10 minutes over rapidly boiling water. Serve hot.

*See page 122.

STUFFED MUSHROOMS

INGREDIENTS

680 ml (24 fl oz) water }
  1 teaspoon sugar   **A**
  ½ teaspoon salt
  1 tablespoon lard

225 g (8 oz) Chinese mustard
  15 big Chinese mushrooms soaked in hot water

  1 egg white, lightly beaten
  ½ teaspoon msg
  ¼ teaspoon salt
  1 teaspoon light soya sauce   **B**
  1 tablespoon cornflour
  Dash of pepper
  1 tablespoon lard
  ¼ teaspoon sesame oil

225 g (½ lb) minced pork with a little fat
455 g (1 lb) prawns, shelled, deveined and   **C**
  finely chopped
  4 water chestnuts, finely chopped
  1 tablespoon spring onions, finely chopped

1. Boil **A**. Add Chinese mustard, cut into pieces. Boil for ½ minute. Drain.

2. Dust underside of mushrooms with cornflour.

3. Mix **B** in a bowl. Add **C**. Mix well.

4. Spread mixture on to dusted side of mushrooms. Steam mushrooms, meat side up, on a greased plate for 7–10 minutes.

Gravy: (A)
¼ teaspoon salt, ½ teaspoon msg, ½ teaspoon sugar, 2 teaspoons light soya sauce, 225 ml (8 fl oz) chicken stock

  1 clove garlic, finely chopped

2 teaspoons cornflour   **B**
2 tablespoons water

1. Mix **A** in a bowl.

2. Heat 1 tablespoon lard in a hot pan. Fry chopped garlic. Pour in **A** and bring to the boil. Reduce heat to low.

3. Add **B** to pan. Stir till it boils. Pour over stuffed mushrooms, meat side up on the boiled mustard. Serve hot.

YAM PUFF

INGREDIENTS

115 g (4 oz) non-glutinous wheat flour
570 g (1¼ lb) yam, steamed and mashed
  2 teaspoons sesame oil

115 g (4 oz) lard
  ½ teaspoon salt
  4 teaspoons fine sugar   **A**
  ¾ teaspoon pepper
  1 level teaspoon msg

Filling for yam puff:
  2 teaspoons oil
  1 teaspoon pounded garlic
115 g (4 oz) prawn meat, deveined and cubed
455 g (1 lb) lean meat, cut into small cubes
 55 g (2 oz) canned button mushrooms, cut into small pieces
  1 egg, lightly beaten
  2 tablespoons cornflour, mixed with
  2 tablespoons water

Seasoning:
½ teaspoon salt, ½ teaspoon msg, ¾ teaspoon pepper, 3 teaspoons fine sugar, 1 teaspoon black soya sauce, 1 teaspoon oyster sauce

METHOD

To prepare yam paste:
1. Blend the wheat flour with 115 ml (4 fl oz) boiling water in a small enamel basin.

2. Add mashed yam in small amounts with sesame oil and knead till smooth. Add in **A**. Mix well.

3. Divide dough into 4 parts and cut each part into small equal pieces, the size of a walnut.

4. Flatten each piece, place filling in centre, fold and seal edges.

5. Deep-fry puffs in a big, flat wire mesh ladle till golden brown. Remove to an absorbent paper to drain. Serve hot.

To cook filling:
Heat oil in pan and fry garlic till lightly browned. Add prawns, pork, mushrooms and stir-fry for 1 minute. Put in beaten egg, stir and pour in the cornflour mixture. Stir well and add seasoning.

TAN TART
(CHINESE EGG CUSTARD TARTLETS)

INGREDIENTS

Lard Dough Ingredients:
115 g (4 oz) lukewarm lard
140 g (5 oz) plain flour
½ teaspoon salt

METHOD

1. Mix ingredients together well in a bowl. Line a 13 × 15 cm tray with tin foil and pour on the lard mixture to spread evenly. Refrigerate overnight.

Plain Dough Ingredients:
170 g (6 oz) plain flour
½ teaspoon fine salt
2 teaspoons sugar
130 g (4½ oz) frozen butter
1 egg yolk
3 tablespoons iced water

METHOD

1. Combine plain flour, salt and sugar in a bowl. Cut frozen butter into 1.5 cm (½ in) squares. Put flour and butter into a food processor and use a steel blade cutter to process till mixture resembles breadcrumbs.

2. Beat the egg yolk with iced water. Remove flour mixture into a mixing bowl and make a well in the centre. Pour egg mixture gradually in centre and combine to form a dough.

3. Remove dough to a lightly floured flat work surface. Knead till dough is smooth. Flatten dough and keep in fridge for ½ hour.

To Roll Pastry:
4. Roll plain dough on a lightly dusted surface to a rectangular 20 × 25.5 cm (8 in × 11 in) shape. Mark dough in 3 equal parts: A, B and C. (see diagram)

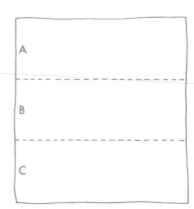

5. Place lard dough on parts A and B. Bring part C over to cover B. Then fold A over to cover B and C. Press open edges firmly to seal and prevent lard from spilling. Cool in fridge for 45 minutes.

6. Place dough with narrow side facing you. Use rolling pin to press lightly at intervals to roll to a rectangular 20 × 25.5 cm. Fold bottom third of dough over and bring top third down. Press narrow edges firmly to seal and cool in fridge for 30 minutes. This is first rolling.

7. Repeat step (6) twice. Cool in fridge after each rolling.

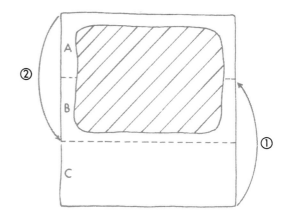

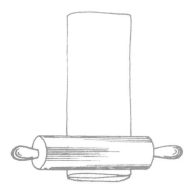

1. Mix custard powder with 1 tablespoon water. Add beaten egg and vanilla. Beat till well blended. Set aside.

2. Combine sugar, 455 ml (16 fl oz) water and condensed milk in a small saucepan. Cook till sugar is dissolved and milk is heated through. Pour the hot milk gradually into the beaten egg mixture and stir well. Cook over low heat for 3 minutes, stirring all the time. Cool before use to prevent bubbles forming while baking. Pour into pastry shells just before baking.

To Bake Custard Tartlets:
1. Preheat oven to 230°C (450°F). Place lined tartlets on a baking tray. Pour in custard to ½ fill the shells. Bake on high heat for 15 minutes, then reduce to 135°C (275°F) to continue baking for another 25–30 minutes or till custard sets and pastry turns light brown.

2. When done, remove from oven to cool for a moment. Place tartlets on paper cups. Serve hot.

Note:
Do not overfill pastry with custard. This will cause the pastry to become soggy and soft.

8. Place dough on a lightly floured surface. Roll till 3 mm (0.1 in) thick. Use a round cutter to cut shapes slightly larger than fluted tartlet tins.

9. Grease tartlet tins lightly and line with pastry. Press lightly on the sides to get impression from the fluted tins. Prick with sharp metal skewer if bubbles appear at base of pastry.

Custard Ingredients:
   2 rounded teaspoons custard powder (Bird's eye brand)
   Water
   4 large eggs, lightly beaten
   1 teaspoon vanilla essence
225 g (8 oz) sugar
   4 tablespoons condensed milk

Savoury Snacks

Beef Curry Puffs

Bun Susi

Cheese Straws

Chee Cheong Fun

Cheesey Beef Patties

Chwee Kuey

Kueh Pie Tee

Lemper Ayam

Minced Pork and Prawn Toast

Morokoo

Prawn Sambal Sandwiches

Rissoles

Pork Rolls

Spicy Prawn Rolls

Soon Kuey

Steamed Fish and Milk Sauce Sandwiches

Clockwise: Kueh Chang Babi, Soon Kuey, Chwee Kuey, Chee Cheong Fun

BEEF CURRY PUFFS

INGREDIENTS

Pastry:
225 g (8 oz) pastry margarine
1 egg
2 tablespoons castor sugar
2 tablespoons lemon juice
1 teaspoon salt
3–5 drops of yellow food colouring
170 ml (6 fl oz) iced water
455 g (16 oz) flour, sifted
115 g (4 oz) butter

METHOD

1. Cut pastry margarine into 2 cm (¾ in) cubes.

2. Mix egg, sugar, lemon juice, salt and food colouring in a bowl. Beat lightly with a fork. Pour in the iced water and stir till well mixed. Chill in a refrigerator.

3. Rub butter into the flour till mixture resembles breadcrumbs. Add the margarine cubes and mix lightly with the flour. Add the egg mixture and mix with both hands to form a dough. Do not knead. Chill dough in refrigerator for 1 hour.

4. Divide dough into two portions. Place one portion on a floured board or flat surface; dredge flour over; flatten and roll out into a rectangle. Fold into three, bringing down one-third of the pastry from the top to fold over the centre. Make a half turn so that the open edges on both ends face you and the fold is at your right. Roll out.

5. Repeat the folding and rolling three more times. Dust board with flour, roll out pastry to 0.5 cm (¼ in) thickness and use a fluted-edged cutter to cut pastry into rounds.

6. Repeat process with the other portion.

7. Place a tablespoonful of filling in the centre of each round. Moisten half the edge with water and bring the other half over to seal.

8. Space curry puffs on a greased tray. Brush with glaze and bake in a very hot oven at 230°C (450°F) or Regulo 10 to 10 minutes. Bake on centre shelf of oven. Reduce heat to 205°C (400°F) or Regulo 8 and bake for another 20 minutes till golden brown. Lift curry puffs on to a wire rack to cool.

To Glaze:
Beat one egg with 2 drops of yellow food colouring.

Filling:
Oil for frying
340 g (12 oz) onions, diced
340 g (12 oz) potatoes, diced
¼ teaspoon salt

1 teaspoon chopped ginger
2 cloves garlic, sliced thinly
8 shallots, sliced thinly
455 g (1 lb) minced beef
4 heaped tablespoons curry powder
225 g (8 oz) grated coconut, to 125 ml (4 fl oz) water, squeezed and strained

Seasoning for curry filling:
2 tablespoons sugar
2 teaspoons salt
1 teaspoon msg

METHOD

1. Heat an iron wok. When very hot, add 4 tablespoons oil and fry onions till transparent. Remove to a plate leaving oil in wok.

2. Add 2 tablespoons oil, stir-fry potatoes with ¼ teapoon salt over a high heat for 5 minutes. Sprinkle 115 ml (4 fl oz) water, stir and cover. Cook over a moderate heat till potatoes are done. Remove and set aside.

3. In a clean iron wok, heat 4 tablespoons oil to brown ginger, sliced garlic, and shallots. Add minced meat and stir-fry for 5 minutes over a moderate heat. Add the curry powder and stir-fry for another 5 minutes. Add the fried onions and cooked potatoes. Mix well then add the coconut milk and the seasoning.

4. Reduce the heat, and cook till meat mixture is almost dry, stirring occasionally. Remove to a large plate to cool.

BUN SUSI
(MEAT BUNS)

INGREDIENTS

Buns:
  30 g (1 oz) or 2 tablespoons fresh yeast
115 g (4 oz) castor sugar
455 g (16 oz) flour, sifted
170 ml (6 fl oz) hot milk
115 g (4 oz) soft butter
  5 egg yolks
  1 egg white, lightly beaten
½ teaspoon salt
225 g (8 oz) bread dough, from bakery
  Flour for dusting

METHOD

1. Dissolve yeast in 3 tablespoons warm water, 1 teaspoon sugar, and 1 tablespoon flour. Let stand for 10 minutes or till frothy.

2. Place hot milk in a mixing bowl, add the butter, egg yolks, egg white, salt, sugar, and 225 g (8 oz) of the flour. Stir till well mixed.

3. Break bread dough into small portions in a big bowl. Add the yeast mixture and the milk mixture.

4. Claw mixture with hand for 5 minutes. Add the rest of the flour to form a dough. Place dough on a flat surface and knead till dough is smooth and leaves palm of hand clean. Place dough in a greased bowl. Cover with a damp cloth and allow to rise in a warm place till double its size.

5. Remove dough to a floured board, dust with some flour and knead for 2 minutes.

6. Divide dough into four parts and shape each into a long roll. Cut into equal walnut-sized pieces. Flatten each piece lightly with the palm of hand, making a well in the centre. Fill with meat filling and shape the dough to form a small bun.

7. Space buns out on a greased tray, allowing room for expansion. Leave to rise in a warm place for 20–30 minutes. Glaze and bake in oven at 205°C (400°F) or Regulo 8 for 10 minutes. Reduce heat to 150°C (300°F) or Regulo 4 and bake for a further 10–15 minutes till golden brown. Cool on a rack.

Filling:
  1 teaspoon msg
¾ teaspoon salt
  3 tablespoons sugar   **A**
  2 tablespoons dark soya sauce
  4 tablespoons water

  3 tablespoons lard or oil
  8 shallots, sliced thinly
  1 tablespoon pounded garlic
680 g (24 oz) minced pork
  2 teaspoons pepper
285 g (10 oz) potatoes, diced and fried
¼ piece grated nutmeg
  3 tablespoons crispy shallots

Thickening:
2 tablespoons cornflour with 4 tablespoons water

METHOD

1. In a very hot pan, heat 3 tablespoons lard or oil to fry the sliced shallots and garlic till brown. Add the minced pork and pepper, stir-fry for 5 minutes. Add the potatoes, cook for 5 minutes.

2. Mix **A** in a bowl for the seasoning.

3. Pour in the seasoning, stir-fry in pan till meat mixture is almost dry. Sprinkle with nutmeg and crispy shallots. Pour in the cornflour mixture and cook for 1 minute. Cool on tray before use.

To Glaze:
Beat 1 egg and 1 egg yolk with 1 tablespoon milk, a pinch of salt, 1 teaspoon sugar and 2–3 drops of yellow food colouring.

Note:
An electric dough hook can be used to knead the dough. Use speed No. 1 or No. 2 for about 15 minutes, or till dough leaves the inside of bowl clean.

CHEESE STRAWS

INGREDIENTS

225 g (8 oz) cheese, finely grated
¾ teaspoon salt
½ teaspoon pepper — **A**
1 tablespoon granulated sugar

170 g (6 oz) butter
225 g (8 oz) flour
2 egg yolks, beaten
1 egg white, lightly beaten for glaze

METHOD

1. Rub butter into flour. Add **A**. Mix well.
2. Pour the beaten egg yolks into the flour mixture. Knead lightly with hand to form a soft dough. Chill dough in refrigerator for ½ hour.
3. Roll dough on a floured pastry board to 0.5 cm (¼ in) thickness.
4. Cut pastry with a pastry wheel into 5 cm (2 in) blocks. Cut each block into strips, so that each strip is 5 cm long by 0.5 cm wide (2 in × ¼ in).
5. Glaze whole blocks of cheese strips with egg white. Place on baking trays and bake in oven at 190°C (375°F) or Regulo 7 for about 20–25 minutes till light brown. Store in an airtight container when cool.

CHEE CHEONG FUN

INGREDIENTS

½ teaspoon salt
2 tablespoons oil — **A**

140 g (5 oz) rice flour
2 tablespoons sago flour
570 ml (20 fl oz) water
4 tablespoons toasted sesame seeds
Crispy shallots

METHOD

1. Mix the two types of flour with 255 ml (9 fl oz) of the water. Add **A** and mix well. Set aside.
2. Bring the rest of the water to the boil and add gradually to the flour mixture, stirring as you pour.

To steam:
1. Grease two 23 cm (9 in) round sandwich trays with oil. Place trays on a perforated rack in an iron wok of rapidly boiling water. Cover trays and heat for 2 minutes. Keep water in wok below the level of the rack at all times during steaming.
2. Stir flour mixture, and pour a ladlespoon or 115–140 ml (4–5 fl oz) of it into the trays. Tilt trays so that the mixture spreads evenly, before steaming. Cover wok and steam for about 1–1½ minutes or till mixture turns transparent.
3. Remove trays from wok and put over a shallow basin of cold water for 1 minute. Use spatula to remove cooked paste. Form into a roll and place on a plate. Repeat with the rest of the mixture.

To serve:
Cut *chee cheong fun* into pieces, sprinkle with crispy shallots and sesame seeds and serve with mushroom soya sauce (*see recipe*) and chilli sauce. Sliced roast pork strips or steamed small prawns can be added if desired.

To make *chee cheong fun* mushroom soya sauce:
1 tablespoon oil
4 slices ginger
2 tablespoons sugar
55 g (2 oz) mushroom soya sauce
55 ml (2 fl oz) water
1 teaspoon msg

In a saucepan, heat oil, sugar and ginger till sugar turns a light brown. Pour in the mushroom soya sauce, water and msg. Bring to the boil and boil for 5 minutes. Serve when cool.

CHEESEY BEEF PATTIES

INGREDIENTS

500 g (18 oz) top-side beef, minced
115 g (4 oz) onions, chopped finely, fried in a little oil till soft — **A**
¼ cup Chinese celery, chopped finely

Seasoning:
(Beaten together)
1 teaspoon fine salt
1 teaspoon pepper
1 teaspoon msg

15 g (½ oz) cheddar cheese, finely cubed
1 kg (2¼ lb) potatoes
Self-raising flour
1 egg, beaten
1 cup dry breadcrumbs
Oil for deep frying

METHOD

1. Place **A** in a large bowl. Add cheese and seasoning; mix till well combined. Divide into 12 portions, shape into flat patties and chill in refrigerator for ½ hour.

2. Wash potatoes and cut deep slits in each to boil gently till tender. Peel skin and mash well whilst hot, adding ½ teaspoon each of fine salt and pepper. Mix well. Divide potato into 12 portions and cover to keep warm.

3. Pat potato around meat patties. Roll patties in self-raising flour; dip in beaten egg and coat with breadcrumbs. Keep in refrigerator for an hour.

4. Heat oil for deep frying. Fry patties till golden. Remove to absorbent paper and serve hot with tomato sauce.

Note:
Make large portions of Cheesey Beef Patties and keep in freezer in a plastic container. Minced pork can be used instead of beef.

CHWEE KUEY
(STEAMED RICE CAKES WITH PRESERVED SALTED RADISH)

INGREDIENTS

565 ml (20 fl oz) water
140 g (5 oz) rice flour
1 heaped tablespoon sago flour
½ teaspoon salt
2 tablespoons oil
170 g (6 oz) lard
2 cloves garlic, lightly bashed
115 g (4 oz) chopped, preserved, salted radish
½ teaspoon msg
Dash of pepper

METHOD

1. Mix well 225 ml (8 fl oz) of the water with the two types of flour and salt in a bowl. Add the oil and beat well with a fork till well blended. Set aside.

2. Bring the rest of the water to the boil and pour gradually into the rice mixture, stirring all the time to prevent lumps forming.

3. Arrange the moulds on a steamer tray over boiling water and steam empty moulds over moderate heat for 5 minutes.

4. Pour rice mixture into each mould and steam for 10–15 minutes or till well cooked. Remove the rice cakes from steamer and allow to cool for about 10 minutes, before taking them out of the moulds.

To cook the radish:
Dice the lard, wash and drain. Cook lard and garlic in a small saucepan till lard turns light brown. Discard garlic and lard, leaving oil to cook radish, msg and pepper, over low heat for ½ hour. Stir occasionally to prevent burning. Place a spoonful of cooked radish on top of the steamed rice cakes and serve. Sweet chilli sauce can be added if desired.

Note:
You can buy the chopped preserved salted radish from any supermarket or grocer's.

KUEH PIE TEE
(SHREDDED BAMBOO SHOOTS IN PATTY CASES)

INGREDIENTS

Patty cases:

1 large egg, lightly beaten	
225 ml (8 fl oz) water	**A**
A pinch of salt	

115 g (4 oz) plain flour, sifted
Oil for deep-frying

METHOD

1. Mix **A** in a bowl.
2. Pour mixture gradually into the flour to form a smooth batter. Sieve into a bowl. Leave to stand for ½ hour.
3. Heat oil for deep-frying.
4. Heat the special patty mould in the hot oil for 2 minutes. Remove the mould, dip it in batter and deep-fry till patty case is light brown and can retain its shape when it slips away from the mould.
5. Place patty cases on absorbent paper. Cool and store in an air-tight container immediately to retain crispness.

Filling:

1.2 kg (43 oz) tender, boiled bamboo shoots	**A**
310 g (11 oz) Chinese turnip	

½ teaspoon·salt	
½ teaspoon msg	
2 tablespoons sugar	**B**
2 tablespoons preserved brown soya beans, pounded	

455 g (1 lb) streaky pork
A pinch of salt
225 g (½ lb) small prawns
225 ml (8 fl oz) water
4 tablespoons lard or oil
2 tablespoons pounded garlic

2 big soya bean cakes, cut into thin strips and fried

METHOD

1. Cook pork in 455 ml (16 fl oz) water and a pinch of salt for ½ hour. Remove and slice pork thinly. Cut again into fine strips. Set aside stock.
2. Shred **A** finely.
3. Shell and devein prawns. Pound prawn shells. Add water and mix well. Strain and set aside stock.
4. Heat lard or oil in an iron wok. Fry garlic till brown, add **B**. Stir-fry for ½ minute. Add shredded ingredients, prawn stock and pork stock. Cook for ¾ hour over a moderate heat.
5. Add prawns, pork and soya bean strips. Stir and cook till almost dry. Cool on tray before filling.

Garnish:
225 g (½ lb) steamed crab meat
225 g (½ lb) prawns, fried with a pinch of salt and cut into small pieces
3 bundles of Chinese parsley, without roots, washed and drained
4 tablespoons pounded garlic, fried crisp
2 eggs, fried into thin pancakes and shredded

To serve:
Fill patty cases with filling. Top with bits of garnish. Serve with chilli sauce.

Note:
Dip shredded turnip in cold water to remove the starch. Drain in colander before cooking.

(50–60 patty cases)

LEMPER AYAM
(STEAMED GLUTINOUS RICE WITH
SPICED SHREDDED CHICKEN)

INGREDIENTS

40 g (1½ oz) shallots 1 stalk lemon grass 2 slices ginger 30 g (1 oz) candlenut	**A**

1½ teaspoons salt 2 tablespoons sugar 2 teaspoons pepper 2 rounded tablespoons roasted ground coriander seeds 2 tablespoons condensed milk	**B** *mixed in a bowl*

605 g (21 oz) glutinous rice, soaked overnight
570 g (20 oz) grated coconut
¾ tablespoon salt
1 level tablespoon sugar
Banana leaves

Filling:
285 g (10 oz) chicken breast
Pinch of salt

3 tablespoons oil
55 ml (2 fl oz) No. 1 milk (*from To prepare glutinous
rice, Step 3*)

To prepare glutinous rice:
1. Wash banana leaves. Cut into 30 cm ×
   10 cm (12 in × 4 in) pieces, and soak in a
   basin of boiling water for 10 minutes to soften.

2. Drain glutinous rice.

3. Squeeze coconut for 200 ml (7 fl oz) No. 1
   milk. Stir in salt and sugar till dissolved.
   Set aside 55 ml (2 fl oz) to cook the filling.
   Add 170 ml (6 fl oz) water to coconut and
   squeeze for 140 ml (5 fl oz) No. 2 milk.

4. Make steam holes in glutinous rice and
   steam over rapidly boiling water for
   20 minutes. Transfer glutinous rice to a
   saucepan, pour in the No. 2 milk, stir and
   leave in saucepan, covered, for 5 minutes.

5. Return glutinous rice to steamer, make
   steam holes and re-steam for 7 minutes.
   Transfer into saucepan again and pour in
   the No. 1 milk. Stir and leave in pan for
   5 minutes. Re-steam for another 5 minutes.
   Remove from heat and keep steamed glutinous rice warm.

To cook filling:
1. Boil chicken breast gently with a pinch of
   salt and 455 ml (16 fl oz) water for ½ hour.
   Remove chicken to cool. Boil stock till it is
   reduced by half.

2. Bash chicken with side of chopper and
   shred finely.

3. Heat oil and fry paste **A** over moderate heat
   till fragrant and light brown. Add the No. 1
   milk, stock and **B**. Stir well, put in the
   shredded chicken and cook over low heat
   till mixture is moist. Cool before use.

To fill *lemper*:
1. Oil hands with boiled coconut oil, put 340 g
   (12 oz) warm glutinous rice on a banana
   leaf. Flatten into a rectangular shape 1 cm
   (½ in) thick.

2. Place 115 g (4 oz) filling in the centre of the
   glutinous rice lengthwise. Roll glutinous
   rice to cover filling. Roll banana leaf tightly
   over glutinous rice and press firmly to flatten. Cut into pieces 5 cm (2 in) long. Wrap
   with grease-proof paper and staple ends.

Note:
Wrapped lemper *can be pan-fried over moderate heat (without
oil) if preferred.*

MINCED PORK AND PRAWN TOAST

INGREDIENTS

225 g (½ lb) minced pork
225 g (½ lb) prawns, shelled, deveined and chopped
115 g (4 oz) chopped pork and ham (mashed)
 1 egg
 2 small boiled potatoes, mashed
 2 tablespoons chopped spring onions
⅛ teaspoon salt
 1 teaspoon sugar
½ teaspoon msg
½ teaspoon pepper

A

 1 big loaf of bread (French loaf), cut into 1 cm (½ in) thick slices
 Oil for deep-frying
 1 egg, beaten with a pinch of salt

METHOD

1. Mix **A** well into a pasty mixture using a wooden spoon.

2. Spread meat mixture on to slices of bread.

3. Dip only the meat side of the bread in the beaten egg. Deep-fry over a moderate heat, meat-side down, for 2 minutes.

4. Turn over once, fry for just half a minute till light golden brown. Remove and place on absorbent paper. Serve hot with tomato sauce or salad cream.

MOROKOO

(BLACK BEAN FLOUR AND COCONUT CRISPS)

INGREDIENTS

455 g (16 oz) rice flour
115 g (4 oz) black bean flour
 2 teaspoon oom seeds (available at Indian grocery shops)
 4 teaspoons cumin seeds, whole
½ teaspoon turmeric powder
 2 level teaspoons salt
55 g (2 oz) grated coconut, white

A

1.2 kg (2½ lb) grated coconut, white
 2 litres (4 pints) oil for deep frying

METHOD

1. Squeeze the 1.2 kg grated coconut for 455 ml No. 1 milk. Set aside.

2. Put **A** into a large mixing bowl. Stir by hand till evenly combined. Pour the No. 1 milk gradually into mixture and knead to form a smooth semi-firm dough. Allow to rest for ½ hour.

3. Put dough in morokoo presser to test for texture. It should flow easily showing a clear pattern.

3. Fill presser with dough and press dough into heated oil in wok. Fry over moderately high heat till golden brown.

PRAWN SAMBAL SANDWICHES

INGREDIENTS

 4 tablespoons oil
 4 tablespoons chopped onions
2–4 tablespoons dried chilli paste
140 g (5 oz) rempah sambal udang (See page 186)
55 ml (2 fl oz) No. 1 milk from 140 g (5 oz) grated coconut
55 g (2 oz) tamarind and 6 tablespoons water, squeezed and strained for juice
 3 tablespoons sugar
170 g (6 oz) dried prawns, pounded very finely
 20 lime leaves, sliced very finely

METHOD

1. Heat 4 tablespoons oil in an aluminium pan and fry onions till light brown. Add chilli paste, rempah udang and coconut milk and stir over moderate heat for 1 minute.

2. Pour in the tamarind juice and sugar, and stir. Add the dried prawns and keep stirring over low heat till mixture is fragrant and almost dry. Mix lime leaves and cool before making sandwiches.

RISSOLES
(MEAT ROLLS)

INGREDIENTS

Batter:

170 g (6 oz) plain flour 2 tablespoons cornflour 3 tablespoons powdered milk	**A**

6 eggs, lightly beaten 425 ml (15 fl oz) lukewarm water A pinch of salt 3 tablespoons oil	**B**

1. Sieve **A** in a bowl.
2. Beat **B** lightly with a fork and pour gradually into flour to make a smooth batter. Strain and leave to stand for 20 minutes.
3. Heat a 20 cm (8 in) base frying pan till very hot. Remove from the heat, grease base of pan with oil once only.
4. Pour in batter, tilting pan to spread batter evenly. Turn pancake out when edges begin to curl. Pile pancakes on a plate.

Filling:

115 g (4 oz) steamed crab meat 225 g (8 oz) boiled bamboo shoots, diced 6 tablespoons boiled green peas 3 tablespoons light soya sauce 1 tablespoon oyster sauce 1 teaspoon sherry ¾ teaspoon salt 1 teaspoon msg 1 teaspoon pepper 2 teaspoons sugar	**A**

1 rounded tablespoon cornflour 6 tablespoons water	**B**

6 tablespoons lard or oil
1 teaspoon garlic, pounded
1 onion, diced small
455 g (1 lb) prawns, shelled, deveined and chopped
455 g (1 lb) minced pork
2 tablespoons spring onions, chopped finely

1. Heat oil in pan, fry garlic till light brown. Add the diced onion stirring till transparent. Add the prawns and cook for 1 minute. Add the minced pork and stir-fry till cooked.
2. Add **A**. Stir well and cook over a moderate heat for 5 minutes.
3. Mix **B** and add to mixture in pan. Stir and cook for 1 minute, then add the chopped spring onions. Stir and remove to a tray to cool.

To make rolls:

1 egg
A pinch of salt
Meat filling
'Paxo' brand golden breadcrumbs
Oil

METHOD

1. Beat egg lightly with salt. Set aside.
2. Place 2 tablespoonfuls of meat filling on each pancake and roll.
3. Brush roll with beaten egg and coat with breadcrumbs. Deep-fry in hot oil for half a minute over a high heat. Place rolls on absorbent paper. Serve hot or cold.

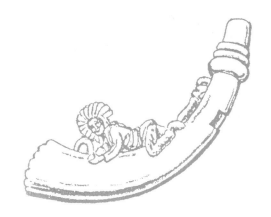

PORK ROLLS

INGREDIENTS

1 tablespoon tomato sauce
½ tablespoon Chinese wine
¾ level teaspoon salt
½ teaspoon Lea & Perrins sauce } **A**

Gravy:
1 tablespoon sugar
1 tablespoon tomato sauce
½ teaspoon Lea & Perrins sauce
½ teaspoon msg
1 teaspoon light soya sauce
½ dark soya sauce
½ teaspoon sago flour in 2 tablespoons water } **B**

455 g (1 lb) pork chop meat

115 g (4 oz) pork fat
115 g (4 oz) pig or chicken liver
115 g (4 oz) bamboo shoots } *boiled and cut into strips*

55 ml (2 fl oz) oil
1 tablespoon lard
A few lettuce leaves

METHOD

1. Cut pork chops into 5 cm strips. Slice each strip horizontally but without cutting through completely.

2. Mix **A** in a bowl and marinate pork for ¾ hour.

3. Spread open each piece of sliced pork on a wooden chopping board. Cut pork fat, liver and bamboo shoots the same length as the pork; put a piece each of these ingredients at one end of pork and roll tightly for frying.

4. Heat a frying pan till hot. Add 55 ml (2 fl oz) oil to fry rolls till brown. Remove.

5. In a clean pan, heat 1 tablespoon lard till very hot. Put in rolls and pour in **B**. Cover pan immediately for ½ minute. Remove from heat and spoon rolls on cut lettuce in serving plate. Pour remaining gravy over rolls. Serve hot.

SPICY PRAWN ROLLS

INGREDIENTS

6 candlenuts
1 thumb-sized piece turmeric
1 teaspoon shrimp paste } **A**

8 tablespoons sugar
½ tablespoon salt
3 tablespoons tamarind in 140 ml (5 fl oz) water, squeezed and strained
340 g (12 oz) dried prawns, soaked and finely pounded } **B**

115 g (4 oz) green chillies
115 g (4 oz) red chillies
115 g (4 oz) garlic
225 g (8 oz) shallots
10 stalks lemon grass, sliced slantwise } **C**

285 ml (10 fl oz) oil
50 pieces Spring Roll skins

Filling:
1 Pound ingredients **A** to a paste. Add **B** and mix thoroughly.

2. Slice **C** finely.

3. Heat an iron wok, then add oil. When oil is heated through, fry the sliced ingredients (**C**) separately till light brown. Set aside.

4. With the same oil, fry the dried prawn mixture over low heat till almost dry. Stir constantly to prevent burning.

5. Add all the fried ingredients and stir-fry for 5 minutes. Remove to a tray and cool.

To Make Prawn Rolls:
1. Cut the Spring Roll skin into quarters. Take one square of skin and scoop 1 teaspoon spicy prawn filling on it. Roll, wrap and seal with flour and water mixture. Repeat with remaining ingredients.

2. Heat oil for deep frying. Put rolls in to fry over moderate heat till lightly browned. Scoop out with a wire mesh ladle onto absorbent paper to drain oil.

3. Store in an air-tight container whilst still lukewarm.

SOON KUEY

INGREDIENTS

300 g (10½ oz) rice flour
570 ml (20 fl oz) water
½ teaspoon salt
  Pinch of *pheng say* (available at Chinese medicine shops)
70 g (2½ oz) sago flour
55 ml (2 fl oz) oil

1. Mix 2 tablespoons rice flour with 170 ml (6 fl oz) water in a cup.

2. Boil the rest of the water in a saucepan with the salt and *pheng say*. Reduce heat, pour in the flour mixture from Method 1 and stir well. Add the rest of the rice flour, and stir with wooden spoon till mixture is smooth. Remove from heat.

3. Transfer to a large basin or tray, add sago flour, oil and knead for 5 minutes.

4. Divide dough into egg-shape sizes, flatten and put in 2 tablespoons filling. Fold dough over filling and seal by pinching the edges together to resemble a curry puff. Place *soon kuey* on an oiled steamer tray and steam for 10–12 minutes. Serve hot with chilli sauce.

Filling:

1 teaspoon pounded preserved soya bean	
1 teaspoon sugar	**A**
½ teaspoon msg	
½ teaspoon salt	

455 g (1 lb) Chinese turnip
3 tablespoons lard *or* oil
1 tablespoon pounded garlic
55 g (2 oz) small dried prawns, washed

1. Cut turnip into thin strips, immerse in water and drain.

2. Heat oil in pan and fry garlic till light brown, add **A** and fry for short while. Pour in 115 ml water, add dried prawns and bring to the boil.

3. Put in the turnip, stir in pan and cook over moderate heat till almost dry. Cool before use.

Note:
170 g (6 oz) fresh prawns can also be added together with the dried prawns.

STEAMED FISH AND MILK SAUCE SANDWICHES

INGREDIENTS

225 g (8 oz) fish (threadfin)
5 slices ginger
1 teaspoon butter
1 teaspoon light soya sauce
2 tablespoons butter for frying shallots
2 shallots or 1 small onion, thinly sliced
1½ tablespoons plain flour
115 ml (4 fl oz) milk
1 tablespoon spring onions, cut finely
1 hard boiled egg, mashed

Seasoning:
½ teaspoon salt
1 teaspoon sugar
½ teaspoon msg
  Dash of pepper

METHOD

1. Cut fish into two; clean. Place ginger slices in an enamel plate, put fish over and dab with butter and soya sauce. Steam fish over high heat for 10 minutes or till fish is cooked. Remove ginger. Set aside fish and fish stock.

2. Heat butter in a non-stick pan to fry sliced shallots till light brown. Add flour and fry for short while. Reduce heat to low, pour in milk and fish stock. Cook for 1 minute and remove to a plate to cool.

3. Flake fish and mix well with flour mixture. Lastly, add spring onions and mashed egg. Stir in seasoning and cool.

Note:
Keep sandwiches covered with a damp cloth till ready to serve.

Sambals, Pickles and Sauces

Chilli Sauce — Hot

Chilli Sauce — Sweet

Chilli Garam Paste

Dried Chilli Paste

Garam Assam Paste

Luak Chye

Rempah Sambal Udang

Salt Fish Sambal

Sambal Belimbing

Sambal Tempe Udang

Sambal Tumis

Sambal Lengkong

Sambal Udang Kering Goreng

Achar (page 148)

CHILLI SAUCE — HOT

INGREDIENTS

625 g (22 oz) red chillies
55 g (2 oz) dried chillies
8 cloves garlic
1 thumb-sized piece ginger, skinned and sliced
5 tablespoons salt
455 g (16 oz) sugar
170 ml (6 fl oz) rice vinegar

METHOD

1. Remove stems from chillies.

2. Boil the dried chillies in a saucepan, using a little water, for 2 minutes. Leave to soak for 5 minutes. Wash chillies till the water is clear. Drain in a colander.

3. Put half of the chillies in a electric blender. Pour in 285 ml (10 fl oz) water and turn the control to high to blend chillies till very fine. Remove and set aside. Repeat process with the other half of the chillies, adding the garlic and ginger.

4. Combine the liquidized chilli mixture and the remaining water in an enamel saucepan. Add the salt and bring to boil over a moderate heat, stirring constantly for 10 minutes.

5. Stir in the sugar. Bring chilli sauce to the boil. Lower the heat and continue simmering for 1½ hours, stirring occasionally.

6. Add the vinegar, stir and continue boiling for 5 minutes. Remove from the heat. Cool before storing in dry, clean bottles.

CHILLI SAUCE — SWEET

INGREDIENTS

115 g (4 oz) dried chilli paste or 55 g (2 oz) dried chillies 1 tablespoon shrimp paste 55 g (2 oz) whitish pale raisins 85 g (3 oz) ginger, sliced thinly 6 cloves garlic, skin removed	**A**

455 g (1 lb) fresh red chillies
1.12 litres (39 fl oz) water
340 g (12 oz) coarse sugar
4 level tablespoons salt
170 ml (6 fl oz) vinegar

METHOD

1. Remove stems from fresh chillies, wash and drain.

2. Blend **A** and half of the chillies in an electric blender till very fine. Add some water if paste thickens. Keep the paste rotating in bowl.

3. Remove from blender. Repeat process with the rest of the chillies.

4. Pour the rest of the water, sugar and salt into a non-stick saucepan or a heavy aluminium saucepan and bring to the boil. Add the chilli mixture and boil over moderate heat for 20 minutes, stirring occasionally to prevent it from sticking and burning at bottom of pan.

5. Lower heat, continue to cook for 1 hour, stirring occasionally till sauce thickens. Pour mixture into an enamel saucepan. Add the vinegar and boil for another 10 minutes. Leave to cool completely before storing in very dry bottles.

Note:
Fill each bottle to the top with chilli sauce and screw on the plastic cover tightly before storing.

If metal cap is used, line it with a piece of wax paper to prevent rust.

Store in a cool place or refrigerator.

CHILLI GARAM PASTE

INGREDIENTS

605 g (21 oz) fresh red chillies
85 g (3 oz) shrimp paste, cut into tiny pieces
225 ml (8 fl oz) oil
2¼ tablespoons salt
2 tablespoons sugar
85 ml (3 fl oz) water

METHOD

1. Pound chillies and shrimp paste together coarsely.

2. Heat oil in pan. Put in the chilli paste and fry over moderate heat till oil bubbles through and smells fragrant. Add the salt, sugar, water and stir-fry till moist and oily. Leave to cool. Cool completely before packing into a plastic container and store in freezer.

Note:
When the chilli paste hardens, cut into cubes of 4 cm (1½ in), then put it back into the freezer. You can then thaw the amount you need each time.

DRIED CHILLI PASTE

INGREDIENTS

225 g (8 oz) dried chillies

METHOD

1. Remove stems from chillies.

2. Place chillies in a saucepan, three-quarters filled with cold water.

3. Bring to a boil and cook for 5 minutes. Cover pan and leave chillies to soak for 10 minutes. Drain. Place chillies in a large basin, wash till water is clear. Drain in a colander.

4. Using an electric blender, blend half of the chillies with 225 ml (8 oz) water till very fine. Remove paste and repeat process with the other half of the chillies and water.

5. Store chilli paste in a plastic container. Keep in freezer until needed.

Note:
Keep chilli paste rotating whilst blending. Add spoonfuls of water if paste is not rotating.

(Makes approximately 32 tablespoonfuls of chilli paste.)

GARAM ASSAM PASTE

INGREDIENTS

340 g (12 oz) sliced galangal
340 g (12 oz) sliced lemon grass
285 g (10 oz) candlenut   **A**
455 g (1 lb) shrimp paste

680 g (1½ lb) fresh red chillies
1.4 kg (3 lb) onions
40 g (1½ oz) turmeric powder
30 g (1 oz) chilli powder *or* dried chillies ground to a fine paste
710 ml (25 fl oz) oil for frying

METHOD

1. Grind or blend **A** to a very fine paste.

2. Pound fresh chillies and onions separately into rough pieces.

3. Combine everything and mix thoroughly till well blended.

4. Heat an aluminium or iron wok till very hot. Heat oil till smoking hot, add half of the mixture and fry over moderately high heat till oil bubbles through, stirring constantly to prevent paste burning. Add the rest of the paste and keep stirring.

5. Lower heat and keep frying till paste is fragrant and almost dry. Cool completely before packing in 455 g (1 lb) packets in plastic bags or containers. Store in freezer for future use.

LUAK CHYE
(MIXED VEGETABLE PICKLE IN MUSTARD SEASONING)

INGREDIENTS

85 g (3 oz) young ginger
1 carrot
2 radishes
$\left.\right\}$ **A**

115 ml (4 fl oz) vinegar
85 ml (3 fl oz) water
4 tablespoons sugar
¾ level teaspoon salt
$\left.\right\}$ **B**

3 teaspoons salt
1 tablespoon sugar
455 g (1 lb) green mustard, thinly sliced
2–3 tablespoons French mustard

METHOD

1. Slice **A** thinly. Season with 1 teaspoon salt and 1 tablespoon sugar, and set aside for ½ hour. Put vegetables into a wire sieve, rinse with water and squeeze dry with a piece of muslin.

2. Spread vegetables on a tray and leave to air in a sunny place for 1 hour.

3. Repeat process with the green mustard, using 2 teaspoons salt.

4. Boil **B** in an enamel saucepan for 1 minute. Remove from heat to cool.

5. Blend a few spoonfuls of the vinegar mixture with the French mustard, then pour in the rest of the vinegar.

6. Mix the sliced vegetables together, put them into a large porcelain jar or glass bottle, pour in the vinegar and stir well. Leave uncovered for 4–6 hours and store in refrigerator for future use. Keep for 1 day before serving.

REMPAH SAMBAL UDANG
(FROZEN SPICY PASTE)

INGREDIENTS

140 g (5 oz) dried chillies
115 g (4 oz) fresh red chillies
905 g (2 lb) shallots *or* onions
4 small cloves garlic
$\left.\right\}$ **A**

455 g (1 lb) grated coconut, white
340 ml (12 fl oz) oil

METHOD

1. Remove stems from chillies, soak dried chillies in hot water for ½ hour to soften. Drain.

2. Grind or blend **A** in an electric blender or food processor to a very fine paste. Remove to a bowl.

3. Use muslin to squeeze coconut for No. 1 milk. Set aside 170–200 ml (6–7 fl oz) in a bowl.

4. Heat an iron or aluminium wok till very hot. Heat the oil, pour in the paste and stir-fry till oil bubbles through and smells fragrant. Add the No. 1 milk and stir for 5 minutes over high heat. Remove paste to a large basin to cool completely. Pack in plastic bags or container when completely cool and store in refrigerator for use.

Note:
Chill in refrigerator or freezer to hasten the cooling process for packing. Stir well so that oil is evenly distributed with paste before packing. This rempah *can be used for fish, prawns and cuttlefish.*

SALT FISH SAMBAL

INGREDIENTS

6 cloves garlic
4 shallots   **A**
1 teaspoon shrimp paste
5 red chillies, seeded

140 g (5 oz) Penang salt fish
170 ml (6 fl oz) oil for frying salt fish
10 red and 10 green chilli padi, stems removed
2 red tomatoes, cut into thin slices
4 tablespoons water

Seasoning:
2 teaspoons sugar
½ teaspoon msg
1 teaspoon vinegar

METHOD

1. Cut salt fish into thin slices; immerse in cold water for 1 minute. Remove to a colander and drain for 10 minutes.

2. Heat oil in a small aluminium pan. Put in salt fish and fry till pale brown. Remove to a wire sieve to drain and cool (approximately 5 minutes).

3. Reheat the oil till very hot. Return fish and stir in pan for 2 to 3 minutes till light golden brown. Drain oil from fish on absorbent paper and keep in container when cooled. Reserve oil for frying sambal.

4. Pound **A** coarsely. Bash chilli padi very lightly.

5. Heat 3 tablespoons oil reserved from (3) till hot. Stir-fry the pounded mixture till fragrant and lightly browned. Add sliced tomatoes and chilli padi to fry till oil bubbles through. Add 4 tablespoons water, seasoning and cook over moderate heat till mixture is thick and oily. Lastly, put in salt fish just before serving.

Note:
Both fried fish and sambal can be prepared ahead and stored. To serve, reheat sambal and add salt fish.

SAMBAL BELIMBING

INGREDIENTS

115 g (4 oz) shallots, sliced thinly
55 g (2 oz) garlic, sliced thinly   **A**
4 red chillies, sliced thinly slantwise
4 green chillies, sliced thinly slantwise

1 teaspoon shrimp paste
2 candlenuts   **B** *pounded to a fine paste*
1 stalk lemon grass, sliced thinly

455 g (1 lb) sour star fruit (belimbing)
2 level teaspoons salt
455 g (1 lb) small prawns
455 g (1 lb) grated coconut, white
Oil for frying

Seasoning:
1 teaspoon salt
1½ teaspoons sugar
½ teaspoon msg

METHOD

1. Remove stems of sour star fruit and slice into thin rounds.

2. Rub salt into fruit and marinate for 1 hour. Rinse and squeeze lightly and set aside.

3. Shell and clean prawns. Set aside.

4. Squeeze grated coconut for approximately 225 ml (8 fl oz) of No. 1 milk. Set aside.

5. Heat oil in kuali. Fry **A** separately till light brown. Remove to a plate.

6. In a clean kuali, heat 4 tablespoons of oil and fry **B** till fragrant.

7. Add fruit and half of No. 1 milk with 4 tablespoons water. Cook for 10 minutes over low heat.

8. Add seasoning, prawns and cook till prawns change colour. Pour and stir in remainder of No. 1 milk.

SAMBAL TEMPE UDANG
(SPICY PASTE WITH FERMENTED
SOYA BEAN CAKE AND PRAWNS)

INGREDIENTS

115 g (4 oz) shallots or onions
   (preferably shallots)
 55 g (2 oz) garlic
115 g (4 oz) red chillies, sliced slantwise
115 g (4 oz) green chillies, sliced slantwise
   4 stalks lemon grass, thinly sliced   **A**

Seasoning:
 2 tablespoons sugar
 1 teaspoon msg
 1 teaspoon salt   **B**

2 tablespoons tamarind, mixed with
   4 tablespoons water and strained   **C**

285 g (10 oz) very small prawns
 10 fermented soya bean cakes (5 packets)
  4 large soya bean cakes
340 ml (12 fl oz) oil
285 g (10 oz) long beans, cut into 3 cm (1¼ in)
   lengths, slantwise
   Pinch of salt
 1 teaspoon sugar
 4 tablespoons oil
2–3 tablespoons dry chilli paste
605 g (21 oz) grated coconut, squeezed for 225 ml
   (8 fl oz) No. 1 milk

METHOD

1. Wash prawns, cut sharp points and tail; drain.

2. Cut fermented soya bean cake into cubes, approximately 1.5 cm (½ in). Immerse in slightly salted water and drain immediately. Set aside. Cut soya bean cake into the same size as the fermented soya bean cake and repeat process. Set aside.

3. Heat 225 ml (8 fl oz) oil in a non-stick frying pan till hot. Fry soya bean cake, fermented soya bean cake and the contents of **A** separately and in order till lightly browned. Set aside in a plate.

4. Add 115 ml (4 fl oz) oil in pan and fry prawns with a pinch of salt till shells are crisp and almost dry. Drain in a colander. Pour oil away, leaving 2 tablespoons to fry the long beans till soft (approximately 2 minutes). Add a pinch of salt and 1 teaspoon sugar. Mix well and remove to a plate.

5. In a clean wok, heat 4 tablespoons oil to fry the chilli paste for ½ minute, add in the No. 1 milk, seasoning (**B**) and tamarind water (**C**). Keep stirring over moderate heat till mixture boils, then put in all the fried ingredients.

6. Increase heat, stir well in pan and cook till almost dry. Spread on to a large tray to cool.

SAMBAL TUMIS
(BASIC SAMBAL)

INGREDIENTS

15 shallots
30 dried chillies *or* 3 tablespoons chilli paste★
 1 tablespoon shrimp paste
 1 clove garlic   **A**

 1 teaspoon sugar
 ½ teaspoon salt
   Pinch of msg
 1 tablespoon tamarind with 55 ml (2 fl oz)
   water, squeezed and strained   **B**

 6 tablespoons oil
115 g (4 oz) grated coconut squeezed with 55 ml
   water for milk

METHOD

1. Grind **A** to a paste.

2. Heat oil and fry paste over moderate heat till oil bubbles through.

3. Add half of the coconut milk and stir for 2 minutes. Add **B**. Cover and cook for another 2 minutes. Add the rest of the coconut milk. Stir for 1 minute and serve.

★See page 185.

SAMBAL LENGKONG
(CRISPY FISH GRANULES)

INGREDIENTS

340 g (12 oz) shallots
  8 candlenuts
  3 red chillies, seeded   **A**
14 slices galangal, weighing 55 g (2 oz)
  6 stalks lemon grass, finely sliced

1.2 kg (43 oz) grated coconut
225 ml (8 fl oz) water
1.2 kg (2 lb 11 oz) wolf-herring, washed
  2 teaspoons salt
  5 tablespoons sugar, mixed with
    3 tablespoons hot water
10 lime leaves

METHOD

1. Pound **A** to a fine paste.

2. Use a piece of muslin to squeeze the coconut for No. 1 milk. Add water to the grated coconut and squeeze for No. 2 milk.

3. Place fish in a deep plate. Pour in the No. 2 milk and steam over a high heat till fish is cooked. Remove and put aside.

4. Mix the fish stock with the No. 1 milk and the paste. Add salt.

5. Debone and flake fish very finely. Add to the fish stock and mix well.

6. Heat an iron wok. Pour in the fish mixture to fry over a moderate heat till almost dry, stirring all the time. Reduce the heat to very low and sprinkle the sweetened water. Add the lime leaves and fry until the fish granules are crispy and light brown in colour, stirring constantly.

Note:
To test if the fish granules are crispy, press them between thumb and finger. They should be grainy. Cool before storing in an airtight bottle. Steamed fish should be mashed till fine whilst still hot. A mincer may also be used.

SAMBAL UDANG KERING GORENG
(FRIED DRIED PRAWNS)

INGREDIENTS

  6 candlenuts
  1 thumb-sized piece turmeric   **A**
  1 teaspoon shrimp paste

  6 tablespoons sugar
½ tablespoon salt
  3 tablespoons tamarind with 140 ml   **B**
    (5 fl oz) water, squeezed and strained
340 g (12 oz) dried prawns, soaked and
    pounded till fine

115 g (4 oz) green chillies
115 g (4 oz) red chillies
115 g (4 oz) garlic   **C**
225 g (8 oz) shallots
  10 stalks lemon grass

285 ml (10 fl oz) oil

METHOD

1. Pound **A** to a paste. Add **B** and mix thoroughly.

2. Slice **C** finely. (The lemon grass should be sliced slantwise.)

3. Heat oil in wok. Fry sliced ingredients separately till light brown. Remove.

4. Leave oil in wok and fry the dried prawn mixture over a low heat till almost dry. Add all the fried ingredients.

5. Stir-fry for 5 minutes and remove to a tray to cool.

Note:
Stir the dried prawn mixture constantly when cooking to prevent it from burning. This dish can be kept for months if stored in a refrigerator. When using an electric blender, do not soak or wash the dried prawns. Blend a little at a time.

Nonya Kueh

Apom Berkuah

Abok-Abok Sago

Kueh Bangket

Kueh Bengka Ambon

Kueh Bengka Ubi Kayu

Kueh Bolu

Savory Kueh Bolu

Kueh Dadar

Kueh Khoo

Kueh Ko Chee

Kueh Ko Swee

Kueh Lapis Batavia

Kueh Lapis Almond

Kueh Lapis Beras

Kueh Lompang

Kueh Pulot Bengka

Kueh Lopis

Kueh Pisang

Kueh Sarlat

Kueh Talam Pandan

Jemput-jemput

Onde Onde

Pulot Panggang

Pulot Tarpay

Pulot Tartar

Sar-sargon

Seray-kaya

Clockwise: Kueh Ko Chee, Bengka Ambon, Apom Berkuah with Sauce

APOM BERKUAH

INGREDIENTS

¾ teaspoon dry yeast (ground to a fine
    powder) or ½ teaspoons fresh yeast
4 tablespoons plain flour   **A**
1 teaspoon castor sugar
5 tablespoons coconut water, lukewarm

340 g (12 oz) rice flour
  2 tablespoons glutinous rice flour   **B**
  1 level teaspoon fine salt
310 ml (11 fl oz) cold water

1.6 kg (3½ lb) coconut, white
285 ml (10 fl oz) coconut water, lukewarm
½ teaspoon lime juice
    Few drops of food colouring

METHOD

1. Squeeze coconut for No. 1 milk. Measure
   285 ml (10 fl oz) for the batter and another
   340 ml (12 fl oz) for the sauce. Put in separate bowls. Add 1.1 litre (2 pints) water to
   the grated coconut and squeeze for No. 2
   milk. Measure 370 ml (13 fl oz) for the batter and another 735 ml (26 fl oz) for the
   sauce. Put in separate bowls and set aside.

2. Mix **A**, stir lightly and set aside for 4–
   6 minutes till frothy.

3. Heat the 285 ml No. 1 milk gently over low
   heat till it turns creamy and thick, stirring
   all the time. Do not overboil. Set aside.

4. Combine **B** in a bowl and pour in the
   370 ml No. 2 milk and **A**. Beat with palm
   of hand till mixture turns to a smooth batter. Add in the 285 ml lukewarm coconut
   water and continue beating for 2 minutes,
   then pour in the creamy No. 1 milk from
   Method 3. Beat till well blended.

5. Cover bowl and leave to stand in a warm
   place for 1–2 hours. Beat lightly with a
   wooden spoon at intervals of 10 minutes.
   To test if batter is ready, take a tablespoon
   of batter and fry in a slightly greased pan.
   Batter is only ready when the cake breaks
   into bubbles and forms holes all over.

6. Pour 140 ml (5 fl oz) of the batter in a cup,
   stir in the food colouring and lime juice. Set
   aside.

To fry the apom (using a special apom berkuah pan)
1. Heat pan till very hot, remove from heat
   and slightly grease each patty pan with oil.
   Return pan to moderately high heat. Stir
   batter well and pour white batter to fill up
   all the patty pans. Take ½ teaspoon of the
   coloured batter and spread in a circular motion over the white batter immediately before it starts to bubble. Reduce heat when
   the cake bubbles and breaks into tiny holes
   all over.

2. Sprinkle water all over pan, cover with lid
   and cook for another 4–5 minutes. Loosen
   cake with edge of knife and place on a cake
   rack to cool. Oil pan each time before you
   fry the rest of the batter.

Sauce for the apom:
  55 g (2 oz) rice flour
    3 tablespoons plain flour   **A**
225 ml (8 fl oz) No. 2 milk

225 g (8 oz) palm sugar, finely grated
140 g (5 oz) coarse sugar
115 ml (4 fl oz) water   **B**
  8 screw pine leaves, cut into short lengths
¾ teaspoon salt

  10 bananas (pisang rajah)
510 ml (18 fl oz) No. 2 milk
340 ml (12 fl oz) No. 1 milk

METHOD

1. Steam the bananas for 7 minutes. Leave to
   cool. Slice.

2. Blend **A** till smooth. Set aside. Combine **B**
   in a saucepan and bring to boil. Boil for
   5 minutes, then add 510 ml No. 2 milk and
   bring to boil again. Strain into a heavy aluminium saucepan.

3. Reduce heat, pour the flour mixture into
   saucepan gradually, stirring all the time.
   Allow to boil gently before adding the 340
   ml No. 1 milk. Add the sliced bananas and
   stir till just boiling. Do not overboil or
   sauce will turn oily and lose its richness.
   Remove the screw pine leaves.

4. Remove from heat, pour sauce into a large
   mixing or china bowl. Stand bowl in a basin
   of cold water to cool, stirring for a moment.

ABOK ABOK SAGO

INGREDIENTS

115 g (4 oz) pearl sago
170 g (6 oz) grated palm sugar
  2 tablespoons coarse sugar
¾–1 teaspoon fine salt
285 g (10 oz) coarsely grated coconut, white
    Few drops of blue food colouring
    4 screw pine leaves, tied into a knot

METHOD

1. Wash and soak pearl sago in cold water for 15 minutes. Drain.

2. Mix the grated palm sugar with the sugar.

3. Sprinkle salt over coconut, mix evenly and combine with the pearl sago in a bowl.

4. Mix one-third of the sago mixture with a few drops of blue food colouring. Put aside.

5. Place the white sago mixture in a shallow oval or round heatproof dish, sprinkle the sugar evenly over it and cover sugar with the blue sago mixture. Place the screw pine leaves on top.

6. Steam over rapidly boiling water for 15–20 minutes.

Using banana leaves to steam:
Wash and scald 10 pieces banana leaves 22 cm × 15 cm (9 in × 6 in). Fold into a cone and staple the edge. Fill with sago mixtures as in Method 5. Put a small piece of screw pine leaf on top before folding over. Secure with stapler and steam for 15–20 minutes.

Note:
Leave a 1.25 cm (½ in) margin round sides of sago mixture when you sprinkle the grated sugar. This will prevent the sugar from melting down the sides of the bowl.

KUEH BANGKET

INGREDIENTS

225 g (8 oz) rice flour
455 g (1 lb) tapioca flour

455 g (1 lb) grated coconut, white, squeezed for 225 ml (8 fl oz) No. 1 milk
  5 eggs
395 g (14 oz) sugar
  ¾ teaspoon salt

METHOD

To prepare the flour:
1. Stir rice flour and tapioca flour separately in a dry iron wok over low heat till very light and fluffy.

2. Mix and sift the two types of flour together into a basin. Leave overnight.

To make biscuits:
1. Using a piece of muslin, squeeze coconut for No. 1 milk. Set aside.

2. Beat eggs and sugar till thick and creamy. Add the salt and No. 1 milk. Beat till well blended.

3. Set aside 115 g (4 oz) of the sifted flour for dusting and 1 teacup of the egg mixture.

4. Mix the remaining egg mixture into the flour to form a dough. Take a handful of the dough and place it on a dusted board or a marble table top. (Keep the rest of the dough covered with a damp cloth.)

5. Flatten the dough with palm of hand. Dust with flour and roll dough out to 0.5 cm thickness.

6. Cut dough with a round pastry cutter. Pinch biscuit, using a jagged-edged pair of pincers (usually used for pineapple tarts), to form a pattern.

7. Mix leftover dough cuttings with another lot of new dough and a little of the beaten egg mixture each time. Mix to a smooth texture before rolling out and repeating process.

8. Place biscuits on greased trays and bake in a moderate oven at 175°C or Regulo 6 for 20–30 minutes. Cool biscuits on a rack before storing in an airtight tin.

KUEH BENGKA AMBON
(HONEYCOMB CAKE)

INGREDIENTS

30 g (1 oz) fresh yeast or
  1 tablespoon dry yeast
  2 teaspoons sugar   **A**
55 g (2 oz) flour
115 ml (4 fl oz) warm water

680 g (1½ lb) grated coconut, white
  6 screw pine leaves, tied into a knot
340 g (12 oz) sugar
170 g (6 oz) sago flour *or* corn flour
  6 eggs, lightly beaten
  ½ teaspoon vanilla essence
  ½ teaspoon salt
  2 drops yellow food colouring

METHOD

1. Combine **A** in a bowl. Stir till batter is smooth and leave in a warm place till frothy (about 15 minutes).

2. Squeeze coconut in small handfuls through a piece of muslin for 340 ml (12 fl oz) No. 1 milk. Set aside in a bowl.

3. Cook coconut milk, screw pine leaves and sugar over very low heat till sugar is dissolved. Stir to prevent burning at the bottom of the pan. Cool. Do not allow the milk to boil. Remove the screw pine leaves.

4. Put sago flour in a mixing bowl. Add beaten eggs, vanilla essence and salt and mix by hand to form a smooth batter. Add the coconut milk mixture, yellow food colouring and stir till well combined.

5. Add the risen yeast dough. Mix till well blended. Rinse mixing bowl with boiling water. Wipe dry and pour batter into bowl. Cover bowl. Put in a warm place and leave for 4-5 hours.

To bake ambon:

Heat brass cake mould over charcoal fire. Brush with corn oil or boiled coconut oil. Stir the batter, fill three quarters of mould and cook over moderate heat till cake bubbles right through to the surface, resembling a honeycomb.

To brown top of cakes:

Place all the cakes on a tray. Put tray 10 cm (4 in) from the heat under a hot grill for 3–5 minutes to brown the surface of the cakes. Cool on a wire rack.

Note:
Bengka ambon can also be baked in a single heavy brass mould or brass 'kueh bolu' mould, uncovered. Charcoal fire is better as the heat is more evenly distributed than in electric or gas rings.

Note: (Coconut oil)
To make oil for greasing patty tins for extra fragrance:— Boil 1 cup oil with 115 g (4 oz) grated coconut and 4 screw pine leaves cut into pieces till coconut turns light brown. Strain and cool before use. When using desiccated coconut, dampen slightly before boiling. Keep in refrigerator for future use.

KUEH BENGKA UBI KAYU
(NONYA TAPIOCA CAKE)

INGREDIENTS

1.4 kg (3lbs) tapioca, finely grated
905 g (2 lbs) grated coconut, white

480 g (17 oz) castor sugar
  3 teaspoons sago or cornflour
  3 eggs, beaten lightly
  1 tablespoon butter, melted   **A**
1½ teaspoons vanilla essence
1½ level teaspoons salt

METHOD

1. Preheat oven to 177°C. Add 1 cup cold water to grated tapioca and squeeze water out with a piece of muslin into a small saucepan. Set tapioca aside and allow tapioca water to stand for tapioca starch to settle at the bottom of pan. After approximately half hour, pour water away carefully to collect starch. Mix tapioca starch with grated tapioca.

2. Squeeze coconut for No. 1 milk. Measure 455 ml (16 fl oz) into a bowl and set aside. Add 170 ml (6 fl oz) water to coconut and squeeze out 170 ml of No. 2 milk. Set aside.

3. Combine Ingredients **A** with No. 2 milk and whisk lightly till blended. Pour mixture into a heavy aluminium saucepan and cook over moderate heat till heated through and sugar dissolves. Add No. 1 milk and cook for another minute.

4. Put grated tapioca into a large mixing bowl. Pour in the hot egg and coconut mixture and stir till well blended.

5. Grease a square baking tin (20 × 20 × 4 cm) on base and sides. Cut a strip of grease proof paper to line the sides of the tin, allowing ½ cm clearance from sides. Grease paper and dust tin with flour.

6. Put tapioca mixture into tin and bake for 10-15 minutes or till cake turns light brown. Reduce heat to 135°C and cook for another 1-1¼ hour or till cake is golden brown.

7. Remove from oven and allow to cool for 10 minutes. Remove cake from tin and allow to cool completely before cutting.

KUEH BOLU
(NONYA SPONGE CUP CAKE)

INGREDIENTS

170 g (6 oz) plain flour
1½ teaspoons baking powder
5 eggs
155 g (5 oz) castor sugar

METHOD

1. Preheat oven to 205°C (400°F). Sift flour and baking powder twice. Divide into two equal parts. Set aside.

2. Beat eggs and sugar till very thick and creamy. Divide into two portions.

3. Sift one portion of the flour over one portion of the egg mixture. Fold very lightly as for sponge sandwich.

4. Spoon batter into greased and heated Kueh Bolu pans till ¾ filled. Bake in 205°C for 5 minutes then reduce heat to 150°C (300°F) till cake turns golden brown. Remove to cooling rack with fork.

5. Repeat with remaining egg and flour. Wait till temperature reaches 205°C before baking. Bake at once when batter is spooned into the moulds. Do not leave to stand.

6. Cool cakes completely before keeping in an air-tight container.

SAVORY KUEH BOLU
(NONYA SPONGE CAKE WITH MINCEMEAT FILLING)

INGREDIENTS

285 g (10 oz) lean pork
55 g (2 oz) shallots, chopped finely
1 clove garlic, chopped finely
2 level teaspoons roasted coriander seeds, ground
4 tablespoons oil
Pork stock, approx. 225 ml (8 oz)

Seasoning:
½ teaspoon salt
3 rounded tablespoons sugar
½ teaspoon pepper
1 teaspoon msg
2–3 teaspoons black sauce

2 large eggs
55 g (2 oz) castor sugar
70 g (2½ oz) plain flour (sifted twice)
2 tablespoons evaporated milk

METHOD

1. Boil whole piece of pork with 285 ml (10 fl oz) water, ¼ teaspoon each of salt and msg for 20 minutes. Remove pork and keep stock. Dice pork into very small pieces.

2. Heat the oil in pan to fry the garlic and shallots till lightly browned. Add in the pork and seasoning, stir well and cook for 2 minutes. Add in the coriander and a third of the pork stock. Stir over moderate heat for 10 minutes.

3. Pour in the rest of the stock and cook till mixture is dry and oily.

4. Beat eggs and sugar till very thick and creamy about 15–20 minutes. Add in the evaporated milk and beat for ½ a minute.

5. Fold in sifted flour gently till blended. Heat bolu pan for 5 minutes, brush with oil and spoon batter to fill ⅔ of each mould. Add in a teaspoon filling and cover filling with batter. Bake in a heated oven for 5–6 minutes till golden brown.

KUEH DADAR

(COCONUT ROLLS WITH COCONUT SAUCE)

INGREDIENTS

Batter:

½ teaspoon salt
2 tablespoons oil
4 large eggs, lightly beaten   **A**
225 g (8 oz) flour
1 tablespoon sago flour

565 g (20 oz) grated coconut, white, for No. 1 milk
Different shades of food colouring

METHOD

1. Extract 225 ml (8 fl oz) No. 1 milk from grated coconut. Set aside. Add 455 ml (16 fl oz) water to grated coconut and squeeze again to obtain 225 ml (8 fl oz) No. 2 milk. Set aside.

2. Blend the two types of coconut milk together with **A** and mix till smooth. Strain into another bowl. Divide batter into three or four portions. Add a few drops of different shades of food colouring to each portion. Stir well. Let stand for ½ hour.

3. Heat an omelette pan. When hot, remove pan from the heat and grease base. Pour just enough batter to cover the base of the pan thinly. Fry pancake till edges curl slightly upwards. Pile pancakes on a plate to cool before filling.

4. Fill each pancake with 2 tablespoonfuls of coconut filling. Fold to enclose filling, then roll.

Filling:

3 tablespoons sugar
285 g (10 oz) grated palm sugar
3 tablespoons water   **A**
6 screw pine leaves

565 g (20 oz) grated coconut, white
1 tablespoon sago flour mixed with 2 tablespoons water

Boil **A** to dissolve sugar. Add coconut, lower heat, stirring till almost dry. Add flour and cook for 5 min. Cool.

Sauce:

680 g (24 oz) grated coconut, white
455 ml (16 fl oz) water
3 tablespoons plain flour
55 g (2 oz) wet rice flour *or* 3 tablespoons rice flour
1 teaspoon salt
1 tablespoon sugar
6 screw pine leaves, tied into a knot

METHOD

1. Squeeze grated coconut for No. 1 milk. Set aside. Add 455 ml (16 fl oz) water to grated coconut and squeeze again for No. 2 milk. Measure milk and add water to bring it up to 855 ml (2 pints).

2. Mix 225 ml (8 fl oz) of the No. 2 milk with the two types of flour. Set aside.

3. Bring the rest of the No. 2 milk together with the salt, sugar and screw pine leaves to nearly boiling point in a saucepan.

4. Remove saucepan from heat. Add the flour mixture gradually to the hot milk, stirring all the time. Add No. 1 milk.

5. Return saucepan to the heat and allow mixture to boil over a very low heat, stirring constantly. Remove and pour sauce into a large bowl to cool.

6. Serve with coconut rolls.

Wet rice or glutinous rice flour:
To 22 oz of fine rice or glutinous rice flour, gradually add 15–17 oz of cold water and stir till it becomes a firm paste. Use the amount required for each recipe and keep the remainder in the freezer for future use. The paste will keep in the freezer for 1–2 months if stored in plastic bags flattened to one inch thick slabs.
Recommended brands: "Superior Quality Thai Rice and Glutinous Rice Flour" (Three Elephant Heads trade mark); "Fine Rice Flour" (Sea Gull trade mark); freshly ground wet rice or glutinous rice flour obtainable from Singapore markets, e.g. Joo Chiat Market.

Note:
For the pancakes, use an omelette pan with a 16.5 cm (6½ in) base.

(22 pieces)

KUEH KHOO

(STEAMED GLUTINOUS RICE PASTE
WITH SWEET GREEN BEAN FILLING)

INGREDIENTS

2 tablespoons sugar
2 tablespoons oil   **A**
½ teaspoon salt

115 g (4 oz) sweet potato
680 g (1½ lb) grated coconut, white
455 g (1 lb) glutinous rice flour
    Red food colouring
20 pieces of banana leaves, cut to fit size of mould

METHOD

1. Peel sweet potato, cut into pieces and boil gently. When tender press through a ricer whilst still hot.

2. Squeeze coconut through muslin for No. 1 milk. Set aside 285 ml (10 fl oz) in a bowl. Add 170 ml (6 fl oz) water to the coconut and squeeze for 170 ml (6 fl oz) No. 2 milk. Add **A** and set aside in a small bowl.

3. Combine the sweet potato with 285 g (10 oz) of the glutinous rice flour in a large mixing bowl. Set aside.

4. Bring the No. 2 milk mixture to the boil in a small saucepan. Add a few drops of red food colouring and remove from heat. Pour in the rest of the glutinous rice flour and stir well.

5. Remove hot dough to flour and sweet potato mixture in mixing bowl. Pour in the No. 1 milk gradually and mix well to form a dough. Place dough on a lightly floured board (using glutinous rice flour for dusting) and knead lightly to form a smooth dough. Put dough in a bowl and cover with a damp cloth till ready for filling.

Filling:
565 g (20 oz) skinned green beans, washed, soaked overnight and drained
  8 screw pine leaves, tied into a knot
625 g (22 oz) coarse sugar

METHOD

1. Steam the green beans till soft\ (20 minutes) and pass through the ricer whilst hot. Set aside.

2. Boil 140 ml (5 fl oz) water in an iron wok. Add the screw pine leaves and sugar and boil over a low heat till the sugar turns syrupy.

3. Add the mashed beans, mix well and cook mixture until almost dry, stirring all the time. Remove the screw pine leaves and let the mixture cool.

4. Form the sweet filling into 20 small balls and place them on a tray till ready for filling.

To mould kuey khoo:
1. Pour 115 ml (4 fl oz) corn or boiled coconut oil (*see page 194*) into a cup. Oil palms of hands and divide dough into 20 equal parts. Roll each part into a ball, make a well in each ball to hold a piece of sweet filling and bring up the sides to cover.

2. Oil palms of hands again and roll cakes till well-rounded. Place each cake in centre of mould and press cake firmly till it fills the mould to obtain a deep impression of the pattern. Turn out each cake on to a piece of banana leaf. Repeat process with the rest of the dough.

To steam kueh khoo:
1. Place the kueh khoos on a perforated steamer tray and steam over medium heat for 7–10 minutes. The water in the steamer must be boiling gently, or cakes will not retain its pattern. Wipe lid of steamer to prevent water dripping down to the cakes.

2. Remove cakes to a rack. Brush cakes lightly with oil whilst still hot. Cover with a big piece of banana leaf till ready to serve. This will keep the cakes soft and moist.

KUEH KO CHEE
(STEAMED GLUTINOUS RICE PASTE WITH COCONUT FILLING)

INGREDIENTS

20 banana leaves, 20 cm (8 in) in diameter
455 g (1 lb) grated coconut, white
115 g (4 oz) sweet potato
395 g (14 oz) glutinous rice flour
    Pinch of salt
  2 tablespoons sugar
  2 tablespoons oil (corn or refined oil)
  2 drops blue food colouring

METHOD

1. Wipe banana leaves with a wet cloth and scald in a saucepan of boiling water for 1 minute. Drain in a colander.

2. Squeeze coconut for 200 ml (7 fl oz) No. 1 milk. Set aside. Add 115 ml (4 fl oz) water to coconut and squeeze for No. 2 milk. Set aside.

3. Boil sweet potato gently till cooked and pass through a potato ricer or mash till smooth. Mix well with 225 g (8 oz) of the flour and set aside.

4. Boil the No. 2 milk, salt, sugar and oil in a saucepan. Add the 2 drops of blue food colouring, remove from heat, and add the remaining flour. Stir lightly. Cool for 1 minute.

5. Put the sweet potato-and-flour mixture in a saucepan, add the No. 1 milk and stir with wooden ladle till it forms a paste. Add mixture from Method 4 and rub the paste lightly to form a smooth firm dough. Add a little flour if dough is too soft.

6. Divide dough into 4 parts and cut each part into 16 pieces. Roll each piece into a ball, put in a knob of coconut filling and seal. Fold each banana leaf into a cone, put in the filled paste, and fold the top over to form a triangle. Staple the ends to secure. Repeat with the rest of the paste and steam over moderately high heat for 15 minutes.

Filling:

  3 tablespoons sugar
285 g (10 oz) grated palm sugar   **A**
  3 tablespoons water
  6 screw pine leaves

565 g (20 oz) grated coconut, white
  1 tablespoon pearl sago, mixed with 2 tablespoons water

METHOD

1. Boil **A** in an iron wok until the sugar turns syrupy.

2. Add grated coconut and lower the heat. Stir mixture constantly till almost dry.

3. Add the sago mixture. Stir thoroughly. Cook for another 5 minutes. Remove to a tray to cool.

Note:
A simpler way of bundling kueh ko chee is to put filling in centre of each piece of paste, cover to form a ball, put on a square piece of softened banana leaf and fold into a neat bundle. Staple the ends and steam.
Store leftover filling in a plastic container in freezer for future use.

KUEH KO SWEE
(RICE CUP CAKES)

INGREDIENTS

285 g (10 oz) wet rice flour⋆
285 g (10 oz) sago flour
570 ml (1¼ pints) cold water   **A**
  3 tablespoons alkaline water

455 g (16 oz) palm sugar
225 g (8 oz) coarse sugar
 10 screw pine leaves, cut into 5 cm (2 in) lengths   **B**
455 ml (16 fl oz) water

455 g (16 oz) grated coconut, white, mixed with a pinch of fine salt

METHOD

1. Mix **A** in a bowl.

2. Boil **B** for 10 minutes.

3. Strain the hot boiled syrup gradually into the flour mixture, stirring with a wooden spoon till well mixed.

4. Steam small empty cups for 5 minutes. Fill cups with flour mixture and steam over a high heat for 7 minutes. Cool and remove cake from each cup. Roll cakes in grated coconut before serving.

To make alkaline water:
625 g (22 oz) white alkaline crystal balls, obtainable from local markets
680 ml (24 fl oz) hot water

1. Place alkaline crystal balls in a porcelain jar. Add the hot water and stir with a wooden spoon till the crystal balls dissolve. Allow to stand overnight.
2. Strain alkaline water through fine muslin. Store the alkaline water in a bottle for future use.

Note:
Prepared alkaline water can be kept for almost a year. Store in a bottle.

*See page 196.

KUEH LAPIS BATAVIA
(INDONESIAN LAYER CAKE)

INGREDIENTS

455 g (1 lb) butter
1 teaspoon mixed spice (see recipe)
115 g (4 oz) flour
17 egg yolks
5 egg whites
255 g (9 oz) sugar
2 tablespoons brandy

To prepare batter:
1. Beat butter till creamy.
2. Sift mixed spice and flour together.
3. Place egg yolks and egg whites in two separate bowls.
4. Beat egg yolks with 200 g (7 oz) sugar till thick.
5. Beat egg whites with the remaining sugar till thick.

6. Fold in alternately, the egg yolk mixture and the egg white mixture to the creamed butter, adding a little flour each time. Lastly, add the brandy.

To bake the cake:
1. Grease bottom and sides of tin with butter.
2. Cut a piece of greaseproof paper in to fit base of tin exactly. Place paper in and grease with butter.
3. Heat grill till moderately hot. Place greased tin under grill for 1 minute. Remove and place in one ladleful of cake mixture. Spread mixture evenly and bake for 5 minutes or till light brown. Remove tin from grill and, using a fine sharp skewer or satay stick, prick top of cake to prevent air bubbles from forming.
4. Add another ladleful of cake mixture. Bake and repeat process as for the first layer, till the cake mixture is used up. Remove cake from tin at once. Turn it over, top side up, on to a cooling rack to cool for ½ hour.

MIXED SPICE

INGREDIENTS

30 g (1 oz) cinnamon bark
20 cloves
1 star anise
20 pieces green cardamom

METHOD

1. Wash cinnamon bark, cloves and star anise. Air in the sun till very dry.
2. Remove the rounded tips from the cloves.
3. Place all the dried ingredients in a heated frying pan to fry over a low heat for 20 minutes.
4. Remove the whitish covering from the cardamom to extract the seeds.
5. Pound the spices together till very fine. Pass them through a fine sieve and store in a clean dry bottle.

KUEH LAPIS ALMOND

INGREDIENTS

85 g (3 oz) SoftasSilk flour
1 teaspoon mixed spice★
255 g (9 oz) castor sugar
375 g (13 oz) butter
2 tablespoons condensed milk
15 egg yolks
5 egg whites
¼ teaspoon cream of tartar
2½ tablespoons brandy
100 g (4 oz) almond powder

METHOD

1. Sift flour and spice 3 times. Divide sugar into 3 portions.

2. Cream butter with 1 part sugar till creamy. Add condensed milk and beat till well blended. Whisk egg yolks with 2nd portion sugar till creamy and thick.

   Whisk egg white with 3rd portion sugar till frothy. Sprinkle cream of tartar and continue to beat till soft peaks form.

3. Scoop butter mixture into a large bowl, fold egg white and flour alternately with the brandy. Fold in almond powder.

4. Grease an 18 cm (7 in) square tin at base and sides with butter. Cut a piece of grease-proof paper to fill base exactly. Dust with extra flour at sides of tin.

5. Heat oven to moderately high. Heat tin for 2 minutes. Scoop about ½ cup of the batter into tin, use spoon to spread evenly then place tin in oven to bake for 5 minutes till light golden brown. Remove tin. Use satay stick to prick holes around cake. Repeat process with the rest of the batter.

6. Remove cake from oven, turn over to cool on cake rack for 20 minutes. Turn over again and cool completely. Cut into pieces to serve.

Note:
Spread batter evenly with a small flattened tablespoon before baking. Piercing holes in cake helps each layer to merge with the next. This will prevent the cake from splitting when cut into thin pieces.

★*See page 199.*

KUEH LAPIS BERAS
(RAINBOW LAYER CAKE)

INGREDIENTS

680 g (24 oz) grated coconut, white
340 g (12 oz) wet rice flour★
225 g (8 oz) sago flour
¼ teaspoon salt
455 g (16 oz) coarse sugar

8 screw pine leaves, tied into a knot
Different shades of food colouring

METHOD

1. Add 570 ml (20 fl oz) water to the grated coconut and squeeze for milk, using a piece of muslin. Add water to bring it to 855 ml (30 fl oz).

2. Place the two types of flour and salt in a bowl; add the coconut milk a little at a time and mix till smooth. Set aside.

3. Boil the sugar with 285 ml (10 fl oz) water and the screw pine leaves for 10 minutes over a moderate heat. Strain the syrup into a bowl. Measure it and add hot water if necessary to bring it to 425 ml (15 fl oz).

4. Pour the hot boiled syrup gradually into the flour mixture, stirring all the time till it is well blended.

5. Divide the flour mixture into four portions. Set aside one portion to remain uncoloured and add a few drops of different shades of food colouring to the other three portions. (Set aside 140 ml (5 fl oz) of the uncoloured mixture to be coloured dark red for the top layer.)

6. Grease an 18 cm (7 in) diameter × 5 cm (2 in) deep cake tin with oil. Place tin in steamer of rapidly boiling water. Pour 140 ml (5 fl oz) of different coloured batters for each layer and steam for 5–6 minutes each time, till mixture is used up.

7. For the final top layer, use the dark red batter. Remove cake to cool for at least 7–8 hours before cutting.

★*See "Wet Rice Flour" on page 196.*

KUEH LOMPANG

(STEAMED RICE CAKES WITH
GRATED COCONUT TOPPING)

INGREDIENTS

140 g (5 oz) rice flour
 1 heaped tablespoon tapioca flour
285 g (10 oz) coarse sugar
 8 screw pine leaves, knotted
 A selection of food colouring
455 g (16 oz) coarsely grated coconut, mixed with a
 pinch of table salt

METHOD

1. Mix the rice and tapioca flour in 75 ml
   (3 fl oz) water. Stir well.

2. Boil sugar and screw pine leaves in 425 ml
   (15 fl oz) water for 5 minutes or till sugar
   dissolves. Pour the syrup gradually through
   a strainer into the flour mixture, stirring all
   the time.

3. Divide the mixture into 3 or 4 portions. Put
   one or two drops of food colouring into
   each portion to make light pastel shades.
   (The colour deepens on steaming so colour
   sparingly).

4. Place small Chinese tea cups in a steamer
   over rapidly boiling water to heat for
   5 minutes. Fill cups with coloured flour
   mixture and steam for 10 minutes. Wipe
   condensation off lid after 5 minutes' steaming.

5. Remove cups and allow cakes to cool for
   about 20 minutes before removing with a
   blunt knife. Roll the cakes in the grated
   coconut and serve.

Note:
*To facilitate filling of small cups, pour mixture from a teapot. Stir
mixture well for an even consistency.*

KUEH PULOT BENGKA

(GLUTINOUS RICE CAKE)

INGREDIENTS

 A 20 cm (8 in) square banana leaf, for lining
 cake tin
680 g (24 oz) grated coconut, white, for No. 1 milk
395 g (14 oz) coarse sugar
 4 screw pine leaves tied into a knot
510 g (18 oz) wet glutinous rice flour★
115 g (4 oz) wet rice flour
 ½ teaspoon salt
340 g (12 oz) coarsely grated coconut, white

METHOD

1. Grease the sides and base of a square cake
   tin, and line it with the banana leaf.

2. Extract 285 ml (10 fl oz) No. 1 milk from
   the grated coconut. Set aside.

3. Cook the sugar, No. 1 milk and the screw
   pine leaves in a heavy-bottomed aluminium
   saucepan over a low heat. Keep stirring all
   the time till the sugar dissolves. Remove
   from the heat.

4. Place the two types of wet flour in a basin.

5. Add the sugary mixture gradually to the
   flour. Mix till well blended. Return the
   mixture to the saucepan, and cook over a
   very low heat, stirring all the time, till the
   mixture becomes thick and gluey (half-
   cooked). Remove from the heat, stir in salt
   and the coarsely grated coconut.

6. Pour mixture into cake tin and bake in oven
   at 190°C (375°F) or Regulo 7 for
   15 minutes. Reduce heat to 175°C (350°F)
   or Regulo 6 and bake for 1–1½ hours or till
   cake is cooked. Leave cake in tin for 20
   minutes before turning it on to a cake rack
   to cool before cutting.

★*See "Wet Rice Flour" on page 196.*

KUEH LOPIS
(GLUTINOUS RICE WITH GRATED COCONUT AND PALM SUGAR SYRUP)

INGREDIENTS

455 g (1 lb) glutinous rice
2 tablespoons alkaline water*
285 g (10 oz) palm sugar
2 tablespoons coarse sugar
5 screw pine leaves cut into pieces
455 g (1 lb) tender grated coconut, white
Pinch of salt

METHOD

1. Wash glutinous rice till water runs clear, place in a container and add water to cover 5 cm (2 in) above level of rice. Add the alkaline water, mix well and evenly and leave to soak for 4 hours.

2. Rinse rice, then drain well, using colander. Set aside for 20 minutes.

3. Make two cloth bags by cutting two pieces of white material measuring 30 cm × 20 cm (12 in × 8 in). Fold the material into halves lengthwise and use running stitch to sew it 0.5 cm from the edge. Use a string to tie one end of the bag 5 cm away from the edge.

4. Pack ½ the rice firmly in 1 bag and tie to resemble a large sausage. Repeat process with the other bag.

5. Put a low steaming rack at bottom of a large saucepan. Add 170 ml (6 fl oz) water and bring to boil. Put in the 2 bags, and boil over constant high heat for 3 hours. Water level in saucepan should always be 8–10 cm above the bags. (Add boiling water when necessary.)

6. Remove bags to cool overnight. Untie bags and use thick thread to slice *lopis* fairly thickly.

To boil the syrup:
Grate the palm sugar, add sugar, water, screw pine leaves and boil in a saucepan for 10 minutes till syrup is fairly thick.

To serve:
Mix the salt evenly with the grated coconut. For each serving, put 2 slices of *lopis* on a plate, and 2 tablespoons of grated coconut on top. Pour some syrup and serve.

*See page 199.

KUEH PISANG
(BANANA CAKE)

INGREDIENTS

625 g (22 oz) grated coconut, white, for milk
6–8 bananas (pisang rajah)
1 packet green bean flour
¾ teaspoon salt
310 g (11 oz) sugar

METHOD

1. Squeeze grated coconut for No. 1 milk. Add 455 ml (16 fl oz) water to grated coconut and squeeze again. Mix both together and add water so that it measures 1 litre (2 pints).

2. Steam bananas with skin on till cooked (about 10–12 minutes). Cool, remove skin and slice bananas (1 cm thick).

3. Place the green bean flour in a heavy-bottomed aluminium saucepan. Add 1 teacup of the measured coconut milk and salt. Stir to blend. Set aside.

4. Cook the sugar and the rest of the coconut milk over a low heat, stirring constantly till nearly boiling. Remove.

5. Stir flour mixture in the saucepan, pour in the hot coconut milk gradually, stirring all the while. Cook it gently over a very low heat till it boils. Let it boil for ½ minute, stirring all the time. Remove from the heat.

6. Add the sliced bananas and mix well.

7. Rinse a square 23 cm (9 in) × 5 cm deep tin. Pour in the mixture to set. Chill in refrigerator.

KUEH SARLAT
(GLUTINOUS RICE CAKE WITH CUSTARD TOPPING)

Coconut milk:
1.6 kg (3½ lb) grated coconut, white
1½ teaspoons salt
  1 tablespoon castor sugar

1. Using a piece of muslin, squeeze grated coconut to obtain approximately 625 ml (22 fl oz) No. 1 milk. Set aside 455 ml (16 fl oz) for the custard topping.

2. Pour the remaining 170 ml (6 fl oz) No. 1 milk into a separate jug for the glutinous rice. Add the salt and castor sugar and stir till dissolved. Set aside. Add 340 ml (12 fl oz) water to grated coconut and squeeze for No. 2 milk. Measure 225 ml (8 fl oz) and set aside.

Custard topping:
  1 tablespoon flour
  1 tablespoon cornflour
  10 screw pine leaves, pounded to a fine pulp
370 g (13 oz) coarse sugar
  10 eggs, beaten lightly
  1 teaspoon green food colouring

1. Mix 4 tablespoons from 455 ml (16 fl oz) of the No. 1 milk with two types of flour till smooth.

2. Add the rest of the milk to the pounded screw pine leaves. Mix well and squeeze with a fine muslin.

3. Blend the milk with the flour mixture. Set aside.

4. Cook the sugar and beaten eggs in a heavy-bottomed aluminium saucepan over a very low heat. Stir constantly till sugar dissolves.

5. Remove from the heat. Add the flour mixture and green food colouring. Stir well and set aside.

Glutinous rice:
625 g (22 oz) glutinous rice, washed and soaked overnight
  6 screw pine leaves, tied into a knot

1. Drain and steam glutinous rice with screw pine leaves over rapidly boiling water for 15 minutes. Make steam holes in glutinous rice using handle of wooden spoon before steaming.

2. Remove glutinous rice to a saucepan, pour in the No. 2 milk. Mix well and cover for 5 minutes.

3. Return glutinous rice to the steamer. Steam for another 7 minutes. Remove to saucepan and mix well with the salted No. 1 milk. Steam again for another 5 minutes.

4. Remove glutinous rice to a round tray, 30 cm (12 in) in diameter and 5 cm (2 in) deep. Press down firmly with a banana leaf or a thick piece of soft plastic.

To steam kueh sarlat:
1. Steam tray of glutinous rice over boiling water for 15 minutes.

2. Re-heat the egg mixture for 2 minutes, stirring all the time. Pour it over the glutinous rice. Cover and steam over a moderately high heat for 15 minutes or till mixture changes colour and sets, forming slight ridges on the surface.

3. Reduce heat to very low and continue steaming for ¾ hour, or till a knife comes out clean when inserted into the centre of top green layer. Remove and place tray on a wire rack to cool completely before cutting.

Note:
Make steam holes each time using a chopstick when re-steaming glutinous rice. From time to time, wipe water collected on the underside of lid of iron wok. Any droplet will cause discolouration of the cake. Add boiling water to iron wok when necessary.

KUEH TALAM PANDAN

INGREDIENTS

Green base layer:

    25 g (1 oz) wet rice flour*
    55 g (2 oz) tapioca flour or cornflour
    28 g (1 oz) grean bean flour (Hoen Kwe Flour)
    ½ teaspoon alkaline water**
    ½ teaspoon green food colouring   **A**

170–225 g (6–8 oz) sugar

    5 screw pine leaves, shredded
    4 tablespoons SANTAN powder dissolved in 400 ml (14 fl oz) water for milk

METHOD

1. Liquidise screw pine leaves with 115 ml (4 fl oz) of milk, squeeze and mix with **A** till smooth.

2. Bring to boil the remaining milk and sugar till sugar is dissolved. Remove from heat.

3. Pour boiling syrup into flour mixture, stirring as you pour.

4. Return flour mixture to cook over low heat till almost boiling. Keep stirring to prevent flour sticking at bottom of pan. Remove and set aside.

5. Place round tray or small cups in steamer for 5 minutes over rapidly boiling water.

6. Pour green mixture into tray or cups (half filled) and steam over high heat for 7–10 minutes. Remove lid, pour in white topping and return to steam for further 6 minutes. Remove to cool completely before cutting.

Note:
Wipe steam from under lid from time to time.

1 tablespoon SANTAN powder is equivalent to 4 oz grated coconut.

Coconut Creme Topping
    ½ 30 g packet SANTAN dissolved in 85 ml (3 fl oz) water for No. 1 milk
    2 tablespoons SANTAN dissolved in 255 ml (9 fl oz) water for No. 2 milk

    1½ rounded tablespoons tapioca flour or cornflour
    1½ rounded tablespoons plain flour   **A**
    1½ rounded tablespoons green bean flour
    2 tablespoons rice flour
    ¾ teaspoon salt
    ½ teaspoon sugar
    2 pieces screw pine leaves, tied into a knot (optional)

METHOD

1. Combine **A** with 85 ml of No. 2 milk till well blended, in a non-stick saucepan.

2. Bring the remaining No. 2 milk to nearly boiling point in a saucepan. Remove from heat. Stir flour mixture before pouring in the hot milk.

3. Return mixture over very low heat and keep stirring till nearly boiling point. Add the No. 1 milk, sugar, salt and screw pine leaves.

4. Keep stirring till mixture begins to thicken. Remove from heat and set aside.

*See page 196. **See page 199.*

JEMPUT-JEMPUT
(BANANA FRITTERS)

INGREDIENTS

200 g (7 oz) grated coconut, white
    4 eggs
225 g (8 oz) sugar
    ½ teaspoon salt
340 g (12 oz) self-raising flour
115 g (4 oz) grated coconut, white
    10 – 12 bananas, (pisang rajah) mashed
    Oil for deep-frying

METHOD

1. Using a piece of muslin, squeeze the coconut for No 1 milk.

2. In a large bowl, beat eggs and sugar to a thick cream. Add salt.

Top: *Kueh Khoo*
On Plate: *(Clockwise) Seray-kaya, Onde Onde, Pulot Tartar*

3. Stir in the flour gradually. Add the white grated coconut, mashed bananas and No 1 milk. Mix very lightly.

4. Heat oil for deep-frying till hot.

5. Drop a few spoonfuls of the batter into the hot oil and fry till light brown. Repeat process till batter is used up.

6. Remove fritters to absorbent paper to cool.

Note:
Turn fritters once over only when one side is brown. Do not pile the fritters when they are still hot.

ONDE ONDE

INGREDIENTS

8 screw pine leaves

300 g (10 oz) glutinous rice flour
1 heaped tablespoon tapioca flour or corn flour
Pinch of salt

Few drops of green food colouring
285 g (10 oz) grated coconut, mixed with a pinch of salt
150 g (5 oz) palm sugar, finely grated and mixed with 1 tablespoon castor sugar

METHOD

1. Pound screw pine pieces till fine, add enough water to bring it to 210 ml (7 fl oz). Add salt and green colouring. Strain and set aside.

2. Boil tapioca flour with 85 ml (3 fl oz) water over low heat, stirring till almost transparent.

3. Pour the tapioca mixture immediately into the glutinous rice flour in a large bowl. Still till well absorbed and gradually add in the screw pine water to form a paste.

4. Place paste on a flat surface. Rub well to form a firm smooth dough. If dough is too soft, add in a little flour. Divide dough in 4 parts. Roll each part into a longish roll and cut into 12 pieces. Keep uncut dough covered with a piece of cloth.

5. Bring a big saucepan of water to the boil. Take 1 piece of cut dough and roll with palms of hands till well rounded. Fill with 1½ teaspoons of the grated sugar in centre.

Put into the boiling water. Repeat process with the remaining dough and boil till each ball surfaces. Keep boiling for 2 minutes to dissolve the sugar.

6. Remove each ball with a tea strainer, dab strainer over dry cloth and roll onde onde in grated coconut. Repeat with the rest of the dough.

Note:
It is very important to keep the balls well sealed to prevent cracking whilst boiling. When onde onde floats to the surface keep boiling for at least 2–2½ minutes.

This will keep the onde onde soft and at the same time turns the grated sugar syrupy.

PULOT PANGGANG
(GRILLED GLUTINOUS RICE WITH DRIED PRAWN FILLING)

INGREDIENTS

Glutinous rice:
35–40 banana leaves, 12 cm × 16 cm (5 in × 6 in)
570 g (1¼ lb) grated coconut, white
2 teaspoons salt
1½ tablespoons castor sugar
905 g (2 lb) glutinous rice, washed and soaked overnight
8 screw pine leaves, tied into a knot

METHOD

1. Scald the banana leaves in a basin of boiling water for 2 minutes and allow to soak for further two minutes before wiping dry.

2. Squeeze coconut for 225 ml (8 fl oz) No. 1 milk. Stir in salt and sugar till dissolved. Set aside. Add 225 ml water to coconut for No. 2 milk. Set aside.

3. Place glutinous rice in a steamer with the screw pine leaves. Make steam holes with handle of wooden spoon and steam over rapidly boiling water for 20 minutes.

4. Remove glutinous rice to a saucepan. Pour in No. 2 milk. Mix well and cover for 5 minutes.

5. Return rice to steamer, make steam holes and steam for another 7 minutes. Remove and mix glutinous rice with No. 1 milk in a

saucepan, cover for 5 minutes and re-steam for 5 minutes. (Make steam holes before steaming.) Remove steamer from heat and leave glutinous rice in the steamer. Cover with kitchen towel to keep warm.

Filling:
170 g (6 oz) grated coconut, white
 85 g (3 oz) dried prawns, pounded finely
  8 tablespoons oil

55 g (2 oz) shallots or onions | *pounded*
8 candlenuts | *to a fine*
1 stalk lemon grass, thinly sliced | *paste*

4 tablespoons sugar
2 teaspoons pepper
1 tablespoon roasted ground coriander

55 ml (2 fl oz) water | *thickening,*
1 tablespoon cornflour | *mixed in a bowl*
2 teaspoons dark soya sauce

To cook filling:
1. Heat an iron or aluminium wok till very hot. Fry coconut over low heat till light brown in colour. Add dried prawns and continue frying for further 20 minutes. Remove to a plate.
2. Heat 8 tablespoons oil in a pan and fry paste till fragrant and lightly browned. Add the sugar, pepper and coriander and stir in pan. Add the fried coconut, dried prawns and the thickening. Stir well so that the fried paste is well mixed with the coconut mixture. Remove to a plate to cool.

To wrap:
1. Wet hands with cool boiled water. Squeeze a small handful of the warm glutinous rice lightly to form a firm oval shape. Use index finger to make a tunnel along the length to hold the filling. Fill and make sure that filling is in the centre. Seal both edges to form a cylindrical shape and wrap with banana leaf. Staple both ends of leaf. Repeat with the rest of the glutinous rice.
2. Heat grill. Put glutinous rice cakes 5 cm (2 in) below grill and grill for 7–8 minutes to brown on all sides. Alternatively, grill over charcoal fire on a satay burner.

Note:
Mixed colours of blue and white glutinous rice can be used. Mix one-third of steamed glutinous rice with a few drops of blue food colouring and 1 teaspoon lime juice. Mix the blue glutinous rice with the white to create a marbling effect.

PULOT TARPAY
(FERMENTED GLUTINOUS RICE)

INGREDIENTS

1.2 kg (42 oz) glutinous rice
140 g (5 oz) rock sugar, pounded finely
170 ml (6 fl oz) hot water
225 ml (8 fl oz) water
1½ pieces *ragi* (Malaysian dry yeast cake) pounded very finely

METHOD

1. Wash glutinous rice and soak overnight.
2. Put the pounded sugar in a bowl. Pour 170 ml (6 fl oz) hot water and stir to dissolve.
3. Drain and steam glutinous rice over rapidly boiling water for 20 minutes. Remove to a saucepan; pour in 225 ml (8 fl oz) water, stir till well mixed, and cover pan for 5 minutes.
4. Return glutinous rice to steamer and steam for another 8 minutes, then remove to a large tray.
5. Set aside 4 tablespoons pounded yeast.
6. Sprinkle the rest of the yeast with the syrup evenly over the warm glutinous rice and mix thoroughly by hand.
7. In a clean dry enamel container or large glass bottle, sprinkle 2 tablespoons of the yeast evenly on base of container. Put the glutinous rice into the container and sprinkle the rest of the yeast evenly on top. Cover container tightly to ferment the glutinous rice. Keep in a warm dark place for 5–6 days.

To serve:
Serve in individual small bowls with chipped ice.

Note:
Separate all the transparent glutinous rice from the chalky rice before steaming. The transparent glutinous rice is harvested before maturity and will leave hardened bits when the tarpay is ready. Do not remove the lid until after the fourth day of fermentation. Keep for a day or two more if it is not fermented.

PULOT TARTAR
(COMPRESSED STEAMED GLUTINOUS RICE WITH COCONUT CREME SAUCE)

INGREDIENTS

605 g (21 oz) glutinous rice
605 g (21 oz) grated coconut, white
  1 tablespoon fine sugar
1½ teaspoons fine salt
  6 screw pine leaves, tied into a knot
Softened banana leaves

1. Soak rice overnight. Drain.

2. Squeeze coconut through a piece of muslin for 200 ml (7 fl oz) No. 1 milk. Stir in the sugar and salt. Set aside. Add 170 ml (6 fl oz) water to coconut and squeeze for No. 2 milk. Set aside.

3. Pour the rice into a colander to drain well before steaming. Steam glutinous rice with the screw pine leaves over rapidly boiling water for 20 minutes. Make steam holes in rice with handle of wooden spoon before steaming.

4. Transfer steamed rice to a saucepan, pour in No. 2 milk, mix well and cover for 5 minutes. Return glutinous rice to steamer, make steam holes and steam for 7 minutes.

5. Stir No. 1 milk to dissolve the sugar and salt and repeat Method 4 using No. 1 milk. Steam for 5 minutes.

6. Line two 10 cm × 15 cm × 10 cm (4 in × 6 in × 4 in) rectangular tins with softened banana leaves. Put half of the glutinous rice into each of the lined tins. Use a piece of banana leaf to press the rice till it is firm and tightly packed in the tin. Leave for 2–4 hours or till completely cool.

7. Cut into slices and serve with coconut creme. Sprinkle castor sugar over if desired.

To make coconut creme sauce:
680 g (24 oz) grated coconut, white
  2 heaped tablespoons plain flour
  4 tablespoons rice flour
  6 screw pine leaves, tied into a knot
  1 teaspoon sugar
  1 level teaspoon fine salt

1. Squeeze grated coconut for approximately 225–285 ml (8–10 fl oz) No. 1 milk. Set aside in a cup. Add 680 ml (24 fl oz) water to the grated coconut and squeeze for No. 2 milk. Set aside.

2. Mix the two types of flour with 225 ml (8 fl oz) of the No. 2 milk. Pour the remaining No. 2 milk into a saucepan, put in the screw pine leaves and cook till nearly boiling point. Add sugar and salt. Stir till dissolved and remove from heat. Stir flour mixture till well blended and pour gradually into saucepan, stirring as you pour. Add No. 1 milk. Stir well.

3. Return saucepan to cook over low heat till sauce comes to the boil, stirring constantly. Remove and pour into a large bowl to cool.

Note:
Mixed colours of blue and white glutinous rice can be used. Mix one-third of steamed glutinous rice with a few drops of blue food colouring and 1 teaspoon lime juice. Mix the blue glutinous rice with the white to create a marbling effect. Stir sauce in pan over a basin of iced water to cool and to prevent it from turning oily.

SAR-SARGON
(CRISPY GROUND RICE AND
COCONUT GRANULES)

INGREDIENTS

605 g (21 oz) No. 1 Thai rice, milled
½ teaspoon fine salt
¼ teaspoon lime paste
3 coconuts, white, coarsely grated
2 eggs, lightly beaten
225–340 g (8–12 oz) sugar

METHOD

1. Wash and soak rice overnight. Drain and dry in sun. When very dry, grind till very fine.

2. Rub salt and lime paste into grated coconut in a large bowl. Pour the eggs over the coconut and mix lightly by hand. Add the rice flour a little at a time and rub between finger and thumb lightly till evenly mixed.

To fry:
1. Heat a wok, pour in the coconut mixture and fry over moderate heat till dry and brittle. Keep stirring to prevent browning.

2. When mixture becomes grainy and free from lumps, reduce heat and stir till it is very crunchy.

3. Add the sugar, stir for 2 minutes and remove from heat. Leave to cool in wok. Taste a spoonful for desired sweetness and add sugar if necessary.

Note:
Charcoal fire and a bronze or brass wok is more suitable for this recipe as it allows the sargon to remain very pale and off-white in colour, yet keeps it very brittle and crunchy as it should be. However if you do not possess a brass or bronze wok, use an iron or thick aluminium wok to fry over charcoal fire.

Lime paste must be very smooth and pasty otherwise it will not mix well with the coconut.

Ready packed ground rice can be substituted for the No. 1 Thai rice.

SERAY-KAYA
(RICH EGG CUSTARD)

INGREDIENTS

905 g (32 oz) grated coconut, white
10 eggs, approx. 565 g (20 oz) in weight
565 g (20 oz) coarse sugar
2 screw pine leaves, tied into a knot

METHOD

1. Using a piece of muslin, squeeze grated coconut to obtain 400 ml (14 fl oz) No. 1 milk.

2. Beat eggs and sugar till well mixed.

3. Heat egg mixture and screw pine leaves in an enamel container over a very low heat to dissolve the sugar (about 10 minutes). Keep stirring all the time with a wooden spoon. Remove from heat. Take away the screw pine leaves.

4. Add the No. 1 milk to the egg mixture. Strain into an enamel container.

5. Stand container of egg mixture on a rack in a saucepan of rapidly boiling water. Keep stirring with a wooden spoon until the egg mixture turns thick like custard cream (¾ hour).

To steam seray-kaya:
1. Wrap lid of container with a dry tea-towel. Place container, with lid on, on rack in a saucepan.

2. Add hot water to saucepan to measure 2.5 cm (1 in) from base of container. Cover saucepan and steam for 3 hours over moderate heat. Do not stir.

3. Dry the underlid of the cover of the saucepan from time to time to prevent discolouration of the seray-kaya.

Desserts

Agar-Agar Cordial

Agar-Agar Delight

Agar-Agar Talam

Au Nee

Almond Creme

Almond Jelly

Bubor Terigu

Bubor Cha Cha

Chendol

Green Beans with Pearl Sago

Groundnut Creme

Kueh Kuria

Lek-Tow-Suan

Len-Chee-Suan

Lotus Seed Fluff

Lotus Seed Paste Mooncake

Mock Pomegranate

Pearl Sago with Mixed Fruit

Red Beans with Coconut Creme Topping

Sago Pudding

Sweet Red Bean and Lotus Seed Soup

Sweet Lotus Seeds and Dried Longan Soup

Agar-Agar Cordial

AGAR-AGAR CORDIAL

INGREDIENTS

1 packet agar-agar powder (Rose brand)
8 screw pine leaves, knotted
85 g (3 oz) sugar

285 g (10 oz) sugar
285 ml (10 fl oz) water   **A**
8 screw pine leaves

½ teaspoon red food colouring
¼ teaspoon rose essence

METHOD

1. Dissolve agar-agar powder in 8 tablespoons cold water.

2. Bring 1 litre water and the agar-agar solution to a boil with the screw pine leaves over moderate heat. Add in sugar, boil till dissolved and continue boiling for 5 minutes.

3. Rinse a mould or square tin. Pour the agar-agar through a nylon sieve into the mould and allow to set. Keep in refrigerator till ready for use.

4. To make syrup, bring **A** to a boil in a saucepan for 15 minutes. Put in red colouring and boil for another minute. Remove from heat. Allow to cool before adding rose essence. Pour syrup into a jar through a piece of muslin.

5. To serve, cut agar-agar into slabs and grate into long strips with a coarse grater. Put agar agar strips into glasses and add syrup. Dilute with cold water to taste. Serve with ice chips.

AGAR-AGAR DELIGHT

INGREDIENTS

½ packet agar-agar powder (Rose brand)
115 g (4 oz) sugar
3 tablespoons condensed milk
225 ml (8 fl oz) evaporated milk
1 tablespoon vanilla
  A few drops green or pink food colouring
2 egg yolks, lightly beaten
3 egg whites, beaten with 1 teaspoon sugar till stiff (but not dry)
1 tin fruit cocktail

METHOD

1. Stir agar-agar in 455 ml (16 fl oz) cold water till dissolved. Bring to the boil and boil for 1 minute. Add in the sugar and cook till sugar dissolves. Keep warm.

2. In another saucepan, bring the condensed and evaporated milk and 400 ml (14 fl oz) water to almost boiling point.

3. Pour 1 cup of the milk mixture gradually into the beaten egg yolks and stir well. Pour this mixture to combine with the agar-agar mixture. Stir and simmer till boiling, stirring occasionally. Add vanilla essence and 2 to 5 drops of food colouring. Simmer for 1 minute.

4. Pour in the egg white, cook gently for ½ minute. Cut to separate the large pieces of egg white. Leave to cook for 10 seconds. Remove from heat.

5. Rinse a shallow, rectangular glass dish and pour agar-agar into the dish allowing the egg white to float evenly. Allow to cool and set before chilling. To serve, cut into small pieces. Garnish with fruit cocktail and serve cold.

Note:
Use ½ of 15 g packet agar-agar powder.

AGAR-AGAR TALAM
(FROSTED AGAR-AGAR)

INGREDIENTS

Bottom layer:
15 g (½ oz) agar-agar, soaked and cut into small pieces
1.4 litres (3 pints) water
6 screw pine leaves, tied into a knot
395 g (14 oz) coarse sugar
     A few drops of red food colouring
3 drops of rose essence

METHOD

1. Press soaked agar-agar lightly to fill one cup.

2. Boil the water and screw pine leaves in a saucepan. Dissolve agar-agar in it. Add sugar and boil till dissolved.

3. Remove from the heat. Stir in the red food colouring and the rose essence.

4. Rinse a round cake tin, 28 cm in diameter and 5 cm deep. Pour the agar-agar into the tin. Allow to set 20–30 minutes, till a thin film forms over the surface, before pouring in the coconut layer.

Coconut layer:
680 g (24 oz) grated coconut, white
1 litre (36 fl oz) water
4 screw pine leaves, tied into a knot
15 g (½ oz) agar-agar, soaked and cut into small pieces
85 g (3 oz) coarse sugar
½ teaspoon salt

1. Squeeze grated coconut for No. 1 milk. Set aside 340 ml (12 fl oz).

2. Boil the water and screw pine leaves in a saucepan. Boil agar-agar and sugar till dissolved.

3. Reduce heat to low, pour in No. 1 milk, stirring well into the agar-agar mixture. Add salt and stir until it comes to a boil.

4. Pour coconut mixture over the red layer, allowing it to run and spread over the surface.

5. Allow to cool and set on a flat surface. Chill in refrigerator. Cut and serve.

AU NEE
(SWEET YAM PASTE)

INGREDIENTS

115 g (4 oz) shelled gingko nuts
227 g (8 oz) sugar
225 g (8 oz) pumpkin cubes, approx. 2 cm
905 g (2 lbs) yam slices (5 cm sq. × 1 cm)
12 tablespoons castor sugar
6 tablespoons lard
3 shallots, sliced thinly

METHOD

1. Wash gingko nuts. Boil with half of sugar in 2 tablespoons water over low heat for 45 minutes till sugar is absorbed into the nuts. Add water a little at a time while cooking. Cool and cut gingko nuts into half, removing centre fibre if any.

2. Cook pumpkin cubes in remaining sugar and 2 tablespoons water over low heat in a heavy-bottomed saucepan. Cook till sugar is absorbed. Add a little water at a time while cooking to prevent sugar from burning. Set gingko nuts and pumpkins aside.

3. Steam yam pieces over rapidly boiling water till very soft. Use a food processor to blend half of the yam, 2 tablespoons lard and half of the sugar till paste is smooth. Remove to a bowl and repeat with remaining yam, lard and remaining sugar.

4. Heat another 2 tablespoons lard in a wok to fry the sliced shallots till very lightly browned. Put in yam paste and stir fry over low heat for ½ minute. Remove to a shallow serving bowl. Place cooked pumpkin cubes around sides of the bowl and gingko nuts over the yam. Serve hot.

ALMOND CREME

INGREDIENTS

285 g (10 oz) almonds
855 ml (30 fl oz) water
285 g (10 oz) sugar to boil in 115 ml (4 fl oz) water

Thickening:
(Mix to a smooth paste)
3–4 tablespoons rice flour
170 ml (6 fl oz) water
170 ml (6 fl oz) fresh milk

METHOD

1. Scald and skin almonds. Drain. Blend till very fine using some of the measured water. Strain through a fine sieve into a saucepan. Blend remaining bits and sieve again. Add remaining water and set aside.

2. Dissolve sugar in the 115 ml boiling water.

3. Bring the blended almonds to a boil over moderate heat, stirring till it boils. Add syrup. Stir thickening and pour gradually into mixture, stirring as you pour.

4. Reduce heat but keep boiling for 5 minutes till mixture thickens. 2 drops of almond essence may be added after removing from heat. Serve hot.

ALMOND JELLY

INGREDIENTS

1 handful of agar-agar strips
4 tablespoons sugar
455 ml (16 fl oz) fresh milk
1 tablespoon condensed milk
3 drops of almond essence

METHOD

1. Soak agar-agar strips in cold water, squeeze out water. Cut agar-agar into very small pieces. Press lightly to fill half a 225 ml (8 fl oz) measuring cup.

2. Boil 510 ml (18 fl oz) water and dissolve the agar-agar in it. Add sugar and boil till dissolved.

3. Pour in the fresh milk and condensed milk. Stir and cook for 2 minutes. Remove from the heat. Add almond essence.

4. Pour into a rinsed jelly mould to set. Cool and chill in refrigerator.

To serve almond jelly:
Place jelly in a deep bowl, add canned longans or lychees and cherries with the syrup. Add chipped ice and serve.

BUBOR TERIGU

INGREDIENTS

115 g (4 oz) coarse sugar	
285 g (10 oz) palm sugar	**A**
225 ml (8 fl oz) water	
8 screw pine leaves	

55 g (2 oz) quick cooking oats	**B**
285 ml (10 fl oz) water	

680 g (1½ lb) grated coconut (white)
¼ teaspoon salt
285 ml (10 fl oz) water
285 g (10 oz) *biji terigu* (without husk)
1.7 litres (4 pints) water

3 tablespoons flour to mix with 170 ml (6 fl oz) water   *thickening*

METHOD

1. Boil **A** for 10 minutes and strain.

2. Mix **B** and cook for 5–7 minutes.

3. Squeeze coconut for No. 1 milk. Add salt and set aside. Add 285 ml water to coconut and squeeze for No. 2 milk.

4. Soak *biji terigu* in cold water for 10 minutes; drain. Pound to break up the *terigu*. Bring it to the boil with the 1.7 litres water till *terigu* is tender and swelling. Reduce heat.

5. Pour **A**, **B** and thickening into the saucepan. Add No. 2 milk, and boil for 2 minutes. Remove from heat.

Note:
Serve in individual bowls with a topping of 2 tablespoons No. 1 milk. Serve hot.

BUBOR CHA-CHA

INGREDIENTS

905 g (32 oz) grated coconut, white
565 ml (20 fl oz) cooled, boiled water for No. 2
   milk
310 g (11 oz) diced sweet potatoes
310 g (11 oz) diced yam
225 ml (8 fl oz) water
   6 screw pine leaves, tied into a knot
140 g (5 oz) coarse sugar
310 g (11 oz) fine quality sago flour
   ½ teaspoon borax, available from Chinese dispen-
   saries
225 ml (8 fl oz) boiling water
   A few drops of red, green and blue food
   colouring
½–1 teaspoon salt

METHOD

1. Squeeze grated coconut with muslin for No.
   1 milk.

2. Add the cooled, boiled water to the grated
   coconut and squeeze again for No. 2 milk.

3. Rinse and drain sweet potato cubes, and
   steam for 5–7 minutes till cooked. Set aside.

4. Steam yam cubes for 5–7 minutes till
   cooked. Set aside.

5. Boil the 225 ml water with the screw pine
   leaves and sugar for 10 minutes. Strain
   syrup into a bowl.

To make sago-flour triangles:
1. Sift sago flour with the borax into a basin.

2. Pour the boiling water over the sago flour.
   Stir with a wooden spoon to combine.

3. Knead to form a firm dough. Flour palms
   of hands with sago flour to prevent dough
   from sticking to them. Knead dough till
   smooth.

4. Divide dough into four parts. Leave one
   part uncoloured. Mix a few drops of different food colouring to the other three parts.
   Knead till colour blends in.

5. Roll each part into thin long strips of about
   1 cm in diameter. Use a pair of scissors to
   cut each strip into small triangles.

6. Bring a saucepan of water to the boil. Place
   the sago triangles in the boiling water, stirring to keep them from sticking together.

Scoop out the cooked sago triangles as soon
as they float to the surface. Soak them in a
basin of cold water for 10 minutes.

7. Drain and place in a bowl. Add
   4 tablespoons sugar and mix to keep the
   cooked sago triangles separated.

To boil the coconut milk:
1. Mix syrup with No. 2 coconut milk in a
   saucepan. Bring to the boil over a low heat,
   stirring all the time.

2. Pour in the No. 1 milk and add salt. Stir
   well. Cook for a moment. Remove from the
   heat and keep stirring for a while to prevent
   mixture from curdling and turning oily.

To serve:
Place a tablespoonful each of cooked sweet
potatoes, yam, and sago triangles in a small
bowl. Add coconut milk to fill the bowl. Serve
hot or cold.

Note:
Clean yam with a brush. Wipe it dry and remove the dark skin.
Do not wash after removing the skin or it will be very slimy and
difficult to handle. Keep diced yam dry.

Place saucepan of boiled coconut milk in a large basin of cold
water and stir to release the heat to prevent curdling when cooking
in big amounts.

CHENDOL

Green Bean Flour Droplets:
Basin of iced water
10 screw pine leaves, pounded to a pulp
¼ teaspoon salt
1 teaspoon green food colouring
1 packet green bean flour, 'Flower' brand

1. Prepare a basin of iced water.
2. Mix the pounded screw pine leaves with 1.2 litres (2 pints) water. Squeeze and strain liquid. Add the salt and food colouring.
3. Blend 225 ml (8 fl oz) of the screw pine liquid with the green bean flour in a bowl. Set aside.
4. Bring the remaining screw pine liquid to the boil in a saucepan. Remove from heat. Stir the green bean flour mixture and pour gradually into the saucepan, stirring all the time.
5. Cook over a low heat till it boils, stirring constantly. Remove from the heat immediately when it boils. Leave to stand for 5 minutes.
6. Place the frame for making green bean flour droplets (see diagram) over the basin of iced water. Pour the hot green pea flour mixture on to the frame. Using a flat Chinese frying slice, press mixture in long, downward strokes.
7. Leave droplets to set in the iced water till firm. Add ice to the water to set droplets faster.
8. Drain in colander. Cool droplets in refrigerator till ready to serve.

Palm Sugar Syrup:
625 g (22 oz) palm sugar, grated
6 tablespoons sugar
225 ml (8 fl oz) water
6 screw pine leaves, tied into a knot   **A**

1. Boil **A** for ½ hour.
2. Strain syrup and set aside till ready to serve.

Coconut Milk:
2 kg (4½ lb) grated coconut
910 ml (32 fl oz) cooled, boiled water
1–1½ teaspoons salt

1. Add water to the grated coconut. Squeeze in small handfuls, using a piece of muslin.
2. Add salt to milk. Stir till thoroughly dissolved and cool in refrigerator.

To serve coconut milk mix:
Spoon green bean flour droplets into glasses, add some crushed ice and pour coconut milk to fill glasses. Serve with palm sugar syrup according to taste. Add salt if necessary.

(20–30 servings)

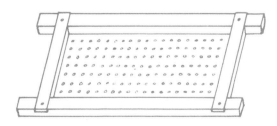

Frame for green bean flour droplets.

GREEN BEANS WITH PEARL SAGO

INGREDIENTS

455 g (1 lb) grated coconut
 85 g (3 oz) pearl sago
605 g (21 oz) green beans
340 g (12 oz) coarse sugar
225 g (8 oz) palm sugar
  6 screw pine leaves tied into a knot
  1 teaspoon salt

METHOD

1. Squeeze grated coconut for approximately 200 ml (7 fl oz) No. 1 milk. Add 455 ml (16 fl oz) water and squeeze for No. 2 milk.

2. Soak pearl sago for 10 minutes. Drain.

3. Boil green beans with 1.14 litres (2 pints) cold water for 20 minutes over high heat.

4. Add 2.27 litres (4½ pints) of cold water and bring to the boil. Reduce heat to moderate and continue boiling till beans are tender and swollen.

5. Put in pearl sago and cook till sago turns transparent. Add No. 2 milk, the two types of sugar and screw pine leaves and cook till it comes to a boil. Add No. 1 milk, salt and cook for 2 minutes. Remove from heat and serve.

GROUNDNUT CREME

INGREDIENTS

625 g (22 oz) groundnuts, shelled
  2 tablespoons rice, washed and drained
  2 litres (4 pints) water
310 g (11 oz) sugar

METHOD

1. Roast groundnuts till light brown. Remove skin.

2. Using an electric blender, blend rice and half of the groundnuts with 455 ml (16 fl oz) water till very fine. Add two or three tablespoonfuls of water if necessary to keep the mixture moving and rotating. Pour into a bowl and set aside.

3. Repeat process using the other half of the groundnuts with another 455 ml (16 fl oz) water.

4. Place the blended groundnuts, sugar and remaining water in a heavy-bottomed aluminium saucepan. Bring to the boil over a moderate heat. Stir mixture all the time with a wooden spoon. Let simmer for 5 minutes, stirring continuously. Remove from the heat. Serve hot or cold.

KUEH KURIA
(TAPIOCA DOUGHNUTS)

INGREDIENTS

455 g (16 oz) grated tapioca, skinned and with
   centre vein removed
170 g (6 oz) grated coconut, white | **A**
  3 tablespoons glutinous rice flour or sago
   flour
  ¾ teaspoon salt

For the sugar coating:
55 ml (2 fl oz) water
225 g (8 oz) coarse sugar
  4 screw pine leaves

METHOD

1. Mix **A** in a bowl.
2. Form mixture into small balls, flatten, and make a hole in the centre as for American doughnuts.
3. Heat oil in iron wok for deep-frying. Fry tapioca rings till golden brown. Remove to absorbent paper.
4. Drain oil from wok. Do not wash. Add the water, sugar and screw pine leaves. Boil till syrup is thick and sticky.
5. Reduce heat to very low and add the tapioca rings. Stir for a minute till they are well-coated with the syrup. Remove wok from heat and keep tossing the tapioca rings in wok till the sugar is dry. Let rings cool on a rack before serving.

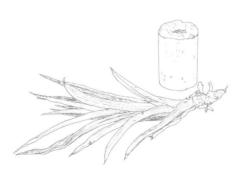

LEK-TOW-SUAN
(GREEN BEAN SOUP)

INGREDIENTS

605 g (21 oz) shelled, split green beans or
  4 packets each of 255 g (9 oz)
  ready-soaked green beans

680 g (1½ lb) coarse sugar
285 ml (10 fl oz) water | **A**
  8 screw pine leaves

115 g (4 oz) sweet potato flour

1.7 litres (4 pints) water | **B**
10 screw pine leaves tied into a knot

METHOD

1. Wash and soak beans overnight *or* for 5–6 hours. Remove loose skin from beans and drain. Bring beans to the boil and boil for 10 minutes. Drain in a colander, immerse in cold water and drain again immediately.
2. Place the beans in a steamer and steam till beans swell and are tender. Do not steam until beans split. Spread beans to cool on a large tray.
3. Boil **A** in a saucepan over moderately high heat for about 10 minutes till sugar turns syrupy.
4. Mix the sweet potato flour with 340 ml (12 fl oz) water. Strain into a saucepan.
5. Boil **B** for 15 minutes. Pour **B** (still boiling) gradually into sweet potato mixture stirring as you pour. Add the syrup, bring to the boil, add the steamed beans, and continue cooking over low heat till mixture boils. Serve hot in small bowls with slices of crispy Chinese crullers.

Note:
Do not oversoak the beans as this will harden the beans and prevent them from being tender when steamed. Ready-soaked beans are much easier to use and can be bought from any supermarket.

LOTUS SEED FLUFF

INGREDIENTS

55 g (2 oz) pearl barley, washed and drained
115 g (4 oz) gingko nuts, blanched and skinned
  (remove centre fibre)

Dried soya bean strips (*see notes on preparation*)
  6 screw pine leaves
510 g (18 oz) sugar
8–10 eggs, beaten with 4 tablespoons water and
  1 tablespoon sugar
Lotus seeds (*see notes on preparation*)

METHOD

1. Bring 3.2 litres (6 pints) water to the boil.
   Add pearl barley and gingko nuts. Boil
   gently for ½ hour.

2. Add the prepared soya bean strips and
   screw pine leaves and let simmer for
   ½ hour. Add the sugar and cook for
   10 minutes.

3. Increase heat to high. Pour in the beaten
   egg mixture gradually, stirring till egg floats
   to the surface. Remove from heat. Lastly,
   add the prepared lotus seeds. Remove screw
   pine leaves. Serve hot.

To prepare dried soya bean strips:
170 g (6 oz) dried soya bean strips
1.4 litres (2 pints) cold water
½ teaspoon bicarbonate of soda

1. Soak soya bean strips in cold water for
   10 minutes. Add bicarbonate of soda, mix
   and allow to soak for 20 minutes.

2. Rinse and soak again in cold water. Drain
   just before use.

To prepare dried lotus seeds:
115 g (4 oz) dried lotus seeds, skinned
¼ teaspoon bicarbonate of soda
2 screw pine leaves
115 g (4 oz) sugar

1. Soak lotus seeds in 595 g (21 fl oz) water
   for 20 minutes. Split lotus seeds and remove
   green centres, if any.

2. Add bicarbonate of soda and allow lotus
   seeds to soak for 3 hours.

3. Rinse and drain lotus seeds and bring to the
   boil with 340 ml (12 fl oz) of the water and
   two screw pine leaves. Let simmer for
   ½ hour. Add remaining water and 115 g
   sugar and cook for another 10 minutes.

LEN-CHEE-SUAN
(LOTUS SEED SOUP)

INGREDIENTS

285 g (10 oz) lotus seeds
  8 screw pine leaves, tied into a knot
170 g (6 oz) sugar

5 tablespoons sugar │ **A**
2 tablespoons water │

2½ tablespoons sweet potato flour, mixed with
  6 tablespoons water

METHOD

1. Soak lotus seeds in lukewarm water for
   4 hours.

2. Split lotus seeds into halves, removing
   greenish centre if any.

3. Boil 565 ml (20 fl oz) water with the lotus
   seeds and 4 screw pine leaves. Lower heat
   and simmer lotus seeds in a covered saucepan for 15–20 minutes, or till tender. Add
   the sugar, stir gently and set aside. Remove
   screw pine leaves.

4. Heat **A** in an aluminium saucepan till light
   golden brown. Add 395 ml (14 fl oz) water
   and the remaining screw pine leaves and
   allow to boil till dissolved.

5. Pour the syrup into the saucepan of lotus
   seeds and bring back to boil over low heat.
   Remove screw pine leaves. Remove from
   heat, stir the sweet potato mixture in bowl
   and pour gradually into saucepan, stirring
   gently. Return saucepan to heat and boil
   gently over low heat. Remove from heat
   and serve hot.

Note:
*To caramelise sugar, boil sugar and water till dissolved. Do not
stir at all after sugar has dissolved, and boil to the colour desired.
Too dark a caramel tastes bitter.*

LOTUS SEED PASTE MOONCAKES

INGREDIENTS

600 g (21 oz) Hongkong soft flour, available at specialist shops catering to restaurants*
170 ml (6 oz) vegetable oil
  1 tablespoon alkaline water**
225 ml (8 fl oz) golden syrup
  2 kg (4 lb) lotus seed paste
115 g (4 oz) melon seeds
115 g (4 oz) olive seeds
 14 salted egg yolks

Glaze ingredients:
1 egg
1 egg yolk
1 tablespoon water
2 teaspoons golden syrup

METHOD

1. Sift flour into a mixing bowl. Pour oil around flour and stir lightly with a fork. Mix the alkaline water with the syrup and pour around flour mixture. Gather dough into a ball and keep covered in bowl for 1 hour.

2. Divide lotus paste into 20 equal portions. Mix seeds and divide into 20 equal portions. Grease palm of hands; take a portion of mixed seeds and knead into a portion of lotus seed paste. Wrap two yolks in each portion. Repeat with remaining ingredients. Set aside.

3. Divide dough into 20 portions. Place each portion between plastic sheets and press to flatten before rolling out thinly. Cut each portion of dough into a large circle to cover lotus seed paste completely.

4. Place a portion of lotus seed paste in your hand and lift a circle of dough to cover paste tightly and evenly, leaving no air pockets. Roll with both hands to form a smooth round ball.

5. Dust mooncake mould with flour. Knock off excess flour and place ball into mould, pressing gently into shape making sure that cake takes up impression from mould. Knock mould gently side to side to release cake. Repeat with remaining ingredients.

6. Preheat oven to moderately high. Glaze mooncakes very lightly on top and side. Place them on a baking tray to bake for 10 minutes. Remove from oven, glaze again and bake for another 10 minutes. Glaze for the third time, reduce heat to low and bake for 20–30 minutes or till golden brown. Remove to cool on a rack. Keep for 3–5 days before serving.

Note:
Glaze cakes very lightly and evenly on top and sides. Do not allow glaze to drip around cakes.
After the third glaze, remember to turn heat to low to prevent cake from cracking.
Use canned golden syrup and not the bottled variety.

Try the one in Lor 27, Sims Avenue.

**See page 199.

Lotus Seed Mooncakes

MOCK POMEGRANATE SEEDS IN COCONUT MILK

INGREDIENTS

455 g (1 lb) fresh water chestnuts or 565 g (1.2 lb)
   canned water chestnuts
  1 teaspoon red food colouring
225 g (8 oz) tapioca flour
  5 tablespoons sugar dissolved in 225 ml (8 fl oz)
   water
1.2 kg (3 lb) grated coconut, white
340 g (12 oz) sugar
  4 screw pine leaves
  1 level teaspoon salt

METHOD

1. Cut water chestnuts into pomegranate seed-sized bits. Add red food colouring, mixing well till colour turns deep pink.

2. Put tapioca flour and water chestnut pieces into a plastic bag. Tie up bag and shake till flour coats chestnuts evenly. Leave in bag for 10 minutes.

3. Bring large saucepan of water to boil. Put chestnuts in and boil till they come to the surface. Stir with chopstick to separate chestnut bits whilst cooking.

4. Scoop out chestnuts and put into a basin of cold water. Drain and pour in more cold water. Stir and drain in colander before putting in sugar solution till ready to serve.

5. To make coconut milk, add 855 ml (30 fl oz) boiling water to grated coconut; cover and leave for 15 minutes. Make syrup with the 340 g sugar, screw pine leaves and 225 ml (8 fl oz) water. Strain and cool.

6. Squeeze coconut for milk into a saucepan and cook over moderate heat to scalding point. Keep stirring whilst cooking. Remove from heat, pour in syrup from (5) and 1 level teaspoon salt. Stir well. Allow to cool and keep in fridge till ready to serve.

PEARL SAGO WITH MIXED FRUIT

INGREDIENTS

  1 packet SANTAN instant coconut cream powder★
    Diced fruit (melon/honey dew or sweet potato/yam)
90 g (3 oz) pearl sago
  6 screw pine leaves, tied into a knot
100 g (3½ oz) sugar
  ½ teaspoon salt
  3 extra screw pine leaves, tied into a knot

METHOD

1. Whisk 1 packet SANTAN with 200 ml (7 fl oz) water. Strain and set aside.

2. Chill in fridge — ½ cup each of diced water melon, rock melon and honey dew. (Alternative: Steamed sweet potato and yam cubes.)

3. Wash and soak the pearl sago for 5 minutes. Drain in colander.

4. Bring 1 litre (2 pints) water to a boil with the 6 screw pine leaves. Continue boiling gently for another 5 minutes. Pour in the pearl sago and cook till it turns transparent.

5. Lower heat, add in the sugar and stir till sugar is dissolved. Pour in the SANTAN milk and salt, stirring as you pour. Put in the extra leaves. Remove from heat and pour into a large bowl to cool.

6. Chill in fridge till ready to serve.

★One 30 g packet of SANTAN is equivalent to 1 lb white grated coconut.

To serve:
Serve the sago coconut sauce in a glass bowl with 1 cup ice chips. Arrange diced fruits over.

RED BEANS WITH COCONUT CREME TOPPING

INGREDIENTS

285 g (10 oz) red beans, washed and drained
½–¾ piece dried orange peel, cut into thin slices (optional)
  6 screw pine leaves — tied into a knot (optional)
250 g (9 oz) sugar
  1 can lotus seed in syrup (455 ml)

METHOD

1. Boil red beans with orange peel and screw pine leaves in 1.5 litres (3 pints) water till soft.

2. Leave to cool for 15 minutes, remove screw pine leaves, then liquidise red beans till smooth.

3. Return liquidised beans into saucepan, add sugar and bring to boil. Add lotus seed and continue to boil gently for 10 minutes.

4. Pour red bean soup into a large serving bowl, pour coconut creme over and serve hot.

Preparation for coconut creme:

30 g (1 oz) SANTAN instant coconut powder 350 ml (12 fl oz) water 1 tablespoon plain flour ¼ teaspoon salt 1 teaspoon sugar	**A**

  3 screw pine leaves, tied into a knot (optional)

1. Blend **A** together and strain into a non-stick saucepan.

2. Put screwpine leaves into SANTAN mixture and cook over moderate heat till boiling point. Keep stirring to prevent lumps from forming.

3. Remove to a basin of icy water to cool completely, chill in fridge till ready to serve.

SAGO PUDDING

INGREDIENTS

120 g (4 oz) SANTAN instant coconut powder*
12 screw pine leaves

½ teaspoon salt **A**
1 tablespoon sugar

285 g (10 oz) pearl sago

¼ teaspoon salt **B**
3 tablespoons sugar

455 g (16 oz) palm sugar **C**
155 g (5 oz) coarse sugar

METHOD

SANTAN milk:
1. Boil 570 ml (20 fl oz) water with 6 screw pine leaves for 5 minutes. Allow to cool. Whisk in SANTAN powder and add **A**.
2. Strain SANTAN milk and cool in fridge.

Pearl sago:
1. Soak pearl sago for 5 minutes. Drain well in colander.
2. Bring 625 ml (22 fl oz) water to boil in a saucepan. Lower heat, and pour in the pearl sago, stirring as you pour. Keep stirring till sago turns transparent.
3. Drain with a strainer and leave to stand under running tap for 3 minutes. Drain excess water and pour sago into a bowl. Add in **B** and stir well. Scoop into a well rinsed jelly mould to set. Chill in refrigerator.

Palm sugar syrup:
1. Boil **C** in 345 ml (12 fl oz) water. Cut 6 screw pine leaves into 1 in lengths and allow to boil together with the syrup for about 10–15 minutes or till mixture turns syrupy. Strain and allow to cool.

To serve:
Top chilled pudding with syrup and chilled SANTAN milk. Serve with a few ice chips.

Equivalent to 4 lb white grated coconut.

SWEET RED BEAN AND LOTUS SEED SOUP

INGREDIENTS

258 g (9 oz) red beans, boiled in 570 ml (20 fl oz) water
1.7 litres (4 pints) water
½ piece dried orange peel, sliced thinly into shreds
225 g (8 oz) sugar
1 can lotus seeds in syrup
4 screw pine leaves, knotted

METHOD

1. Boil the red beans for ½ hour rapidly. Drain and rinse with cold water in a colander.
2. Put beans and the 1.7 litres water into a pressure cooker and boil for 45 minutes. Leave beans in cooker for ½ hour to release pressure.
3. Remove cover from cooker, pour in another 1 litre water, dried orange peel and screw pine leaves. Bring to a boil, stirring till beans become blended with liquid.
4. Reduce heat. Boil gently till soup thickens; add sugar and lotus seeds with syrup and continue boiling for ¾ hour. Keep stirring occasionally to prevent beans sticking at bottom of cooker. Serve hot.

Note:
Dried orange peel can be bought from Chinese medicine shops.

SWEET LOTUS SEED AND DRIED LONGAN SOUP

INGREDIENTS

455 g (16 oz) treated lotus seeds
 85 g (3 oz) dried longans or 1 can sweet longans
905 ml (2 pints) water
  4 screw pine leaves, knotted
    Sugar to taste

METHOD

1. Cook treated lotus seeds in 250 ml (9 fl oz) water and 125 g (4 oz) sugar for 10 minutes.

2. Wash dried longans and drain immediately. Soak in 285 ml (10 fl oz) boiling water to allow to swell for ½ hour.

3. Boil sugar and screw pine leaves in water for 10 minutes over moderate heat. Remove leaves and add longans and water. Boil for another 2 minutes. Do not overboil or longan will lose its natural flavour.

4. Add lotus seeds and syrup or canned longans. Boil over gentle heat for 5 minutes. Remove from heat. Serve hot or chilled.

Cakes

Banana Cake

Butter Cake

Cheesecake

No Bake Lemon Cheesecake

Chocolate Chiffon Cake

Coffee Walnut Cake

Fruit Cake

Ginger Cake

Lemon Sponge Cake

Pandan Chiffon Cake

Pound Cake

Rose Marie Cake

Semolina Cake

Sponge Sandwich

Super Light Sponge Sandwich

Sultana Cake

Swiss Roll

Walnut Cake

White Christmas

Cheesecake

BANANA CAKE

INGREDIENTS

455 g (16 oz) bananas
455 g (16 oz) butter
  4 tablespoons condensed milk
455 g (16 oz) castor sugar
½ teaspoon salt
  1 teaspoon banana essence
  1 teaspoon vanilla essence
  9 eggs
340 g (12 oz) self-raising flour, sifted

METHOD

1. Mash bananas with a fork.

2. Cream butter, condensed milk and half of the sugar for 5 minutes. Add salt, banana essence and vanilla essence.

3. In a clean mixing bowl, whisk eggs with the rest of the sugar till thick and creamy.

4. Fold in one cup of the egg mixture to the creamed butter till well mixed. Add the rest of the egg mixture, mashed bananas and lastly the flour, stirring as lightly as possible.

5. Pour into a greased cake tin. Bake in oven at 150°C (300°F) or Regulo 4 for 1–1¼ hours.

BUTTER CREAM

For a 20 cm (8 in) cake:
115 g (4 oz) butter
 55 g (2 oz) sifted icing sugar
  2 teaspoons rum
½ teaspoon vanilla essence
  2 egg yolks

1. Place all the ingredients in a dry mixing bowl.

2. Beat at moderate speed for about 7–8 minutes till mixture turns to a smooth cream.

3. Chill in refrigerator until ready for icing and filling cake.

Note:
To make coffee-flavoured butter cream, dissolve 2 tablespoonfuls of 'instant' coffee powder in 2 tablespoonfuls of boiling water. Cool completely. For chocolate flavour, add 115 g (4 oz) plain chocolate, grated. Beat into the creamed butter, continue beating for 1–2 minutes till well blended. Chill.

BUTTER CAKE

INGREDIENTS

310 g (11 oz) flour
 10 egg whites
310 g (11 oz) sugar
  2 teaspoons baking powder
 10 egg yolks, lightly beaten
455 g (16 oz) butter
  6 tablespoons condensed milk
  2 drops almond essence
  2 teaspoons vanilla essence
  2 teaspoons brandy

METHOD

1. Sift flour twice.

2. Beat egg whites, sugar and baking powder till thick. Add the beaten egg yolks, a little at a time, and continue beating till thick and creamy. Remove to a basin.

3. Place butter and condensed milk in a mixing bowl. Beat till well blended, about 5 minutes. Add almond and vanilla essence and brandy. Beat till blended.

4. Add one cup of egg mixture and mix thoroughly. Fold in flour lightly with the rest of the beaten egg mixture. Pour batter into a greased cake tin and bake in moderate oven at 175°C (350°F) or Regulo 6 for 10 minutes. Reduce heat to 135°C (275°F) or Regulo 3 and bake for further 45–50 minutes or till done. Turn cake on to a cake rack.

To make Rich Marble Cake:

1. Set aside one-third of the cake mixture in a bowl. Sift 2 tablespoons cocoa and stir lightly into the mixture.

2. Pour and spread half of the white batter into a greased cake tin.

3. Place and space out small heaps of the cocoa mixture over batter in tin.

4. Add the rest of the white cake mixture to cover the cocoa mixture completely. Bake as for Butter Cake.

CHEESECAKE

INGREDIENTS

170 g (6 oz) digestive biscuits
55 g (2 oz) butter
3 tablespoons canned syrup
30 g gelatine
1 small can evaporated milk, chilled
455 g (16 oz) cottage cheese
115 g (4 oz) castor sugar
35 ml (1 fl oz) double cream

METHOD

1. Lightly grease a 24 cm (10 in) deep cake tin with a removable base.

2. Crush biscuits till fine. Melt butter in a saucepan, and stir in crushed biscuits. Press the mixture in the base and side of tin. Leave to set in fridge till well chilled.

3. Place 3 tablespoons of canned syrup in a saucepan and sprinkle on gelatine. Place over a pan of hot water over low heat and stir till dissolved.

4. Whisk chilled evaporated milk until thick. Set aside. Beat cottage cheese with the castor sugar till smooth and fold in the gelatine mixture and chilled milk. Leave mixture in a cool place until just to the point of setting (approximately ½ hour). Whisk double cream till thick, stir till well mixed and pour into tin. Chill till well set in fridge.

Note:
Use the syrup of canned peaches or pineapple. For added flavour, add bits of the canned fruit to cream cheese mixture just before chilling.

Decorate cheesecake with fruit slices.

For best results, leave cheesecake in fridge overnight.

NO BAKE LEMON CHEESECAKE

INGREDIENTS

1 packet digestive biscuits
1 tablespoon icing sugar
115 g (4 oz) melted butter, hot

Ingredients for filling:
1 tablespoon gelatine crystals
2 tablespoons hot water
115 ml (4 fl oz) boiling water
1 teaspoon lemon rind
1 tablespoon lemon juice
1 tin evaporated milk, chilled overnight
225 g (8 oz) Philadelphia cream cheese
5 tablespoons condensed milk

Ingredients for topping:
½ can sliced peaches
2 tablespoons gelatine crystals
55 ml (2 fl oz) boiling water

METHOD

1. Crush biscuits till fine; mix with icing sugar, add hot melted butter and stir till well mixed. Press biscuit mixture to bottom and sides of low cake tin. Chill for 2 hours.

2. Heat gelatine and water over low heat till dissolved. Combine gelatine solution with 115 ml boiling water, lemon rind and juice. Set aside.

3. Whip chilled evaporated milk till thick, remove to a bowl. Add cream cheese to condensed milk and stir till combined.

4. Mix together gelatine mixture, whipped evaporated milk and cream cheese mixture. Beat till mixture is well combined and smooth.

5. Pour filling into biscuit crust in tin and decorate with sliced peaches. Dissolve 2 tablespoons gelatine in water over low heat. Allow to cool for a while and pour over peaches. Chill overnight to set.

Note:
Pour boiled gelatine over peaches when gelatine is about to set.

CHOCOLATE CHIFFON CAKE

INGREDIENTS

200 g (7 oz) flour
  4 level teaspoons baking powder   **A**
  1 level teaspoon fine salt

  55 g (2 oz) cocoa
  2 tablespoons 'instant' coffee powder   **B**
225 ml (8 fl oz) boiling water

370 g (13 oz) castor sugar
170 ml (6 fl oz) corn oil
  8 egg yolks
  1 teaspoon vanilla essence
  9 egg whites
  1 teaspoon sugar
  1 teaspoon cream of tartar

METHOD

1. Sift **A** together.
2. Blend **B** and let cool.
3. Place sifted flour and sugar in a mixing bowl. Make a well in the centre.
4. Pour oil, egg yolks, vanilla essence and cooled cocoa mixture into the well. Blend and beat slowly till smooth (5 minutes).
5. In a separate bowl, whisk egg whites with 1 teaspoon sugar and 1 teaspoon cream of tartar till very stiff (20 minutes).
6. Fold the egg white mixture lightly into the beaten mixture till well blended.
7. Place in an ungreased tube cake tin. Bake in a hot oven at 205°C (400°F) or Regulo 8 for ½ hour. Reduce heat to 175°C (350°F) or Regulo 6 and bake for another ¾–1 hour. The cake should spring back when lightly touched.
8. Invert cake and allow to cool before removing from pan.

Note:
Sift in the cream of tartar to the egg whites while whisking to mix it evenly. Pre-heat oven before use.

COFFEE WALNUT CAKE

INGREDIENTS

255 g (9 oz) flour
  1 teaspoon baking powder
½ teaspoon salt
170 g (6 oz) chopped walnuts
225 g (8 oz) butter
200 g (7 oz) sugar
  5 eggs

2 tablespoons 'instant' coffee powder mixes
  with 1 tablespoon hot water
3 tablespoons evaporated milk mixed with   **A**
  3 tablespoons water

  1 teaspoon vanilla essence

METHOD

1. Grease and flour cake tin.
2. Sift flour, baking powder and salt into a basin. Add the chopped walnuts. Set aside.
3. Beat butter and sugar till light and creamy. Add eggs, one at a time, beating well after each egg.
4. Mix **A** in a cup.
5. Divide flour into three portions and fold each portion one at a time into the creamed butter mixture. Lastly, add **A** and the vanilla essence. Mix lightly.
6. Pour batter into cake tin and bake in slow oven at 165°C (325°F) or Regulo 5 for 1–1½ hours or until cake is done. Leave cake in tin for 5 minutes to cool on a cooling rack.

FRUIT CAKE

(CHRISTMAS CAKE)

INGREDIENTS

285 g (10 oz) flour
1 teaspoon salt   **A**
2 teaspoons mixed spice★

225 g (8 oz) currants
225 g (8 oz) sultanas
225 g (8 oz) raisins
115 g (4 oz) candied peel   **B**
115 g (4 oz) almonds
115 g (4 oz) glace cherries

3 tablespoons sugar
2 tablespoons water
6 tablespoons evaporated milk
225 g (8 oz) butter
175 g (6 oz) sugar
5 eggs, lightly beaten
1 teaspoon vanilla essence
4 tablespoons brandy

METHOD

1. Sift **A** together. Chop **B** into small pieces.

2. Rub sifted flour into the chopped ingredients. Set aside.

3. Grease an 18 cm (7 in) square cake tin. Line with greaseproof paper at base and sides. Grease paper.

4. Caramelize the sugar and water to a dark brown. Add the evaporated milk and stir over a low heat to dissolve the caramel. Cool in refrigerator.

5. Cream butter and sugar till light. Add beaten eggs a little each time and beat till well blended.

6. Add the vanilla essence, caramel and 2 tablespoons of the flour to the egg mixture. Beat lightly till well blended.

7. Fold in the remaining flour-fruit mixture and the brandy. Stir well.

8. Pour batter into cake tin and bake in oven at 175°C (350°F) or Regulo 6 for 1–1¼ hours or till cake is done. Leave cake to cool in tin before turning out on to a cake rack.

★*See page 199.*

GINGER CAKE

INGREDIENTS

4 egg yolks
85 g (3 oz) sugar
85 g (3 oz) butter
55 ml (2 fl oz) black treacle
4 egg whites with 1 teaspoon sugar
½ teaspoon cream of tartar

140 g (5 oz) flour
2 teaspoons ginger powder
½ teaspoon mixed spice★   **A**
1 teaspoon bicarbonate of soda

1 tablespoon brandy or rum
55 ml (2 fl oz) evaporated milk

METHOD

1. Grease and flour a cake or loaf tin. Pre-heat oven to 190°C (375°F) or Regulo 7.

2. Beat egg yolks with sugar till very thick and creamy.

3. Heat butter till almost boiling point, and add slowly to the beaten egg yolk. Pour in the black treacle and beat to blend.

4. Whisk egg whites with sugar till frothy. Sift in cream of tartar and continue whisking until mixture becomes stiff and can hold its shape.

5. Sift **A** together three times. Combine and fold in the egg white mixture, egg yolk mixture, brandy and milk. Mix well.

6. Pour into cake tin and bake in moderate oven at 175°C (350°F) or Regulo 6 for 20 minutes. Reduce oven heat to 135°C (275°F) or Regulo 3 for another 20 minutes or until cake springs back when pressed with finger. Remove and turn cake over on to rack to cool for 15 minutes.

★*See page 199.*

LEMON SPONGE CAKE

INGREDIENTS

12 eggs
1 cup castor sugar
1½ cups flour
115 g (4 oz) butter, melted and warmed
1 teaspoon vanilla essence
½ teaspoon fresh lemon juice
½ teaspoon cream of tartar

METHOD

1. Pre-heat oven to 205°C (400°F). Separate egg yolks from whites.

2. Beat egg yolks and sugar till creamy. Add flour and butter, stir till well blended. Add vanilla essence, lemon juice and mix well. Set aside.

3. Beat egg whites till frothy. Sieve in the cream of tartar and beat till stiff but not dry.

4. Pour in the egg yolk mixture and fold lightly into egg whites till well blended. Pour into an ungreased chiffon cake pan.

5. Bake for 10 minutes at 205°C for 10 minutes. Reduce heat to 177°C (335°F) and bake till cake is done (approximately 25–30 minutes). Test when cake leaves side of pan; cake should spring back when pressed gently with finger.

6. Remove cake from oven; invert pan and leave to cool for 10 minutes before taking out from pan.

PANDAN CHIFFON CAKE

INGREDIENTS

455 g (1 lb) grated coconut, white
9 egg whites
1 rounded teaspoon cream of tartar

2 tablespoons screw pine juice, from 12 screw pine leaves
1 teaspoon green food colouring

8 egg yolks
255 g (9 oz) castor sugar   **A**
170 ml (6 fl oz) corn oil
1 teaspoon vanilla essence

140 g (5 oz) 'Softasilk' or 'Silksifted' flour   *sifted twice*
2 heaped teaspoons baking powder
½ teaspoon fine salt

METHOD

1. Pre-heat oven to 170°C (350°F).

2. Squeeze coconut for 170 ml (6 fl oz) No. 1 milk. Cook over low heat till it boils and thickens like cream, stirring all the time. Cool.

3. Beat egg white till frothy, sieve the cream of tartar on to egg white and continue beating till very stiff but not dry. Set aside.

4. Combine **A** in a bowl and beat lightly.

5. Put flour in a mixing bowl. Make a well in centre, and pour in **A**. Bring in flour from sides and beat with batter beater till smooth.

6. Add the screw pine juice, green food colouring and coconut cream. Stir till blended.

7. Fold in one-third of the egg white to the egg mixture and blend well. Then add the rest of the egg white and fold in lightly with rubber spatula till well blended.

8. Pour into an ungreased 25 cm × 10 cm (10 in × 4 in) chiffon cake tin and bake for 45–50 minutes or till cake springs back when pressed with finger. Remove from oven, invert cake tin and leave for ½ hour before transferring to a wire rack to cool.

Pandan Chiffon Cake

POUND CAKE

INGREDIENTS

225 g (8 oz) butter
1 teaspoon vanilla essence
3 drops almond essence
6 egg yolks
225 g (8 oz) sugar
6 egg whites beaten with 1 teaspoon sugar

170 g (6 oz) flour   **A**
¼ teaspoon salt

METHOD

1. Cream butter till fluffy. Add vanilla and almond essence to blend.
2. Beat egg yolks and sugar till thick.
3. Whisk egg whites with 1 teaspoon sugar till stiff.
4. Sift **A** together. Mix with egg yolks and creamed butter. Fold in the egg whites and mix thoroughly.
5. Pour cake mixture into a greased cake tin and bake in slow oven at 150°C (300°F) or Regulo 4 for 1–1¼ hours. Turn on to a rack to cool.

ROSE MARIE CAKE

INGREDIENTS

20 egg yolks
170 g (6 oz) sugar
340 g (12 oz) butter
1 teaspoon vanilla essence
6 egg whites beaten with 1 tablespoon sugar

85 g (3 oz) flour
170 g (6 oz) Marie biscuits, finely pounded
    and sifted   **A**
1½ teaspoons baking powder
½ teaspoon mixed spice★

METHOD

1. Beat egg yolks with 85 g (3 oz) of the sugar till thick and creamy.
2. Cream butter with the remaining sugar till fluffy. Beat in the vanilla essence.
3. In a clean and dry bowl, whisk egg whites and 1 tablespoon sugar till stiff.
4. Sift **A**. Fold the sifted ingredients, egg yolks and whites into the creamed mixture.
5. Pour mixture into a greased cake tin and bake in oven at 150°C (300°F) or Regulo 4 for 15 minutes. Reduce heat to 135°C and bake for another ¾–1 hour.

SEMOLINA CAKE

INGREDIENTS

455 g (16 oz) butter
225 g (8 oz) semolina
12 egg yolks
5 egg whites
255 g (9 oz) sugar
140 g (5 oz) flour
½ teaspoon mixed spice★

4 tablespoons brandy
3 drops almond essence
1 teaspoon vanilla essence   **A**
3 drops rose essence

225 g (8 oz) almonds, chopped coarsely

METHOD

1. Beat butter for 15 minutes; add the semolina and continue beating for another 10 minutes. Leave in bowl to stand for 4 hours.
2. Beat egg yolks, whites and half of the sugar together till creamy. Add the rest of the sugar and beat till very thick.
3. Sift flour and mixed spice twice.
4. Mix creamed butter and semolina with 225 ml (8 fl oz) of the egg mixture and **A** till well blended. Then fold in the flour and the chopped almonds alternately with the rest of the egg mixture.
5. Pour into a greased tin and bake in a very slow oven at 135°C (275°F) or Regulo 3 for 1–1½ hours.

★*See "Mixed Spice" on page 199.*

SPONGE SANDWICH

INGREDIENTS

12 egg yolks
200 g (7 oz) castor sugar
5 egg whites
140 g (5 oz) butter

140 g (5 oz) flour | sifted
1 teaspoon baking powder | together

2 teaspoons brandy
1 teaspoon vanilla essence
Apricot jam, warmed

METHOD

1. Pre-heat oven to 190°C (375°F).

2. Brush two 20 cm (8 in) sandwich tins with butter and dust with flour.

3. Beat yolks with three-quarters of the sugar till thick and creamy.

4. In a dry clean bowl, beat egg whites with the rest of the sugar till stiff.

5. Bring the butter to a boil in a saucepan.

6. Fold egg white and flour, in parts, to the yolks adding brandy, vanilla essence and the boiling butter gradually. Stir lightly till well blended. Pour batter into two sandwich tins and bake till golden brown for about 20–25 minutes or till done.

7. Turn cake over and whilst still hot spread the warmed jam to sandwich cakes.

Note:
Level the cake batter in tin and with back of spoon make a slight dent in middle of cake so that cake will be level after baking.

SUPER LIGHT SPONGE SANDWICH

INGREDIENTS

5 eggs and 2 egg yolks
225 g (8 oz) castor sugar

30 g (1 oz) or 2 tablespoons butter |
55 ml (2 fl oz) or 4 tablespoons boiling | A
water |
Pinch of salt |

140 g (5 oz) self-raising flour, sifted twice

METHOD

1. Grease and dust with flour three 20 cm (8 in) round sandwich tins.

2. Pre-heat oven to 165°C (325°F).

3. Beat eggs and sugar till thick and creamy, about 15–20 minutes.

4. Put **A** in a small saucepan and bring to the boil. Pour gradually into the egg mixture and beat lightly. Add small amounts of flour and fold it in.

5. Pour batter into tins and bake for 25–30 minutes or till cake springs back when pressed lightly with finger. Bake to a light golden colour.

6. Remove from oven, loosen cake by scraping sides of cake tin with a knife and turn over on to a wire rack immediately. Turn over once more to let cake cool.

7. Sandwich cake with warmed apricot jam, butter cream or whipped cream as desired.

Butter cream filling:
2 small egg yolks
85 g (3 oz) icing sugar
1 tablespoon rum *or* 1 teaspoon vanilla essence
170 g (6 oz) unsalted butter

Beat all ingredients over moderate speed for 5 minutes.

SULTANA CAKE

INGREDIENTS

3 tablespoons brandy
400 g (14 oz) sultanas

255 g (9 oz) plain flour
55 g (2 oz) self-raising flour — *sifted together*
Pinch of salt

115 g (4 oz) chopped almonds
225 g (8 oz) butter, semi-frozen
200 g (7 oz) castor sugar
5 eggs
2 teaspoons vanilla essence
6 tablespoons fresh milk
10 whole almonds, halved

METHOD

1. Sprinkle the brandy over the sultanas and mix well. Leave to soak for 1 hour. Rub in 1 cup of the sifted flour and set aside. Mix 3 tablespoons of the flour with the chopped almonds.

2. Beat butter and sugar together till light and creamy. Add eggs one at a time, beat for about 5 minutes for each egg. Beat five more minutes after the last egg. Add the vanilla essence and 3 tablespoons of the milk and beat till just blended.

3. Fold in the rest of the flour with the rest of the milk, the sultanas, and the chopped almonds. Using a spatula, mix batter by folding from bottom of bowl till evenly mixed.

4. Grease and line cake tin with greaseproof paper. Pour the mixture into tin and bake in moderate oven 135°C (275°F) for 1½–1¾ hours or till done. Leave in tin for ½ hour before turning out on to a wire rack to cool. Keep cake for at least a day or two before serving.

Note:
Bake cake for 10 minutes before placing the halved almonds on top to prevent them sinking into cake. Continue baking till cooked.

SWISS ROLL

INGREDIENTS

200 g (7 oz) sugar
8 eggs
2½ tablespoons evaporated milk
1 teaspoon vanilla essence
130 g (4½ oz) flour

METHOD

1. Grease and flour two Swiss roll tins.

2. Beat sugar and eggs till very thick and creamy. Add evaporated milk and vanilla essence. Beat till well blended.

3. Fold flour lightly into egg mixture. Pour cake mixture into tins. Bake in a hot oven at 205°C (400°F) or Regulo 8 for 7 minutes.

4. Place cakes on a damp towel and roll using the towel. Leave for 1 minute, unroll and spread with jam. Roll again. Cool before cutting into pieces.

WALNUT CAKE

INGREDIENTS

115 g (4 oz) self-raising flour
55 g (2 oz) plain flour — **A**

4 tablespoons evaporated milk
4 tablespoons milk — **B**

140 g (5 oz) butter
170 g (6 oz) fine sugar
3 egg whites and 1 egg yolk
170 g (6 oz) finely chopped walnuts

METHOD

1. Cream butter and sugar till light and fluffy.
2. Add eggs, one at a time, beating well.
3. Sift **A** together. Mix **B** together.
4. Fold the flour, milk and walnuts lightly into the egg mixture.
5. Bake in a moderate oven at 175°C (350°F) or Regulo 6 for 20–30 minutes.

WHITE CHRISTMAS
(MIXED FRUIT AND COCONUT
CANDY BARS)

INGREDIENTS

250 g (9 oz) icing sugar, sifted
250 g (9 oz) full cream milk powder, sifted
250 g (9 oz) desiccated coconut, toasted lightly
250 g (9 oz) mixed fruit   **A**
  2 cups rice crispies
  65 g (2½ oz) walnuts, chopped coarsely
  65 g (2½ oz) toasted almonds, chopped
    coarsely

250 g copha★
  1 teaspoon vanilla essence

METHOD

1. Stir **A** in a mixing bowl to mix evenly.

2. Heat copha in a heavy bottomed pan till it melts. Add vanilla essence. Pour copha mixture into **A** and stir till well combined.

3. Pour mixture into a lightly greased 25 × 20 cm (10 × 8 in) baking tray or glass baking dish. Press top of mixture to smoothen till firm. Chill in refrigerator for two hours before cutting into fingers. Store in refrigerator.

Note:
★Copha is solid cream of coconut available in specialty supermarkets.

Biscuits, Cookies and Pastries

Special Almond Biscuits

Almond Raisin Rock Cookies

Cat's Tongues

Cheese Cookies

Chocolate Eclairs/Cream Puffs

Custard Tartlets

Fruit Scones

Melting Moments

Pineapple-Shaped Tarts

Pineapple 'Open' Tarts

Sponge Fingers

Spritches Butter Biscuits

Sujee Biscuits

Sweet Corn Fritters

Selection of cookies with Cheese Cookies
(middle) and Sugee Biscuits (in canister and foreground)

SPECIAL ALMOND BISCUITS

INGREDIENTS

680 g (24 oz) plain flour
170 g (6 oz) icing sugar
455 g (16 oz) butter, chilled in refrigerator
3 egg yolks, lightly beaten with 1 teaspoon vanilla essence
1 egg and 1 yolk, lightly beaten
115 g (4 oz) almonds, blanched and chopped coarsely

METHOD

1. Sift flour and icing sugar into a basin.

2. Rub butter into the flour till mixture resembles breadcrumbs. Pour the beaten egg yolks into the flour mixture. Mix lightly to form a soft dough. Chill in refrigerator for ½ hour.

3. Knead dough very lightly. Roll out to 0.5 cm (¼ in) thickness on a lightly floured board or marble table top.

4. Using a fancy cutter, cut dough and place on greased baking trays. Glaze with beaten egg and sprinkle top with chopped almonds. Bake in moderate oven at 150°C (300°F) or Regulo 4 for 20 minutes. Cool on a rack and keep in an airtight container.

Note:
Divide dough into three or four portions. Flatten the dough with palm of hand before rolling out to cut. Lift dough gently with a spatula and space apart on baking trays.

ALMOND RAISIN ROCK COOKIES

INGREDIENTS

225 g (8 oz) self-raising flour
½ teaspoon mixed spice* (optional)
Pinch of salt
2 teaspoons baking powder
85 g (3 oz) butter, chilled
115 g (4 oz) sugar
55 g (2 oz) chopped almonds, roasted
55 g (2 oz) raisins
2 eggs lightly beaten with 1 teaspoon vanilla essence

METHOD

1. Sift the spice, salt and baking powder into a bowl.

2. Rub butter into flour mixture till it resembles breadcrumbs.

3. Combine the flour, sugar, almonds, raisins and the beaten eggs to form a soft dough. Do not rub or knead.

4. Space dough out in small heaps on a greased tray and bake in a moderate oven at 150°C (300°F) or Regulo 4 for 20–25 minutes until brown.

5. Cool on a wire tray.

See "Mixed Spice" on page 199.

CAT'S TONGUES

INGREDIENTS

455 g (16 oz) flour
  2 teaspoons baking powder
455 g (16 oz) butter
455 g (16 oz) sugar
  2 teaspoons vanilla essence
12 egg whites beaten with 1 teaspoon sugar

METHOD

1. Grease baking trays evenly with butter.

2. Sift flour and baking powder.

3. Beat butter and sugar till light and creamy. Add vanilla essence and beat till well blended.

4. In a very dry and clean bowl, beat egg whites and sugar till stiff, but not dry.

5. Fold one-quarter of the egg whites lightly into the creamed mixture. Fold (in three parts) the flour, and the rest of the egg whites lightly into the creamed mixture.

6. Scoop batter into an icing tube with a plain 1.3 cm icing nozzle. Press batter out in small heaps or in 5 cm lengths, 2.5 cm apart, on to greased trays.

7. Bake in oven at 150°C (300°F) or Regulo 4 for 20–25 minutes till pale brown. Remove from oven, take biscuits off trays immediately to cool on rack for 5 minutes. Keep in airtight containers immediately when cool.

Note:
Remove cat's tongues immediately from tray to cake rack after taking them out of the oven. Place them flat on a cake rack to prevent them from curling.

CHEESE COOKIES

INGREDIENTS

  1 tablespoon castor sugar
225 g (8 oz) self-raising flour
  ¼ teaspoon pepper
  ¼ teaspoon chilli powder (optional)
225 g (8 oz) butter, chilled
225 g (8 oz) cheese (preferably fully matured), grated
115 g (4 oz) desiccated coconut for rolling cookies

METHOD

1. Sift all dry ingredients into a mixing bowl; add butter, mix with fingertips to resemble breadcrumbs. Add cheese to flour mixture and knead lightly to form a dough. Chill in refrigerator for ½ hour.

2. Divide dough into 4 parts. Roll each part into thin logs and cut into equal pieces the size of a candlenut.

3. Spread the desiccated coconut onto a tray; roll cheese balls in desiccated coconut and space balls well apart on biscuit trays. Use a fork to flatten ball slightly and to form a pattern. Bake in moderate oven, 135°C (275°F), for 25–30 minutes till pale brown. Cool on cake rack before storing in an airtight container.

Note:
Cheese cookies should be very pale in colour but crunchy right through.

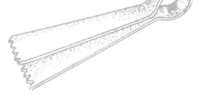

CHOCOLATE ECLAIRS/ CREAM PUFFS

INGREDIENTS

Choux Pastry:
170 g (6 oz) flour
 1 teaspoon baking powder
115 g (4 oz) butter
285 ml (10 fl oz) water
 5 eggs

METHOD

1. Pre-heat oven to 230°C (450°F) or Regulo 10.
2. Sift flour and baking powder.
3. Bring butter and water to the boil in a pan.
4. Stir in the sifted flour all at once and cook till mixture is smooth and leaves sides of pan.
5. Remove from heat and cool in mixing bowl. Beat in eggs, one at a time, till smooth and shiny.
6. Place cooked mixture in piping tube and press batter out in small heaps on a well-greased tray.
7. Bake in a hot oven at 230°C (450°F) or Regulo 10 for 15 minutes. Reduce heat to 175°C (350°F) or Regulo 6 and bake for another 15 minutes till golden brown.
8. Cook on cake rack. Split puffs at sides and fill with custard cream.

INGREDIENTS

Filling:
 3 eggs
115 g (4 oz) sugar
 3 tablespoons flour, heaped
 1 teaspoon custard powder

225 ml (8 fl oz) evaporated milk | **A**
225 ml (8 fl oz) water

 2 tablespoons condensed milk
 1 teaspoon butter
 1 teaspoon vanilla essence

METHOD

1. Beat eggs, sugar, flour and custard powder together in a heavy-bottomed saucepan.
2. Bring **A** to near boiling point.
3. Pour condensed and hot milk gradually into egg mixture. Cook mixture over a low heat, stirring continuously till mixture is thick.
4. Remove from heat. Stir in the butter and vanilla essence. Cool before filling.

For chocolate eclairs:
1. Pre-heat oven to 205°C (400°F) or Regulo 8.
2. Using a large plain piping tube, pipe the Choux pastry into 7.5 cm (3 in) lengths on a lightly greased baking tray.
3. Bake for 20–25 minutes until golden brown.
4. Slit each eclair horizontally. Then leave to cool on a wire rack.
5. When thoroughly cold, fill with custard cream and coat the top with chocolate butter icing. (See recipe)

CHOCOLATE BUTTER ICING

INGREDIENTS

55 g (2 oz) plain chocolate, grated
½ teaspoon 'instant' coffee powder
 1 tablespoon rum
55 g (2 oz) butter

METHOD

1. Stir grated chocolate, 'instant' coffee powder and rum in a bowl over saucepan of simmering water till chocolate turns into a smooth cream. Remove and set aside to cool.
2. Beat butter, adding the melted chocolate till mixture is of spreading consistency.
3. Spread on top of eclairs.

CUSTARD TARTLETS

Pastry:
225 g (8 oz) flour
  A pinch of salt
  2 tablespoons icing sugar
170 g (6 oz) butter
  1 egg, separated
4–5 tablespoons iced water

1. Sift flour, salt and icing sugar together.
2. Rub butter lightly into sifted flour till mixture resembles breadcrumbs.
3. Add egg yolk and water to form a dough.
4. Chill dough in refrigerator for ½ hour. Roll dough out thinly and cut to line greased patty tins. Prick pastry with fork and brush with egg white.
5. Bake 'blind' in hot oven at 150°C (300°F) or Regulo 4 for 10 minutes.
6. Remove from oven and fill with custard.

Note:
To bake 'blind' is to bake unfilled pastry shells.

Custard:
  4 eggs
  2 tablespoons condensed milk
    A pinch of salt
225 ml (8 fl oz) evaporated milk
340 ml (12 fl oz) water
  55 g (2 oz) sugar
  1 teaspoon vanilla essence
    Grated nutmeg

1. Beat eggs, condensed milk and salt lightly in a bowl.
2. Heat evaporated milk with water and sugar. Pour gradually into the egg mixture. Add vanilla essence and strain. Spoon custard into pastry cases.
3. Sprinkle with grated nutmeg and bake in oven at 150°C (300°F) or Regulo 4 for 20–25 minutes or until custard is firm.

FRUIT SCONES

INGREDIENTS

  1 egg, lightly beaten
    Pinch of salt
  1 cup milk
  2 cups self-raising flour
  ½ cup sugar
  ½ cup sultanas
  2 tablespoons lemon peel
100 g (3½ oz) butter

METHOD

1. Pre-heat oven to 175°C (350°F). Mix egg, salt and milk in a bowl.
2. Combine flour, sugar and fruits in a mixing bowl and rub in butter.
3. Pour the egg mixture gradually into the flour mixture to form a soft dough.
4. Dust top and bottom of dough with a generous portion of flour. Put between pieces of wax paper and roll lightly till 2 cm thick. Cut with scone cutter and place in a sandwich tin to bake for 15–20 minutes or till done. Serve hot with butter and jam.

MELTING MOMENTS

INGREDIENTS

455 g (16 oz) self-raising flour
225 g (8 oz) coarse sugar
225 g (8 oz) butter
  2 eggs
115 g (4 oz) cherries, diced

METHOD

1. Mix flour, sugar, butter and eggs in a large basin.
2. Mix lightly with fingertips to form a soft dough.
3. Place portions (each the size of a hazel nut) of the biscuit mixture on a greased baking sheet. Top each with a piece of cherry. Bake in oven at 150°C (300°F) or Regulo 4 till light golden brown for about 20–30 minutes. Cool on rack before storing in an airtight container.

PINEAPPLE-SHAPED TARTS

INGREDIENTS

565 g (20 oz) flour
  2 teaspoons baking powder   **A**

340 g (12 oz) butter, chilled

  2 tablespoons castor sugar
  3 egg yolks
  1 teaspoon vanilla essence
  3 drops of yellow food colouring   **B**
  ½ teaspoon salt
  8 tablespoons boiling water

  Flour for dusting
  Cloves

METHOD

Glaze:
Beat 1 egg and 1 yolk with 2 drops of yellow food colouring.

1. Sift **A** into a basin.
2. Rub butter lightly into flour with tips of fingers till mixture resembles breadcrumbs.
3. Beat **B** lightly in a bowl.
4. Pour egg mixture into the flour mixture. Add boiling water and mix with both hands to form a pastry dough.
5. Chill in refrigerator for ½ hour.

To shape the tarts:
1. Divide pastry into two or three parts. Place each part on a well-floured board or marble table top. Knead for a moment till smooth. Flatten pastry with palm of hand and dust with flour. Roll pastry out to 0.5 cm (0.2 in) thickness.
2. Cut pastry pieces with an oval pastry cutter.
3. Place a piece of pineapple jam on one half of the pastry and fold the other half over it. Press the edges together, using finger and thumb. Roll tart so that one end is tapered. Insert a clove (without pit) at the broad end, to resemble a pineapple stalk.

4. Using a small pair of scissors, snip tiny 'v' shapes on the front half of the tart. Snip in rows.

5. Place tarts on greased trays, leaving space for expansion. Glaze and bake in oven at 175°C (350°F) or Regulo 6 for 10 minutes. Reduce heat to 150°C (300°F) or Regulo 4 and continue baking for another 15–20 minutes, till light brown.

Pineapple filling (to be made the day before):
6 pineapples, preferably Mauritian
Coarse sugar (See note below)
3 cloves
1 piece 5 cm (2 in) cinnamon stick
3 segments of star anise

1. Remove skin and 'eye' from pineapples.

2. Grate pineapples coarsely. Use muslin to squeeze out juice from pineapples. Do not squeeze too dry. Chop grated pineapples till fine. (Wear rubber gloves)

3. Place chopped pineapples, sugar, cloves, cinnamon and star anise in a heavy-bottomed aluminium saucepan.

4. Cook over moderate heat till almost dry (about 1 hour). Continue cooking over a low heat, till mixture is thick. Keep stirring all the while.

5. Cool. Store overnight in refrigerator.

6. Make into long rolls of 2.5 cm (1 in) diameter and cut into 1 cm (1½ in) pieces. Roll each piece to resemble a quail's egg.

7. Place jam pieces on a tray to chill in refrigerator till ready for use.

Note:
Amount of sugar should be exactly the same as amount of pineapple e.g. 1 cup sugar to 1 cup pineapple.

PINEAPPLE 'OPEN' TARTS

INGREDIENTS

680 g (1½ lb) flour
  1 teaspoon fine salt
  2 tablespoons fine sugar
455 g (1 lb) butter
  1 egg

55 ml (2 fl oz) iced water   **A** *mixed*
2 teaspoons vanilla essence   *together*
3 drops of yellow food colouring

METHOD

1. Sift flour with salt and sugar.

2. Rub butter into flour till mixture resembles breadcrumbs.

3. Beat egg lightly, add to the flour. Add Ingredients **A** to form a pastry dough. Chill for ½ hour.

4. Roll pastry to 0.5 cm thickness on a floured board or marble table top.

5. Cut with a special tart cutter.

6. Fill tarts with pineapple filling.

7. Pinch a small neat frill or pattern around the edge of tart. Cut thin strips from left-over pastry to decorate top.

8. Place tarts on a greased tray and bake in a hot oven at 175°C (350°F) or Regulo 6 for 15 minutes.

9. Reduce heat and bake for another 10-15 minutes till light brown.

10. Turn tarts out to cool on a wire rack before storing in an airtight container.

Note:
Use special brass pincers to pinch frill for tart. For pineapple filling see Pineapple-Shaped Tarts

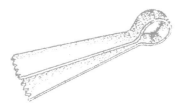

SPONGE FINGERS

INGREDIENTS

Butter for greasing
Flour for dusting
  4 egg yolks
115 g (4 oz) sugar
  1 teaspoon vanilla essence
  4 egg whites
A pinch of salt
  2 teaspoons sugar
 85 g (3 oz) 'Softasilk' flour
 85 g (3 oz) sugar, to sprinkle over sponge fingers

METHOD

1. Grease trays with butter; dust with flour.

2. Beat egg yolks and 115 g sugar till very thick and creamy. Add vanilla essence, beat till very well blended.

3. Beat egg whites till frothy; add the salt and 2 teaspoons sugar and continue beating till mixture is stiff, but not dry.

4. Lightly fold in one-third of the egg white mixture to the egg yolk mixture. Sift in one-third of the flour and stir very lightly to blend well. Repeat the process twice with the rest of the flour and the egg white and egg yolk mixture.

5. Spoon batter into an icing tube. Squeeze on to prepared greased trays to form finger shapes 10 cm (4 in) long and 2.5 cm (1 in) wide. Place sponge fingers 2.5 cm apart to prevent them from sticking to one another whilst being baked.

6. Sprinkle sugar over fingers and bake in oven at 150°C (300°F) or Regulo 4 for 20–25 minutes till light brown.

7. Remove fingers immediately from baking trays after taking them out of the oven. Place on cake rack to cool. Keep in an airtight container.

SPRITCHES BUTTER BISCUITS

INGREDIENTS

910 g (32 oz) plain flour
455 g (16 oz) flour
455 g (16 oz) butter
455 g (16 oz) icing sugar
  8 egg yolks
  2 teaspoons vanilla essence
  4 egg whites and 1 teaspoon sugar

METHOD

1. Sift the two types of flour together into a basin.

2. Beat butter, sugar and egg yolks to a cream. Add vanilla essence and mix.

3. In a separate bowl, whisk the egg whites with 1 teaspoon sugar until thick.

4. Mix the creamed butter mixture with the flour and the whisked egg whites to form a soft dough.

5. Press dough through a biscuit pump using any design. Space biscuits out on a greased tin and bake in moderate oven at 150°C (300°F) or Regulo 4 for 25–30 minutes, or till light golden brown. Cool on rack before storing in an airtight container.

Note:
Beat egg whites in a very clean and dry mixing bowl.

SUJEE BISCUITS

INGREDIENTS

455 g (1 lb) ghee
340 g (12 oz) icing sugar
795 g (1¾ lb) plain flour

METHOD

1. Cream ghee and sugar for 5 minutes, add flour and knead into a soft dough. Leave covered for 4 hours.

2. Pre-heat oven at 120°C (250°F).

3. Divide dough in 4 parts. Shape each part into a roll and cut each roll into 50 pieces, the size of a marble. Press each piece lightly, put on a greased baking tin spaced well apart and bake in a moderate oven for 20–25 minutes. Cool on a wire rack and keep in an airtight container.

Note:
Bake biscuits to a pale cream to get the buttery taste of ghee. This recipe makes 200 biscuits.

SWEET CORN FRITTERS

INGREDIENTS

2 egg yolks
1 small can whole sweet corn
55 g (2 oz) breadcrumbs
  Pinch of salt   **A**
  Dash of pepper
1 teaspoon baking powder

2 egg whites

METHOD

1. Mix **A** in a bowl.

2. Whip egg whites till stiff. Fold in the sweet corn mixture. Leave to stand for ½ hour.

3. Drop spoonfuls of fritter batter into hot oil to deep-fry till golden brown or pour batter thinly into a frying pan and fry as for pancake.

List of some ingredients

ENGLISH	MALAY	CHINESE
agar-agar	agar-agar	石花菜
alkaline water (clear)	ayer abu (puteh)	白鹼水
alkaline water (yellow)	ayer abu (kuning)	黃鹼水
anchovies	ikan bilis	江魚仔
aniseed	jintan manis	大茴香
basil leaf	daun kemangi	羅勒菜
bean sprouts	towgay	豆芽
bird's eye chilli	chilli padi	指天椒
borax	tingkal	硼砂
cabbage	kobis	包菜
candlenut	buah keras	馬加拉
cardamom	buah pelaga	豆蔻
cashew nut	biji gajus	檳如果
Chinese celery	seladeri	芹菜
Chinese mustard greens	sawi	菜心
Chinese parsley	pasli	芫荽菜
Chinese turnip	bangkuang	無菁
chives	kuchai	韭菜
cinnamon bark	kayu manis	桂皮
cloud ear fungus	chendawan kering	木耳
clove	bunga chengkeh	丁香
coriander leaf	daun ketumbar	香菜
coriander seed	ketumbar	香菜子
cray fish	udang katak	蝦婆
crispy Chinese cruller	yu char kway	油條
cumin seed	jintan puteh	小茴香
curry leaf	daun kari	咖哩葉
cuttlefish	sotong karang	墨斗
dorab	parang-parang	西刀
dried bean curd wrapper	tauhu kering	大腐皮
dried chillies	chilli kering	辣椒乾
dried tamarind slice	kulit assam	羅望片
fennel seed	jintan hitam	茴香子
fenugreek	halba	茴香花
five-spice powder	serbok lima rempah	五香粉
flat rice noodles	kwayteow	粿條
fried spongy bean curd	tauhu bakar	豆腐泡
galangal	lengkuas	藍薑
garlic	bawang puteh	蒜
ginger	halia	薑
gingko nut	peck kway	白果
glutinous rice	pulot	糯米
gold-banded scad	selar kuning	君冷
granulated sugar	gula pasir	砂糖
green beans	kachang hijau	綠豆
green bean flour	tepong hoen kwe	綠豆粉
grouper	kerapu	石斑魚
Indonesian black nuts	buah keluak	巴克拉
lemon grass	serai	香茅
lime leaf	daun limau purot	檸檬葉
lime paste	kapor	石灰乳
local lemon	limau nipis	星檸檬
local lime	limau kesturi	酸柑
mint leaf	daun pudina	薄荷葉
monosodium glutamate	serbok perasa	味精
mustard seed	biji sawi	芥辣子
nutmeg	buah pala	荳蔻
onion	bawang besar	洋葱
palm sugar	gula melaka	椰糖
peppercorn	biji lada	胡椒子
phaeomaria	bunga kantan	香花
polygonum	daun kesom	古蒿葉
pomfret	bawal tambak	島鯧
poppy seed	biji kas-kas	罌粟子
prawn paste	petis	蝦膏
preserved bean curd	tauhu asin	腐乳
preserved soya bean	taucheo	豆醬

ENGLISH	MALAY	CHINESE
red beans	kachang merah	紅豆
red snapper	ikan merah	紅雞
rice noodle	kway teow	粿條
rice vermicelli	bee hoon	米粉
rock sugar	gula batu	冰糖
saffron	safron	黃薑色
sago flour	tepong sago	西米粉
salted plum	plam asin	鹹梅
salted radish	lobak asin	菜脯
screw pine leaf	daun pandan	香葉
sesame seed	bijian	胡麻子
shallot	bawang merah kechil	葱頭
shark	yu	沙魚
shrimp paste	belachan	馬來羹
snapper	ikan tanda	記魚
soya bean	kachang soya	黃豆
soya bean cake	tauhu keping	豆腐乾
soya bean strip	tauhu kering	腐竹
soya sauce	kichap	醬油
spanish mackerel	ikan tenggiri	鯖魚
spring onion	daun bawang	葱
star anise	bunga lawang	八角
star fruit	belimbing	羊肚
sweet red sauce	kichap manis merah	海鮮醬
sweet thick black sauce	kichap pekat manis	甜醬
tamarind	assam	羅望子
threadfin	kurau	午魚
transparent bean vermicelli	tang hoon	粉絲
turmeric	kunyit	黃薑
turmeric leaf	daun kunyit	黃薑葉
water chestnut	sengkuang China	馬啼
water convolvulus	kangkong	旱菜
wet rice flour	tepong beras basah	濕米粉(占)
white bean curd (soft)	tauhu	豆腐
white radish	lobak puteh	蘿蔔
wolf herring	ikan parang	西刀魚
yeast	ragi	酵母
yellow noodle	mee	麵

Kitchen Equipment

Aluminium frying pans:

Suitable for deep-frying as they retain a steady heat and give food a nice golden brown colour. Frying chilli paste in an aluminium pan will give the mixture a natural bright colour whereas an iron wok (kuali) will turn it darkish and may give it a slight taste of iron.

Aluminium saucepan:

The heavy flat-bottomed pan is the best buy. It is suitable for both the electric or gas stove. Food is cooked easily without burning. A thin saucepan will buckle when it is overheated and will not be in contact with the electric hot plate.

Enamel saucepan:

Enamel saucepans are more suitable for soups and certain types of food that contain acid like tamarind or vinegar. Chipped enamelware is vulnerable to rust.

Iron wok (kuali):

Most Chinese prefer the iron wok to the aluminium one chiefly because the iron wok can retain extreme heat before the other ingredients are added. Ingredients will cook in a shorter time, keep their taste, and retain their crispness. The most important point to remember is that fried food and pounded ingredients will not stick to the bottom of the wok when it is well heated.

To season an iron wok:

Boil some grated coconut and water till dry [the water should fill up three-quarters of the wok.] Stir occasionally till the coconut turns black, approximately 3–4 hours.
Daily care: Do not use any detergent. Wipe wok well after each wash. If it is to be stored for a long period, grease wok lightly to prevent rust.

Stainless steel pans:

Stainless steel pans look attractive and are easily cleaned, but do not heat evenly. Food burns easily, too.

Copper pans:

Copper pans are rarely used in Asian recipes. For instance, salted mustard turns a very bright green colour when boiled in a copper pan. They are very rarely used, also, as they are very expensive.

Non-stick pans:

There are many brands of non-stick pans to select from. Choose carefully. Whenever possible, buy the best quality products as they are the cheapest in the long run.
Some points to remember when using non-stick pans:
1. Non-stick pans are ideal for frying fish and soft soya bean cake. In a non-stick pan, food that is to be braised or simmered needs less liquid. Food does not burn easily in a non-stick pan nor does the gravy evaporate as fast as in an ordinary pan.
2. The Teflon in a non-stick pan should not be heated through. If this happens, then the pan would lose its non-stick qualities. Since stir-frying requires that it is done over a high heat, do not stir-fry in a non-stick pan. It is always best to stir-fry in an iron wok.
3. Do not use the non-stick pan as a steamer, since this will again damage the Teflon, making the pan less likely to be non-stick.
4. Never use a metal slice on a non-stick pan.
5. Always pour in the oil or gravy first before putting on the heat.

China clay pot:

Braising and stewing of chicken and pork are usually done in the China clay pot. It simmers food very nicely without burning and has a lower rate of evaporation than other saucepans. It also retains any special flavour of the food and is widely used in Chinese homes. It is also used to cook rice and porridge. Buy one with a smooth, glazed finish.

Pounder (pestle and mortar):

Insist on local granite which is white with black/grey spots. To season the pounder, grind a small handful of fine sea sand in the mortar until both the pestle and mortar are reasonably smooth.

INDEX

abalone
    chinese mustard with   129
    steamed chicken and   96
abok abok sago   193
achar   148
agar-agar
    almond jelly   214
    cordial   212
    delight   212
    talam   213
almond
    creme   214
    jelly   214
anchovies
    crispy, with sambal   140
    fried, and groundnuts   152
apom berkuah   192
assam gulai   34
au nee   213
ayam
    buah keluak   34
    goreng assam   36
    kari   46
    kleo   36
    lemper   177
    merah   38
    risa risa   38
    satay panggang   151
    sioh   39
    tempra   39
babi
    assam   40
    chin   40
    pong tay   42
bak pow   160
bak wan kepiting   43
barbecued spareribs   82
bean
    sprouts with crispy salted fish, fried   128
beans
    green, with pearl sago   217
    red, with coconut creme topping   223
    spicy soya bean paste   109
    sweet red bean soup   224
beehoon
    vegetarian   134
beef
    balls, steamed   166
    braised in dark soya sauce   89
    brisket   89
    claypot   70
    curry   88
    curry puffs   172
    dry curry   88
    fillet steak   92
    rendang   142
    serondeng   146
    shin with mixed vegetables   70
    steak, Chinese   90
    with celery   90
belly pork
    soya bean cakes and eggs in soya sauce, braised   138
bengka ambon   194
biscuits
    special almond   240
    spritches butter   247
    sujee   247
buah keluak   34
buah paya masak titek   42
buns
    for braised pork   83
    susi   173
bubor
    cha cha   215
    terigu   214
butter
    cake   228
    cream   228
cakes
    banana   228
    butter   228
    cheese   229
    chocolate chiffon   230
    coffee walnut   230
    fruit   231
    ginger   231
    lemon sponge   232
    no bake lemon cheesecake   229
    pandan chiffon   232
    pound   234
    rose marie   234
    semolina   234
    sultana   236
    walnut   236
cat's tongues   241
cauliflower
    and long beans in creamy sauce   128
chap chye masak titek   44
char siew   84
char kway teow   12
chee cheong fun   174
cheese
    cakes   229
    straws   174
chendol   216
chicken
    and corn soup   76
    abalone   96
    almond curry   97
    bon bon   98
    braised ginger   96
    coconut curry   97
    curry   156
    curry devil   99
    flavoured, rice   54

fried spring   12
fried with dried red chillies   99
in claypot   71
in the basket   100
lemon curried   101
macaroni soup   77
paper wrapped   101
porridge   52
rice   53
salt baked   102
seven minute crispy   104
spicy, fried   144
stew   105
turmeric   105
chilli
dried paste   185
hot sauce   184
garam paste   185
sweet sauce   184
chinese mustard
with abalone   129
with crab meat sauce   132
chocolate
butter icing   242
eclairs   242
chop suey   129
chwee kuey   175
claypot
beef shin with mixed vegetables   70
braised beef brisket   70
chicken   71
fish head   71
seafood   72
tofu and crabmeat   73
tofu with pork and prawns   73
cold dish salad   122
cookies
almond raisin rock   240
cheese   241
cockles, spicy   117
crabs
baked   108
in spicy soya bean paste   109
in tomato chilli sauce   109
mustard with crab meat sauce   132
tofu and crabmeat   73
crayfish mornay   116
cream puffs   242
curry
chicken   156
chicken almond   97
chicken coconut   97
chicken devil   99
dry fish   110
fish head   111
mutton in tomato   85
puffs, beef   172
vegetarian   134
custard tartlets   243

cuttlefish
chilli   116
stuffed, soup   117
desserts   212-225
dhal char   150
duck
shredded, and fruit salad   124
steamed stuffed   104
eggplant
in spicy sauce   130
with pork and prawns   130
fish
and milk sandwiches   181
dry, curry   110
head curry   111
head in claypot   71
salt, sambal   187
fritters
prawn   163
sweet corn   247
gado gado   123
garam
assam   186
chilli, paste   185
goreng ikan terubok   44
groundnut
and fried anchovies   152
creme   217
grouper
braised, with black soya bean sauce   108
gulai, assam   34
hae mee   14
har kow   161
hati babi bungkus   45
hum sui kok   162
ikan
masak assam pekat   45
masak kuah lada   111
rendang   112
terubok, goreng   44
itek tim   46
jemput-jemput   204
ju her eng chye   15
kai chok   52
kai see ho fun   66
kari ayam   46
kee chung   162
kon loh mee   15
kueh
bangket   193
bengka ambon   194
bengka ubi kayu   194
bolu   195
bolu, savoury   195
dadar   196
khoo   197
ko chee   198
ko swee   198
kuria   218

lapis almond   200
lapis batavia   199
lapis beras   200
lompang   201
pulot bengka   201
lopis   202
pie tee   176
pisang   202
sarlat   203
talam pandan   204
kuey
    chap   138
    chang babi   164
kway teow
    beef   64
    char   12
    teochew   67
laksa
    lemak   16
    penang   17
lek tow suan   218
lemper ayam   177
len chee suan   219
loh hon chye   131
loh kai yik   152
loh mee   19
long bean
    omelette   154
    with minced meat   131
lotus seeds
    and dried longan   225
    fluff   219
    paste, mooncake   220
    sweet red bean and   224
luak chye   186
macaroni   77
mee
    goreng   20
    hae   14
    hokien   65
    kon loh   15
    loh   19
    rebus   21
    siam   22
melting moments   243
morokoo   178
minyak, nasi   151
murtabak   23
mushroom
    soya sauce   174
    stuffed   167
mutton
    braised ribs   85
    in tomato curry   85
    ribs with vegetables in spicy gravy   150
nasi
    briani ayam   56
    kuning   55
    lemak   138

lemak kuning   55
lontong   146
minyak   151
pilau   58
ulam   58
ngoh hiang   24
nonya
    birthday noodles   62
    kueh   192-209
    mahmee   67
    salad   123
    specialties   34-49
noodles
    birthday, nonya style   62
    crispy, with prawns   63
    fried   64
onde onde   206
otak otak
    panggang   25
    puteh   25
    rhio   140
ox tail stew   92
pearl sago
    green beans with   217
    with mixed fruit   223
penang
    laksa   17
    salted fish with steamed minced pork   154
pickle
    cucumber   142
poh pia   26
pomegranate, mock   222
pomfret steamed   112
pong tauhu   47
pork
    braised in tamarind sauce   40
    braised in dark soya sauce   40
    braised in soya sauce   83
    braised with crunchy black fungus   82
    instant minced   52
    minced and prawn toast   178
    minced with crab and bamboo shoot soup   43
    roast, strips   83
    rolls   180
    satay   47
    stewed   42
    sweet and sour   84
porridge
    taiwan   152-155
pow
    bak   160
    char siew   160
prawns
    chilli   114
    fritters   163
    glassy   114
    in soya sauce   114
    spicy, rolls   180
    sweet sour   115

tempura   115
pulot
   bengka, kueh   201
   panggang   206
   tarpay   207
   tartar   208
rebong masak lemak   132
rempah
   sambal udang   186
rendang
   beef   142
   ikan   112
rice
   chicken   53
   flavoured chicken   54
   fried   54
   pineapple   59
   steamed glutinous   59
rissoles   179
rojak
   Chinese   120
   Indian   120, 121
roti jala   156
sago pudding   224
salad
   cold dish   122
   nonya   123
   shredded duck and fruit   124
sambal
   belimbing   187
   goreng   147
   lengkong   189
   prawn, sandwiches   178
   salt fish   187
   telor   144
   tempe udang   188
   tumis   188
   udang kering goreng   189
sandwiches
   prawn sambal   178
   steamed fish and milk sauce   181
sar-sargon   209
satay
   ayam panggang   151
   babi   47
   beef   28
   chelop   27
sayor nanka masak lemak   47
seafood
   claypot   72
   dishes   108-117
scones
   fruit   243

sharksfin soup   78
seray kaya   209
siew mai   166
soon kuey   181
sop kambing   78
soto ayam   79
soups
   bak kut teh   76
   chicken and corn   76
   chicken macaroni   77
   hot and sour   77
   thom yam   79
soya bean
   spicy, paste   109
soya sauce
   braised beef in dark   89
   braised grouper   108
   braised belly pork   138
   braised pork   83
   prawns, in   114
   streaky belly pork, in   138
   threadfin, fried with   155
spring rolls
   vegetarian   133
spritches butter biscuits   247
sponge
   fingers   246
   sandwich   235
   superlight, sandwich   235
sultana cake   236
sweet corn fritters   247
swiss roll   236
tauhu masak titek   49
tarts
   pineapple open   246
   pineapple-shaped   244
   tan   169
tofu
   and crab meat   73
   with pork and prawns   73
thom yam soup   79
turkey roast   102
turmeric chicken   105
udang kuah pedas nanas   49
vegetarian
   bee hoon   134
   curry   134
   spring rolls   133
wan tan, fried   161
white christmas   237
yam puffs   167
yong tau fu   30
yue sung   124

Fiona MacCarthy

British Design since 1880

A Visual History

Lund Humphries · London

Copyright © 1982 Fiona MacCarthy

First edition 1982
Published by
Lund Humphries Publishers Ltd
26 Litchfield Street London WC2

SBN 85331 447 0 (paperback)
SBN 85331 461 6 (casebound)

Designed by Herbert and Mafalda Spencer
Printed in Great Britain by Jolly & Barber Ltd, Rugby

Photographic acknowledgements:

BBC   105

David Carter Associates   219

Dinah Casson   206

Christie's   33

Clareville Studios Ltd   26, 149, 151, 153, 155, 182, 185, 192, 193, 208, 211

Keith Collie   218

Conran Associates   28, 179

Lucienne Day   165

Design Council   156, 161–4, 166–9, 172, 174, 177, 178, 184, 186, 191, 194–9, 216, 220, 221, 226

Mark Fiennes   214

Kenneth Grange   227

Heal & Son Ltd   106

David Higham   3, 5, 6, 11–14, 17–24

London Transport Executive   125, 127

John Maltby   201

Mann Studios   147, 183

Gordon McLeish   1, 2, 7, 8, 9, 10, 15, 16, 27, 41–6, 49, 53–8, 64, 67, 68, 70–8, 82–5, 87–9, 94, 96, 98, 103, 108–13, 119, 120, 121, 122–4, 128–35, 137, 140, 141, 142, 145, 152, 157, 160, 170, 171, 173, 202, 207, 212, 213, 215

William Morris Gallery, Walthamstow   4

Ogle Design   223

Plush-Kicker   176

Race Furniture   144

John Rose & John Dyble   146

Gordon Russell Ltd   148

Leiga Siegelmann   203

Sotheby's Belgravia   102

Victoria & Albert Museum   38, 40, 99, 204

Josiah Wedgwood & Sons Ltd   136, 138, 158, 159

Robert Welch   187

Contents

page 7   Preface

10   Acknowledgements

11   The British Tradition in Design

13–20   *Colour plates 1–15*

33–40   *Colour plates 16–28*

53   The 1880s

65   The 1890s and early 1900s

85   The 1910s and 1920s

103   The 1930s

123   The 1940s and 1950s

143   The 1960s

163   The 1970s

187   Into the 1980s

191   British design books and exhibition catalogues

203   British design collections

225   Index of designers

227   General index

Preface

For a century or more, from William Morris onwards, there has been an easily identifiable strain in society in Britain concerned with the improvement of the objects which we use and live with. This movement for reform has, through the years, developed certain ideas on the designer's social role as well as recognisable criteria on aesthetics. From the Arts and Crafts movement of the late nineteenth century, the Design and Industries Association campaigns between the wars, through to the post-war Council of Industrial Design (now the Design Council), a tradition has evolved which is, I would claim, particularly British: a tradition in the approach to designing and a tradition in reaching the solutions, amounting to a long succession of products, both handmade and mass-produced, with a common visual character. Indeed, the idea that consistent standards are both practically possible and morally desirable, that design solutions can be measured against a sense of ideal rightness, both functional and aesthetic, has dominated much of British design thinking over the past century. It is a concept in which, from the 1930s onwards, the British government has been investing ever-increasing resources, especially in the education of designers, and since the war it has been at the very centre of activities in government-approved design.

The design movement of the past hundred years has created its own *species humaniores*, the genus which in the early days was known as 'art adviser' but which we are more likely now to designate 'designer'. The designer's professional status has become increasingly sophisticated, but the basic role remains that of problem solver, reconciler of conflicting demands and outside pressures. When it comes down to it, it is the designer who makes the creative leap, the visual synthesis. Designers finally decide how things shall *be*.

The degree of pure creativity, the freedom allowed to the designer in arriving at the object, of course is variable. With a one-off piece of pottery, handmade in a craft workshop, extra-aesthetic pressures are relatively minimal: attention must be paid to techniques and to materials and (possibly) to function and (possibly) to marketing; but the art-content is the factor which is dominant. Moving on to, for instance, a chair for mass production there are wider considerations, far beyond the basic requirements of techniques and materials: functioning and marketing acquire much more importance; there are the added pressures of company image and corporate investment. In this kind of context, the aesthetic contribution is one of many elements, though still a major one. By the time one reaches the designer's contribution to, say, a machine tool or microprocessor, the purely aesthetic aspects are in effect subsidiary; the designer's role is a collaborative one, working in conjunction with the engineer, providing a relatively small, though still essential, element of visual and functional coherence from within a whole network of alternative criteria. And yet, in the end, is the process very different? Though different in degree, in the extent of its restraints, the process of arriving at the ultimate decision is, I would argue, much the same in kind whether one is designing a piece of handmade silver or acting as design consultant for the High-Speed Train. It is still a question of aesthetic judgment, the designer is still making the creative leap, the synthesis, and it is the broad base of this reconciling talent, the designer's special role in each successive period in bringing the various conflicting design factors to the optimum visual and functional solution, which is one of the basic tenets of this book.

The idea for the book came from an exhibition – 'Homespun to Highspeed: A Century of British Design 1880–1980' – which I organised in 1979 for Sheffield City Art Galleries. This was not so much a collection of the objects I most like (though personal predilections do, of course, come into it), as an attempt to collect together what I saw as the key pieces in the British design movement, by which I mean the élite, progressive movement, over the past century. I wanted to assemble the designs which seemed important in their day, objects then approved of by the cognoscenti, as well as things which still seem very good solutions to their particular set of design pressures, expressions of the vitality and excellence of their particular period of design. By collecting together many hundreds of examples of designers' work over this long period, I hoped to discover – and indeed to reveal – some salient facts about designers, their aims and aspirations, what they felt they were about. This visual record, based on the selection of exhibits, attempts a distillation of what is, to me anyway, an infinitely interesting aspect of recent British culture. I hope others think so too.

I feel it is important to mention in passing the continuing, perhaps even increasing, elusiveness of actual examples of British design of the immediate past period. This seems strange when one considers contemporary concern for the national artistic heritage in general, and the recent growth of interest in design history at both amateur and academic levels. But the cavalier attitude towards major design-historic acquisitions, chaotically organised and erratically catalogued even in some areas of our best-known national collections, is surely a cause for some concern. Admittedly this gave my own research a certain piquancy, a sense of the excitement which must be quite familiar to archaeologists at work on a new site, as, for instance, past Design Centre Awards were excavated from the cellars of South Kensington and a massive hoard of 1930s glass and ceramics, still packed in the tea-chests in which it was delivered, was uncovered in the store-rooms of one of the most famous of provincial city art galleries. There are, of course, exceptions: the superbly well-kept and immaculately documented collection of textiles at the Whitworth Art Gallery in Manchester; the displays of furniture by Gimson and the Barnsleys at Leicester and at Cheltenham, crucial national collections which still retain a very individual quality, reflecting the enthusiasms of their keepers; the beautiful, small-scale Bath Crafts Study Centre; the logically organised, professionally catalogued modern silver collection at Goldsmiths' Hall in London.

These collections are all models of their kind. There are also some signs of an increasing sense of responsibility towards their own past products by such manufacturers as Warner and Sons Ltd, continuously building up a comprehensive archive, and Gordon Russell Ltd whose small design museum at their factory in Broadway is so personal and evocative it almost undermines institutionalised collecting. But these examples are very isolated. The fact is that many historic designs, including some which I had hoped to show in this recent exhibition, are already disappearing. This is especially true of products of the 1920s period and those of the 1940s and 1950s. These post-war designs in a sense appear so recent that their potential importance is neglected. There is much to be located before it is too late.

At the end of the book I have made a brief location list, based upon my travels, an outline indication of the major collections up and down the country. They are terribly far-flung. For the basic problem, which still seems no nearer a solution, is the all too obvious lack of a central British modern design collection where the main developments can be viewed in context as part of a whole historic sequence. So far, the collections all tend to be fragmented. The Crafts Council collection, though excellent, is totally craft-orientated. The Conran Foundation's Boilerhouse project, though again a highly welcome enterprise, is concentrated on industrial design. Apart from the Victoria and Albert Museum, where the British modern collections are richly comprehensive but displayed in such a random way as to be daunting to anyone except the most intrepid historians, there is nowhere in the country where one can follow through the pattern of modern design in all its aspects, the interaction of hand and machine production which has been so formative to the development of British design over the past century, in many ways the source of its great individuality and strength.

Fiona MacCarthy
November 1981

Acknowledgements

As well as the many owners of the objects illustrated, whose generosity is acknowledged in the picture list, I should like to thank Frank Constantine, Julian Spalding and James Hamilton, and other staff of Sheffield City Art Galleries, organisers of the 'Homespun to Highspeed' exhibition, without whom this book would never have materialised. Their enthusiasm has been very much appreciated.

I should also like to express our gratitude for the considerable and very expert contribution made by Gordon McLeish to the photographic content of this book. This is detailed in the photographic credits on page 4.

My view of British design has built up slowly, over many years, and I am very grateful to the dozens, if not hundreds, of people who have endlessly – and usually enjoyably – discussed the subject with me. Indeed, this applies to almost everyone I know.

For special information relating to this book I need to thank the following: Nick Butler, Frank Height, Tom Karen, Bridget Kinally, Rodney Kinsman, Mary Mullin, James Pilditch, Robert Strand.

The British Tradition in Design

If anybody asked me to make up a short-list of the ten most British designs of the past century, this would be it:

One of Christopher Dresser's startlingly innovative metalwork designs of c.1880: British design at its most brilliant and precise.

A William Morris chintz.

A Gimson ladderback chair in ash, epitome of the ruralist traditional, homely yet very subtle, dominating British design till 1930.

A pre-war Murphy radio cabinet, designed by R.D.Russell.

Maybe (and this is, I suppose, an outside entry, but surely defensible as a prime example of the affectionate and quirky tendencies in the character of British design), one of the decorative pottery designs which Eric Ravilious did for Wedgwood in the 1930s.

A Race chair, as seen at the Festival of Britain, 1951.

A lighting design by Robert Heritage for Rotaflex, an admirable example of the reappearance of old Design and Industries Association principles of common-sense and rightness in product designing in the post-war period.

A Shirley Craven fabric, superb illustration of mid-1960s jollity and style.

A spectacular piece of Craft Revival furniture of the 1970s, when the decorative individualistic urges, surprisingly, resurfaced.

A High-Speed Train.

All these, I would maintain, have a common basis in a particular, peculiarly British tradition of designing, and most are illustrated later in the book.

What this tradition is, what ideas most inspired it, are the things I shall be analysing in this introduction. They were important ideas which had their origins in the Arts and Crafts movement of the late nineteenth century and which can be followed right through to present-day British design practice. In attempting to explain them, I can do no better than to start quite near the middle, with the words of Frank Pick, the famous Chief Executive of the London Transport Passenger Board in the period between the two World Wars, Chairman of the DIA, Chairman of the Council for Art and Industry (precursor of the Design Council) in the 1930s, for whom design was almost a religion. Speaking to the DIA in Edinburgh he said:

'Everything is made for a use. The test of the goodness of a thing is its fitness for that use. So that boots eked out with canvas or paper, or fashioned of porous leather, are no good, for the essence of a boot is to keep the foot dry. So that flower-vases with narrow bottoms that topple over and make a mess are no good. So that a salt-pot in metal that corrodes with the natural dampness of the salt is no good. So that posters ornamented and confused until the words cannot be read at a glance (the main requirements of a poster) are no good. If you will keep an alert mind you can multiply examples from the common objects you meet with everyday. The test of the goodness of a thing is its fitness for use. If it fails on this first test, no amount of ornamentation or finish will make it any better; it will only make it more expensive, more foolish.'[1]

So much of what he says is central to the thinking of the British design movement. The functional aesthetic: the relation of practicality to beauty. The preoccupation with small things of daily life: the flower-vases, salt-pots and the boots which keep the rain out. (Boots were also an obsession with W.R.Lethaby.) The common-sense approach, homely yet highminded; the emphasis on plainness; the rejection of extravagance, dismissal of the foolish. The tone of voice so kindly and so certain. Solid stuff.

Good design is really a statement of the obvious. This perception of a fact which has proved not altogether as plain as one might think has been one of the main principles of the design reformers. It helps illuminate the good sense and moderation in British design in the past century. The insistence on fitness for use as a means to and a correlation of beauty can quite well be traced back from Frank Pick to William Morris. Like Pick, William Morris was concerned with humble detail, with making the daily round more orderly and seemly, as part of his whole urge to reorganise society, his large hopes for getting rid of the superfluous and pompous. Ideals of simple usefulness of course abounded in the Arts and Crafts movement and they find their best expression in the speeches and writings of W.R.Lethaby, disciple of Morris and a master of the aphorism. (He once said: 'Gothic cathedrals are as natural as birds' nests'.) Lethaby had some strong views on the role of the designer, maintaining that the best design was basic, never showy. Here he is at his most forthright, in some lines from *Art and Workmanship*:

'Art is not a special sauce applied to ordinary cooking; it is the cooking itself if it is good. Most simply and generally art may be thought of as *the well-doing of what needs doing*. If the thing is not worth doing it can hardly be a work of art, however well it may be done. A thing worth doing which is ill done is hardly a thing at all.'[2]

It was Lethaby's view that a machine-made product should be designed in such a way as to show quite obviously that it is the child of the machine; it is, he explains, the pretence and subterfuge of most machine-made things which make them so disgusting. A sense of the importance of honest sense of purpose, of calling a chair a chair, a boot a boot, together with distaste for the false and the effusive, characterises both the work and the pronouncements of the design reform groups of those early days.

One can also follow this same feeling going forward in British design history from Pick to Gordon Russell in his influential post as Director of the Council of

1
'Peacock' dish by William De Morgan, late 19th century,
painted in fashionable Persian colours. Typically rich
and fanciful De Morgan treatment of the Peacock motif,
so powerful a symbol of the Aesthetic Movement.
Victoria and Albert Museum.

2
Aesthetic pots with greeny-ochre glazes made by
Linthorpe Art Pottery, c.1880, probably designed by
Christopher Dresser, Art Designer to the pottery from
its foundation in 1879. Handled flask from Stoke-on-
Trent City Museum and Art Gallery; little jar from the
collection of Mr and Mrs H.Ovenall.

3
'Medway' or 'Garden Tulip' block-printed chintz, designed by William Morris, 1885, and printed at Merton Abbey. An example of the nearness-to-nature theme which obsessed Morris. He used the same design to make a wallpaper. Whitworth Art Gallery, University of Manchester.

4
'Wey' block-printed chintz, designed by William Morris, 1884. The name is taken from one of the tributaries of the River Thames beside which Morris lived (both in Oxfordshire and London): this is one of his many river patterns of the period. William Morris Gallery, Walthamstow.

5
'Tulip and Bird' reversible double-cloth, wool and silk, designed by C.F.A.Voysey, manufactured by Alexander Morton & Co., c.1896. One of the most beautiful of Voysey's long series of formalised bird-and-plant patterns. Whitworth Art Gallery, University of Manchester.

6
Embroidered table runner by May Morris, late 19th century. William Morris's younger daughter May took charge of the embroidery workshops of the Morris firm in 1885, when she was 23. Her patterns tend to be more static than her father's, more heraldic. William Morris Gallery, Walthamstow.

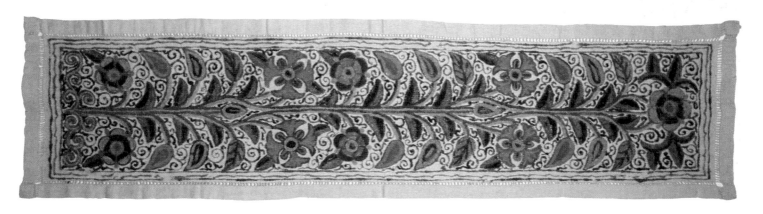

7
Bowl with flambé glaze by Bernard Moore, 1908.
Bernard Moore, working in North Staffordshire,
produced a succession of experimental glazes –
comparable with Pilkington's and Ruskin at that same
period – of an intense richness and great decorative
effect. Leicestershire Museums.

8
Large hand-painted porcelain 'Bird and Harebell' bowl
designed in 1908 by Hugh Thackeray Turner, Arts and
Crafts architect and designer, and Morris's successor as
secretary of the Society for the Protection of Ancient
Buildings. Victoria and Albert Museum.

9
Pottery with floral decoration, c.1920. The basic Wedgwood shapes were hand-painted by Grace Barnsley, daughter of Sidney Barnsley; the freshness and delicacy of design is still very close to the Arts and Crafts in feeling. From Mr and Mrs A.C.Davies's loan collection in Leicestershire Museums.

10
Large dish with spotted deer, characteristic of the widespread interest in *l'art sauvage* in the early 1920s, designed by Truda Carter, hand-painted at Poole Pottery and exhibited at the British Empire Exhibition in Wembley in 1925. Museum Collection, Poole Pottery.

11
'Diagonal' cotton furnishing fabric by Phyllis Barron and Dorothy Larcher, one of many most original and confident designs for hand-block printed textiles, the work of a remarkably productive partnership of the 1920s and 1930s. Crafts Study Centre, Bath.

12
'Howarth' furnishing fabric in cotton and worsted/fibro designed by Marianne Straub for Helios, 1939. This particular shade of rusty-brown, so popular among the designers of that period, makes a final appearance among the Utility textiles of World War II, before giving way to the more acid-orange tones of the Festival of Britain. Marianne Straub.

13
'Wessex' hand-tufted wool rug from Wilton Royal
Carpet Manufacturing Co., c.1935; a swirling abstract
pattern unmistakably by Marion Dorn, mistress of the
modernist rug. Mrs J.Pruskin.

14
Hand-tufted wool rug by John Tandy, c.1937, one of a
sequence of artist- and architect-designed rugs – by
McKnight Kauffer, Ronald Grierson, Marion Dorn,
Marian Pepler etc. – commissioned for limited production
by the Wilton Royal Carpet Manufacturing Co. from
1930 onwards. Note designer's signature in the bottom
corner, a very 1930s touch. Mrs J.Pruskin.

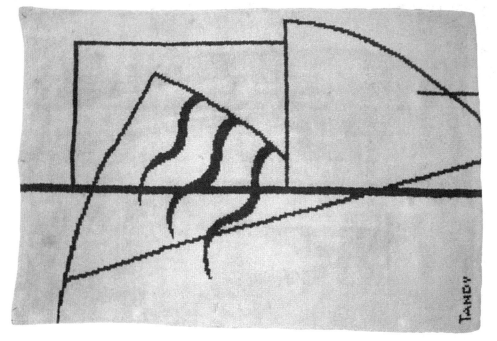

15

'Garden Implements' jug and lemonade beaker, designed
by Eric Ravilious for Wedgwood, 1937–8. This
decorative pattern, on standard Wedgwood Queen's
Ware shapes, was printed in sepia, with lustre decoration.
If Keith Murray's designs for Wedgwood in the 1930s
show the architect's approach to pottery, then this shows
the painter's: Ravilious at his most subtle and evocative.
Wedgwood Museum collection.

Industrial Design, from 1947 onwards. Gordon Russell's design philosophy was deeply practical, and British design, as approved by the Council of Industrial Design in the fifteen years which followed World War II, was indubitably honest and restrained and understated. It had to measure up to the Gordon Russell concept of 'the decent job', by which he meant a useful thing made well in the most suitable materials. The qualities of design admired by Gordon Russell were reflected in the choice for the Design Centre Awards given by the COID from 1957. The adjectives of praise bestowed on the first award winners range from 'practical', 'well-organised', 'agreeable' and 'pleasing' to 'plain but handsome', 'fresh and gay'. As Frank Pick had been much earlier, the judges of the 1950s were impressed by functional effectiveness and basic practicality, denoting a cast-iron room heater as 'an efficient appliance with a clean appearance which will fit appropriately into most surroundings', describing a range of pendant lampshades as 'light, durable and easily cleaned with soap and water' and praising the fitness for purpose of a new design in Melmex plastics tableware: 'The Judges were favourably impressed with the positive location of the cups in their saucers'. Good design was indeed, back in 1957, the statement of the obvious. But it was evidently something else as well. There is a definite sense of moral earnestness in the good design pronouncements of the day. Again, this is a tendency going back to Pick and Lethaby. Again, one reads it clearly in the comments of the judges of those first Design Awards: a set of cutlery, for instance, is praised highly for 'an elegance of style and an individuality of character which could only have developed from the careful consideration of the essential form of each article, coupled with a knowledge of the best of the past and a disciplined avoidance of those self-conscious departures from tradition characteristic of many contemporary designs'. This is surely a quintessentially British judgment on aesthetics, not just in its stress on elegance and unostentatious individuality (both favourite criteria of that early post-war period) but also in its ideas of humility and rightness, the belief that designers are not there to make a statement. A concept of good manners, of what is and is not done, a code which was soon challenged by the brashness of the 1960s, gives 1950s design its rather poignant sense of certainty, its comforting conviction of the lasting social value of the decent job well done.

The strongly moral bias of high design in Britain has its origins in the mid-Victorian reforming movements, in particular John Ruskin's passionate outcry against the prevailing conditions of work and standards of workmanship in an increasingly industrialised environment. His optimistic vision of the inherent beauty and potential creativity within society, only waiting to be rediscovered and released, was a powerful inspiration to the designers and design theorists of the Arts and Crafts movement. Ruskin saw the best design as a civilising instrument, a force for the good both of the man who makes the object and the society which ultimately uses it, and he puts forward a prophetic view of the importance of the designer's analytic way of working, a calm and measured, very systematic method, the basis of which is a true perception of human joy and humanitarian usefulness. Ruskin wrote:

'Without observation and experience, no design; without peace and pleasurableness in occupation, no design; and all the lecturings, and teachings,

and prizes, and principles of art in the world are of no use as long as you don't surround your men with happy influences and beautiful things.'[3]
In the writings of Ruskin one first finds this most beguiling idea of the designer as a benign influence within society, the solver of problems, smoother out of difficulties: the person whose large job it is to look at things afresh.

The long connection, from the Ruskin period onwards, with the radical political movements of the time gave British design a lasting sense of moral force and social purpose. The Arts and Crafts provided furniture for the New Life. There were strong links between many of the Arts and Crafts architects and designers and contemporary groups aligned to upturn the old order; these covered the whole spectrum of free-thinkers, from political and educational reformers to the people dedicated to new diet and new dress. Morris himself, of course, was politically active, increasingly so as he grew older, and his idealism, his view of the designer as reformer, as a kind of social catalyst, was transmitted to many Arts and Crafts designers. (I have always thought it particularly apt that the furniture designer Ernest Gimson, as a very young man, was first introduced to Morris after a meeting of the Leicester Secular Society: it was just that sort of world.) Morris's attitudes to the business of designing were shaped by his whole hatred of capitalist principles; as explained by J.W.Mackail, his first biographer: 'He carried on his business as a manufacturer not because he wished to make money, but because he wished to make the things he manufactured.' This purist view of the role of the designer, the rejection of the profit motive for the sake of impulses of social benevolence, a principle which has had so great an influence, for better or for worse, on British design development, comes pounding through in Morris's many speeches on art and life and their ideal interrelation, in none of them more strongly than his famous address on 'The Beauty of Life', given in Birmingham in 1880, in which he looks forward to 'the victorious days when millions of those who now sit in darkness will be enlightened by an *art made by the people and for the people, a joy to the maker and the user*'. He describes himself, and colleagues, as the servants of a cause.

Servants of a cause; bearers of the light; marchers with the banner; strikers of the colours: the British design movement over the past century has frequently been delineated in terms of battle and, rather intriguingly in view of the stalwart agnosticism of many of its leaders, has often been described in the images of muscular Christianity. It has been seen, simplistically, as a crusade: the powers of goodness ranged against commercial darkness. It has upheld principles of usefulness and beauty, appropriateness, simplicity and practicality as the proper birthright of the British people. From the early days of the Arts and Crafts it was, in theory at least, a very democratic movement. As Lethaby once put it: 'beauty can only be brought back to common life by our doing common work in an interesting way', and it was this democratic impulse which encouraged the cult of simplicity in Arts and Crafts aesthetics and inspired the late nineteenth-century peasant arts revival. The principle of common social responsibility, 'work of each for weal of all', was strikingly embodied in the Arts and Crafts guilds, the largest and best known of which, the Guild of Handicraft formed in 1888 by C.R.Ashbee, was conceived as an experiment in democratic practice. It was founded with an almost overwhelming sense of mission. Ashbee, over-ambitiously as it turned out, saw the Guild as the first phase of the regeneration of the nation, a revival which would spring from a new standard of beauty, new ideals of democratic work and life.

Though it never again reached such passionate expression, the idea that high standards of design are of importance to civilised life, the conviction – to put it at its baldest – that good design is a good thing, persisted. It is there in the campaigns of the DIA, from its foundation in 1915 onwards: the propaganda is replete with zeal and fervour; the members are undoubtedly still servants of the cause. One finds it just as strongly in the avant-garde design world of the 1930s, when the network of modern designers, manufacturers and shopkeepers tended to refer to themselves as 'real believers' and Alastair Morton of Edinburgh Weavers pointed out, at a DIA meeting, 'we cannot expect well-designed fabrics in an unstable or badly-designed society'. The designer's creative integrity was seen as a bulwark against commercial exploitation, the antithesis of Americanised 'styling' which so much shocked the British design pundits of the 1930s. The traditional British purity of purpose, the belief in design as a force for social betterment, gathered conviction in the years immediately after World War II, the heady period of 'Britain Can Make It' and the Festival of Britain, when the Council of Industrial Design saw itself empowered with the almost sacred charge of improving standards for the great mass of British people. Good design was seen to have a serious social purpose; the best design was clean and plain, not wayward or eccentric. The aim was to achieve a style accessible to everyone, a democratic style which was never ostentatious, not consciously 'designed' but real, simple and direct.

Although in recent years these principles have been much sabotaged, first by the jokers and then the profiteers, the altruistic elements within design in Britain have never been obliterated altogether. Even in the cynical and disillusioned 1970s, Professor Misha Black could still argue with conviction that it was the duty of designers to make certain that every system or object they initiated should celebrate the dignity of man. In an important article 'Fitness for what Purpose?' he argued that a humble, highly disciplined approach became, in a time of stringency, more, not less, essential; designers should renounce any formal preconceptions:

'We should approach each new problem from the base of practicality – how can it most economically be made, how will it function most effectively, how can maintenance be simplified, how can the use of scarce materials be minimised? An absolute concern with practicalities will produce new formal solutions as technology constantly develops: when alternatives present themselves during the design process, the aesthetic sensitivity of the designer will determine his selective decision but this should remain a searching process and not be seen as the opportunity for imposing a preconception of formal appropriateness. The difference between an arrogant conscious aesthetic and a conscientious searching for the most elegant solution is fundamental to my argument.'[4]

He wrote this in 1975. Not long ago.

British design has always been pervaded by a consciousness of what is the most natural solution to any given problem. This again goes back to Ruskin and his theories of the creative strength to be derived from the natural phenomena around us, and Morris's obsession with the English rural scene and with country traditions of sturdiness and honesty. The Arts and Crafts movement developed a romantic and indeed a highly sophisticated way of looking at the country life of England. The nearness to nature, to the rhythms of the seasons, the cycle of the harvest: the basic facts of rural life were almost glorified. There was a feeling that rural life was real life and that rural values, handed down the generations, were the truest and the purest. Rural quietness and slowness, the lack of incident, which was, to many country people, a privation, was to most of the Arts and Crafts architect-designers a source of inspiration. Their intense appreciation of the details of the English rural landscape – English villages and churches, English cottages and manors, the vernacular tradition in design and decoration, the use of country motifs, English flowers in English meadows – was important in its day and productive in its influence. From the Arts and Crafts emphasis on soundness and straightforwardness, the dignified and natural, there developed a whole attitude, belief in lasting values, which, one way or another, has been a constant element in British design practice.

The ruralist factor in design in Britain has often been bound up with the ideals of the simple life, the recurring conviction that civilisation has become so over-complex that the time has now come to sweep away the old accretions. To many supporters of the movement this implied not only simplified relationships, the breaking-down of age-old social barriers, but also simplified conditions of living, most ideally in a cottage in the country, with minimum possessions. Morris, Marshall, Faulkner & Co., Fine Art Workmen, founded in 1861 with the intention of protesting against prevailing styles of decoration, attempted a simplification by recreating a basic mediaevalism; Walter Crane described their aims as 'a revival of the mediaeval spirit (though not the letter) in design; a return to rich and suggestive surface decoration, and simple constructive forms'. Edward Carpenter, most famous of the British simple lifers, lived in a state of exemplary plainness in his cottage at Millthorpe in Derbyshire, from which he ruthlessly cleared out all unnecessary objects: 'the absence of THINGS' was noted with approval by Janet Ashbee, C.R.Ashbee's wife, who went to visit him. The impulse towards the free, untrammelled life was strong at the turn of the century, a period amazing for its variety of social experiment: 'At the bottom of my mind', wrote Lethaby, 'I long for the experience of standing up free and possessionless'. (This *cri de cœur* was heard again in the mid-1930s as visions of the minimum cottage were supplanted by the counter-attractions of minimum flats.)

For many early members of the Arts and Crafts societies, the love of rural life was mainly theoretical. But as the back-to-the-land movement gathered force, at the end of the nineteenth century, the exodus began: Gimson and the Barnsleys, and then Ashbee, to the Cotswolds; Godfrey Blount to Haslemere; and later Eric Gill to Ditchling. These, and other, rural communities of craftworkers, subscribing – more or less – to the old Ruskinian theory that lovely works of art can only be arrived at in a setting of corresponding truth and beauty, had enormous influence on the British design ethos. In particular, the furniture of Gimson and the Barnsleys, and the rural idioms which they adopted, the ruralist regard for sturdy, unpretentious structure, the countryman's tricks of champfering and chipcarving, contributed greatly to the sane and forthright character of twentieth-century design in Britain, creating the cult of the profoundly ordinary which has since then almost become the national style. Gordon Russell, as a young man working in the Cotswolds, was indubitably influenced by Gimson's furniture and by Gimson's whole approach to the design and making of it: his overall control of the details of the product through his own deep knowledge of materials and techniques.

In British design one finds great qualities of patience, the kind of doggedness one has to have to be a craftsman. The early DIA in fact exemplifies this outlook. Though their mission was improvement of design in British industry, several of the founders had their roots in rural craftsmanship. One thinks of Harry Peach, proprietor of Dryad handicrafts, earnest in his check tweed cap, his pockets stuffed with design pamphlets, embodiment of DIA right-thinking. Or Harold Stabler, as his colleague Hamilton Temple Smith described him: a man of wide vision and imaginative commonsense: 'He came of Westmorland and yeoman stock and remained a countryman all his life: perhaps it was an inherited instinct for doing things in their right season that gave him his flair for producing the idea for a new activity at the psychological moment when it could be most effectively undertaken.'[5] Ambrose Heal was a countryman *manqué*. Even Pick, chief prophet of Efficiency Style, had strong traces of the country-dweller's almost mystic attitude to nature and the land, a Wordsworthian sense of the unity of all living things, the harmony of man and nature.

'The vital and miraculous result is this', he told the DIA one day in Edinburgh, 'if we seek efficiency in production, which is industry, and if we seek efficiency in the product, which may be summed up in design, and if the efficiency that we seek leads us to a vast harmony of all things, then all things must become alive, part of the living world.'[6]

It is interesting how the English countrified tradition, which descends directly through the woodworkers, the potters and handweavers of the 1920s to the multifarious craft workshops of today, has also, less directly, perhaps, but just as deeply, affected the progress of design for British industry. Here the key figure, of course, is Gordon Russell who began as a designer in the Cotswold craft tradition but who, in the mid-1920s, made a gradual transition so that, by 1930, the furniture made in his factory in Broadway was almost all designed for quantity production. As Nikolaus Pevsner explained it:

'Gordon Russell suddenly turned modern . . . Speaking from personal memory,' (for Pevsner once worked with Gordon Russell), 'I would say that the furniture of between 1935 and the war, in its entirely contemporary, never mannered, and never showy style, equalled the best on the Continent, and its workmanship was more perfect than any I saw in the Continental shops I visited. The fact that the men who made these pieces, however much of the rough and preliminary work machines were gradually taking off them, were still the same men who had been the craftsmen of the 1920s bore fruit.'[7]

Pevsner liked, and understood, the essential Englishness of Gordon Russell's attitudes, the attitudes which sprang from his deep feelings for the countryside. (Utility was, after all, a kind of country furniture.) Gordon Russell's own designs, and the designs which he promoted, have a specially British quality of reticence, the virtue which Sedding once described so accurately as the 'imaginative handling of the commonplace'. This consistent understatement, a creative kind of modesty, is central to the British tradition of designing, stretching back to Philip Webb, the

25

architect and friend of Morris, who always felt unhappy, he claimed, if his work looked anything but ordinary, and forward to the furniture designers of the 1950s (trained at the Royal College of Art by R.D.Russell) and the best of the industrial designers of today.

The British tradition, derived as it was from the Arts and Crafts movement of the late nineteenth century, was very much a workshop tradition of designing. By this I mean a process of design through making. Many of the most famous of the Arts and Crafts designers were themselves obsessive makers: one thinks of William Morris, his arms deep into the dye-vats; Sidney Barnsley selecting and then sawing his own timber for the furniture he made in his workshop in the Cotswolds. The whole period was a great time of rediscovery of technical skills and the artistic possibilities which sprang up from them. It was an age of excitement and delight both in the skills themselves, the sheer technical achievements, described in vivid detail in interminable essays by the designer-craftsmen of the time, and also in the leeway which these skills gave the designers in fulfilling what they saw to be their role within society, for setting the standards which they felt to be the right ones, for seeing through their theories of art and labour, the civilised relationship of work and life.

This implied a certain relaxation and open-mindedness. As Morris himself analysed it after his return from a visit to Edward Carpenter at Millthorpe:

'it seems to me that the real way to enjoy life is to accept all its necessary ordinary details and turn them into pleasures by taking an interest in them: whereas modern civilisation huddles them out of the way, has them done in a venal and slovenly manner till they become real drudgery which people can't help trying to avoid.'[8]

Joy in all life's simple things, and leisure to explore them, seemed to many of the followers of Morris essential components of a well-balanced human life. To work at their own pace and standard, free from outside pressures: this was seen not as an opting-out, a form of self-indulgence, but rather the reverse, a form of positive experiment, a pattern for society as it might one day be. No one took these ideas further, of course, than C.R.Ashbee, whose experiment in Campden, (thoroughly, though sadly, described in his own book *Craftmanship in Competitive Industry*), stretched the doctrine of creative work and useful leisure to what turned out to be its ultimate conclusion. His passionate belief in doing things as well as possible, whatever their status in the usual scale of values – mending a wall or designing a cathedral, singing a catch or delivering a treatise – came as a revelation to some of his Guild craftsmen (and, it must be said, remained a mystery to others). Its importance in British design history is obvious: not just in the emphasis which Ashbee places on workshop practicality, on closeness to materials, but also in his stress on the creative need for calmness, with the time to think, to judge, to discuss and to amend.

From the Arts and Crafts movement and on right through the century, to the 'nearness to need' preoccupations of the 1970s, one finds signs of the idea that the best design is the result of human carefulness. 'Every real work of art', wrote W.R.Lethaby, 'looks as if it was made by one person for another', and this concept of personal integrity, responsibility for all the detail of the making, which applies at its most literal to the single craft-made object, also had a wider meaning in relation to design for mass production, the areas in which the trained designer, as the century progressed, was increasingly involved. It has always been crucial to the British tradition for designers to be close to actual methods of production. John Sedding once made the very sensible pronouncement:

'Our manufactures must be of good materials and make. The designs must be good and well suited to the necessities of modern methods of production. Note, moreover, that it is not enough to get good designs, but the designer should, more or less, superintend their making at the factory. The designer should be part of the working staff of the factory, see his design take shape, and be consulted as required. We have had enough of studio designs.'[9]

This was very British thinking. Dated 1893.

The overlap of craft into machine production is, to me, one of the most unique and interesting aspects of the whole development of design in Britain. Only in Scandinavia has there been a comparable balance between workshop and factory designing. Gordon Russell, in a lecture which he gave in 1948 on the work of Royal Designers for Industry, listed a group of the designers in this category (of which he himself was, of course, a prime example). As well as Harold Stabler, designer of silver, glass, medals and enamels, for one-off as well as for quantity production, he mentioned Duncan Grant and Allan Walton, whose textile designs were first produced by hand to be translated into machine processes; and also Ethel Mairet, described as 'specialising in first-rate hand-woven and hand-spun textiles, but also interested in making experiments for machine weaving'. This was only the beginning of a tendency which was to become still more important in the early post-war period, as the workshop tradition was encouraged and expanded by the regimes at the COID and the Royal College of Art. In the next two decades the list of Royal Designers included such convinced hand-and-machine practitioners as Margaret Leischner, Marianne Straub, Enid Marx, David Mellor, Robert Welch.

This was 'doing-is-designing' philosophy in action. As Russell had explained it, it was, for instance, Eric Gill's close knowledge of each individual letter of the alphabet, a knowledge gained by actually drawing and cutting letters for years at a size far larger than ordinary type size, which made him such an efficient and sensitive designer of typefaces for the Monotype Corporation. Similarly, it was Robert Welch's training as a silversmith, his basic understanding of and feeling for the metal and the possibilities it allowed to the designer, which shaped his whole approach to the design of stainless steel and other industrial products in the 1950s.

It is, I think, this merging of hand and machine values, this fusion of technical expertise and deep instinctive feeling, the result of many years of craft connection, which gives British design a good deal of its conviction. Frank Pick, in the days of the Pick Council, once defined the national design character as:

'modest and not too grandiose in scale . . . not too logical in form . . . a reasonable compromise between beauty and utility, neither overstressing beauty till it degenerates into ornament, nor overstressing utility until it becomes bare and hard.'[10]

Not stark, but never sloppy; precise, but not inhuman. Up to a point, Frank Pick's description still rings true, even when applied to pure industrial designers. Through the long development of design for engineering, from the 1930s pioneers to Kenneth Grange and David Carter, British design has kept a certain sense of balance, a getting to the point, an avoidance of mere 'styling', which has its base, perhaps, in the old workshop practicalities and, over the years, has been a major source of strength.

The human quality in design, which Frank Pick noted, has always been a part of the British national character. Often this has meant not just good sense and moderation but individuality and strangeness and inventiveness. It has led to all those human quirks, the oddity and fantasy, affection and banter, with which design in Britain has been so much imbued. This was a tendency the Arts and Crafts made much of. Morris and Brother Rabbit; William De Morgan ('the whimsical De Morgan', as C.R.Ashbee called him), with his fantastic sequences of birds and beasts and fishes; Walter Crane, who so much loved the quaint and magical and childish, even dressing up his wife as a sunflower for a party: the Arts and Crafts were full of these inventions and surprises. They took up the motifs of the picture book and folk tale, the most beautiful example of which is the Baillie Scott commission, in 1898, to design a royal tree-house for the Crown Princess Marie of Romania in the woods on the family's summer estate. This house, a wooden cabin, was designed to be supported by a group of eight trees twenty-five feet above the ground. The Arts and Crafts delight in the *faux naïve* and fairytale, a childlike perspicacity and sense of wonder, comes over most consistently in the designs of Voysey. His work is, I think, an extraordinary instance of commercial application of a highly personal vision. In his book *Individuality* he lays great stress on personal development:

'Let us assume,' he says, 'that there is a beneficent and omnipotent controlling power, that is perfectly good and perfectly loving; and that our existence here is for the purpose of growing individual characters.'

He sees it as essential to the civilised community to preserve individual creativity and even individual idiosyncrasy in the face of advancing tendencies of standardisation and bureaucracy:

'. . . if we would train character and preserve individual responsibility, we must most jealously guard individualism. Especially in these days, when the state has degenerated into a machine for producing armies of officials, with volumes of rules and regulations stereotyped and settled to suit given conditions, which by the laws of Nature must be for ever changing and developing.'[11]

This individualism Voysey carried through not just in the design of his personal and changeable and somehow childlike houses, but also in the details of his furniture and ironwork; his use of homely symbols, like the ever-present heart; the birds and flowers entwining in the patterns of his textiles and his wallpapers, giving them a character so English (and so Voysey-like) it sometimes seems as if they verge on the surreal.

English individuality has only sometimes taken a form of ornate richness: as, for instance, in the breathtakingly complex, neo-Byzantine metalwork of Henry Wilson. It has usually had a much more everyday emphasis in which the originality consisted in a new interpretation of the normal things around us. Back again to William Morris and Morris's conviction that peasant art was the best and most *English* form of decorative art. There has been a strong tradition in British design thinking, from

Gimson's hay-rake stretchers to Keith Murray's famous beer-mugs, of sophisticated treatment of the basic equipment of ordinary living. There has also been a knowledgeable cultivation of basic English folk art, and especially the art of the fairground and the popular theatre. What was seen as the natural exuberance of folk art, the instinctive sense of pattern, the joyful uninhibited use of brightest colours, in some reckless combinations, delighted the designers of the 1920s in particular. One can see the influence in Lovat Fraser's textiles and in the Poole pottery of that same period. Concurrent was the widespread interest in puppeteering in the advanced design circles of the 1920s, and the highly-cultivated low-life habits of the era – the visits to the village pub, pursuit of local pastimes – which related to the theory, held by Eric Gill and others, that an artist or designer was an ordinary chap.

Enid Marx has been particularly keen on the folklorique. As recounted in the introduction to the catalogue of her retrospective exhibition in London in 1979, she very early on in her career began collecting examples of English popular ephemera: the chap books, broadsheets, pattern papers, toy theatre sheets, and so on. She also soon became intrigued with the continuing vitality of English popular decoration and craftwork: the Staffordshire pottery, the corn dollies, barge furniture, wrought-iron work and English inn signs, the images with which we feel so much at home that we have almost ceased to recognise their value. These themes recur not only in her work, for her textiles and her graphics are themselves ideal examples of traditional Englishness, but also in the books which she has written on the subject – *English Popular and Traditional Art*, in 1946; *English Popular Art*, in 1951.

English popular art has been so very much in favour among the design cognoscenti through the century not just on account of its sheer decorative qualities but also because of its intrinsic moral purity. Peasant art (and even savage art) was seen to be a good art, springing from the real and not the artificial values. Such artefacts as the painted gipsy wagon – the symbol of the freedom of the open road, as used by Augustus John and family – became, in design circles, the favourite exemplars of the human attributes of primitive designing, the exuberant directness so admired by design pundits. Even Frank Pick, chief-executive-to-be of London Transport, not perhaps the man most likely to fall for the charms of horse-drawn locomotion, could be heard extolling the humanity and honesty of caravans and hay-wains and happy barge-men's cabins. Said Pick, with feeling:

'The gipsy caravan has its close-set ribs and frame, notched and carved and painted with gay lines and dabs of colour, red or green or blue, on its yellow surface; the farmer's wain away in the far country is the same; the little cabin in the stern in which the barge-dweller lives is still bright and joyous.'

In contrast, he depicted the falsity of styling of the delivery van then in use by a large London store. The body of this van had an eccentric curve, not, judged Pick, because the curve followed necessarily from structure, but because the curve had been consciously sought as being odd and distinctive. He went on:

'It shows no structure at all, but is encased in shiny sombre green and bears on its smooth finished surfaces the name of its proud possessor in precise and gilded letters. Such is the difference between the individual seeking the great adventure of self-expression heedless of the goal of distinctiveness and the individual seeking after the goal of distinctiveness heedless of the great adventure.'[12]

Which came, in later years, to be seen as the distinction between the true industrial designer and the stylist.

The details of the English scene entranced not only Pick but many of his fellow-members of the DIA. The English landscape, both the countryside and townscape, was a passion to Clough Williams-Ellis, architect of fantasy and author of so many of the inter-war campaigns to save the face of the land from desecration. His quizzical, affectionate attitude to England, his love of the visual absurdities as well as the English scenic splendours, and his longing to preserve them, was, in its time, extremely influential. The same feeling of enchantment with the oddities of England can be glimpsed in the design work of Ravilious and Bawden in the 1920s and 1930s: Edward Bawden's tiles for Carter, Stabler, Adams, and mugs and jugs and bowls and urns for Wedgwood by Ravilious, with their Boat Race scenes and vistas of the crowds in Piccadilly, share this quality of quiet conviviality, this curiosity and pleasure at the passing scene. The feeling re-emerges at the Festival of Britain: the Lion and Unicorn Pavilion was full of it, a large-scale celebration, designed by Robert Goodden and R.D. Russell, of the British national character and British way of life which stressed, as well as British dignity and British doggedness, the national predilection for whimsy, eccentricity and a kind of gentle urge for self-congratulation. This was very much the impulse of the time, a hopeful era. When in 1948 Robin Darwin became Principal of the Royal College of Art, he made the wish that his forthcoming students should be literate, articulate, of broad intelligence, with minds that were 'amused and well-tempered'. The term well-tempered maybe seems a little baffling. The spirit of Ravilious was what I think he meant.

The idiosyncratic tendencies within the British design tradition, so superbly realised in Robert Goodden's silver in the early post-war period, had a later re-revival in the work of Gerald Benney and Louis Osman in the 1960s, the lavishness of which often verges on the jokey, and the flamboyantly eccentric work of Makepeace, whose furniture combines the strangely classical and freakish. The small craft-workshop movement of the past few years has provided a whole sequence of new individual statements. The Crafts Council has collected quite a number of the best ones. From the Crafts Council collection my own favourite is a teapot. A teapot by Jill Crowley. In fact a green-leaf teapot. A teapot or a cabbage? Or a comment on a nation which drinks tea and consumes cabbages? All that is certain is that when it comes to tea and cabbages, the national symbolism becomes tortuous indeed.

British design, at first sight so sane and simple, reveals an unexpected aspect of complexity the harder one looks at it. The rational and symbolic instincts co-exist to an astonishing degree. Look at Lethaby, for instance. What a man of rationality, a downright nuts-and-bolts man, with his practical reflections on viaducts and bicycles, and yet, at the same time, what a wild amazing thinker with his theories of egalitarian architectural symbolism. In his book *Architecture, Mysticism and Myth* (which Lethaby, half-jokingly, used to call 'the Cosmos'), he creates a whole new language of designing through a sequence of associative visual ideas: pavements like the sun, ceilings like the sky, labyrinths, and golden gates, the jewel-bearing tree; a literary language, with images from folklore, and dominated by the very symbol of creation. Some of his contemporaries wondered what to make of it. But others found it totally rewarding and inspiring. Robert Weir Schultz maintained that, for him, it opened up an undreamed-of world of romance in architecture, and May Morris, embroidery and jewellery designer, said that she had fallen on the book with much delight. Certainly, accumulative symbolism, layers of meaning, by the later 1890s were increasingly apparent in the metalwork and bookbindings, the textiles and the hangings of the more expressionist wing of Arts and Crafts.

The element of ecstasy should never be discounted in British design tradition. One way or another, it has always been recurring, onwards from Ruskin and 'All great Art is praise'.

First, the ecstasy of sheer creative possibilities: from John D.Sedding, 1886.
'By his divine craft the priest of form can fold in one the magic in nature and man's emotion – he can steal nature's seal and print it upon his work – he can put the glamour of the woods into his timber roofs or stone vaultings, can bring the might of the tall cliffs into his walls and fluted columns, can entice the soul of the tangled thicket into the mazes of his carved beaten work, can give to the temple of God such an air of religiousness – fill its recesses with such an air of mystery and stillness, that you get a strange thrill of expectancy as you enter, and say, involuntarily, "surely the Lord is in this place".'[13]
And also the ecstasy of personal creativity, the joy of actually making (ideally on a fresh and sunny morning in the springtime): from A.Romney Green, c.1946.
'There is no lovelier exercise in the world than that of planing up a figured oak board with a wooden jack plane . . . It taxes every muscle in your body from the soles of your feet to the tips of your fingers. The workshop is soon full of the acrid scent of the newly cut oak (or the aromatic scent of pine or cedar) as the shavings come, almost whistling, through the mouth of your plane and fall in foam about your feet.'[14]
And then the ecstasy of mastery of a technology, a feeling which developed from the Arts and Crafts preoccupation with skill and with technique towards the sense of glory in technology which seemed so to obsess the designers of the 1970s. This quotation comes from a cult book of that period, *Zen and the Art of Motor Cycle Maintenance*, quoted within another cult book of the 1970s, Dr Patrick Nuttgens' *Learning to Some Purpose*, 1977:
'if you have to choose among an infinite number of ways to put it together then the relation of the machine to you, and the relation of the machine and you to the rest of the world, has to be considered, because the selection from among many choices, the art of the work, is just as dependent upon your own mind and spirit as it is upon the material of the machine. That's why you need the peace of mind.'[15]
The spiritual and almost ludicrously practical; emotional and reticent, highminded, sentimental; the ornate and the symbolic and the plain and the straightforward; the mixture of radical and innovative urges with a deep conservatism: the contrasts of British design character are obvious, and have helped to shape its subtle individuality. But what is not so obvious, perhaps, yet fascinating – a trait which is, I think, peculiar to Britain and of very great importance to the national design story – is the way the individualism, almost always, is contained within the group, is exerted in a context of group aims, collective attitudes. This has always been the

British background of designing. There has always been a pattern of groups forming and reforming, aims discussed, action plans made, papers read, committees meeting, a man's world of bonhomie, of friendly, moderate efficiency, which has had great influence on the whole history of design.

William Morris was, of course, the first and greatest exemplar of gregarious designing. He began, as a young man, with the streak of amateurism which has often been endearingly apparent in British design practice, by making some rough sketches for a settle and some tables and chairs for the house in Red Lion Square which he was sharing with Burne-Jones. These were constructed by a local carpenter. On the panels of the high-backed settle, and the chairbacks, Dante Gabriel Rossetti, another friend of Morris's, painted scenes of Sir Galahad and Dante. Morris then designed a wardrobe which Burne-Jones decorated with figures from *The Prioress' Tale* by Chaucer. When William Morris married and moved into Red House, the house in the country which Philip Webb had designed for him, Webb also designed furniture, brass candlesticks, grates, fire-irons and table glass (besides a gothic wagon for touring round the countryside): Burne-Jones designed decorative stained-glass windows; Morris himself designed embroideries and hangings, gradually carried out by the ladies of his circle. These early exercises in collective creativity, the idea of the value of the pool of expertise, which is indeed still with us, in modern design practices, encouraged the formation, in 1861, of Morris, Marshall, Faulkner & Company. The other partners were Webb, Burne-Jones, Rossetti and Ford Madox Brown. The work they undertook, according to the first prospectus, was a superior form of decoration, what would now be termed a co-ordinated interior design service: they offered to carry out and supervise whole schemes involving wall paintings, decoration, stained glass, metalwork and jewellery, sculpture, embroidery and all kinds of furniture for houses and for churches 'at the smallest possible expense'. As it turned out, the expense was sometimes great, and even then the profits could often be derisory. The motivation of Morris, Marshall, Faulkner & Co. was not, needless to say, primarily commercial. It was a venture in which the spirit of camaraderie was stronger than the interest in marketing, a scale of values characteristically English, with results which I shall hope to follow through.

William Morris was the centre of a network of design-reforming groups in the late nineteenth century. The Society for the Preservation of Ancient Buildings, founded in 1877; the Art Workers' Guild, in 1884; the Arts and Crafts Exhibition Society, in 1888. Not surprisingly, perhaps, since these societies had many members in common – a nucleus of architects and craftsmen, painters and sculptors of a progressive, though sociable, mien – the atmosphere within them was really very similar: sincerity, good comradeship (remarked on by May Morris), gentlemanliness, an earnest form of jocularity. Lethaby described it nicely, referring to his own acceptance into this charmed circle, and his attendance at the weekly meetings of the SPAB:

'It was Gimson who introduced me to the Society and the circle in 1891. For a time – a great time to me – we attended meetings, from 5 to 7, and then went across the Strand to Gatti's for an evening meal: Morris often, Webb always, and two or three of a number of younger lesser people, Gimson, Emery Walker, Sydney Cockerell, Detmar Blow and myself; here were stories, jokes, real talk.

17
'Ticker Tape' printed furnishing fabric designed by
Lucienne Day for Heal Fabrics, 1954. A very successful
post-Festival of Britain pattern (comparable with
Lucienne Day's more well-known 'Calyx', no.165), with
a subtle use of that favourite designer's colour of the
period, Thames Green. Whitworth Art Gallery,
University of Manchester.

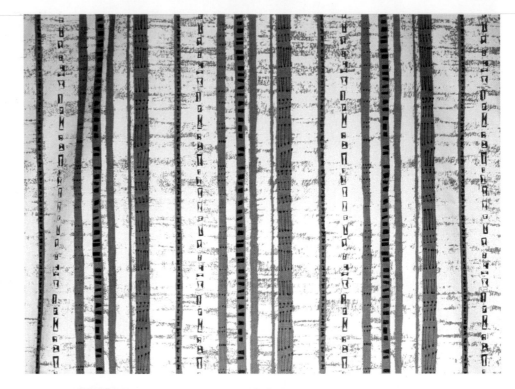

18
'Flamingo' furnishing cotton designed by Tibor Reich
and manufactured by Tibor, 1957. The 'Fotexturprint'
technique used in arriving at the pattern much impressed
the judges at the Council of Industrial Design and the
fabric was included in the first of the Design Centre
Awards. Tibor Reich.

19
'Five' printed linen and cotton furnishing fabric designed by Shirley Craven for Hull Traders, 1966. Whitworth Art Gallery, University of Manchester.

20
'Shape' printed furnishing cotton designed by Shirley Craven for Hull Traders, 1964. Whitworth Art Gallery. University of Manchester.

21
'Reciprocation' printed furnishing cotton designed by
Barbara Brown for Heal Fabrics, 1963. Whitworth Art
Gallery, University of Manchester.

22
'Glenaffric Check' woven furnishing fabric designed by
Peter Simpson for Donald Brothers, 1962. Peter Simpson.

23
Rag rug, hand-dyed and hand-woven by John Hinchcliffe, 1977. The use of traditional techniques to new effect: a classic product of the workshop revival of the 1970s. Private collection.

24
'Maze' printed cotton designed by Hans Tisdall for Tamesa Fabrics, 1978. A large-scale design, but softer in character than the big, brash textiles of the 1960s, more in keeping with the new vernacular buildings of the period. Tamesa Fabrics.

25 and 26
Woven Irish linen for a range of kitchen textiles
developed by the hand-weavers Roger Oates and Fay
Morgan for large-scale production by David Mellor,
1981. Roger Oates.

27
Cabinet with ebony, holly and dyed beech veneer, 1972,
designed by Michael Gurney, then a student at the
Royal College of Art. (He died tragically young in that
same year.) A spectacular piece, prophetic both of the
considerable revival of hand-made furniture later in the
decade, and also the reawakened interest in Oriental art
and design. College collection, Royal College of Art.

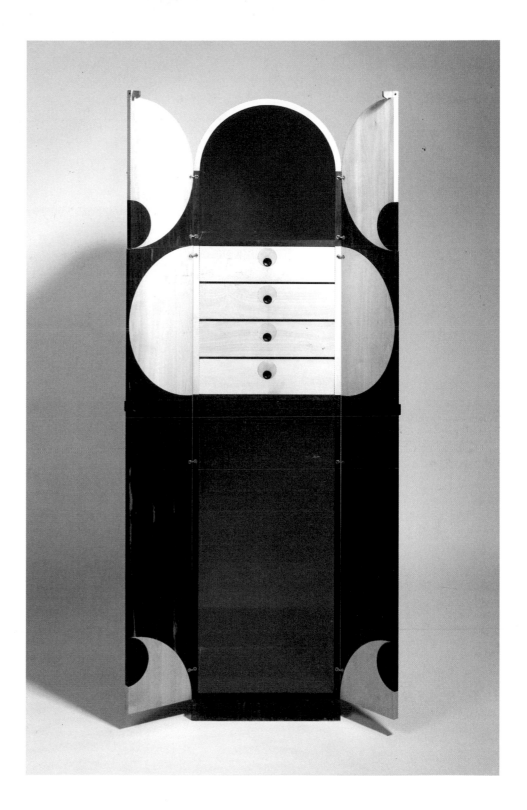

28
The Crayonne 'Input' range, first launched in 1973 by
Airfix Plastics and Conran Associates: the first serious
attempt to apply high-design principles to everyday
household plastics, the forerunner of many similar
collections, and a long-term commercial success. Conran
Associates.

There was a kindly old waiter from North Italy whom we call Ticino, who smiled at us like a host.'[16]

There was something very schoolboyish about these Arts and Crafts groups. The Art Workers' Guild, although very shy in public, almost pathologically nervous of publicity, was different in private, full of badinage and boisterousness. *The Art Workers' Guild* history, written by H.J.L.Massé in 1935, year of the Guild's half-century, has many references to past Art Workers' Guild festivities and the good-natured chaff and banter these engendered. Some became the stuff of legend. Reginald Blomfield, in his memoirs, mentions the Shrovetide revels of 1892, the year that William Morris was in the chair. Wrote Blomfield:

'George Frampton, who, whatever his merits as a sculptor, possessed a most droll humour, acted the little Blondel donkey, with somebody else behind, George being the head. I was bowled over in cock-fighting by T.R.Spence, architect, while E.P.Warren, architect, an old friend of mine, watched us with solemn and immovable dignity. Many years later Frampton and I were able to help Spence at the Royal Academy.'[17]

The point I want to make is not just that many major designers of the day were good at being silly, but – a feeling emphasised by Blomfield's final sentence, in which he talks of helping Spence at the Academy – that collective loyalty, the sense of shared experience, between many of the leaders of design in that far-off period, created a strong code, almost a kind of a freemasonry, which, it could be argued, has continued to exist.

The Arts and Crafts movement was in fact a whole succession of groups within groups. For instance, the young architect-designers of Shaw's office (where, once again, the horseplay was very much in evidence): Lethaby, Mervyn Macartney, Edward Prior, Robert Weir Schultz and Sidney Barnsley; the young architect-designers who worked with John D.Sedding: Ernest Barnsley, Henry Wilson, Ernest Gimson, Alfred Powell, John Paul Cooper. These groups split off and reassembled through the period. Some of the members later re-met in the Cotswolds. But earlier, in 1890, five of these designers   Gimson, Lethaby, Blomfield, Macartney, Sidney Barnsley – had joined in setting up a small experimental workshop, Kenton & Co., in Bedford Row, in London. They designed the furniture and employed professional craftsmen who made it up for them. They enjoyed themselves immensely and were totally unbusinesslike:

'We made no attempt', wrote Blomfield, 'to interfere with each other's idiosyncrasies. Lethaby's and Gimson's inventions ran to simple designs of admirable form in oak. I recollect a mirror frame, rather Persian in design, inlaid with mother-of-pearl, by Sidney Barnsley and much admired by Leighton. Macartney followed the elegant motives of the eighteenth century, and I indulged myself in solid rosewood.'[18]

Kenton & Co., which was in effect a forerunner of the co-operative craft workshops of the 1970s, in that the designers, although sharing all the overheads, were working independently, closed down two years later. Though they had hardly hoped to, they had not made a profit, and divided up the furniture among themselves to repay their original capital investment. Mostly they chose their own designs. But Lethaby selected an oak cabinet by Blomfield with an inlaid pattern of rabbits eating lettuce.

The main motive of Kenton & Co. had been the pleasure of the founding partners. Design for entertainment. This was just as true of the Omega Workshops, although the style of product was altogether different. The Omega was founded in 1913 by Roger Fry, the art critic and painter and, incidentally, in years gone by, a friend of Ashbee's, though Fry had never had the same belief in craftsmanship. Indeed, the Omega in a sense was anti-craftsmanship: Fry was apt to buy a Dryad chair and paint it red (*Venetian* red, the favoured colour of the Omega). The idea of the Omega was a gathering of artists – Fry himself, Duncan Grant, Vanessa Bell and others – aiming to express their individual sensibility through the decoration of normal household objects, the cups, the chairs, the tables people often take for granted. It was a group project, though the group around the Omega seemed particularly prone to upheavals and reversals; it was, in a way, the working-out of Fry's own theory that 'the greatest art has always been communal, the expression – in highly individualised ways no doubt – of common aspirations and ideals'.[19] Its spirit of experiment reminds one of the joie de vivre, and the naivety, of Morris & Co. at the beginning; and in its iconoclastic urges, its will to shatter the complacency and dullness of the capitalist manufactured product by showing an alternative set of design values, it was, as it turned out, an extraordinary foretaste of the anarchic design movement of today.

The Design and Industries Association, meanwhile, also had its eye on British chairs and English teapots. But it had a relatively steady bourgeois theory, viz. that if a thing were unaffectedly made to fulfil its purpose thoroughly, then it would be good art: a very reasonable surmise. The DIA in those days, in the years between the Wars, was the chief, indeed the only, design group of any substance. 'It was not', wrote John Gloag once, 'a society for Art twaddle'. Art, or any other, twaddle was not its line at all. The DIA was supremely conscientious; as much, if not more so, than the Arts and Crafts societies which, in a sense, gave birth to it and from which it drew so many of its members. It was a group with admirable fixity of purpose. As the Yearbook for 1926 so well expressed it: 'Fashion ebbs and flows, but DIA principles remain true'. Like the Arts and Crafts societies before it, it had its own built-in hierarchy: first W.R.Lethaby became the father figure, revered theorist and spokesman, and then Frank Pick took over. Ranged round them were the henchmen – the Heals, the Harry Peaches, the Curwens and the Stablers – good-natured men of principle, their hearts in the right place. The DIA, of course, had its own robust code of honour, and shared the Arts and Crafts distaste for self-publicity. Like the Arts and Crafts, as well, it had its private jokes, its banter, its rather unremitting hail-fellow-well-met atmosphere. Even more, perhaps, than Arts and Crafts, the DIA mid-period, the tucket-sounding years of the 1920s and 1930s, exudes the tweedy sense of well-meaning masculinity, the predilection for the predictable and clubbable, which lasted so long in British design life.

This is not to say that the design groups were immovable. Though set in their ways, the emphasis within them shifted quite considerably according to the period. In the early years of the Arts and Crafts societies, painters and sculptors, besides architects and craftsmen, were included in the grouping. This was the whole intention: the Art Workers' Guild and the Art and Crafts Exhibition Society were set up to establish a common ground between the fine artist and the craftsman: 'an honest and sincere attempt', as Blomfield put it, 'to find a common standpoint from which all the graphic and plastic arts and crafts should be approached'.[20] The DIA evinced a comparable catholicity: its membership, though hardly bursting at the seams with sculptors, covered a very broad spectrum of designing and drew in other members from ancillary professions, from writing, journalism and even the more reputable advertising agencies, as well as the captains of industry which it cultivated with enormous assiduity. During the 1930s the groupings changed again, not least with the foundation of the Society of Industrial Artists, the professional society, in 1930. But the atmosphere remained, it seems, astonishingly constant. The design groups were still very much a band of brothers. Here is James Holland, in his Jubilee history of the SIA, describing those early scenes of camaraderie:

'the embryo Society amounted to a select group of artists, designers and craftsmen – later becoming several groups – meeting regularly and convivially, to discuss the pursuit of their stated aims and to listen to lectures and discourses by colleagues and guest speakers. My earliest personal recollection of encountering the SIA is of a friendly evening of talk, darts and bitter in a south London pub, a tweedy, pipe-smoking occasion much in keeping with the character of that pre-war decade'.[21]

One important feature of the SIA in those days was its link, once again, to the fine artists. In the 1930s, according to James Holland's perspicacious Jubilee analysis, a quite surprising number of fine artists were actively involved in the Society's working structure. In 1932–3, Paul Nash was President; Frank Dobson, Graham Sutherland and Allan Walton, among other well-known artists, were members of the Council. Partly, this reflected an ideal: the new conception of the potential role of the artist in relation to machine production, as the theories of the Bauhaus gradually percolated through to Britain. (It was, wrote Paul Nash in 1932, in a mood of some intoxication, the duty of the artist to invade the house as a designer in materials ranging from 'stone, paper, glass, steel, wood, cardboard, rubber, leather, fabrics and endless synthetic and artificial patent compositions',[22] and he foresaw that 'the professional artist of the future would be a professional designer'.[23]) But as well as an ideal, the feeling for the merging of art into design reflected a reality: the 1930s were becoming a great period for patronage, and artists were employed (as designers) quite consistently by such entrepreneurs as Frank Pick at London Transport, Jack Beddington at Shell, Stephen Tallents at the GPO and Tom Heron of Cresta. There were famous 1930s projects like the Foley range of pottery designed by artists (Paul Nash in fact was one of them); and Edinburgh Weavers' collection of textiles commissioned from painters (another enterprise with which Paul Nash had been connected). The proximity of design groups and fine artists in the 1930s, a time when design education theories were surfacing, encouraged the conviction that training for designers should be carried out in art-orientated schools and colleges: a belief which only now is beginning to be questioned.

In the 1930s, the links were also very architectural. The design world and the architects were close together because, in many cases, the designers *were* the architects. The few actual industrial designers of the period, designers edging into such areas as furniture, ceramics, glass and engineering – Wells Coates, Serge Chermayeff, Robert Goodden, R.D.Russell, Jack Howe, Keith Murray – were all architects by training. Many of the members of the design groups proper, the DIA and SIA, had strong affiliations with the progressive architectural group practices, Tecton for instance, and also with the MARS group. The ex-Bauhaus architects Walter Gropius and Marcel Breuer arrived in London in the mid-1930s, refugees from Nazi Germany. A home was offered to them by Jack Pritchard at Lawn Road Flats in Hampstead. This building, completed in 1934, had been designed for Jack and Molly Pritchard by Wells Coates, and it is now regarded as a classic of its period, one of the few landmarks of the British Modern Movement. The social centre of Lawn Road was the Isobar, which Breuer had designed, and to which naturally gravitated architects, designers and what counted as the international modernists of England.

The groupings within groupings, the complex interweavings, of British design history are nowhere more apparent than in the Faculty of Royal Designers for Industry, which was set up by the Royal Society of Arts in 1936. This relatively small and élite body of designers, self-elected, from quite varied design disciplines, astonishingly English in its structure and its attitudes, forms a kind of microcosm of the whole design profession. In 1948, twelve years after it was founded, Gordon Russell gave a paper, 'The Work of the Royal Designers for Industry', analysing in most fascinating detail the major design groupings, as they then appeared. What is striking is not just the sheer profusion, the multiple approaches to industrial designing, but the energy and zest for corporate activities among many of the Royal Designers of that period. He lists the architectural group within the Faculty, the many RDIs in architectural practice. He lists the RDIs who, at the same time, are fine artists – painters, etchers or lithographers – and puts a special emphasis upon the stage designers, Anna Zinkeisen, Gordon Craig and Laurence Irving. He defines the exhibitions group (Gardner, Gray, Coates, Gordon Russell himself); the typographic group (Meynell, J.H.Mason, Percy Delf Smith); the all-round-designers group (Robert Goodden, Harold Stabler); the more specialist furniture and radio designers (Ambrose Heal, Wells Coates again and R.D.Russell, Gordon Russell's brother). He contrasts the pure engineering group (Sir Geoffrey de Havilland, Barnes Wallis and Charles Nicholson) with the more craft-minded hand-to-machine designers (Duncan Grant, Allan Walton, Ethel Mairet, Robert Goodden, and two past Royal Designers, James Hogan, glass designer, and Eric Gill, described by Gordon Russell as 'the outstanding figure of this class'). He goes on to consider the designer-manufacturer (RDIs like Allan Walton, Susie Cooper) and the designer-manufacturer-and-shopkeeper (of which the one example he can find is Ambrose Heal). There are other groups to come. The design directors' group: Reco Capey of Yardleys, Ashley Havinden of Crawfords, A.B.Read of Troughton and Young Lighting. The design-in-education group. The list of Royal Designers who sit on myriad design advisory committees (this group totals seventeen, almost as much as half the Faculty). Many of the RDIs belong in two or three compartments, interconnecting to outside design strongholds. No less than ten had been involved at one time or another, Gordon Russell notes with awe, in design commissions from Frank Pick at London Transport; several had been working under the aegis of the Utility Furniture Design Panel (of which Gordon Russell himself had been the Chairman). In this early post-war period, the network of designers, as Gordon

Russell points out with immense pleasure – for networks suited Gordon Russell – was considerable. Milner Gray, SIA President, was a Royal Designer. Gordon Russell, at the time of his paper, was both Master of the Faculty and Director of the Council of Industrial Design.

Gordon Russell had great hopes, the hopes which we have seen before among reformers of design in Britain, of the moral efficacy of designing, the designer's role in helping to regenerate the nation. He ended his paper on the Royal Designers, touchingly, on a note of highest visionary fervour, seeing design as one of the prime factors in the post-war revival of the country:

'I think you will agree with me', he said, 'when I say that one would be optimistic indeed to believe that wars lead to an improvement in manners. The exact opposite is the case. Over great areas of the world we find today the most elementary rules of courtesy flouted and, not unnaturally, human relationships do not survive the strain. The standard of industrial design in a country is one of the visible signs of its standard of manners and of its general approach to life. Never was it so important to hold fast to real values. Here we are determined that the Faculty shall play its part, albeit a very small one, in the great revolution we are witnessing.'[24]

In 1951, year of the Festival of Britain, many of these heartfelt hopes were still extant. The Festival, although perhaps one should not view it as the sign of a new civilisation evolving, was certainly a very effective morale-booster in that bleak period of post-war austerity and a quite enormous stimulus for innovation in architecture and design. The artistic control of the whole Festival, from the use of the site to the selection of the teaspoons, involving a hundred architects and designers, working in groups and sub-groups, was an extraordinary exercise in teamwork which confirmed the British talent for corporate designing. One also gathers, from the stream of reminiscence which has since then poured from those who took part in the Festival (the Festival has now acquired an element of folklore), that, for the designers, it was not just very valuable experience, put to good use later, but the most enormous fun. It was a perfect period for the groupings and regroupings which have occurred so rhythmically in British design history. A good many Royal Designers were designers for the Festival: Hugh Casson RDI was architectural Director. Many Festival designers had also been recruited for the Royal College of Art, just then beginning in its new incarnation under Robin Darwin. Festival figures reassembled in new guises: Professor Sir Hugh Casson; Professor Robert Goodden; Professor R.D.Russell; Professor Misha Black.

Possibly by then it had just become a habit. But one senses that the impulse towards corporate designing is more deeply allied to British character and outlook, and the post-war growth of multi-talent design offices has not been unrelated, although it has become increasingly less purist, to the joy in camaraderie of early design periods. The idea of working groups of artists and designers, complementary in talents, who enjoyed each other's company, has been so very central to the national tradition – from Morris, Marshall, Faulkner & Co. onward – that it does not need much stretch of the imagination to connect this through to the latter-day design groups. Design Research Unit was really the first of the professional large-scale design consultancies, formed in 1942, and drawing on the skills, in its early years, of the designers Milner Gray and Misha Black and Norbert Dutton, architects Frederick Gibberd and Sadie Speight, the structural engineer Felix Samuely, with Herbert Read as the Director. DRU explained its arguments for a group practice in an early leaflet:

> 'Like every aspect of modern industry, design should be a co-operative activity, and the function of DRU is to focus on every project it undertakes the combined knowledge and experience of several creative minds since it believes that only by pooling the talents of a team of designers is it possible to offer a service capable of meeting every demand from the wide and varied field of present-day activity.'[25]

The pool of talent theory has had an immense influence, since then, on the development of British design practice: there are dozens of examples in the post-war period of which the most convincing is Pentagram, perhaps.

British designing, a bit like British cooking, has absorbed a lot of foreign influences through the ages: assimilated them and created something new, and often in the end intensely British. The DIA, for instance, founded on the model of the Deutscher Werkbund, the German design pressure group, emerged very far from German, somehow almost doubly English. The original foreign influence, absorbed, made something different. Frank Pick, in 1930, much admired design in Denmark, the consistent design standards, on the large scale and in detail, in the streets of Copenhagen; this very much affected his London Transport policy, but Frank Pick's way of doing things remained completely British. British designers were receptive to the influence of both the USA and Scandinavia in the 1950s, Germany and, to some extent, Italy as well during the 1960s; and yet these were decades in which national design, far from being swamped, was actually strengthening. One could argue that this propensity towards design influence from abroad implies a marked degree of national tolerance and confidence. It can perhaps be seen as the natural extension of the British group tradition, the whole, large, settled structure of designing in this country, and related to the relative ease with which designers from abroad, in particular the many refugees from Europe in the 1930s, were absorbed not just into the professional design groups but also the whole hierarchy of design in Britain.

The coherence and conviction of design in Britain, as well as allowing the absorption of outside influence, has worked the other way: from inside outwards. The theories and the actual artefacts of Arts and Crafts made an extraordinary impact all through Europe and, as Pevsner pointed out so long ago, the reverberations from this period continued. The DIA delight in simple things fit for their purposes – farm implements and garden tools and sports equipment, from the golf club to the ultra-functional croquet mallet – was a source of fascination to many Scandinavians early in the 1930s and certainly encouraged the special design tendencies, the mixture of efficiency style and artful homeliness, in Swedish industrial design as it developed. The British Design Council, of course, has been the model for innumerable international design organisations, and the post-war British educational system for designers has, in scope and in ambition, been a source of wonder, much the most highly-developed in the world. The attributes, the virtues, of design in Britain have been coming under a new and intense scrutiny as British design services themselves have been exported with very great success. But there are few surprises. The qualities which make British design services covetable – so much so that some consultancies now claim that they are doing half their work away from Britain – are the traits which for so many years have been totally familiar: moderation, efficient, lucid thinking, commonsense.

And yet, has moderation been as far as we could get? Has moderation, in fact, been absolutely beneficial? Or have the obvious virtues of the national tradition, the honesty, the reticence, the care and equanimity, in fact, in some respects, almost been a liability? In the past few years – a major turning-point, it seems, in British design history, with many long-held values beginning to be challenged, and many old-established ways of doing things dismantled – much attention has been focused on the whole design tradition. It was obviously in many ways a generous tradition; there was a great deal which it encouraged and included. But doubts have been accumulating: was its tolerance so total? In fact hasn't there been also quite a lot which it shut out?

Certainly, through the years, its qualities of human niceness, relaxation, wit and whimsy, leisure and repose, have militated against rigorous professionalism. Professionalism has been a little suspect in the British tradition of designing. There has always been a certain nervousness of overdoing things, a gentlemanly horror of being seen to go too far. Frank Pick, for instance, criticised the lack of human quality in German design of the World War I period. He related how Professor Neumann of the Deutscher Werkbund urged the German architects 'to seize upon the house and create it in a German style . . . I remember reading once upon a time,' Pick added, 'how the colour of the cat was included in the prescription for a German home'.[26] His Art Workers' Guild audience would have seen this as preposterous: the colour of the cat could never be prescribed in Britain. It was totally against the British design ethos, then or later; the easy-going, civilised, comfortable, convivial, humorous, half-amateurish outlook on designing which has sometimes resulted in that British self-indulgence of designing rather less for one's clients than one's peers.

Certainly, too, the streak of cosy insularity in the British design movement made it terribly suspicious of anything it saw as even faintly strange and foreign. The room which E.W.Godwin designed in 1884 for Oscar Wilde fell well within this category: this was Anglo-Japanese in style, bare white and grey; the sparse furniture was white, except for one red lampshade. Walter Crane, the epitome of Englishness, denounced it, in the *Daily News*, as 'needlessly Spartan – there was a hair-shirt vigour about it opposed to all geniality and prandial humours'.[27] The English country background to the Arts and Crafts, the sense of fellowship, the love of the familiar and natural and wholesome, which brought about so much that was creative in that period, also led to an undoubted nervousness of novelty, amounting to a kind of a stick-in-the-mud quality, which lasted for many decades. This, together with the tendency for William Morris worship, was ridiculed quite sharply by Sir Lawrence Weaver in his introduction to the DIA Yearbook in 1927:

> 'No one is heard in disrespect of William Morris fabrics or tapestries or type. These things are English: they come from Hammersmith and Merton (where Lord Nelson abode) and had the flavouring name of Kelmscott. But Munich – à bas les Boches!'

A bas les Boches indeed. The traditions of the workshop, which had so much
dominated the British design movement, the cult of works of art made by one
human for another, the whole stress on individuality, the quirks and oddnesses
which seemed to make the life of England very much worth living, meant that
British design leaders of the 1920s and 1930s found international rationalism
difficult to stomach: robot modernism, as John Gloag crossly called it.

> 'It is', wrote Philip Morton Shand in 1930, 'a melancholy and humiliating
> confession for an Englishman to make that the great movement towards
> standardisation of design in terms of functional fitness, to which the genius of the
> German people is now applying itself, should find no echo in the country which
> has initiated the Industrial Age. But it has to be candidly admitted that no nation
> has more stubbornly resisted rationalisation in industry: To none – not even the
> French – are standardisation and mass production more abhorrent.'[28]

Although Philip Morton Shand over-dramatised the problem, and the rationalist
movement did make certain inroads into Britain by the middle of the 1930s, there
was still something about it which made the British anxious. When it came, the
British Modern Movement was a mild one. Rationalism, in its strictest form, was,
simply, just not British: it contravened too much in our tradition of designing, the
build-up of a deep feeling, the associationism.

It has always been intriguing how British design tradition, so positive in some
ways, is so negative in others; progressive, but also so inbred and so conservative;
receptive and yet in some ways curiously stubborn; welcoming and yet ironically
prone to exclusivity. Its virtues almost always seem to have another side to them.
The sturdy masculinity, in many ways so admirable, to which one can attribute the
conviction and the vigour, the congeniality, of much of Arts and Crafts designing,
was remarkably successful (albeit quite unconsciously) in setting up a pattern of
anti-feminism within the British tradition in designing, of which there are still
traces. The male-dominated world of Arts and Crafts has been exhaustively, and
chillingly, described in Anthea Callan's *Angel in the Studio*. In the gathering of
confrères, the women are irrelevant: the social pattern so stalwartly established in
the Art Workers' revelries (the 'Eve-less Paradise' depicted by May Morris) extended
to, for instance, the SPAB in Gatti's, the SIA pipe-smoking tweedily in the Cock
Tavern. A pattern which, while not actually hostile towards woman, has scarcely
been encouraging, and partially explains the considerable imbalance within the
design profession even now.

British design is not much good at the erotic. Perhaps this is because of its early
sense of purity, its aura of self-conscious bonhomie resulting in an attitude to
women one can only term as puerile; in any case, eroticism has not featured greatly
in the national tradition. Indeed, from time to time, it has seemed positively scaring.
The erotic connotations of *art nouveau*, especially, left British commentators in a
state of some confusion. 'Shows symptoms of pronounced disease',[29] as Lewis
F. Day muttered, at the sight of *art nouveau* in October 1900. 'The majority of the
exhibits were not only crude but meaningless', wrote Arthur Liberty in 1909,
reporting on a visit to an exhibition of *art nouveau* paintings and drawings in
Budapest: 'Nearly all the few clever ones were either obtrusively revolting in subject
. . . or else erotic imaginings of morbid brains depicted with a mastery of technique

only too wickedly perfect.'[30] In the clean, fresh atmosphere of mainstream British thinking, even the Glasgow School designers seemed too strange and esoteric: a reaction one might criticise as rather unimaginative. For it must be faced that in their long pursuit of sturdiness and plainness (both qualities quite simply seen as tantamount to goodness), the British have from time to time been very narrow-minded. They have shown, for instance, very little feeling for the glamorous: significantly, Eileen Gray, who had great sense of glamour, spent much of her career working outside Britain. There has also been consistent British mistrust of sheer brilliance which perhaps, in retrospect, has not been altogether wise.

British design has lacked a certain sense of stylishness. Again, this was a conscious rejection, going back to the Arts and Crafts ideals of basic honesty. 'Avoid', said Lethaby, 'the false smiles of the sham styles'. Avoiding the false smiles has had some curious effects, like the falling over backwards in the almost manically modern-minded 1950s to pour scorn on the creative neo-Georgian of the 1920s (a style the DIA had then, ironically, approved of). Only now has the design world started saying yes to Lutyens. Fixity of purpose; or shutting out of influence which might have been of value? Though there is no final answer, it does seem very likely that honesty and truthfulness cannot go on for ever, that the cult of the commonplace has rather overreached itself: at least in design markets in which fashion is an element. British design indubitably lacks sophistication beside, say, the very best Italian furniture today.

Anarchy is something else at which the British have not been too expert. This is not just a case of commonsense and sanity; for British design has had its mystics and its freaks. But the tenor has been more assimilative than rejective; the British have not had a lot of truck with the debunkers. No Studio Alchymia; no equivalent of Ettore Sottsass. Few anarchic revolutions: anyway not many yet.

The British tradition on the whole has been much gentler. The ideals which have formed it, though radical in some ways, have been calmer and more kindly. The reforming ideas, developed with such consistency from Ruskin, Morris, Lethaby to Pick and Gordon Russell, are intensely visionary and also deeply human. They have sprung from a real love of English countryside and British people. They show a strength of purpose, a generosity and an imaginative fervour which one cannot help admiring. And yet one also senses that this moralistic bias, the idea of basic rightness in designing, the conception of the designer as reformer, the bearer of the message, the bringer of the light, has set up a whole sequence of most complex inhibitions, the dangers of which are maybe only now being realised, and has started long debates about the values and the future of the British tradition of design.

It seems a fair conjecture that the highly moralistic, and indeed, at the beginning, anti-capitalist, leanings of British design, the whole intense, elaborate, self-righteous philosophy, has resulted in what one might call a lack of gumption in tackling modern problems of design for the world markets. An instinctive distrust of publicity and marketing; even a lingering suspicion of commerce. It also seems likely that the British group tradition, the networks of designing, the hierarchic patterns, have encouraged a pleasant, but insidious, complacency, a group tendency to make the best of things and not to question the generally accepted attitudes and values. 'We keep jogging along in our quiet way', as the DIA once mentioned in an early Yearbook. How charming, modest, British. But, also, how self-satisfied. Did they ever ask themselves, jogging towards what?

In the succeeding chapters of this book I shall be attempting to take a closer look at the evolution of the British tradition, period by period, and along the route from homeliness to eccentricity, from 1880s fantasy to 1980s deadpan, from conviviality to ecstasy, to outline the main tendencies within design élitism over the past century and to trace through the sequence of events which has, it now appears, resulted in the kind of crisis of identity, both personal and national, with which the design profession is confronted.

It is easy to see, from just a quick glance through these pages, that the British tradition, as it has built up over this long period, has been based on individual flair and creativity. It is a tradition, in a way, of star performers: such innovative talents as, in the early period, E.W.Godwin and Christopher Dresser; Morris and De Morgan; Ashbee, Voysey, Gimson, Mackintosh and many others working in the individualistic manner of the Arts and Crafts. The Arts and Crafts movement was indeed mainly responsible for the whole principle of designer-as-individual, designer as maverick, licensed to set up in opposition to society: the role filled in the years between the two World Wars by Eric Gill and also, less ostentatiously, by Bernard Leach. In the 1930s, under influence from the United States, designers in Britain became very nearly superstars: Wells Coates, Bernard, Chermayeff, were almost design idols. And in the post-war period, encouraged by the early promotional policies of the COID and by the design journalism of that period, the idea of the designer's individual contribution came across to a wide public. No wonder that designers now feel a little baffled. Over the past decade, the pattern has much altered. The designer-as-individual is less convincing. Design offices are larger, with new emphasis on teamwork. Design commissions too are much bigger and more complex. The tradition of personal design patronage is weakening in an era of industrial rationalisation, takeover and merger. Innovation is rarer, risks are much less often feasible; there is a general atmosphere of drawing-in, of caution, which designers, not unnaturally, find disorientating. In this context it is maybe too early to discern whether the craft revival of the past few years, the move back to the individual workshop, is important, a meaningful new phase of the tradition of personal experiment, or just an aberration. In the climate of the times it is an unexpected and, one may well find, an over-optimistic trend.

The other obvious question which emerges from these pages, the sequence of design from William Morris to Pentagram, is just how far a national style continues to be valid. Looking through the illustrations, one must admit the Britishness, strong in the first three sections, up as far as 1930, from then on becomes progressively more watered-down, more modified. The designs which illustrate the 1960s and the 1970s, though still I think quite characteristically British, are gradually acquiring internationalist identity. Is this, one has to wonder, good, bad, or just inevitable? Will there *be* British design by the early 1990s? Or, in years to come, will the national tradition almost cease to have any relevance at all?

References

[1] Quoted Christian Barman: *The Man Who Built London Transport: A Biography of Frank Pick* (Newton Abbot, David & Charles, 1979)

[2] W.R.Lethaby: *Form in Civilisation: Collected Papers on Art and Labour* (London, Oxford University Press, 1922)

[3] Quoted J.D.Sedding: 'Our Arts and Handicrafts,' paper read at Liverpool Art Congress, 1888, and reprinted in *Art and Handicraft* (London, Kegan Paul, Trench, Trubner & Co., 1893)

[4] Misha Black: 'Fitness for What Purpose?' Article in *Design* magazine, January 1974

[5] Hamilton Temple Smith: 'The History of the DIA: The Early Years.' Article in *Design for Today*, May 1935, reprinted in *DIA Yearbook* 1975

[6] 1Quoted Christian Barman: *The Man who Built London Transport*, ibid.

[7] Nikolaus Pevsner: 'Gordon Russell'. Article in *Architectural Review*, CXXXII, 1962

[8] Quoted Philip Henderson: *William Morris, his life, work and friends* (London, Thames and Hudson, 1967)

[9] J.D.Sedding: 'Our Arts and Handicrafts', ibid.

[10] Quoted Christian Barman: *The Man Who Built London Transport*, ibid.

[11] C.F.A.Voysey: *Individuality* (London, Chapman and Hall, 1915)

[12] Quoted Christian Barman: *The Man Who Built London Transport*, ibid.

[13] J.D.Sedding: 'Religion and Art,' paper read at Portsmouth Church Congress, 1886, and reprinted in *Art and Handicraft*, ibid.

[14] A.Romney Green: fragment of autobiography (unpublished), in MS collection of the Victoria and Albert Museum

[15] Quoted Dr Patrick Nuttgens: *Learning to Some Purpose* (London, Society of Industrial Artists and Designers, 1977)

[16] W.R.Lethaby: 'Ernest Gimson's London Days', chapter in *Ernest Gimson, His Life and Work* (Stratford-upon-Avon, Shakespeare Head Press, 1924)

[17] Sir Reginald Blomfield: *Memoirs of an Architect* (London, Macmillan, 1932)

[18] Sir Reginald Blomfield: *Memoirs of an Architect*, ibid.

[19] Roger Fry: *Vision and Design* (London, Chatto & Windus, 1920)

[20] Sir Reginald Blomfield: *Memoirs of an Architect*, ibid.

[21] James Holland: *Minerva at Fifty: The Jubilee History of the SIAD, 1930 to 1980* (Westerham, Hurstwood Publications, 1980)

[22] Paul Nash: 'The Artist in the House'. Article in *The Listener*, 16 March 1932

[23] Paul Nash: Article in *The Times*, May 1933, quoted in *Paul Nash as Designer* by Susan Lambert (London, Victoria and Albert Museum, 1975)

[24] Gordon Russell: 'The Work of the Royal Designers for Industry'. Lecture given to the DIA, 6 October 1948, and reprinted from *The Journal of the Royal Society of Arts*, October 1948

[25] Quoted John Blake: *The Practical Idealists* (London, Lund Humphries, 1969)

[26] Quoted Christian Barman: *The Man Who Built London Transport*, ibid.

[27] Walter Crane: Interview in *Daily News*, 20 October 1896

[28] Philip Morton Shand: 'Type Forms in Great Britain'. Article in *Die Form*, Berlin, 1930, quoted Stephen Bayley: *In Good Shape* (London, Design Council, 1979)

[29] Lewis F.Day: Article in *Art Journal*, October 1900

[30] Quoted Alison Adburgham: *Liberty's: A Biography of A Shop* (London, George Allen & Unwin, 1975)

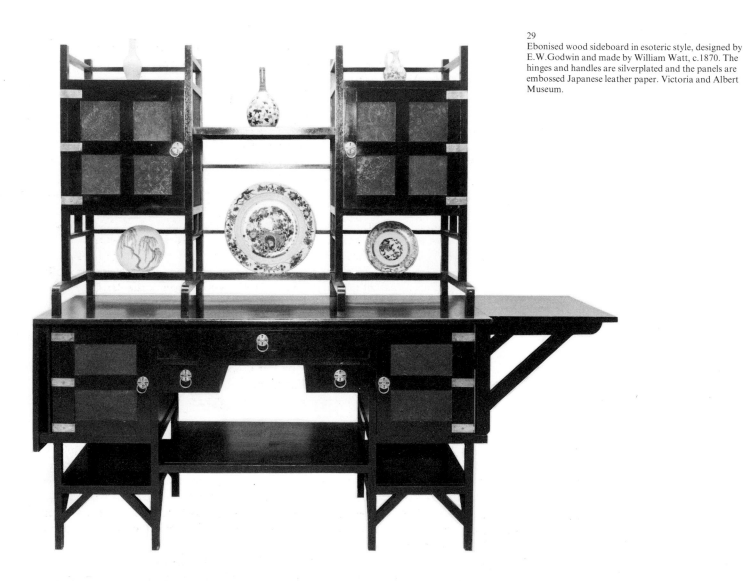

29
Ebonised wood sideboard in esoteric style, designed by
E.W.Godwin and made by William Watt, c.1870. The
hinges and handles are silverplated and the panels are
embossed Japanese leather paper. Victoria and Albert
Museum.

The 1880s

30
Ebonised oak table, designed by E.W.Godwin and made
by William Watt, c.1870. City of Bristol Museum and
Art Gallery.

The 1880s was a period of extraordinary activity in the visual arts and a time at
which many of the basic elements of the next hundred years' development of design
in Britain are first discernible.

An idea of 'the spirit of true design' was in the air, and this implied the shedding
of historic precedents, traditional superfluities, and aiming for a new style of
freshness, directness and simplicity. Through this decade, the principles of
functional efficiency, the fitness-for-purpose doctrines which were destined to
dominate British design theory for many years to come, found their most persuasive
expression in the metalwork of Christopher Dresser. E.W.Godwin's astonishing,
stark, geometric furniture, made by William Watt, whose catalogue, *Art Furniture*,
was published in 1877, helped to popularise the intellectual pared-down style.

At the same time, a small foretaste of the many contradictions of British design
history and indeed in some ways a reflection of the paradox embodied in the
dominating figure of the decade, William Morris, the mood of high ideals and
austerity was balanced by a style of unprecedented richness, even fantasy, especially
in textile and pottery design. The purity and reticence of much of the design of the
Aesthetic Movement, obviously influenced by the art of Japan, was offset, as time
went on, by the relative robustness, the self-conscious Englishness, of early Arts and
Crafts design. The decade in which Dresser did much of his best work was also the
decade in which Morris established his textile printing works at Merton Abbey on
the Wandle; in which Walter Crane made patterns in many different media –
wallpapers, textiles, ceramics, illustration – most of them entrancingly ingenious
and elaborate; and William De Morgan was decorating pottery with unsurpassed
exuberance and idiosyncrasy.

It was in the 1880s that the choice of special objects with which to live surrounded,
one's furniture and furnishings, one's wallpapers and carpets, glass, pottery and
silver, became established, in sophisticated circles, as a considerable skill, if not an
art. Many handbooks of good taste were published, and believed in. Many old-
established firms appeared in new aesthetic guises, calling themselves Art Furniture-
makers or Art Potters. New aesthetic shops, emporiums of life-style, were set up for
the assistance of the doubtful or faint-hearted, performing rather the same function
as Habitat stores much later on.

Liberty's of Regent Street, founded in 1875 as an importer of Eastern
merchandise, had by 1883 opened its own furnishing and decorating studios under
the direction of Leonard F.Wyburd who rapidly built up a large, stylistically

53

31
Side table in ebonised oak, designed by E.W.Godwin and made by William Watt, c.1870. City of Bristol Museum and Art Gallery.

32
Oak writing desk, designed by A.H.Mackmurdo for the Century Guild, 1886. William Morris Gallery, Walthamstow.

33
Rush-seated chair in ebonised beech, a revival of a traditional Sussex design sold by Morris, Marshall, Faulkner & Co. from the mid-1860s onwards. This chair, in its own period, was extremely popular and it started an important ruralist tradition of chair design, British and international, Gimson to Magistretti. Wrote J.W.Mackail, Morris's first biographer: 'of all the specific minor improvements in common household objects due to Morris, the rush-bottomed Sussex chair perhaps takes the first place'.
Private collection.

coherent collection of designs in many different materials, some made in Liberty's own workshops, some made under contract by outside factories. There was even a Costume Department supervised by the avant-garde architect E.W.Godwin, and the aim was to sell goods with a consistent visual image, a kind of design package, to Liberty's aesthetically-conscious clientele. A similar exercise, an early example of corporate image-making, was well under way by the later 1870s and early 1880s not far from Liberty's, in Lower Regent Street, where Howell & James, originally metalwork specialists and general furnishers, had become the most prestigious suppliers of art pottery, claiming to be internationally known for their efforts to popularise works of high art and good taste. In those years of prosperity, art metalwork continued to be made in their own workshops, but pottery was manufactured to their specification by outside firms such as Doulton and Minton, and marked with the Howell and James stamp. Another remarkable example of

34
'Tulip' chintz designed by William Morris and originally printed by
Thomas Wardle at Leek, 1875. William Morris Gallery, Walthamstow.

35
'Cromer Bird' cretonne designed by A.H.Mackmurdo
for the Century Guild, c.1884. William Morris Gallery, Walthamstow.

36
'Wild Tulip' wallpaper designed by William Morris and
hand-printed by Jeffrey and Co., 1884. William Morris
Gallery, Walthamstow.

what was later to be known as 'design management' was the development of
W.B.Simpson, a relatively humble firm of London housepainters and decorators,
into a well-known company of art-tile painters, who commissioned a succession of
reputable artists to decorate their tiles and design tile murals (which included the
tiled refreshment room and grill room at the Victoria and Albert Museum.) Tile
blanks were supplied by commercial factories, painted, glazed and fired in Simpson's
workshops, and marked W.B.Simpson. Jeffrey & Co. of Islington printed a special
series of art wallpapers for Simpson. Some of these were designed by Lewis F.Day.

As successful as Liberty's in terms of public image was William Morris's own
company, which started in 1861 with the title Morris, Marshall, Faulkner & Co.,
Fine Art Workmen, later to become Morris & Co. The basic idea, the result of a
fruitless search by Morris and his friends for congenial furnishings for their own
houses, was to set up a 'manufactory of all things necessary for the decoration of
the house', and the founder partners included Ford Madox Brown, Dante Gabriel
Rossetti, Edward Burne-Jones and Philip Webb, the architect. In such an era of
aesthetic enterprises, the idea of a working band of brother artists (though Morris
in fact was the only really active member of the group), linked with the concept of
the moral worth of handicraft (though many of Morris's designs were, of course,
produced commercially in large quantities), had obvious attractions. The Firm, as it
was known in Morris circles, moved to premises of its own in Queen Square in
1865, and in 1877 opened a showroom in Oxford Street. By the 1880s, 'Morris' had
become a household word, as potent as Laura Ashley in the 1970s. Morris products
appealed most to the thinking middle classes, the kind of people who were moving
into Norman Shaw houses in Bedford Park, the first of the Garden Suburbs which

55

was then under construction, and soon, as Walter Crane recollected later, 'no home
with any claim to decorative charm was felt to be complete without its vine and fig
tree so to speak – from Queen Square'. Besides the William Morris wallpapers and
textiles, the Morris Sussex chair became almost a cult object which, by the 1880s,
was an established feature of the interiors of the cognoscenti: a forerunner of
quantities of peasant-inspired furniture in Britain and America over the next
century, a symbol of sophisticated simple life.

William Morris was an early, and unique, example of the designer entrepreneur,
a man whose considerable creative impulses led him to work in the commercial
world, as designer, as manufacturer, as retailer. (The fact that, as a socialist, he
much despised general commercial practice makes his achievement all the more
extraordinary.) It was obviously a time of great artistic optimism. In the early
1880s, Christopher Dresser, the most original designer of the day, was involved in
multifarious commercial ventures: an oriental import firm, Dresser and Holme; an
aesthetic shop in Bond Street, the Art Furnishers' Alliance, which was formed 'for

39
'Poppy' dessert doily in silk and linen damask, one of a set entitled 'Flora's Retinue' designed by Walter Crane, 1893. William Morris Gallery, Walthamstow.

40
'Single Flower' cretonne designed by A.H.Mackmurdo for the Century Guild, c.1882. On account of Mackmurdo's swirling foliage, this design makes an almost statutory appearance in books on the origins of *art nouveau*. William Morris Gallery, Walthamstow.

the purpose of supplying all kinds of artistic house-furnishing material, including furniture, carpets, wall-decorations, hangings, pottery, table glass, silversmiths' wares, hardware, and whatever is necessary to our household selection'. Every item for sale was subject to approval by the art director, Dr Dresser, who, at this same period was acting as designer, on a freelance basis, to Hukin & Heath and James Dixon, manufacturers of metalwork, and Linthorpe Pottery. Though not all Dresser's enterprises were successful, the Art Furnishers' Alliance going into liquidation in 1883, the sheer range of his design-work is impressive: cast iron, silver, pottery, glass, woodwork, textiles for at least a dozen factories. He was also writing some influential books, among them *Japan*, published in 1882.

It is possible to see the 1880s as the period of origin for the design profession, although the designer of those days would be entitled 'art adviser' or 'art superintendent'. But his role was beginning to be defined. Its commercial importance was beginning to be recognised. Walter Crane, painter, printmaker and illustrator, was, for instance, also greatly in demand as a designer for wallpapers and fabrics, printed, woven and embroidered, for pottery and tiles. Like Morris, Walter Crane had become a name to conjure with. As Mark Girouard points out in *Sweetness and Light: The Queen Anne Movement*, a Walter Crane frieze in the drawing room, Crane tiles and wallpapers throughout the house and even Walter Crane picture books in the nursery, had become *de rigueur* in many of the fashionable houses of the period, and in 1880 Crane was appointed Art Superintendent of the London Decorating Company. Another famous professional designer, Lewis F.Day, a formidable precursor of the twentieth-century design consultant, had set up his own office in London in 1870, branching out from his first speciality, stained glass, to design for the wallpaper and textile industries as well as pottery, furniture and glass. He became art director of Turnbull & Stockdale, the textile manufacturers, in 1881. In the 1880s and 1890s, especially through his widely distributed wallpapers and textiles – designs as evocative of their period as those of Claud Lovat Fraser in the 1920s, Lucienne Day in the 1950s – he had a very direct influence on public taste. In 1884, another very early example of commercial freelance design studio was opened by Arthur Silver. The Silver Studio, which sold designs successfully on the Continent as well as in Britain, was professional in outlook rather than pioneering, bringing good design to the bourgeoisie. It lasted until 1963.

The dawning art consciousness of industry showed itself in many forms in the late nineteenth century, the most immediately significant of which was the highly popular Art Pottery movement. Remnants of this are still around us. Art Pottery, of course, was very much a feature of the Aesthetic period. In the early 1870s, Henry Doulton of Doulton of Lambeth, the mainstay of whose production then consisted of stoneware drain-pipes and conduits, had yielded to persuasion from John Sparkes, head of the School of Art at Lambeth, for a number of students from the school, under Sparkes' supervision, to decorate experimental ranges of Doulton's salt-glazed stoneware. This policy continued and developed and by the 1880s Doulton's studio was employing over 200 artists, male and female. At almost the same time, Minton had opened Art Pottery Studios in South Kensington. The biscuit pottery was brought from Minton's factory in Stoke-on-Trent for decoration and impression with the mark 'Minton's Art Pottery Studio, Kensington Gore'. In

41
Copper and brass kettle designed by Christopher Dresser
and made by Benham & Froud, c.1885. Victoria and
Albert Museum.

42
Stand for 6 eggs, electroplate, designed by Christopher
Dresser and made by Hukin & Heath, c.1878. Victoria
and Albert Museum.

43
Teapot, electroplate, with ebony finial and handle,
designed by Christopher Dresser and made by Hukin &
Heath, 1878. Robertson collection at the Royal Pavilion,
Art Gallery and Museums, Brighton.

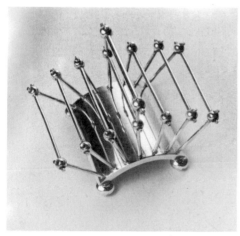

44
Folding toast-rack, electroplate, designed by Christopher
Dresser and made by Hukin & Heath, 1881. Robertson
collection at the Royal Pavilion, Art Gallery and
Museums, Brighton.

45
Ebony-handled teapot from electroplate tea service
designed by Christopher Dresser for James Dixon, 1880.
Dresser was designing regularly for this Sheffield firm in
the early 1880s and their contemporary catalogue
illustrates dozens of designs of an extreme stylistic non-
conformity. Victoria and Albert Museum.

46
Tall jug and beakers in salt-glazed stoneware, made by
the Martin Brothers, c.1893. The three potter brothers,
who set up their joint studio in Southall in 1877, are best
known for their grotesque birds, modelled by Wallace
Martin. But they were prolific potters, and their more
classic pieces are interesting too. Victoria and Albert
Museum.

47
Three-legged soup tureen in silverplate with ebony
handles, designed by Christopher Dresser for Hukin &
Heath, c.1880. One of Dresser's most famous and
original designs: similar soup tureens are in the collections
of the Worshipful Company of Goldsmiths in London
and the Museum of Modern Art, New York. Sheffield
City Museums.

the late 1870s, Wilcock and Company, a Leeds manufacturer of drain-pipes and
firebricks, had introduced a new kind of art pottery, Burmantofts Faïence, which
was sold by Howell & James in Lower Regent Street. Through the 1880s, there were
many more art potteries to come. This same pattern of the large industrial firm
supporting, and in ideal cases being stimulated by, an experimental craft studio was
developed with particular conviction in Scandinavia from the 1920s onwards.

As well as such commercially-sponsored art potteries, there was a growing number
of independent, individualistic potters. This was really the first sign of the modern
studio-pottery movement which was to dominate the coming century of British craft
activity. In Devon, in the 1880s, C.H.Brannam, a potter who had been to School of
Art in Barnstaple, had begun producing the well-known and peculiarly artistic
'Barum Ware', for which Liberty's became the agents. At this period, too, the
Martin Brothers were at work in Southall, producing their very distinctive, often
startlingly eccentric pottery designs in salt-glazed stoneware. At Clevedon Court,
near Bath, Sir Edmund Elton was experimenting, from 1880, with shapes and glazes
many of which were extraordinarily innovative. (He once said of himself, rather
endearingly, that 'if an ignorant country baronet set to work to make mud-pies and
didn't know anything about it, and used plenty of glazing he was bound to turn out
something queer'.) From 1882, William De Morgan was installed at Merton Abbey,
having erected his own buildings and kilns beside the disused print works which
William Morris had converted for the manufacture of his chintzes. Though De
Morgan's pottery shows a multitude of influences, Spanish, Italian, Persian, as well

as contemporary English-Aesthetic, its decorative qualities are thoroughly original. De Morgan was almost obsessively involved in workshop experiments, in technical development, a bias typical of advanced artistic thinking in this first great era of fine art workmanship.

Technique was to become one of the very central interests, a kind of watchword of the times, as the decade progressed and the preoccupations of the Aesthetic Movement gradually gave way to the ideals of Arts and Crafts. William Morris's theories of truth to material, the idea that designers should work to get the most from their material 'in such a way as honours it most', began to come into general artistic currency, together with the principle, to be developed greatly by later design theorists, that not only should it be altogether obvious to the beholder what that material is, but that the material should have received some special treatment which served to exploit its intrinsic qualities: as Morris maintained, something should have been done with it which is specially natural to it, something that could not be done with any other. William Morris was a toweringly influential figure in the artistic circles of the time, referred to reverentially as 'the Master Craftsman', and it was generally acknowledged that his example stimulated the very widespread interest and activity through the 1880s and 1890s not only in the central craft areas, in weaving, in woodwork, in metalwork, in pottery, but also in the more esoteric crafts, from the revival of embroidery and bookbinding to stained glass and plasterwork, inlay and intarsia, gesso and sgraffito.

The late Victorian individual workshop movement, in some ways very similar in spirit to the workshop movement of the 1970s, was of course a protest movement, a movement of revulsion against prevailing taste and current manufacturing practice. It was in a way rather amateur in concept. Morris, Marshall, Faulkner & Co. was founded in a spirit of camaraderie, a group of friends of the same outlook who liked the idea – in the early years at least – of co-operative working. The Century Guild, founded in 1882 by A.H.Mackmurdo, architect and self-taught craftsman, a disciple of Ruskin's, had similarly wide-ranging aims, the intention to 'restore building, decoration, glass painting, pottery, wood-carving and metal to their rightful place beside painting and sculpture', and a comparably loose and rather dilettante structure. Again, it was a gathering of more or less like-minded artists and designers, among them Selwyn Image, Herbert Horne and Clement Heaton. William De Morgan, Heywood Sumner and C.F.A.Voysey were, also, from time to time, working with the Guild, which, typically in an age of the all-round designer, an age in which William Morris composed epics while weaving tapestries, produced its own quarterly magazine, *The Hobby Horse*. Some of the work, especially the textiles and the furniture designed by Mackmurdo himself, is peculiarly innovative, strangely blending Japanese and English eighteenth-century influences. But the Guild itself in the end came to very little and in 1888 it was disbanded.

That same year, as the Century Guild dwindled away, another Guild, the Guild of Handicraft, was started. This was to be a larger, more ambitious venture, the pattern of the other Guilds to come. It was set up in the East End of London by a young architect-idealist, C.R.Ashbee, whose aim was not just to improve aesthetic standards, to make buildings and the objects which went into them more beautiful, but also, more importantly, to improve the standards of life of the workmen, the producers. The Guild of Handicraft, founded on the Ruskin tenets of joy in handicraft, of man's innate creative instinct, had a solemn moral purpose. It was educational, with a School of Handicraft working alongside it, and a full programme of cultural activities planned to enlarge the horizons of the craftsmen. Its reputation and influence grew quickly and its repertoire of crafts expanded from base metalwork, furniture, interior decorating, modelling to wrought ironwork and the wonderfully original silver and jewellery for which C.R.Ashbee is now so widely known.

By the end of the 1880s, the moral issues of art and craftsmanship seemed almost to be outweighing the aesthetic ones: the relation of the fine artist and the craftsman; the relation of the handicrafts to machine production; the whole wide role of the artist-craftsman in society. These were all subjects under long discussion at the earnest, convivial and, needless to say, male-dominated meetings which were so much a feature of this period. Gatherings of the Art Workers' Guild, founded in 1884, and including in its membership almost all the leading artist-craftsmen (and craftsmen-artists) of the day; meetings of the Arts and Crafts Exhibition Society, formed in 1888 with Walter Crane as President declaiming confidently that 'the true root and basis of all Art lies in the handicrafts'. A constant theme in the writings and speeches of these groups, the membership of which in fact was fairly interchangeable, was that of the importance of the personal element in art, a claim for the rightful recognition of the individual designer. This idea of individual artistic responsibility, a strongly moral concept, also turned out to have considerable commercial advantages in that it identified particular designers, giving them a public image, a glamour and a kudos. The 'personal element' was to develop greatly in the full-blown Arts and Crafts movement of the next two decades.

48
Inlaid oak chest designed in the late 1890s by Ernest
Barnsley. Although rarer than that of his younger
brother Sidney, for he spent most of his life in
architectural practice, Ernest Barnsley's furniture has
much of the same quality and character: a similar love of
straightforward, sound construction; a comparable
fascination with countrified traditions, as exemplified in
the domed lid and inlaid chevrons of this masterly piece
of Arts and Crafts design. Leicestershire Museums.

The 1890s and early 1900s

The Arts and Crafts movement dominates the period from 1890 to 1910, two decades of almost bewildering richness, both in terms of individual creative energy and also sheer range of design activity. It was a period of marvellous inventiveness and confidence, during which British prestige abroad was at its height.

The visual style stretched from the extremely plain and simple, the box-like construction of the pseudo-peasant furniture joked about so much by its detractors, to the highly ornate, associative and symbolic Arts and Crafts artefacts, especially the metalwork. From the basic rural idiom so popular in Europe – exemplified by the clarity and sweetness, the perfectly-judged prettiness of C.F.A.Voysey's designs for wallpapers and textiles – it ascends to the very urbane sophistication of much of the metalwork designed by C.R.Ashbee, the high-flown fantasies of Henry Wilson's silver. It was in some (though not in all) ways a hugely tolerant, imaginative period in British design history. And if in the end, as the nationalistic forces of *Jugendstil* spread over Europe, the Arts and Crafts in Britain tended to recede into a rather sentimental Celtic-inspired quaintness, this should not be allowed to obliterate the quality and force of the movement in its early years nor to belittle the considerable influence of Arts and Crafts on what came later.

Design at this time of course was deeply rooted in the architectural movement of the day. Architecture was regarded in progressive design circles as the 'mother Art', the centre of activity, and it is significant that most of the successful designers of the period had had an architectural training. William Morris himself, acknowledged by so many of the younger architect-designers as their prophet and their mentor, had worked with G.E.Street, and although he did not afterwards practise as an architect, his view of design was always architecture-orientated. His friend and contemporary, Philip Webb, who was also much respected by the younger generation and who must be held at least partly responsible for the cult of the commonplace in Arts and Crafts, was an architect obsessively concerned with detail. His belief that the architect should control totally all aspects of a building, structural and decorative, practical and spiritual, had immense and obvious influence on the philosophy and practice of such Art Workers' Guild architects as W.R.Lethaby, Ernest Gimson, E.G.Prior. This idea of design totality, coherence of all visual aspects of a building, can be seen in the work of many Scottish architect-designers of the period, sometimes sublimely so in C.R.Mackintosh's buildings. Another especially interesting example is the work of Frank Brangwyn, the painter and designer, whose decorative schemes, though few survive intact, seem to have been *tours de*

force of Arts and Crafts perfectionism, with as much attention lavished on the patterns for the ashtrays as on the designs for the furniture and murals.

The craft experiments, the fascination with techniques, which had been so characteristic a feature of the 1880s, continued unabated through the 1890s. *The Studio*, founded in 1893, almost a house magazine for Arts and Crafts, carried detailed reports of these developments. In its first issues, for instance, it included 'Notes on Gesso Work' by Walter Crane, a commentary on T.J.Cobden-Sanderson's new bookbinding, and a feature on the progress of Alexander Fisher's early attempts at mastering enamelling (described as 'a very arduous undertaking, being more the work of a chemist than an artist'). It was still the age of individual artist-craftsmen, enthusiasts, inventors, almost showmen. In his old age, William Morris, inveterate experimenter, focused his attention on the revival of hand printing

50
Wash-stand in oak, with block-printed curtain, designed c.1895. This is the first known piece of furniture by Ambrose Heal, in the basic cottage style he was later to make famous, an idiom so unpopular with Heal's employees they tended to refer to it as 'prison furniture'. Heal collection, Heal and Son.

51
Domino table and barrel-shaped chairs in oak with
brown stain finish, designed by Charles Rennie
Mackintosh for the Argyle Street Tea-Rooms, 1897. The
top surface was for playing dominoes, then a very
popular Glasgow pastime; the lower shelves were meant
to hold the coffee cups and the unspent dominoes of four
players. The design proved so functionally successful
that it was revived for the Ingram Street Tea-Rooms
fourteen years later. Mackintosh collection, Glasgow
School of Art.

52

Macassar ebony cabinet on stand, inlaid with mother-of-pearl, designed by Ernest Gimson, c.1907. Gimson's reputation for unsurpassing honesty, well deserved as it was, tends to obliterate his love of decoration; his penchant for the courtly; the elaborate and urbane style of much of his production. This cabinet shows Gimson at his most ornate and formal; yet somehow it avoids all sense of blandness or pomposity. It has a kind of innocence, self-confidence and sweetness which makes it one of the great classics of its period. Leicestershire Museums.

and in 1890 set up the Kelmscott Press in Hammersmith. In 1894, Harold Rathbone had established the Della Robbia Pottery in Birkenhead, and four years later, W.Howson Taylor founded the Ruskin Pottery in Smethwick, producing a whole range of experimental glazes. The individual innovative urge was very strong in many design areas in the 1890s. But gradually, alongside these triumphs of technique, a new preoccupation began to spread infectiously, a new interest not just in the work but in the workshop, in life as well as craft, in the idea of communities of working craftsmen. When in 1890 the Birmingham Guild of Handicraft was founded, on the model of C.R.Ashbee's Guild in London, one of its main concerns was the well-being of the workmen, a well-being which, it was felt by the founders, conscientious citizens who had read their Ruskin, was likely to result from civilised conditions of working life, especially the pleasure gained from making things by hand.

53
Ladderback chair in ash with rush seat, adapted by Ernest Gimson from a traditional country design, late 19th century. Inspired by Philip Clissett, the Herefordshire chair bodger who supplied chairs to the Art Workers' Guild in London, Ernest Gimson himself learned the basic skills of chair-making and designed a number of variations of the turned wood country chair, which soon became the standard seating of the Arts and Crafts movement. This particular chair, with its unusually decorative back, was used by the bookbinder Katharine Adams at her bindery in Broadway. Mr and Mrs Michael Rossiter.

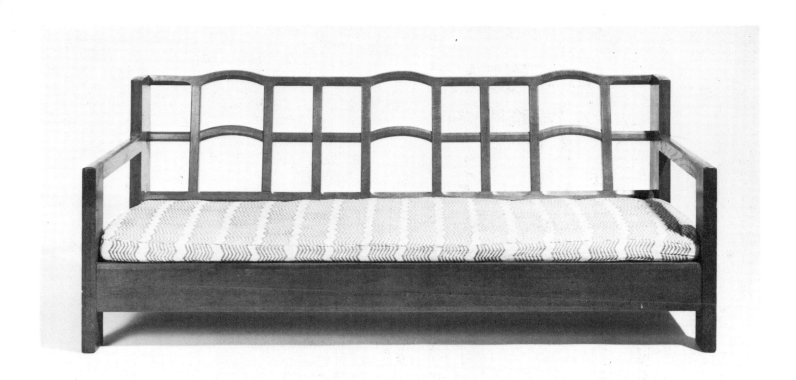

54
Lattice-backed oak settee with cushion seat by Sidney
Barnsley, c.1919. A handsome (though hardly
comfortable) piece of furniture made for the sculptor
and carver William Simmonds in simplest Barnsley style,
with subtle detailing. Cheltenham Art Gallery and
Museum.

The love of rural life which has had such a strong impact, for better or for worse,
on twentieth-century design development, is easy to trace back to the idealists of
this period, the back-to-the-land craftsmen and the simple-life protagonists. In
1893, three years after the formation of Kenton & Co., experimental furniture
workshops in London in which they had both been founder-partners, Ernest Gimson
and Sidney Barnsley travelled out to the Cotswolds to set up their own craft
workshops, where they were joined by Sidney's brother, Ernest. Both in terms of
the visual style which they established, and in terms of their whole approach to art
and workmanship, Gimson and the Barnsleys have had an influence above and
beyond their own small individual output. In 1896, with a comparable instinct to
revivify the rural traditions, similarly inspired by a congenial country setting,
Godfrey Blount was to establish the Haslemere Peasant Industries, promoting
weaving, embroidery, simple furniture and other country crafts and forming an
associated Peasant Arts Society. It was Haslemere too, then something of a centre
for small handweaving workshops, which Edmund Hunter, who was later to become
a well-known designer in the textiles industry, chose as the ideal site for his own
enterprise, St Edmundsbury Weaving Works, in 1901. The following year, a venture
which even in that era of artistic optimism seems astonishingly romantic and
ambitious, C.R.Ashbee and the craftsmen of the Guild of Handicraft, their wives
and children, in all 150 people, moved out from the East End of London to start

working in the peaceful rural setting of Chipping Campden, Gloucestershire. Ashbee
hoped he would improve both his craftsmen and their craftsmanship by bringing
them in touch with 'the elemental things of life'.

Considering the widespread concern with handicrafts among the more progressive
designers and design theorists of the time, it was perfectly predictable that when the
LCC, through its Technical Education Board, decided to open a new school, the
Central School, in London, this should turn out to be a school of craftsmanship.
Up to then the design courses in the colleges of art, the Royal College of Art in
London and the provincial colleges, had concentrated on two-dimensional design,
on pattern-making, and in fact they had specialised in training teachers. But the
Central School, which opened in 1896, was altogether different, a new species of art
school. The co-Principal, to start with, was W.R.Lethaby, architect, designer and
by then a leading figure in Art Workers' Guild circles, a respected spokesman for
Arts and Crafts principles. He managed to gather around him a teaching staff
which, from the first, included many of the most distinguished craftsmen and
designers, such Arts and Crafts practitioners as Halsey Ricardo, the architect;
Douglas Cockerell, the bookbinder; R.Catterson Smith, who taught wallpaper and

textile design; Edward Johnston who taught lettering and illuminating and whose department was soon to be developed to cover book design and printing. (His students included Eric Gill, Noel Rooke and Graily Hewitt.) The success of the Central School, which very quickly established itself as the most progressive and best-organised school of design in Europe, must mainly be attributed to Lethaby's own gentle powers of leadership, his total conviction, expressed in his most famous essay 'Art and Workmanship', that 'a work of art is first of all a well-made thing'. In 1900 Lethaby also became the first Professor of Design at the Royal College of Art, holding both appointments simultaneously in the period up to World War I. He was in a position of extraordinary influence on the new generation of designers, and his ideas of the importance of handcraftsmanship as the basis of designing, the essential element in the training of designers, helped to shape the design education of the time. These views affected education on the Continent, especially in Germany: they are obvious in the workshop structure of the early Bauhaus. They were still in force in art colleges in Britain, including the Royal College of Art, until well into the 1950s.

Although the Arts and Crafts movement seems clear-cut in its theories, acknowledging its debt to Ruskin and Morris, it interpreted these principles, as Morris did himself, with some sophistication. In practice, Arts and Crafts were a great deal less dogmatic than might have been imagined. Except by the most doctrinaire of fine-art workmen, the crafts were not seen as an end in themselves.

56
Armchair in walnut, inlaid with mother-of-pearl, designed by George Walton and made for Liberty & Co. by William Birch, c.1899. Victoria and Albert Museum.
57
Ebonised dining chair with cane seat and back, designed by George Walton, c.1903. Victoria and Albert Museum.
58
Three-sided oak cupboard with brass handles, designed by Ernest Gimson, c.1906. Leicestershire Museums.

They were regarded as more of a potential force for the good of society at large. The
idea of interaction of hand and machine, the role of the craftsman as the humanising
factor, the controller of standard, in industrial production, was becoming a popular
tenet of this period and a recurring theme in the deliberations of the National
Association for the Advancement of Art and its Application to Industry, a society
founded in 1887, whose members included leading Arts and Crafts designers.
Through the 1890s, a number of designers whose origins and loyalties lay with the
Arts and Crafts movement were to be seen designing for machine production with
no apparent self-consciousness or anguish. W.A.S.Benson, for instance, an associate
of Morris and a founder of the Art Workers' Guild, built up a highly mechanised
small factory in Hammersmith to produce his metal lamps, vases, dishes and so on
in considerable quantity. ('He preferred', said his *Times* obituary, 'to approach his
subject as an engineer rather than a hand-worker; to produce beautiful forms by
machinery on a commercial scale rather than single works of art'). From 1895,
C.F.A.Voysey was working prolifically as a designer for James Morton of Alexander
Morton & Co., the textile firm, establishing a pattern of close co-operation over a

61
Smoker's cabinet, oak with dark stain finish, designed
by Charles Rennie Mackintosh, with repoussé copper
panels by his wife, Margaret Macdonald, c.1900. This
cabinet, which was shown at the Secessionist Exhibition
in Vienna, was, in its very idiosyncratic character, with
its touches of eroticism, the antithesis of mainstream
English Arts and Crafts, much closer in feeling to the
Expressionist design tradition which developed on the
Continent. Mackintosh collection, Glasgow School of
Art.

62
Oak armchair with inlaid decoration, designed by
E.G.Punnett, made by William Birch, 1901. This chair,
manufactured in High Wycombe, is one of many
interesting examples of the way in which Arts and Crafts
ideas about design – forthrightness of structure, fitness
of decoration – percolated through to commercial
production. Victoria and Albert Museum.

63
'Purple Bird', silk and wool double cloth, designed by
C.F.A.Voysey for Alexander Morton, c.1899.
Manchester College of Art collection, The Whitworth
Art Gallery, University of Manchester.

long period between enlightened patron and his 'art adviser', an important element
in twentieth-century British design history.

By 1896, *The Studio* was commenting: 'Now a "Voysey wallpaper" sounds almost
as familiar as "Morris Chintz" or a "Liberty Silk".' The cult of personal style, the
singling out of special objects, the trick of recognising individual designers: all these
tendencies, clearly discernible in the 1880s, became even more pronounced by
the later 1890s. The prime experts in house style, Liberty & Co., extended their
successful policy, marketing their famous range of pseudo-Saxon furniture, designed
in their own Studio, as well as commissioning furniture from well-known freelance
designers, such as Voysey and George Walton. From 1899, they developed 'Cymric'
silverware and 'Tudric' pewter, designed in craftsman's style by professional
designers, Archibald Knox and Rex Silver in particular, and mostly made for
Liberty's by Haseler's in Birmingham. They also added to their reputation as
leading dealers in art pottery by introducing Moorcroft's 'Florian' collection, as

64
Coffee-pot, hot milk jug and cream jug, electroplate, probably designed by Arthur Dixon, made by the Birmingham Guild of Handicraft (motto: 'By Hammer and Hand') between 1902 and 1908. Private collection.

65
Silver sugar bowl with double handles, each set with a green chrysoprase, designed by C.R.Ashbee, made by the Guild of Handicraft, 1902. The long, thin, looping handles are typical of Ashbee, often used in his silverware, to great effect. The Worshipful Company of Goldsmiths.

66
Brass lamp designed by W.A.S.Benson, c.1895, and
manufactured in the small-scale factory which Benson,
an important link between the Arts and Crafts and mass
production, set up in Hammersmith in the early 1880s.
Victoria and Albert Museum.

well as rural pottery from Farnham (listed in Liberty's contemporary catalogues as
'Green Ware'), and the range of garden pots made especially for Liberty's at the art
pottery at Compton, Guildford, Surrey, founded and run by Mary Watts, wife of
G.F.Watts, the famous painter.

67
Silver christening mug designed by C.R.Ashbee for his daughter, Felicity, 1913. The mug, with its 'Wise Old Owl' quotation, shows the Arts and Crafts delight in decorative inscription, a tradition handed on to Eric Gill and his adherents. Felicity Ashbee.

68
Silver carriage clock with enamelled face, made for Liberty & Co., 1900. The wry inscription, 'TEMPUS FUGIT', is a characteristic Arts and Crafts device. On loan to City of Bristol Museum and Art Gallery. .

Heal style, in direct competition to 'Stile Liberty', first got underway in 1898, when the first catalogue of furniture designs by Ambrose Heal, a range of bedroom furniture in oak, was circulated. The family firm of Heal in Tottenham Court Road was already well-established as a manufacturer of bedding and supplier of traditional furniture. Ambrose Heal, a member of the new generation (like Geoffrey Dunn of Dunn's of Bromley in the 1930s) pursued the more progressive design thinking of his time. He trained with a cabinet-maker, and this workshop experience influenced his designs for furniture which, compared with the fanciful urbanities of Liberty's, were more consciously countrified, designed for plainer living: the commercial consequence of Arts and Crafts. In 1900, a Heal bedroom was assembled

69
Firedogs in brass and steel, designed by Ernest Gimson
and probably made by Alfred Bucknell, foreman of
Gimson's smithy at Sapperton, c.1905. The pierced
decoration based on the carnation, with its strong
associations of sweet summers, English gardens, is true
to the feeling of ruralist nostalgia in the Arts and Crafts
movement. Leicestershire Museums.

70
Cutlery, electroplate, designed by Charles Rennie
Mackintosh for the Ingram Street Tea-Rooms, 1903.
Glasgow Museums and Art Galleries.
71
Cutlery, electroplate, designed by C.F.A.Voysey and
made by C.W.Fletcher, Sheffield, c.1902.
Mrs J.Wellington.
72
Silver cutlery, designed by George Walton and made by
W.Comyns, 1902–3. Victoria and Albert Museum.
73
'Dewdrop' finger-bowl and tumbler, made for Liberty &
Co., c.1902. Victoria and Albert Museum.
74
Casket, silverplate and copper with cedarwood lining,
made by the Birmingham Guild of Handicraft, early
20th century. Private collection.
75
One of a pair of brass candle-sconces, designed by
Ernest Gimson and made by Alfred Bucknell, c.1907.
Cheltenham Art Gallery and Museum.

for the Paris Exhibition. The furniture, in oak inlaid with figured ebony and pewter, was designed by Ambrose Heal: the setting was by his cousin Cecil Brewer, the architect (later co-founder of the DIA). The room-set shows remarkable attention to detail, down to tapestry bed-hangings by Godfrey Blount of Haslemere Peasant Industries, and the *Architectural Review* commented: 'It almost goes without saying that the materials have been very carefully selected, and the work, which has been carried out under Mr Heal's personal supervision, is a triumph of craftmanship'.

In fact, as it developed, Heal's plain oak furniture was perhaps not so much a triumph of craftsmanship (though standards of craftsmanship were never less than decent) as it was a triumph for commercial acumen. The market at that time was absolutely ready for it. The British middle classes have always had a craving for a somewhat spurious peasant style of living – a tradition one can follow through from

76
Silver casket set with opal matrix, designed by Archibald Knox for Liberty & Co., 1903, in the quasi-Celtic idiom so popular in turn-of-the-century art metalwork. Victoria and Albert Museum.

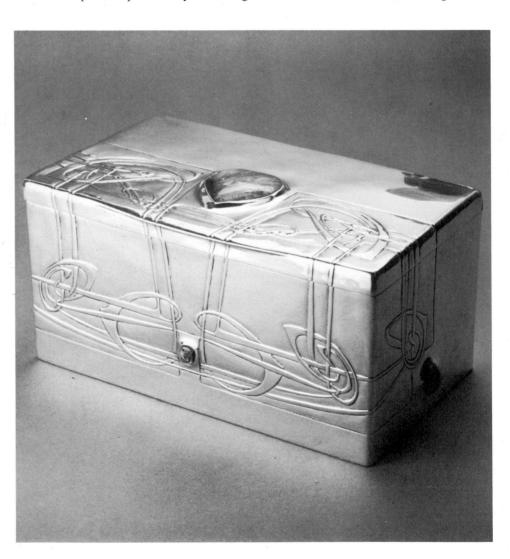

82

Heal in 1900 to Habitat much later. This was a form of furnishing especially in fashion in the Edwardian era in the new high-minded homesteads of the Garden Cities and the Garden Suburbs around London, and just as the denizens of Bedford Park had welcomed William Morris wallpapers and fabrics and rush-seated country chairs, so now the prospective residents of Letchworth were eager for the reasonably-priced oak of Ambrose Heal: the dressers and the bookcases, the wheelback dining chairs, the china racks, the coal scuttles, the Cottage Table Wares. Before long, Heal acquired a great many imitators, most of them less sensitive to visual consistency, and the catalogues of furnishing shops throughout the country, from Glasgow to Bristol, began promoting furniture which was a curious hybrid of English country style and Continental *art nouveau*.

In the end, needless to say, this did the Arts and Crafts no good. In the face of

77
Large double-handled jar by Della Robbia Pottery, late 19th century. This design, with its rich green and yellow decoration, shows the admirably courageous fusion of Italian Renaissance style with English Arts and Crafts. Victoria and Albert Museum.

83

such proliferation of Arts-and-Crafts-style products, the individuality was gone, the idea meaningless. The Arts and Crafts had lost their purity and mystery. The Arts and Crafts, in fact, had become a bit banal. William Morris had died in 1896; the movement had lost its impetus and focus. It was generally obvious that Arts and Crafts Exhibition Society shows in 1903 and 1906 were less convincing than the exhibitions of the previous decade; and later exhibitions were felt to be still worse. Commercial competition, the cynical development of factory production imitating craftwork, was undermining the more conscientious workshops, upholders of the Arts and Crafts hammer-and-hand values. This, at a time of general trade depression, was certainly a factor in the final liquidation of Ashbee's Guild of Handicraft, a *débacle* which did nothing to restore the confidence of Ashbee's brother art workers. By the end of the decade it was becoming clear that the time was coming for some form of realignment. It began to be seen as the duty of designers to get out of the workshops and into the factories, an idea which became a principle and a fixation, indeed a sort of war-cry, in the naïve optimism of the period ahead.

The 1910s and 1920s

This was the period in which the concept of design for industry began to be important. In the years surrounding World War I, and even, surprisingly, while that War was raging, one can watch the evolution from Arts and Crafts ideas to a kind of a crusade to improve the standards of design for mass production, led by the Design and Industries Association. The philosophy of 'decent design for ordinary people', which the DIA propounded with such earnestness, was the dominant principle of these two decades, and indeed was still adhered to in the government efforts to influence design in British industry after World War II. But an interesting facet of this period, a development largely ignored by historians, who find it convenient to trace progress neatly from Arts and Crafts to DIA to modernism, was the resurgence, as the 1920s progressed, of an immense amount of craft activity. This was less of a formalised craft movement, more of a spontaneous springing-up of individual workshops, and the interrelation between craft and industry, hand and machine production, give this peculiarly fascinating period a character and influence very much its own.

The feeling of the time is very even, very gentle. Compared with the stylistic idiosyncrasies of Arts and Crafts design, the recurring images of DIA design are altogether steady and predictable. The Heal's weathered oak sideboards, the Dryad cane chairs, the early morning tea-sets by Carter, Stabler, Adams: such perennial favourites of the design cognoscenti of the period have an understated homeliness, a pleasant kind of primness, very much related to the (DIA-approved) reconstituted Georgian buildings of the era. This overall consistency and reticence of style makes the many sudden bursts of the exotic and the quirky all the more endearing and astonishing: the impractical Expressionism of the Omega Workshops, set up by Roger Fry and his group of artist friends, antidote to all the DIA good sense and soundness; the 'potterie sauvage' designed for Poole by Truda Carter; the dazzlingly inventive Foxton textiles of the 1920s designed by such professionals as F.Gregory Brown, Minnie McLeish and (before his early death) Claud Lovat Fraser, illustrator and stage designer, whose attraction to the fairground and the chap-book, puppet shows and pantomimes, the popular theatrical tradition, with its emphasis on colour and humour and directness, also had its influence on the contemporary scene.

The Design and Industries Association was founded formally in 1915. It was a pressure group modelled, broadly speaking, on the Deutscher Werkbund, and it introduced itself, in its first propaganda leaflet, as *A New Body with New Aims*. In a

78
Polished deal cupboard chest with black edges, designed by Ambrose Heal, c.1918. This design, a standard Heal's product included in the Cottage Furniture Catalogue, exemplifies the principles of unobtrusive decency propounded by the Design and Industries Association, of which Ambrose Heal had been a founder. Heal collection, Heal and Son.

79
Tallboy chest in English oak with laburnum handles, designed by Gordon Russell, c.1926. Up to the mid-1920s, Gordon Russell's furniture was strongly Arts and Crafts in character, obviously influenced by Gimson and Sidney Barnsley. Compared with the (slightly earlier) Heal's cupboard, no. 78, this is very much a craftsman's piece of furniture, beautiful but, in a sense, by then a little antiquated. Museum collection, Gordon Russell.

sense one should see it less as a totally new departure than a logical development, a realigment; for many of its members, including such important early committee members as Harold Stabler, Ernest Jackson, Ambrose Heal and Cecil Brewer, had been leading figures in the Arts and Crafts societies. W.R.Lethaby, a member of the Council and the *eminence grise* of the Association, was very much attuned to the precepts and the attitudes of Philip Webb and William Morris. Many of the theories of the DIA, such doctrines as the right use of materials, the proper place for ornament, the beauty of the commonplace, were all close to the most basic principles of Arts and Crafts; and almost all its aims, its belief in the national importance of improved design standards in factory production, had been under discussion for many years before. But what was new about the DIA was its insistence on the need

80
Boot cupboard in Honduras mahogany, designed by
Gordon Russell, 1925. The change in style from the Arts
and Crafts tallboy chest of the same period, no. 79,
is remarkable: instead of the old frame-and-panel
construction, the cupboard has flush fronts; the doors
are veneered blockboard; the piece has a pared-down,
completely functional appearance; and this was the
idiom which Gordon Russell, over the next few years,
successfully pursued. Museum collection, Gordon
Russell.

for urgent action and the way it was able, early on in wartime, by pointing out the
comparable excellence of German industrial products, to enlist government interest
and support. In 1915, the Board of Trade had organised an exhibition at Goldsmiths'
Hall in London under the convincing title 'Exhibition of German and Austrian
articles typifying successful design'. The accompanying leaflet, which praised
co-operation between German manufacturers and designers and the resulting
'appropriateness, technical perfection and honest workmanship' of German
products, gave the DIA a great initial impetus in its campaign for British 'Efficiency
Style'.

Lethaby, the most inspiring theorist of his period, saw it as the DIA's function to
impose some sort of visual order and serenity on a world which had become, as he

81
Oak chair with leather seat, designed by Gordon Russell, 1924. Museum collection, Gordon Russell.
82
Trolley made by the Dryad Cane Furniture Works, c.1915. Mr and Mrs S.H.Nichols.

83
Oak dining chair with bun feet and latticed back, designed by Ambrose Heal and made by Heal's from c.1926. Heal collection, Heal and Son.

saw it, a pawnshop 'full of old junk'. This urge to tidy up the visual scene, to rationalise, to simplify, was deeply sympathetic to the design-conscious industrialists and businessmen, mostly of a younger generation than Lethaby's, who joined the DIA in its early years. Of these the best known and in some ways most remarkable was Frank Pick, then a rising manager with London Underground and later Chief Executive of the London Passenger Transport Board. He was DIA Chairman from 1921. By then, with a typical solemnity and thoroughness, he had developed his own design convictions, the principles of fitness for use which he reiterated with a passionate belief. Frank Pick's work for the Underground and then for London Transport, the posters he commissioned, the classic Sans Serif typeface designed by Edward Johnston (dating back to 1916), the long collaboration with the architect Charles Holden on the underground stations and headquarters offices, the calling in of specialist designers for such details as ticket machines, directional signs, litter bins and wall-tiles, moquettes for the seat covers of LPTB vehicles: all this was an advertisement of the DIA principles on an enormous scale. It was also an early and enviable example of the science of design management in action, a justification for corporate identity before that much-overworked term had been invented. Most of all, perhaps, it has to be seen as the expression of one man's sense of vision, Pick's own sense that visual rightness was the moral thing to strive for: for these, in their own way, were still idealistic years.

The spirit of that time, its fervour and gregariousness, its dogged sense of mission, is very well recorded by Noel Carrington in *Industrial Design in Britain*. It is also referred to by Sir Gordon Russell in his autobiography, *Designer's Trade*, in which he describes his DIA induction in the early 1920s when, as a young man, he was just beginning to make furniture in Broadway, on a very tiny scale. 'I had come across

84
Cane chair, c.1910, made by Dryad, the cane works established by Harry Peach in Leicester in 1907. Though Dryad acknowledged its debt to the cane furniture then being produced in Austria and Germany, the designs arrived at through the collaboration of Peach and his friend B.J.Fletcher (head of Leicester College of Art, co-founder of the DIA) emerged as unmistakably English, British design classics. All the more unfortunate that, because of the nature of the material, few of them survive in good condition. Pat Kirkham.

85
Oak chair with chip-carved decoration and pigskin seat designed by Romney Green, most intellectual of craftsmen, c.1925, and possibly made by Stanley Davies, his assistant at the time. Romney Green's furniture, handmade and highly detailed, is always interesting and inventive but, compared with the best of the Cotswold designers, tends to be more self-conscious and over-wrought. Cheltenham Art Gallery and Museum.

86
Silver tea-set, octagonal in form, designed by Harold
Stabler, made by Wakely and Wheeler, 1928. The
Worshipful Company of Goldsmiths.

87 (*right*)
Silver sauceboats designed and made by Ramsden and
Carr, 1909–10, and engraved, with typical Ramsden
ostentation, 'OMAR RAMSDEN ET ALWYN CARR ME
FECERUNT'. Ramsden was the most successful craft
silversmith – and one of the best showmen – of the
century. The output of his workshop was great, its style
uneven; but this pair of sauceboats is a superb example.
Victoria and Albert Museum.

this body', he writes, 'only recently and I cannot say how much I owe to its early
members, men like Harold Stabler, Crofton Gane, Ben Fletcher, Frank Pick,
Charles Holden, Ambrose Heal, Noel Carrington, Harry Peach, Hamilton Smith,
Herbert Simon, Harold Curwen, Alfred Read and Leslie Mansfield, all of whom
were willing to share their experience with a greenhorn.' It was from the DIA, as he
soon makes clear, that Russell absorbed many of the ideas and the principles
exemplified in his own furniture and propounded, much later, in his propagandist
role as Director of the Council of Industrial Design: the notion that the choice of
good design instead of shoddy is better for the chooser and better for the nation,
which springs from his belief, a moralistic attitude not far removed from Ruskin
and the Arts and Crafts philosophers, that quality – quality of design, of material
and of workmanship – is 'the outward and visible sign of good health'.

   In its pursuit of Efficiency Style, the DIA was extremely energetic on many
different fronts. Though its membership was small – only 200 to begin with, only
602 by 1928 – it managed to be relatively influential because it was well organised

and sensible and practical in its campaigns. Its membership was broadly based. The
DIA stalwarts listed by Gordon Russell include architects and shopkeepers, designers,
manufacturers, printers, writers and an educationalist. This set-up tended naturally
to be a bit incestuous: Stabler worked for Pick, Fletcher designed for Peach, Noel
Carrington wrote copy for Heal's catalogues, and Ambrose Heal, DIA retailer par
excellence, purveyed the products of his colleagues. Heal's catalogues from 1918 to
the late 1920s are replete with designs which, if not actually made by DIA members,
would have met with their approval: from the cheerful clean pottery with simple
decoration to the clear crystal glassware, including coloured vases in 'butterfly-wing
blue', and the sensible furniture for people of discernment. There is obvious
avoidance of the showy and the wayward, a contrasting concentration on the
decent and the modest, the pleasant and the comely, the practical and the
workmanlike, well made and well proportioned: public manifestation of the main
DIA tenets, the commercial stamp on DIA right-thinking. How much nearer to need
would it be possible to get?

For the first time in its history, design in Britain had an official, or at least a semi-
official, framework. It was gradually acquiring the first of the committees,
memoranda, conferences, reports, propaganda exhibitions and information bureaux
which feature so prominently, and at times so comically, in its later years. The DIA
membership was at that time particularly orientated towards typography and

90
Ceremonial cigar box, grey shagreen with silver mounts, designed and made by John Paul Cooper, c.1927. The Worshipful Company of Goldsmiths.

91
Silver cigarette box with blue enamel decoration designed by Harold Stabler, 1923. For Stabler, leading member of the DIA, fitness for purpose did not necessarily mean plainness and this large cigarette box shows his interpretation of fitness for purpose on the most luxurious level. The Worshipful Company of Goldsmiths.

92
'Dolphin' bowl in silver, designed and made by Omar Ramsden, 1929. The Worshipful Company of Goldsmiths.

printing, the legacy of its origins in Arts and Crafts, and 'Design and Workmanship in Printing' was the theme of the first DIA exhibition held in London in 1915. Further exhibitions in this early series showed exemplary pottery and textiles; a small exhibition of well-designed furniture was held by the DIA in 1919 in Shoreditch, strategically placed to convert East End manufacturers; a larger 'Exhibition of Household Things' – 'designed', of course, 'primarily to serve their purpose' – was held in Whitechapel in 1920. From 1916 onwards the DIA was publishing spasmodic Journals and Newsletters, and then, from 1922, a series of DIA Yearbooks appeared regularly. These reflect quite interestingly the changing emphasis of DIA reforming instincts in this period: the early concern with individual household objects, from the storage capacities of wardrobes to the pouring qualities of teapots, has by the late 1920s, burgeoned out to include the whole of town and country planning. It has turned into an urge to redesign the whole environment. This was the heyday of Clough Williams-Ellis's well-known *Cautionary Guides*.

Though it was hard for any government department to emulate the emotional commitment, the reforming effervescence, of the DIA in those days, there was plenty of DIA conviction in the pamphlet *Art and Industry* published in 1919 by the Ministry of Reconstruction, containing such DIA-indoctrinated comments as 'Art is indispensable in life and therefore in education and work'. The following year, as a result of this report, the British Institute of Industrial Art was set up in London.

93
'The Sea Beaker', a small silver vase symbolic of the sea,
designed by R.M.Y.Gleadowe, made by H.G.Murphy,
with exceptionally fine engraving by George Friend,
1929. The Worshipful Company of Goldsmiths.
94
Silver tea-caddy made by A.E.Jones, Birmingham, 1918.
On loan to Birmingham City Museums and Art Gallery.
95
Facetted silver mug designed by Edward Spencer for the
Artificers' Guild, 1926. The Worshipful Company of
Goldsmiths.

96
Earthenware plate and jug with hand-painted decoration
designed by Susie Cooper for A.E.Gray, 1929. Before
she set up her own pottery, Susie Cooper worked for
Gray's, a small firm in Stoke-on-Trent, as a painter and
designer. These florals in soft colours, with their dots
and multi-banding, are very prophetic of her later work.
Manchester City Art Gallery.

97
Silver alms dish designed and made by R.M.Y.Gleadowe
and H.G.Murphy for the Goldsmiths' Hall collection,
1930. The large dish was raised in one piece, with
spectacular pictorial engraving by George Friend. The
Worshipful Company of Goldsmiths.

98
Stoneware coffee service with deep green speckled glaze,
designed and manufactured by William Moorcroft,
c.1916. A design so simple and cylindrical that it could
quite easily have been mistaken for a late-1950s Design
Centre Award-winner. Victoria and Albert Museum.

98
Stoneware coffee service with deep green speckled glaze, designed and manufactured by William Moorcroft, c.1916. A design so simple and cylindrical that it could quite easily have been mistaken for a late-1950s Design Centre Award-winner. Victoria and Albert Museum.

This was a permanent exhibition of 'good design', as the DIA would see it, together with an information service, and although it was rather unconvincing and short-lived, it set the pattern for government involvement in approving design standards. In 1920, too, the Federation of British Industries formed an Industrial Art Committee which gave itself the task of considering 'the question of industrial art in this country' (a question which recurs as the century progresses). A Designers' Register and Employment Bureau – again the first of many – was opened by the Federation of British Industries in 1924.

At this stage of the narrative of design in Britain, the enlarging network of committees, associations, and institutes, what one might call the mainstream propaganda movement, can easily camouflage the force and influence of smaller-scale and more individual enterprises. But one must remember that this was not only the age of Efficiency Style, it was also a time of its absolute antithesis, a period of spiritual reassessment and social experiment in which a belief in the regenerative values of handwork once again loomed large. Nowhere was this more manifest than at Ditchling, Sussex, in Eric Gill and Hilary Pepler's Guild of St Joseph and St Dominic, described by Gill, who had himself by then become a Dominican

99

'Harvest' earthenware pattern designed by Frank Brangwyn for Doulton in 1930. This lushly decorative free-hand pattern, in greens, blues, pinks, yellows, rich browns, on honey buff, obviously very closely allied to Brangwyn's painting, attracted great critical acclaim when Doulton first produced it but, although the price was kept 'within the reach of people of quite moderate means', the pattern was never a commercial success. Richard Dennis.

Tertiary, as 'primarily a religious fraternity for those who make things with their hands'. (The Eric Gill view of fitness for purpose, which in the end perhaps is not so far removed from Pick, is that work should be fit both for one's God and for one's neighbour: 'Good quality is therefore twofold: work must be good itself and good for use'.) The idea of the moral worth of handwork and the value of crafts to the community, in effect the old Ruskinian doctrine, was revived, in a new setting, in such intellectual-artistic communities of the mid-1920s as Dartington in Devon and Gregynog, northern Powys, in the life of which a central place was given to music and the crafts.

In 1920, Bernard Leach, the potter, returned from a long period of study in Japan to set up his own pottery at St Ives in Cornwall. This, a fresh example of the reawakened interest in the more metaphysical aspects of design, for Leach returned immersed in the philosophy of pottery, had an enormous influence on the development of British twentieth-century ceramics. The first students to be trained at St Ives were Michael Cardew, Katharine Pleydell-Bouverie and Norah Braden, all of whom of course became considerable potters in their own right. A comparable spiritual intensity is obvious in the work and in the teaching of the other major

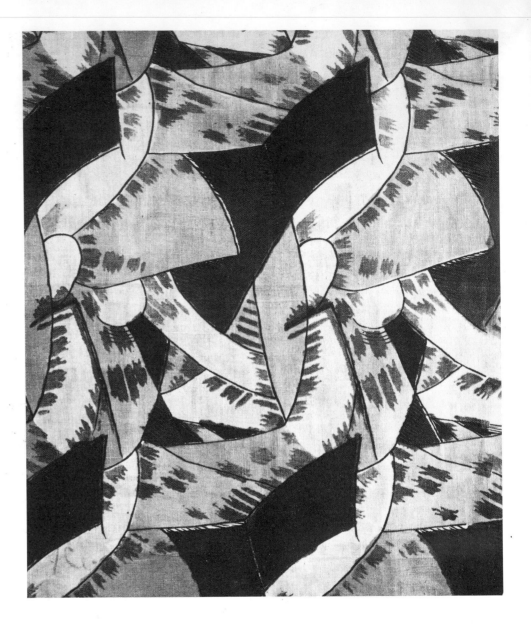

potter of this period, William Staite Murray, an orientalist who was one of the
earliest English converts to Buddhism. In 1925, he was appointed Head of Ceramics
at the Royal College of Art. On the one side from Leach, the deeply convinced
craftsman, on the other from Staite Murray, the emphatic artist-potter, involved
widely with the fine-art movements of his day, one can trace a dual tradition in craft
pottery in Britain: the useful and the abstract, the domestic and the sculptural, a
dichotomy which even now persists.

The mid-1920s were a time of renewed movement in the craft world. Edward

Barnsley, son of Sidney, the Arts and Crafts woodworker whose furniture was one
of the great glories of that period, had opened his own workshop in Petersfield in
Hampshire; A.Romney Green, poet, mathematician and social reformer as well as a
very innovative craftsman, was by then working in Christchurch; his pupil Stanley
Davies, an adherent of Romney Green's theories of 'Structural Design', had by the
mid-1920s moved up to the Lake District. Links with the Arts and Crafts movement
were still strong. The cluster of craft workshops in and around Ditchling retained,
according to C.R.Ashbee (who visited them in 1923), much of the old spirit of the

102
Oak dresser designed by Frank Brangwyn and made by
J.W.Stenning. Many years before his reputation as a
painter was established, Brangwyn had been immersed
in the Arts and Crafts: as a boy, he had worked for
William Morris; he was a lifelong friend of
A.H.Mackmurdo. In his later career, there was a
constant correlation between painting and the
decorative arts. This large, well-proportioned and very
English dresser, designed in the mid-1920s, shows the
Arts and Crafts influence still strong. Private collection.

Guild of Handicraft in Chipping Campden. They included the weaving workshop known as Gospels where Ethel Mairet, most remarkable twentieth-century practitioner and theorist, worked for many years and trained other well-known weavers. In her sphere, her influence was comparable with that of Bernard Leach. Ethel Mairet's husband, Philippe, once one of Ashbee's Guildsmen, set up The New Handworkers' Gallery in Percy Street in London, a characteristic 1920s enterprise; here as well as selling craftwork he admired, such as Michael Cardew's pottery, he distributed craft tracts, for instance his own pamphlet 'The Idea Behind Craftsmanship', Ethel Mairet's view of 'Weaving' and 'A Potter's Outlook' by Bernard Leach. A similarly esoteric London shop which specialised in craftwork, selling among other things, the hand-block printed textiles of the Barron-Larcher partnership, was The Little Gallery in Chelsea, opened by Muriel Rose in 1928.

The craft of silversmithing then, as later, took its impetus mainly from the Worshipful Company of Goldsmiths in London. From 1926, with George Hughes as Art Secretary (a role later taken on by his son, Graham), the Company promoted a long series of competitions and exhibitions of modern silverwork, placing a succession of commissions and stimulating a huge interest in the craft. The silversmith-designers on whom Goldsmiths' Hall, in the late 1920s, focused most attention were John Paul Cooper and H.G.Murphy, both highly original exponents of the craft of silversmithing; R.M.Y.Gleadowe, whose designs for engraving on to silver are surely among the very finest of the period; and Harold Stabler, a versatile designer who had been one of the founders of the DIA. Stabler, an important figure of his day, one of the partners in Carter, Stabler, Adams, saw his role as designing for machine production as well as for handmaking. All through the 1920s, this was quite a usual view.

And in fact it was this very flexibility, the way in which designers, far from being hidebound, moved easily between craft and machine production, which created a free and optimistic climate, encouraging to many of the major developments of the next decade. It was a climate in which the work done by Alec Hunter in the small experimental weaving unit set up in the late 1920s by James Morton of Morton Sundour Fabrics led logically on to the Edinburgh Weavers of the 1930s. A period at which the pottery designer, Susie Cooper, hand-decorating one-off pieces for Gray's Pottery, was acquiring the techniques and the confidence to set up her own firm which very soon became well known. This was the time when Enid Marx, whose early designs were strongly influenced by Barron and Larcher, hand-block printers, with whom she worked as an assistant, began to develop her own original thinking and her interest in craft-into-industrial-design, leading on to her work for London Transport and Utility. It was also the decade in which one sees how Gordon Russell, up till then a craft furniture-maker in the superb Cotswold Arts and Crafts tradition took the first steps towards the machine production which made his firm so famous in the 1930s. With so much activity in such varying directions, the 1920s was a period of magnificent transition, and many of the themes and ideas it generated only find their resolution a good deal later on.

The 1930s

After the fairly even tenor of the 1920s, the 1930s was a decade of sudden, obvious change: a shift of visual style, a change of fundamental attitude. In this period, modernism came to Britain, if not in as extreme a form as it was visible in other parts of Europe, certainly as a positive and vigorous new influence. In the 1930s in Britain, as in the rest of Europe, design and architecture were very much related: this was part of the Modern Movement rationale; design was seen largely as a by-product of building, the industrial designers of the period were mainly architects by training. The 1930s were nothing if not open-minded and this was also a notable decade for the cross-fertilisation of fine art and design. Most remarkable of all, by the end of the decade, was the way in which the work of the élite designers, the contemporary idiom of the progressives, had gradually percolated down and become popular, almost part of the everyday culture of the time.

Traditional English reticence of course was still about; the strong element of craftsmanship continued through the 1930s. But added to this there was awakened social purpose, a revived energy to experiment with new techniques and new materials, particularly the techniques of mass production. Ideas altered. This was partly the result of a whole influx of foreign designers and architects who started work in Britain, some temporarily, some permanently, through the 1930s. The Europeanisation of design was first noted in the *Journal* of the DIA by John C.Rogers in 1928. He described the exhibition of modernist furniture at Waring & Gillow, designed by Serge Chermayeff, as 'by far the best thing yet done in this country', going on to say that it was 'not at all on the lines of those whose creed is the teaching of Gimson and the Barnsleys'. It was this new breed of architect-designers which produced such archetypal products of the 1930s as the Isokon Long Chair, in laminated birchwood; the well-known matt-glazed pottery from Wedgwood; the marvellous succession of modernist rugs. Because by this time the frontiers of design were widening quite rapidly, designers soon became involved in more engineering-orientated projects of the period: adjustable reading lamps are typical, and radio cabinets in bakelite.

Around this time, design first began emerging as an organised profession. The main professional association, the Society of Industrial Artists, was founded in 1930. One must not be misled about that early title (later changed to Society of Industrial Artists and Designers), for its original membership included industrial designers, as we would now describe them, as well as graphic specialists and illustrators. The fact that designers still considered themselves artists is perhaps an

Weathered oak desk by Ambrose Heal, with leather-seated chair in green, 1931. In contrast to Heal's simple cottage furniture, this desk was marketed as a prestige piece, a signed edition aimed probably at the rising businessman: the central cupboard opens to reveal a telephone. Heal collection, Heal and Son.

indication of the feeling of the time: at that stage, the precise professional status of designers was rather less clear-cut than it was later to become. The profession was much smaller and more experimental: the visual sense was seen as multi-purpose; designers simply tackled any job that came along, graphics, exhibitions, architecture, products. At the same time, designers had a serious sense of mission: one of the avowed intentions of the SIA was 'to assemble the resources of design as a vital factor in British industry'. (The debates on how to do it continued through the decade.) By 1936 the Royal Society of Arts was discussing the creation of the distinction Designer for Industry, and two years later the first Royal Designers for Industry were appointed. These were Douglas Cockerell (for bookbinding), Eric Gill (for typography), James Hogan (for glass), J.H.Mason (for printing and typography), H.G.Murphy (for gold and silver), Keith Murray (for glass and pottery), Tom Purvis (for commercial art), Harold Stabler (for pottery and silver), Fred Taylor (for commercial art), C.F.A.Voysey (for interior decoration, and furniture and fabric design), George Sheringham, who died before the day of the appointment ceremony (for stage and interior decoration and costume and textile design). The first honorary Royal Designer, E.McKnight Kauffer, was appointed simultaneously 'for services to Commercial Art', which ranged from his posters to his esoteric abstract 1930s rugs. A highly individual, eclectic group of people, in themselves a comprehensive history of British design attitudes.

104
The Isokon Long Chair designed by Marcel Breuer,
originally made in laminated birch in 1936, and still in
production. Jack Pritchard.

105
Tubular steel stacking chairs with canvas seat and back,
designed by Serge Chermayeff for Pel, 1932, and used in
the new Broadcasting House, London. Pel.

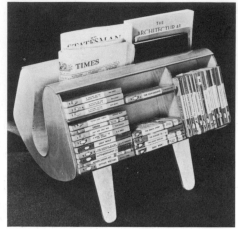

106
Chair in laminated birch designed by Gerald Summers
for the Makers of Simple Furniture, c.1934. Victoria and
Albert Museum.
107
The Isokon Penguin Donkey, Mark One, in birch
plywood, designed by Egon Riss, 1939. Jack Pritchard.
108
Isokon nesting tables in birch plywood, designed by
Marcel Breuer, 1936. Jack Pritchard.

109
'Shipton' dressing table and stool in black walnut and
chrome, designed by W.H.Russell for Gordon Russell,
1930. By the 1930s, the Gordon Russell factory was
largely adapted to techniques of mass production; design
work was done mainly by W.H.Russell (not a member of
the family) and by Gordon Russell's architect brother,
R.D.Russell. Museum collection, Gordon Russell.

110
Buffet in macassar ebony and burr walnut, designed by
Serge Chermayeff for Waring & Gillow, 1928. One of the
first examples in Britain of the swishly sophisticated
Continental style which was continued through the
1930s by such designers as Betty Joel, Ian Henderson,
Charles Richter. Royal Pavilion, Art Gallery and
Museums, Brighton.

Through the 1930s, a succession of committees of enquiry, some official, some
set up by industry itself, were discussing the whole question of Art and Industry.
Its national importance by then had been well recognised. The most far-
reaching of these investigations was the one by the Board of Trade committee on
Art and Industry, set up in 1931 under Lord Gorell. This led to the formation in
1933 of the Council for Art and Industry. The Chairman was Frank Pick and the
Council (popularly known as the Pick Council), with its brief to encourage good
design, 'especially in relation to manufactures', was an early blue-print for the post-
war Council of Industrial Design. In 1937, on the recommendation of the Pick
Council, a National Register of Industrial Art Designers was established by the
Board of Trade. This promotional work, the linking up of designers and
industrialists, has always been seen by the official propagandists as crucially
important and indeed it is still being carried out both by the Design Council and the
SIAD. In these and other ways, in particular the preoccupation in the 1930s with
designers' education, which, it was felt, should be a lot more realistic, one sees
increasingly serious concern with design standards from the point of view of the
national economy. Here were the early stages of official design policy as it developed
in the years after the War.

Perhaps it seems peculiar that at such a time of acute financial crisis so much attention should have been lavished on the problems of design for industry. But in fact, of course, this is a recurring pattern, as relevant to the 1980s as the 1930s: a crisis (or a war) frequently provides the stimulus to plan ahead, to reassess. In furniture, for instance, the declining market for special one-off pieces in the early 1930s encouraged Gordon Russell to direct the major energies of his firm into design for mass production. With this specific aim, Gordon Russell's brother, R.D.Russell, went to train at the Architectural Association, returning to the Cotswolds to produce a whole series of designs for Gordon Russell Furniture which, although quintessentially British, could compete on the same terms as international modern. In the more uncompromising atmosphere of Hampstead, Jack Pritchard, a young engineer-economist and an intrepid patron of the Modern Movement, had set up a company called Isokon, committed to the idea of promoting buildings, furniture and fittings of a strictly functional modern design. Wells Coates, the architect, was a co-founder of Isokon. Walter Gropius, then a refugee from Nazi Germany, became Controller of Design in the Isokon Furniture Company; Marcel Breuer designed furniture for Isokon; Laszlo Moholy-Nagy designed some of the sales leaflets: this, by far the most convinced attempt in Britain to emulate the

111
Tubular steel-frame dining furniture made by Pel in the mid-1930s for Prudential Assurance. Tubular steel furniture had by this time become popular: Bauhaus austerity combined with Hollywood-style glamour. Victoria and Albert Museum.

112
Walnut dresser with spectacular inlaid pattern, designed
by Frank Brangwyn and made by E.Pollard in 1930; one
of a whole series of modernist designs for furniture,
carpets, textiles, ceramics and glass commissioned from
Brangwyn at this period. The contrast with his Arts and
Crafts oak dresser of the previous decade, no. 102, is
emphatic, and the new sense of 1930s stylishness
remarkable in a designer born in 1867. William Morris
Gallery, Walthamstow.

113
Silver tea service with wood handle, ivory and wood
finial, designed by Harold Stabler and made by Adie
Brothers, 1935. This modernist tea-set, of which there
was also an electroplated version designed to fit on a
bakelite tray, contrasts interestingly with Stabler's more
Art Deco 1920s service, no 86. Victoria and Albert
Museum.

114
Silver bowl with stepped-up lid and ribbed ivory finial,
designed and made by H.G.Murphy, 1936. This
decorative use of ivory with silver was very much in
fashion with the 1930s silversmiths. The Worshipful
Company of Goldsmiths.

115
Tall fluted silver vase, one of a set of six by
R.M.Y.Gleadowe and H.G.Murphy, 1935. The Worshipful Company of Goldsmiths, (as 116, 117 and 118).
116
Small silver box with jet and ivory handle, designed and made by Cyril Shiner, 1933.
117
Silver bowl with niello decoration, designed and made by Bernard Cuzner, 1933.
118
Silver tea-caddy with ivory knop, designed by
A.E.Harvey and made by Hukin & Heath, 1933.

international rationalist movement, was memorably satirised by Osbert Lancaster as Twentieth Century Functional style. The Isokon Long Chair, in intellectual circles, had a distinct cachet, but in terms of popular success was soon outdone by the ubiquitous Pel tubular steel stacking chair with canvas seat and back, shortly to be found in every village hall in England, achieving a renown and instant recognition perhaps comparable only with the Hille polypropylene chair of the early 1960s.

In 1932, Alastair Morton, son of James Morton, first became involved in directing an experimental textile unit within the large Morton Sundour firm. This became famous as Edinburgh Weavers, whose fabrics form another potent image of the 1930s. In his role as artistic director, Alastair Morton, himself a painter with many artist friends, with modernist ideals of relating art and architecture, commissioned an extraordinary collection of textiles, perhaps the most remarkable to be produced this century: the 'Constructivist Fabrics' launched in 1937 included designs by Ben Nicholson, Ashley Havinden and Barbara Hepworth. Hans Aufseer, Marion Dorn and John Tandy were also designing regularly for Edinburgh Weavers at this period. Meanwhile, Alec Hunter, Alastair Morton's predecessor at Edinburgh Weavers in its very early days, had by now moved on to Warner's in Braintree, where, as production manager, he acted as controller of design and encouraged the development, in 1935, of a department for exclusive handwoven fabrics under the weaver Theo Moorman. Another influential figure of 1930s textile design was Allan Walton, architect and painter and interior decorator as well as director of his own textile manufacturing firm: he too commissioned textile designs from well-known artists of the period. (He was about to be appointed Professor of Textiles at the Royal College of Art when, in 1948, he died.) Two important freelance textile designers came to work in Britain in the 1930s: Margaret Leischner, a hand-weaver from the Bauhaus, and Marianne Straub, whose industrial experience in her native Switzerland was augmented by the time she spent with Ethel Mairet in her hand-weaving workshop in Ditchling, Sussex. Both these designers remained to work in Britain in the post-war period, strengthening the tradition of hand and machine.

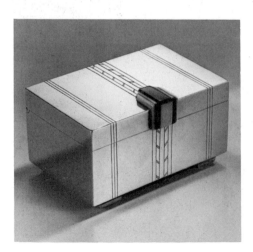

119
'Ridgeway' cutlery, silver plate, made by Roberts and Belk, c.1935. Lent by Sheffield City Museums.

120
Coffee-set in earthenware, with white 'Moonstone' glaze, designed by Keith Murray for Wedgwood, c.1934. Keith Murray's background as an architect perhaps accounts for his coolness and precision: his was the very opposite of craftsman's pottery. Victoria and Albert Museum.

121
Early morning tea-set in earthenware, black and brown on a grey ground, made by Poole Pottery, about 1937. The 'Streamline' shape was designed by John Adams, the pattern by Truda Carter. Victoria and Albert Museum.

122

China plate with the 'Mayfair' decoration designed by Milner Gray for E.Brain (Foley China), 1935. An elegant example of nostalgic witticism which tempered British modernism at this period. Milner Gray.

In 1931, Susie Cooper moved her pottery firm, founded two years earlier, into its permanent home, the Crown Works, Burslem. Here too the interaction of hand and machine – for instance, the use of both hand-painting and lithographic techniques for decoration – was much in evidence all through the 1930s, a period of considerable success for Susie Cooper. (Even Queen Mary bought a Susie Cooper tea-set.) Susie Cooper's 'Kestrel' shape with 'washband' decoration, 'Polka Dot' and 'Wedding Ring'; Poole Pottery's 'Streamline' with its two-tone 'Mushroom' glazes; the 'Vogue' and 'Mode' shapes produced by Shelley Potteries: such developments as these, so evocative of their particular period, had an obvious effect on the industry in general. Some of the most progressive designs were emanating from the Wedgwood factory, where Victor Skellern was appointed Art Director in 1934. The design pundits of the time praised Keith Murray, the architect (who also designed glass for Stevens and Williams and silver for Mappin and Webb) for his very rational matt-glazed Wedgwood pottery: 'better', said Herbert Read of the

123
Decanter and glass designed by Keith Murray for
Stevens & Williams, c.1935. Another good example
(cf. no. 120) of Keith Murray's architectural approach to
tableware. He also designed very successfully in metal.
Leicestershire Museums.

124
'Cactus' cut-glass vase, designed by Keith Murray for
Stevens & Williams, c.1938. The cactus was of course at
the time a well-known feature of the modernist interior:
(see Osbert Lancaster, *Homes Sweet Homes*, 'now the
cactus sprouts where once flourished the aspidistra and
the rubber plant'). Manchester City Art Gallery.

matt-straw Wedgwood beer mug, 'than anything else in modern ceramics'. Many of
Wedgwood's major decorative designs were the work of the artist and illustrator
Eric Ravilious, in his picturesque, affectionate and very English style. In glass, some
particularly interesting pieces were developed for Chance, for industrial production,
by Robert Goodden, the architect-designer, whose 'Asterisk' wallpaper was also a
beautifully characteristic pattern of that time

One of the most striking advances in the 1930s was the increased involvement of
designers in industrial product design: not just in the traditional craft-orientated
areas of furniture, textiles, ceramics, glass and so on, but also, gradually, in the
newer technology-based industries. There was, for instance, a sudden influx of
designer-designed radios: E.K.Cole commissioned new radio cabinets in plastics
from Serge Chermayeff, Wells Coates and Misha Black, while Murphy developed a
now classic range of cabinets in wood with Gordon and Dick Russell. As Gordon
Russell records in his autobiography, these were planned to reflect function, designed

125

Upholstery moquette designed for London Passenger
Transport Board by Enid Marx, 1937. The designer's
brief was exacting: strong contrasting tones had to be
used to keep the seat cover looking fresh after hard
wear; but the design must avoid dazzling the passengers
in moving vehicles. The scale of the repeat was dictated
by the economics of cutting out the fabric for differently-
sized seats. Enid Marx.

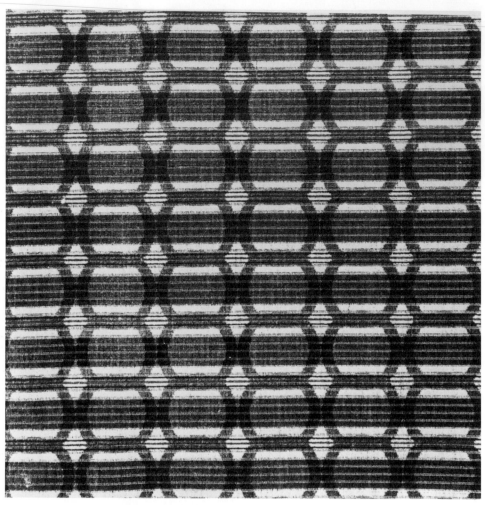

126
'Fugue' screen-printed linen designed by Paul Nash,
1936. Victoria and Albert Museum.

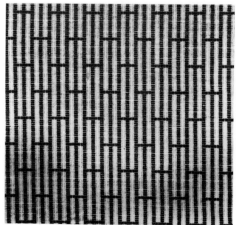

127
Upholstery moquette designed by Enid Marx for London
Passenger Transport Board, 1937. Enid Marx.

116

128

'Vogue' lightweight suitcase in cowhide, designed by
John Waterer for S.Clarke & Co., manufacturers of
Watajoy Luggage, c.1937. Note the innovative zipper
fastening. An interesting example of designers'
involvement in new areas of product design in the 1930s;
patterned linings for John Waterer's luggage were
purpose-designed by Enid Marx. Leathercraft collection,
Northampton Museum.

from the inside outwards: a DIA-inspired fundamentalist approach which, at that
period, was very far from usual. In terms of what came later, as industrial design for
engineering was developed, the products of the 1930s seem very small beginnings: a
convector heater here, an Anglepoise light there. But they were important, not only
because of the intrinsic quality of some of the finest 1930s design solutions, but also
as proof of the designer's capabilities, his value to society. More and more, this
began to be recognised by industry: for instance, by Troughton & Young, the
lighting manufacturers, who had now appointed A.B.Read, a Royal College-trained
designer, as their Design Director. It was also the conviction behind the formation
of the first of the corporate design groups in the 1930s. In 1935, the Bassett Gray
partnership, founded by Milner Gray and Charles and Henry Bassett in the early
1920s and at that time mainly preoccupied with graphics, reconstituted itself as a
new group, Industrial Design Partnership, with enlarged emphasis on product
design. Misha Black, one of the partners, was to be a crucial figure in the immense

129
Ekco radio cabinet in bakelite, designed by Wells
Coates, winner of competition for a modern plastics
wireless cabinet organised by E.K.Cole in 1932. This
design, which has become almost a symbol of the 1930s,
was first brought out in 1934, in walnut brown and
black; later it was also made in ivory and onyx. Patrick
Cook.
130
Ecko radio cabinet in bakelite, designed by Serge
Chermayeff and first made by E.K.Cole in 1934. Besides
designs by Wells Coates and Serge Chermayeff, E.K.Cole
produced wireless cabinets by Jesse Collins, in 1936, and
Misha Black, in 1938. Patrick Cook.

131
Electric convector heater with chromed finish, designed
by Christian Barman for HMV, 1934. Victoria and
Albert Museum.
132
Radio cabinet in light walnut designed by R.D.Russell
for Murphy Radio, 1937. Perhaps the best of the long
line of Murphy cabinets, mass-produced by Gordon
Russell through the 1930s, which had so obvious an
influence on the design-awareness of other
manufacturers. Museum collection, Gordon Russell.

133
Thermovent electric convector heater designed by Wells
Coates for E.K.Cole in 1937. Several versions of this
heater were produced, in dark brown or black plastic,
and production continued for some years after the war.
Victoria and Albert Museum.

134
Anglepoise lamp designed for Herbert Terry by
G.Carwardine in 1932. The idea was a simple one: for a
lamp based on the mechanism of the human arm,
infinitely adjustable. The Anglepoise, little altered, is still
in production, and makes an unfailing appearance in all
exhibitions of design classics. Science Museum.
135
The Bestlite was designed by R.D.Best for his family
firm, Best & Lloyd of Birmingham, 1930. Though
evidently inspired by Bauhaus principles, this lamp has
a trace of traditionalism which ends up by making its
appearance very English: in its time, it was much
admired by the pundits, and like the Anglepoise, no. 134,
the Bestlite is still in production. Museum collection,
Gordon Russell.

post-war expansion of design for engineering. Industrial Design Partnership later
developed into Design Research Unit, the leading design group in Britain in the
years after the War.

The 1930s was a memorable time for design patronage. Designers, later on, came
to look back with nostalgia on the early design entrepreneurs, such strong
enthusiasts as Alastair Morton at Edinburgh Weavers; Frank Murphy of Murphy
Radio; Jack Pritchard and Isokon. Frank Pick, appointed in 1933 Vice-Chairman
and Chief Executive of the London Passenger Transport Board, was an almost
legendary design patron of the 1930s; London Transport design policy became a
kind of marvel, the envy of artistic foreign visitors to Britain. And all through the

136
'Tree of Life', left, and 'Spirals', right: two earthenware patterns designed by Susie Cooper and first produced in 1938. Susie Cooper Pottery.

137
Electric fire designed by Wells Coates for Jack and Molly Pritchard's own apartment in Lawn Road Flats. Hampstead, 1934. University of East Anglia Collection.

decade, a time described in retrospect by Enid Marx as 'that halcyon period when all the arts flowered in such profusion', new patrons were emerging. For instance, Colin Anderson, a young director in his family shipping firm, the Orient Line, commissioned not only new ships – the *Orion*, 1935 and the *Orcades*, 1937 – but also a whole range of new interior fittings, from the carpets to the cutlery, substantial orders in a firmly modern idiom which helped to set new standards in the corresponding industries.

Essential patrons of design in the 1930s were the shopkeepers. In 1929, Gordon Russell's firm had opened a shop in Wigmore Street which sold, as well as furniture from Broadway, a whole collection of related products such as textiles, glass and pottery; from 1936 there was a larger shop as well, a few doors down the street, where for several years the merchandise was chosen by Nikolaus Pevsner, the art historian, a recent refugee from Nazi Germany. Another influential individual shop was Dunbar Hay, opened by Cecilia Dunbar Kilburn (later Lady Sempill) and Athole Hay in Grosvenor Street. Dunbar Hay was especially successful in promoting the work of Eric Ravilious and other staff and students from the Royal College of Art in London, where Athole Hay was Registrar. New designs were being encouraged by such Modern-Movement furnishers as Gane's of Bristol, early patron of Marcel Breuer, and Dunn's of Bromley in the pre-war pioneering days of Geoffrey Dunn. In 1938, Dunn, Crofton Gane and Gordon Russell formed the Good Furniture Group, a small association of enterprising retailers - 'a few real believers', as Dunn later described them - who commissioned designs and had them

138
'Polka Dot', 'Exclamation Mark', and 'Wedding Ring': three tableware designs, moderately modern and generally popular, produced by Susie Cooper at her pottery in Burslem in the early 1930s. Susie Cooper Pottery.

139
'Crayon Swirl' decoration on 'Curlew' shape earthenware, designed and manufactured by Susie Cooper from 1935. Susie Cooper Pottery.

manufactured. By this time, a number of modern design tendencies, especially the vogue for unit furniture, began coming into evidence in some of the large stores.

In the 1930s, the scene seemed to be beginning to be set for the 'new spirit of design' which had been prophesied for the past half century. By the mid-1930s, the idea had been well publicised by a whole succession of books and exhibitions, most notably at Dorland Hall in 1933. Modern design had become a much-used concept, the subject of discussion programmes on the BBC. The modern design movement had acquired its own philosophers, the most widely read of whom was Herbert Read, whose classic *Art and Industry*, published in 1934, was seized on both as handbook and as bible by the modernists. The rational aesthetic, the minimalist outlook – always tempered by a British moderation and good humour – was just about beginning to be seen to be convincing. It is tempting to speculate about the course of history had it not been for the intervention of the War.

The 1940s and 1950s

At the end of World War II, in the general mood of hope for a regenerated nation, two developments took place, both of which soon proved of particular importance to design in Britain: the formation, in 1944, of the Council of Industrial Design (now known as the Design Council); and the reorganisation of the Royal College of Art by Robin Darwin, appointed Principal in 1948. After the War, as a symptom of the idealistic socialism of the time, the main preoccupation was design for mass production, the idea of good design for the great mass of British people. An almost euphoric sense of optimism, stimulated by the Festival of Britain, is discernible in much of post-war design thinking, as the design profession gathered strength.

The character of British design was altered brusquely as the pre-war 1930s experimental style which, however rational, had had a kind of glamour, a self-confident urbanity, gave way to the unadulterated plainness of Utility, in which the back-to-basics idiom had been dictated as much by sheer shortage of materials as by any intellectual functionalist theories. Utility style has an obvious solemnity, almost a kind of smugness, as of Arts and Crafts austerity pushed to its utmost limit. Perhaps as a result, the post-war *volte-face*, Festival style as it soon came to be described in a tone of affectionate nostalgia, was determinedly lightweight, more self-consciously flippant. The element of whimsy which crept in in the 1950s can be beautifully observed in such Festivaliana as the Race Antelope chairs and the crystal-structure textiles, and it carries on through to the end of the decade to the classic early collections of Design Centre Awards.

In October 1942, the first Utility Furniture was shown to the public at the Building Centre. From then on until several years after War had ended, Utility was the only furniture permitted to be made in Britain. The Utility episode is so significant not just because of the historic antecedents of the Utility style, its origins in Arts and Crafts and DIA right-thinking, but also because it was a quite unprecedented example of state intervention in regulating standards of design. The chief influence, indeed to some extent the mastermind, behind Utility was Gordon Russell, first a member of the Board of Trade's Advisory Committee on Utility Furniture and then, from 1943, the Chairman of its newly-appointed Design Panel. The brief, to ensure 'a supply of furniture of the best quality available, at controlled prices, to meet a real need' was, it seemed to some (including Gordon Russell), a rare chance for reforming by example of what was possible in the least auspicious circumstances. Utility appeared an almost godsent opportunity to raise the whole level of national design standards. Arguments are still in progress, almost forty

140
Utility furniture prescribed by the Board of Trade in
World War II: the dining chair, designed in 1942, was
included in the original Utility catalogue; the 'Cotswold'
dining table, in mahogany or oak, was introduced in
1946. Geffrye Museum.
141
Utility tallboy chest in light oak, 1942. Gordon Russell
was an original member of the Board of Trade Advisory
Committee on Utility Furniture, later Chairman of the
Design Panel, and many Utility designs show a
remarkable stylistic similarity to Russell's early pieces:
compare this Utility tallboy with Russell's own tallboy
chest of the mid-1920s, no. 79. Geffrye Museum.

years later, about how well Utility in fact succeeded: were the standards too high-
minded, or were they perhaps too lenient? But what, in retrospect, seems altogether
clear, is that Utility design was a successful expression, a convincing affirmation, of
the standards of British commonsense and moderation which Gordon Russell could
be seen wholeheartedly pursuing a few years later as Director of the Council of
Industrial Design. By the time that Utility furniture production ended officially in
1952, there was some regret, even in trade circles which had at the beginning been
bitterly opposed to it. Since, because of the stringency of the regulations it was
practically impossible to produce a shoddy piece of furniture, Utility had by then,
ironically in view of the shortage of materials and labour, gained a widespread
reputation for quality. Aspects of its appearance, its sensible proportions, its sturdy
masculinity, its total lack of flashiness, had an obvious impact on modern British
furniture of the post-war period.

The Council of Industrial Design came into being at the end of the War, December
1944, as a result of the Weir Report on Industrial Design and Art in Industry made
to the Post-War Export Trade Committee of the Department of Overseas Trade.
The Council was established as a grant-aided body financed by the Board of Trade,
and the fact that it was founded by a coalition government, independent of inter-

124

142
Oak sideboard, designed in the post-Utility period
between 1948 and 1951, when restrictions had been
partially lifted and manufacturers were allowed to
design their own furniture within the Utility guidelines.
Geffrye Museum.

143
Dining chair in pre-cast aluminium designed by Ernest
Race for Race Furniture, 1945. These chairs, designed
with great ingenuity in the years of post-war shortage,
when conventional materials were strictly limited, were
shown in the 'Britain Can Make It' exhibition and
continued in production until 1969. Sally Race.

party policies, was to stand it in good stead in later years. The first Director was
S.C.Leslie, followed by Gordon Russell in 1947; the commitment of the Council
was, broadly, 'to promote by all practicable means the improvement of design in
the products of British industry'. In spite of its small size – it began with just ten
staff – and in spite of the misgivings of contemporary free-thinkers who resented the
idea of government intervention in aesthetics, the Council set about its vast task
with zest and confidence which, from this distance, seems both touching and
amazing. The early publications of the Council, patient and painstaking in their
exposition, are full of earnest visions of a better-designed Britain, a country made
more practical, for the man at his work, more dignified and pleasant for the woman
in her kitchen, for the children in their schools. Perhaps, in a sense, it had all been
said before. The aims and statements of the Council of Industrial Design were quite
familiar to the veterans of the many past design campaigns. The middle-of-the-road
ideals and principles reflected a whole history of British design attitudes through
the years of propaganda from the early DIA to the Pick Council of the 1930s. But
because it was official and, as it enlarged, was quite generously financed, the
Council of Industrial Design was more effective than its predecessors in propagating
the views which it believed in, and the opportunities it was to open out for post-war

125

British designers were enormous. As it developed, it was to be the model for design
organisations throughout the world.

Early on in the Council's life, in 1946, it was asked to stage a major exhibition,
ambitiously intended 'To intensify the interest of manufacturers and distributors in
industrial design and their awareness of the desirability of rapid progress; to arouse
greater interest in design in the minds of the general public, as consumers; and to
stage a prestige advertisement before the world for British industry, industrial
design and standards of display'. This exhibition was 'Britain Can Make It', the
first major government-sponsored exhibition of design ever to be held, colloquially
known as 'Britain Can't Have It', since many exhibits, at a time of great austerity,
were either prototypes or being made for export only. Though many doubts were
cast on the wisdom of Sir Stafford Cripps, then President of the Board of Trade, in
insisting that this was a propitious or even a practical time to display British
achievement in industrial design, his judgment was vindicated by the usefulness of
the exhibition in assessing the national potential in design and in setting the

145
Wing settee designed by Ernest Race for Race Furniture, 1948. With its companion chair, this button-backed design – modern but far from outrageous – was a favourite choice for many middle-brow interiors. Robert Race.

146
'Hillestak' chair with moulded plywood seat and back, designed by Robin Day for Hille, 1957. Royal Pavilion, Art Gallery and Museums, Brighton.

147
Convertible bed-settee designed by Robin Day for Hille in 1957 and included that same year in the first selection of Design Centre Awards. Amstad Systems.

148
Mahogany sideboard with Bombay rosewood veneer, designed by David Booth for Gordon Russell, 1951. The machine-cut decoration – a routed groove exposing the white birch below – is typically 1950s. Douglas Barrington.

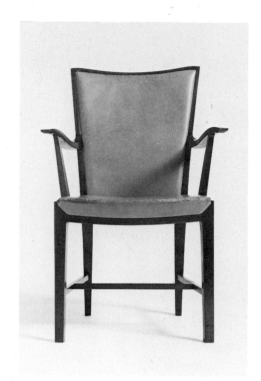

149
Mahogany dining chair with leather upholstery designed by Ronald Carter for the Royal College of Art Senior Common Room, 1951. Ronald Carter.

150
Mahogany dining chair designed by W.H.Russell for Gordon Russell in 1949 and in continuous production ever since. Its success stems, perhaps, from its unobtrusive confidence, its style of moderation, even from its touch of dullness: qualities of the British tradition through the ages. Gordon Russell.

dialogue in motion between the Council and many British industries. For 'Britain Can Make it', 3,385 manufacturers were contacted and 1,297 were chosen to exhibit. Altogether, 5,259 products were selected to be shown at the Victoria and Albert Museum in settings specially designed by James Gardner, Chief Exhibition Designer, his assistant Basil Spence, Robert Goodden, Misha Black and others (many of whom were to reassemble later as designers for the Festival of Britain). Most of all, Sir Stafford Cripps' idea in staging such a large-scale exhibition was justified by the public response, which was both unexpected and extraordinary. Contemporary photographs show people queuing in their hundreds down Cromwell Road to see it. In its fourteen-week run, 'Britain Can Make It' was visited by 1,432,546 members of the public, sixty per cent under forty. This dawning public interest in a modern design idiom – 'contemporary style' as it soon came to be depicted – was, once again, a foretaste of the Festival of Britain, five years later.

'Britain Can Make It' was the very first attempt, on any serious level, to put over to the public the idea of the designer; it identified the designer's special skills, the combined attributes of artist, scientist and technician which make the contribution of the designer so essential to the process of industrial development. The traditional rift in British education between the arts and sciences, the cerebral and practical, academic as opposed to visually-based training, had been analysed and deprecated by Robin Darwin, Education Officer of the Council of Industrial Design, in his report on the training of designers in 1946. When, two years later, Robin Darwin was appointed Principal of the Royal College of Art in London he had a unique

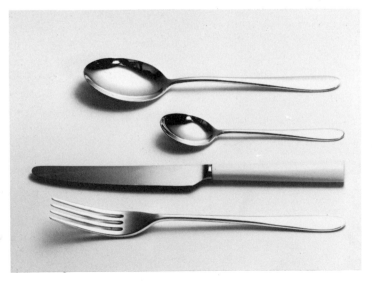

chance to reverse many of these tendencies, with a success which is by now almost a legend. His determined revitalisation of the College, which after the War was in a state of disarray; his appointment of a sequence of Professors who were themselves experienced architects and/or designers; his clear sense of the purpose of the College as primarily an institution for the training of designers for industry: all this, in its day, was so effective that by the late 1950s, a good proportion of RCA-trained designers were occupying key positions as staff designers, mainly in the craft-based industries, or else were setting up their own design consultancies. In the 1950s, on the model of design in Scandinavia, these were mainly on a small and personal scale.

The year of the Festival of Britain, 1951, was a landmark for British architecture and design. National events focused on four main areas: arts, science, technology and industrial design. The South Bank exhibition, the centre of attention, proved effectively to many disbelieving critics that modern design could be a popular success. In a corporate-image exercise on a hitherto unprecedented scale, the Council of Industrial Design was empowered to co-ordinate design throughout the Festival. The Council was responsible for all the manufactured objects included in the Festival, in all 10,000 products, and no smallest detail, from the litter bins and signposts to the cafe chairs and tables seems to have escaped its official surveillance. It was a job which delighted Gordon Russell, with his strong convictions that design was omnipresent in a civilised society, that design should be a facet of ordinary living. One especially typical Festival development, poignant in its mixture of earnestness and levity, was the series of decorative patterns promoted by the Council through the Festival Pattern Group: these were applied to such products as textiles, lighting fittings, dinner plates and wine glasses, and were the forerunners of innumerable experiments in patterning and texturing in the immediate post-Festival period (the war-time restrictions on decoration were finally lifted in 1952). But beyond the crystal-structure fabrics, the splayed legs and the ball finials, the Festival ephemera, there were some more fundamental signs of influence: a solid core of interest in the idea of design management and a new concern with standards of environment and the designer's role in attempting to control them, preoccupations which reappear so constantly in the ideologies of the next two decades.

In this post-war period, design became a cult. The publicity it attracted was enormous. But one must remember that, compared with later developments in British design history, the aims and actual achievements of the movement were, at this stage, at least up to the mid-1950s, relatively limited and narrow. It was still very much a pioneering period, still very much a matter of individual enterprise. The scene was dominated by descendants of the early DIA progressives, by people with a cause. One of these was Ernest Race, the furniture designer, who from 1945 was Director of Design for Race Furniture Ltd, an engineering-orientated company producing the most innovative of post-war British furniture. Another important post-war pioneer was Hille, an old-established East End manufacturer of furniture which, in 1949, commissioned its first designs from Robin Day, beginning a historic collaboration. At Edinburgh Weavers, from the mid-1950s onwards, reflecting the relief at the ending of restrictions, Alastair Morton commissioned the now famous series of large artist-designed abstract textile patterns which were so true to the feeling of that time.

131

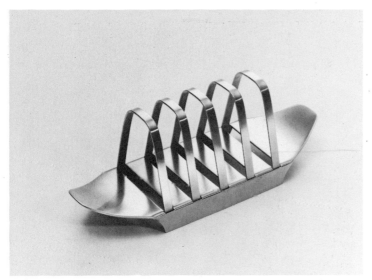

155
Stainless steel toast-rack designed by Robert Welch for
Old Hall, 1955 Robert Welch.

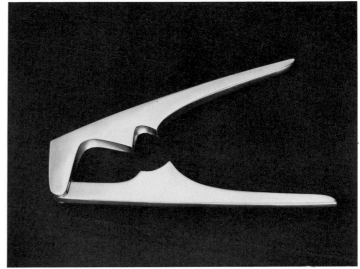

156
Stainless steel nutcrackers designed by Robert Welch for
Old Hall, 1958. The Worshipful Company of Goldsmiths.

154 (*left*)
Silver coffee-pot designed and made by Gerald Benney,
1957. The tall tapered cylinder form much cultivated by
the craft silversmiths of the late 1950s, was just as
popular with the pottery designers of the period, see
no. 157. The Worshipful Company of Goldsmiths.

157
Spode 'Apollo' bone-china tableware, designed by Neal
French and David White, then Royal College of Art
students, and produced by W.T.Copeland in 1959. The
following year Spode 'Apollo' won the Duke of
Edinburgh's annual Prize for Elegant Design. The Spode
Museum.

In stimulating public awareness of design, the rash of small design shops of the late 1940s and 1950s was important. These reflected their proprietors' own conscientious choice and set a kind of standard for household style and judgment which one can see leading inexorably on to the Habitat stores of the later 1960s. The first of these highly personal small shops of the early post-war period was Primavera in Sloane Street in London, opened in 1945 by Henry Rothschild. It gained a reputation for its modern textiles and also, increasingly, for its British craft work, an area of design which, although eclipsed in the post-war concentration on design for mass production, would soon be re-emerging.

'I am never for forcing the pace', wrote Gordon Russell in his days at the Council of Industrial Design: limited advance and then consolidation was his motto, and

159
Queen Elizabeth II Coronation Mug, designed by
Richard Guyatt for Wedgwood, 1953, continuing the
whimsical Ravilious tradition. The Wedgwood Museum.

this sums up very nicely the feeling of the period, high-minded and low-key, perhaps
a bit self-congratulatory, as Design Week followed Design Week, as *Design* magazine
began its publication, and as design standards for 'consumer goods', the furniture
and fabrics, the pottery and glassware, the cooking pots and lighting fittings which
at this period were the Council's major target, slowly but undeniably improved. In
1956, the Design Centre was opened in the Haymarket in London, followed the
next year by the Design Centre in Glasgow. In 1957, the first of the Design Centre
Awards were given to such exemplary products as Melmex plastic tableware and
Rayburn room-heaters, as fit for their purpose as could be. The early batches of
Design Centre Awards, which at the time attracted public interest on a scale
unimaginable later, helped greatly to consolidate the reputations of the new RCA-

160
Shallow bowl in stoneware with sgraffito decoration, c.1954. Lucie Rie had arrived in England from Vienna in 1938, and in the post-war period, together with Hans Coper, she quite rapidly established a new tradition in craft pottery in Britain, in many ways the opposite to that of Leach and Cardew. Leicestershire Museums.

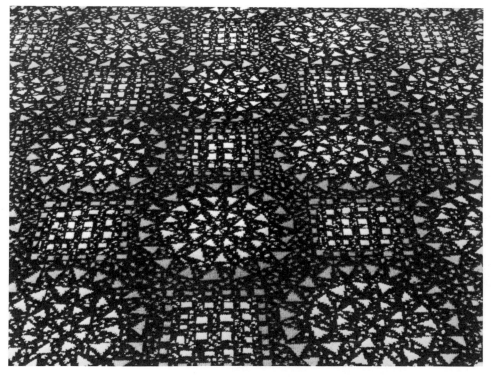

161
'Mandala' Wilton carpet designed by Audrey Tanner for Carpet Manufacturing Co., 1959. This pattern, an early Design Centre Award-winner, was one of the most widely-used carpets of its period, to be found in innumerable hotel foyers, cinemas and contemporary-style conference halls. Victoria and Albert Museum.

162
'Piazza' plastics-coated fabric designed by Eddie Pond
for Bernard Wardle, 1958. Eddie Pond.

163
'Royal Gobelin' Axminster carpet designed by Neville and Mary Ward
for Tomkinson's, 1958. Victoria and Albert Museum.

164
'Impasto' wallpaper designed by Audrey Levy for The
Wallpaper Manufacturers, 1956. Audrey Levy.
165
'Calyx' screen-printed linen designed by Lucienne Day
for Heal Fabrics, 1951. The Whitworth Art Gallery,
University of Manchester.

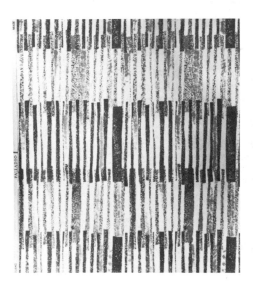

166
Bus shelter, galvanised steel with vitreous-enamelled
panels, designed by David Mellor for Abacus, 1957.
Abacus Municipal.

167
'Prestwick' leather suitcases designed by K.H.Paterson
for S.E.Norris, 1957. Victoria and Albert Museum.

168
Street light designed by Richard Stevens for Atlas
Lighting, 1959. From the late 1950s, as the Council of
Industrial Design began to involve itself increasingly in
engineering design, the sphere of influence for
professional designers enlarged greatly: see especially the
area referred to rather picturesquely as 'street furniture'.
Lantern, Victoria and Albert Museum; lighting column,
Abacus Municipal.

169
Television set designed by Robin Day for Pye, 1957.
Victoria and Albert Museum.
170
Chair in beech, designed by Christopher Heal in the
semi-Utility period, 1948–51. Geffrye Museum.

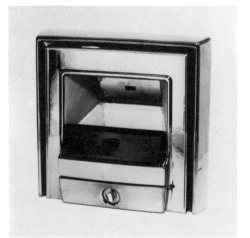

171
Jewel casket in black leather, designed by John Waterer,
1956. Leathercraft collection, Northampton Museum.

172
'Rayburn' solid fuel heater, designed by David Ogle for
Allied Ironfounders, 1956. Victoria and Albert Museum.

173
Bedside clock in copper with synchronous movement,
designed by Jack Howe for Gent & Co., 1948. Jack Howe.

trained designers and the companies they worked for: David Mellor and Walker & Hall cutlery, Robert Heritage and Archie Shine furniture, Robert Welch and Old Hall stainless steel.

The early post-war scene was gentlemanly, rather cosy, not so far away from the Arts and Crafts in atmosphere. But by the late 1950s, there were signs of growth and change and a much-enlarging area of influence for designers. This was partly the result of COID initiative, its growing involvement in design for capital goods: the first of a series of COID conferences, 'Industrial Design and the Engineering Industries', was held in Birmingham in 1958, and *Design* magazine was by this time including regular reviews of engineering products, stressing the role of the industrial designer as an integral member of the development team and emphasising the designer's potential contribution not only to the visual aspects of the equipment, its final appearance, but also to its practicality in use, the areas defined as the ergonomic factors. Ergonomics was a term which came into constant use, and as the campaign grew for the employment of designers, trained in visual perception and ergonomic skills, in the development of heavy engineering machinery and equipment and such areas as large-scale transport projects, the historic names of Stephenson, Brunel and Fowler, designers on a massive scale, were frequently invoked.

By the late 1950s, too, the role of the designer was beginning to be recognised within the public sector. It began to be seen as an important factor both in its direct benefits to the quality of life of the community and in its usefulness in public image-building. The airport authorities had, by this time, become convinced users of designers' services, a policy which still continues. British Railways, in 1956, established its Design Panel, appointing its first Director of Design. London Transport, too, was advised by a Design Panel, though it never again quite achieved the standards of coherence set for it, single-handed, by Frank Pick. From the 1950s onwards, the Ministry of Public Building and Works (later the Department of the Environment) pursued a systematic design policy, both in employing its own designers and commissioning designs from outside specialists. The Ministry of Transport, in an interesting example of attempted political control of visual standards, subsidised the lighting on trunk roads on condition that the authorities concerned had selected their lighting columns from those pre-approved by the COID.

The whole pattern of designing in Britain could be seen to be altering, subtly and gradually. The relative amateurism of the 1930s and the early post-war period, the small-scale, very personal, often craft-orientated design offices, working along Scandinavian lines, were soon to be overtaken by much larger, multi-purpose, more Americanised design consultancies. The first of these, Design Research Unit, had been founded in 1942 with the intention of presenting 'a service so complete that it could undertake any design case which might confront the State, Municipal Authorities, Industries or Commerce'. Under its leading co-partners, Misha Black and Milner Gray, it had flourished in the intervening period, benefiting from 'Britain Can Make It' and the Festival, dominating corporate design practice in Britain until the mid-1950s when, in the prevailingly expansionist mood, the sense of increasing possibilities in large-scale designing, other equally ambitious design combines began emerging. These included Ogle, founded in 1954, which quickly

174
'Knifecut' pruner designed by Hulme Chadwick for Wilkinson Sword, 1956. Wilkinson Sword.

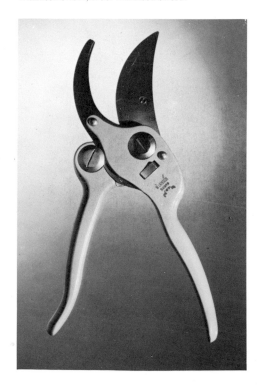

175

Mini Minor designed by Alec Issigonis for British Motor Corporation and first produced in 1959. Sturdy, functional, trim, tidy, unpompous, rather jolly: by the mid-1960s the Mini, then world-famous, had become almost synonymous with the best in British design. British Leyland Heritage collection.

acquired its current reputation as the most professional transport design consultancy; Conran, which began in 1955 with furniture and fabrics, shops and exhibitions; and Allied Industrial Designers, founded in 1959.

When, in 1959, Sir Gordon Russell retired from the Council of Industrial Design, there was a certain sense that an era had then ended, a link in the long tradition had been broken. With some questions as to whom, or to what, they owed allegiance, designers in Britain girded themselves ready for the period of increased professionalism and aggrandisement, together with a gathering self-doubt, which lay ahead.

The 1960s

The 1960s was the period in which design in Britain reached its zenith of self-confidence. There was a great deal happening: an increasing public recognition and even, one might say, adulation of designers; a vast expansion in the design profession and also in design education, massively reorganised after the Coldstream Report on Art Education, from 1960 onwards. There was an obvious feeling of the new day dawning and a sudden, reckless, very general enthusiasm, even among the erstwhile caretakers of purism, for the fashionable, ephemeral and zany. British design had never got quite so near vulgarity. Maybe, indeed, the transition proved too rapid, the exuberance too sudden to be easily digested, for by the late 1960s a reaction had set in, leading to a period of painful reappraisal: disquiet among the design student population, which began to question the whole basis of its training; a noticeable edginess in the design profession as new doctrines of design for social usefulness abounded; and, logically in this growing mood of conscientiousness, a reawakened interest in the crafts.

The style of the times was, at its most apparent, a rather knock-out style of ostentatious verve and jollity. Among its attributes was the quality of bigness: large Heal prints, 'Big Circle' carpets and huge Collins & Hayes sofas. The quality of brightness: shining chromed-steel chairs and tables, like those made by Plush Kicker. The quality of jokeyness exemplified by Conran. The cult of carefree youthfulness – 'the hunt for the young' as defined (and encouraged) by *Queen* magazine who in 1967 devoted a whole issue to the Royal College of Art – resulted in a widespread fascination with the images not only of pop and the contemporary drug culture but also with a multiplicity of newly-rediscovered, newly-reworked bygone fashions. Meanwhile, less ostentatious but just as typical, was the large-scale build-up in the 1960s of products designed with an increasing expertise, the design which got Design Awards: such archetypal 1960s prize designs as Kenneth Grange's 'Courier' electric shaver, Robert Heritage's 'Quartet Major' light fittings, the Hille polypropylene chair, the Moulton bicycle, the Adamsez bathroom suite, the famous Friedland chimes. A kind of middle-ground design was seen to be developing. Finally, there was the rising of the Anti-Design movement, identified revealingly by Misha Black in the *Queen* RCA issue, as a post-post-modernism, an idea that the sober, rational and unobtrusive was after all acceptable and even necessary. For as Misha Black pointed out, what use is the eccentric if there is no normal standard with which one can contrast it? His view at the time amounted to an affirmation of the value to society of designers relatively placid in their outlook

176
Tubular steel table and chairs designed by Peter
Wigglesworth and R.V.Exton for Plush Kicker, 1968.
This shiny chromed-steel furniture with its intertwined
curved frame was unmistakably a 'Swinging Sixties'
product. Peter Wigglesworth.

and more plodding in their practice, designers producing objects which 'in their
quiet dignity could provide a domestic and industrial environment in which the gay,
fashionable, nonsensical and exciting would be more enhanced'.

One could say that the 1960s was the period in which design was first recognised
over a wide area. 'Design' was a word which was forever cropping up, used (and
abused) in a profusion of contexts. 'Design' was, at its simplest, the pattern on the
wallpaper. But 'design' was also used for much more complex processes within the
areas of design for engineering, the world of ergonomics and systematic methods in
which the industrial designers of the 1960s were becoming increasingly involved.
For the designer, things were much less straightforward than they had been in the
days when 'good design' seemed mainly a matter of aesthetics: the idea, so current
in the 1950s, that in any visual question the designer's word was final. In the 1960s,
design processes began to be de-mystified. This was the result of the growing

recognition of the relevance of principles of human science, and especially ergonomics, to product design. As John Blake has pointed out in *The Practical Idealists*, his history of Design Research Unit (one of the design practices most obviously attuned to systematic methods), the stress on ergonomics from the early 1960s onwards influenced designing in three main directions. 'First, it emphasised that, in the design of products, the needs of consumers were more important than those of the designer; second, it put forward the, then, rather novel idea that such needs can be determined by scientific means, rather than by guesswork or intuition; and third, it provided a systematic framework for the design activity.' Indeed it can be seen to have influenced a whole new way of thinking about design for industry.

The first articles on systematic methods of designing appeared in *Design* in 1958, and in the next few years the theories of Bruce Archer, J.Christopher Jones and others working in design methodology were widely circulated and discussed. They were not, it must be said, immediately palatable to the design profession: for their basic proposition that design was less a matter of aesthetic intuition than of scientific method, their suggestion that design effectiveness in fact was measurable, undermined the age-old concept that good design is godgiven, a trace of which, of course, has always been a factor in the British tradition of designing. But one outcome of these much-publicised attempts to apply scientific methods of analysis in areas from which they had been noticeably absent, a result of obvious benefit to the design profession, was the way in which design seemed suddenly much more approachable, more comprehensible, more relevant to people who up till then had regarded with suspicion vague assertions of the importance of the visual values. A common language had begun to be discovered. The first conference on systematic methods in designing, held at Imperial College in 1962, a conference which has come to be regarded as something of a milestone in British design history, emphasised how much, in human terms, would be achieved by this breaking down of barriers, the divisions which separated scientist from artist, artist from designer, designer from engineer, engineer from the common man, the user. Design was seen to be the missing link between these sectors. The designer's role had new, important social force.

Design in Britain in the 1960s was much influenced not only by the study of behavioural sciences but also by the techniques of scientific management which had reached Britain from America and which were by now becoming an essential factor in the management of large-scale British industry. Since the War there had been many attempts by the COID to convince industry that design was a top-level management responsibility. At the time of the Festival of Britain – which was, in itself, such a convincing demonstration of the skills of design management the Council recommended – the first tentative Design Management Congress had been held, and there was a much more major one in 1956. The idea that good design is indivisible, that good design should ideally extend to all activities within a company, from the products, packaging and publicity material to the visual standards of the whole working environment (a favourite theme with Gordon Russell), had over the decade been argued with persistence. But it was only in the mid-1960s, undoubtedly encouraged by evidence of new tangible bases for designing, the disciplined approach allied to scientific management, that industry began, at last, to seem convinced. One

145

177
Flexible chair designed by Nicholas Frewing for Race
Furniture, 1964. Steel mesh seat and back hook into the
beech frame: an ingenious design for home assembly,
typical of that period of knock-down, blow-up furniture.
Alec Gardner-Medwin.

146

178
Polypropylene stacking chair designed by Robin Day for
Hille, 1961. This, perhaps the most instantly recognisable
of post-war British chairs, was the first to have a rigid
shell in polypropylene: a technological innovation of
importance. Hille International.

179
Bed-sofa with beech frame and striped cotton mattress, designed by Terence Conran for Conran Furniture, c.1962. The Conran idiom of the 1960s was basic, solid, cheerful, much in the tradition of Heal's Cottage Furniture of the early 1900s. Terence Conran.

180
Children's furniture in corrugated fibreboard, bright red or royal blue, by Polycell Design Group, 1967. This was sold packed flat, half furniture, half toy. Polycell.

181
Chromed tubular steel chair with leather seat and back, designed and made by OMK Design, 1967. A fashionable 1960s chair, without the starkness of Marcel Breuer's 'Wassily' to which it is indebted. OMK Design.
182
Chair in beech designed by Clive Bacon and made by Design Furnishing Contracts, 1963. One of several versions of linking/stacking seating developed at this period for conference halls and churches. The oak chair by Gordon Russell made originally for Coventry Cathedral is similar in style. Design Furniture Group.

of the results of this was the emergence of a new kind of designer (or a new kind of executive) entitled Design Manager, or, at best, Design Director, broadly responsible for visual liaison within the company: by 1965, the SIA, or the SIAD as it was by then rechristened, was working towards the setting up of a new category of members to cover Design Managers, and this became official in 1968. Another sign of the times was the establishment in 1964 of the Royal Society of Arts Presidential Awards for Design Management: the first winners, predictably enough, were Heal's, Conran, Hille, London Transport, Gilbey, Jaeger, firms which had, as the judges put it, 'made a contribution' (a good phrase of the day). With this growing involvement in management and marketing, the importance of which was stressed with greater urgency as Britain prepared to join the Common Market, the designers' traditional role was shifting delicately and, as some saw it, perhaps a little dangerously. The designer, in this context, was inevitably less of the questioner of accepted values, the reformer, more of the interpreter of social aspirations, raising very complex questions of morality indeed.

Reading through the design publications of the period one is very often struck by the much-increased professionalism of designers. Whereas in the 1950s it was easy to identify the gentlemanly, British quality of relaxation, a lingering sense of pre-war hopeful amateurism, by the 1960s the profession had begun to look quite different, a change of outlook marked, in 1963, by the SIA decision to rename itself Society of Industrial Artists and *Designers*. In the image-conscious atmosphere of the mid-1960s, designers were reluctant to present themselves as artists, and Dorothy Goslett's well-known manual, *Professional Practice for Designers*, published in 1963, became much thumbed. In this mood of general professional expansion, design offices themselves were getting bigger: in 1967 Design Research Unit had a staff of 60, including a newly formed design group specialising in product and engineering design. Although the design offices were still very much geared to smaller-scale domestic items – the transistors, the alarm clocks, the food mixers of that period – some were also well-equipped to design much larger products. Ogle

183
'Form' unit seating designed by Robin Day for Hille in
the late 1950s and winner of a Design Centre Award in
1961. Tania Slowe.

184
Wall storage unit in veneered pine designed by Robert Heritage for Archie Shine. Robert Heritage trained at the RCA with Professor R.D.Russell and continued much of the Russell tradition – that peculiarly English combination of self-assurance and self-effacement – into the 1960s. Victoria and Albert Museum.

Design, for instance, were working in the 1960s on such complex projects as the Ogle Mini, the Electric Taxi, the Raleigh Chopper bicycle, the Reliant Scimitar; and by 1968, they had set up their own research and product development department. BIB Design Consultants, formed in 1967, a specifically product design-orientated group, found that a surprising number, in fact the great majority, of their early clients came from the area of capital goods.

For this was one direction in which design was moving by the mid-1960s. From the small beginnings, the early pioneering work in design for the engineering industries done by the COID in the late 1950s, the possibilities had by now increased immeasurably. This was a development consistently encouraged by Paul Reilly, who had succeeded Gordon Russell as Director of the COID in 1960, and it was an area on which general attention had been focused by the publication, in 1963, of the report of the government committee, chaired by G.B.R.Feilden, on mechanical-engineering design. Two years later, a follow-up report, *Industrial and Engineering Design* (again, produced by a committee chaired by Feilden), was published by the Federation of British Industries. The report examined in great detail the ways in which the functions of the designer concerned with the appearance, form and ergonomics of a product and of the designer concerned with the mechanical and technical aspects overlapped – 'and, at best, merged'. This clear and concise apologia for the particular expertise of the industrial designer working in the engineering industries had, in its period, considerable influence. By the end of the decade, the number of firms making plant and equipment who used industrial design services had risen from a negligible figure to a total of some hundreds, and from 1968 the

COID included a Capital Goods section in its annual Design Awards. The establishment, in 1966, of the Engineering Design Centre at Loughborough, and, in 1969, of the Computer-Aided Design Centre in Cambridge, opened out still further prospects for the integration of industrial design.

185
'Thrift' cutlery, stainless steel, designed by David Mellor for the Ministry of Public Buildings and Works, 1965. After commissioning tableware for embassies (see no. 186), the Ministry turned its attention to cutlery for government canteens, hospitals and HM prisons. This led to an economy design in stainless steel in which the customary 11 pieces were reduced to a basic 5-piece setting and the number of production operations were relatively minimal. David Mellor.

186
'Embassy' teapot in silver with black fibre handle, designed by David Mellor for the Ministry of Public Buildings and Works, 1963. This teapot was part of an extensive collection of sterling silver, china and glass specially commissioned for use in British embassies, an interesting example of 1960s government conversion to the 'modern'. The Worshipful Company of Goldsmiths.

187
'Alveston' stainless steel teapot designed by Robert Welch for Old Hall, 1963. The Worshipful Company of Goldsmiths.

153

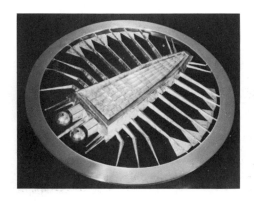

188
'Beetle' bowl in silver, gilt inside, designed and made by
Gerald Benney, 1962. The Worshipful Company of
Goldsmiths.
189
Stoneware table pottery, designed by Robin Welch in
1968 for production in an individual craft workshop,
an example of small-unit production. Robin Welch.

190
Cast-iron candlesticks with matt black finish, designed
by Robert Welch, 1962. Robert Welch.

154

191
Table glass designed by Frank Thrower for Dartington, late 1960s. The Dartington factory, set up in 1967 at Great Torrington in Devon under the aegis of the Dartington Trust, filled an obvious gap in middle-ground design; its medium-modern style was an immediate success. Dartington Glass.

But where were the industrial designers coming from? One feature of the 1960s, developing in parallel with the expansion of the design profession, was reorganisation and substantial upgrading of design education, involving a considerable national investment. In 1961, as a result of the Coldstream Report on Art Education, which had recommended the replacement of the National Diploma in Design with a more liberal, more highly academic system of training for designers, the National Council for Diplomas in Art and Design was established. The Dip AD was a 'degree-equivalent' award (not long afterwards replaced by an honours degree proper); and its implementation, through the decade, led to an enormous enlargement of facilities and a corresponding increase in teaching staff The Dip AD system covered the whole spectrum from the Fine Arts to Industrial Design, allowing considerable freedom to individual colleges, within the general framework of a nationally-administered system, in the development of their own courses. Some of these were still relatively craft-based, becoming more, not less, so in the craft renaissance of the succeeding decade: one thinks, for example, of Sheffield silversmithing or the very successful craft-based textiles course at Camberwell. But, not surprisingly in this period of reassessment and expansion, there was also much development in more scientifically-orientated courses for industrial designers. Whereas before the War, there had been the smallest handful of quite generalised courses in the large industrial centres – at Leicester, for instance, and at Birmingham – by the early 1960s the emphasis on training in industrial design was becoming more widespread, and more specific. The Industrial Design School at the Royal College of Art, a department

192
'Courier' electric shaver designed by Kenneth Grange for Milward, 1963, and well-known winner of the Duke of Edinburgh's Prize for Elegant Design. Kenneth Grange.

which developed from the Wood, Metal and Plastics School of the early years of the RCA revival, had a notably productive period in the 1960s under Misha Black, then the Professor, and Frank Height; and it was during this regime that the Industrial Design Research Unit, directed by Bruce Archer, was first established in 1961.

Interestingly enough, although this was a period for such extensive schemes and super-sized design commissions (*Design* magazine, at the time, seemed to be full of pictures of Design Award-winning earth-moving equipment), it was also a time when the climate for more experimental and esoteric enterprises had never seemed more right. OMK Design was a typical example: a small, experimental and remarkably successful furniture-manufacturing company founded in 1966 by three ex-students of the furniture department of the Central School, Jurek Olejnik, Bryan Morrison and Rodney Kinsman, hence OMK. Osborne-Little Wallpapers began in 1968, again a very small-scale, individual operation which continued and expanded through the 1970s. The tenor of the times, as one sees it from so many contemporary publications on design, was not only one of systematic methods and level-headed planning, but also quite the opposite: the 1960s also had an extreme naïve self-confidence, a touching faith in visual flair and intuition, which was, of course, being boosted – as it had, indeed, been earlier, back in the 1880s – by a supporting body of design-conscious consumers, sophisticated people on the track of special objects with which to enhance the reputation of their life-style. This was much to the advantage not only of the older-established design-minded shops like Heal's and Dunn's of Bromley, but also of the newly-modernised large stores, of which Woollands, Knightsbridge, was the supreme example. There was a sudden spate of new, small, personal design shops, some of which, in fact, were being opened by designers in a new role (or a role only new since William Morris) of simultaneous designer, manufacturer and shopkeeper. One of these was Terence Conran, who opened the first Habitat in Fulham Road, South Kensington, in 1964.

It is difficult, perhaps, for those who never knew it to understand fully the impact of that Habitat. It was so very much a symbol of that period, an expression of the youth cult, much attuned to swinging Chelsea, a fascinating mixture of the amateur and knowing, the naïve and the cynical, the sensitive and brash. The inordinate success of Mary Quant's Bazaar in Knightsbridge, which Conran had designed in 1963, encouraged Terence Conran to open Habitat, a 'shop for switched-on people', as his press release described it. And really Habitat and Bazaar were very similar; they serviced (and indeed half-created) the same life-style. What more perfect 1960s vision, for worldly London people, than sitting on a Conran sofa dressed in clothes by Quant? Besides the furniture, which was made at Conran's factory in Thetford, one of the *raisons d'être* of the first Habitat, the shop also sold lighting, fabrics, china, glass and kitchenware, household equipment immaculately chosen but displayed with a brilliantly-calculated randomness. The overall image was sophisticated peasant, for although the individual objects were quite purist, sound enough to have passed muster with the early DIA, the general atmosphere was cheery, rather homely, and this was very much a part of its success. The point was that 'good design', as it had been put over for so many years by the official propagandists and the private devotees, had, to many people, seemed a little daunting: somehow it had a certain element of grimness. But Conran, almost by

156

193
Traffic signal system designed by David Mellor with the
Ministry of Transport, installed nationally from 1969.
As a result of the Worboys Report, the traffic signal
system was overhauled and rationalised: the optical
system was intensified, and plastics or plastics-coated
materials were introduced to minimise maintenance
costs. Plessey Controls.

194
Moulton bicycle designed by Alex Moulton and
manufactured by Moulton Bicycles, 1964. A radical
rethinking of bicycle design, superbly well engineered.
Moulton Bicycles.

195
Garden shears with beech handles, designed by Hulme
Chadwick for Wilkinson Sword, 1964. Victoria and
Albert Museum.
196
'Barbican' hand-rinse basin designed by Chamberlin,
Powell and Bon with Twyfords, 1966. Victoria and
Albert Museum.

some sleight of hand, succeeded in gaining acceptance from a fairly general public
for principles the experts had been trying to put over for so long so relatively
ineffectively: good design could, at last, be seen to be accessible; good design could
even be proved to be amusing. And even if, as Habitat succeeded Habitat (for by
1968, four new stores had opened), the idea, inevitably maybe, lost its freshness, its
totally convincing sense of personal vision, it was still one of the 1960s most
remarkable phenomena and set a whole new standard of retailing in Britain.

The pursuit of individuality, which has been a constantly recurring theme within
design in Britain, was clearly on the increase from the mid-1960s onwards. Perhaps
this should be seen as a necessary safety valve in case the systematic methods grew
oppressive, an inbuilt corrective against encroaching dullness. In this decade, for
instance, there was a quite remarkable, and in many ways completely unexpected,
revival of the craft of silversmithing. This can be attributed partly to the influence
of Robert Goodden, a notably effective RCA Professor of Jewellery and
Silversmithing, partly to the energetic practical support of Graham Hughes, the Art

197
Door bells, chimes and buzzers, designed by Norman
Stevenson for Friedland, early 1960s. A determined
attempt to impose 'sixties-modern' styling on the
traditional door-chimes of English bourgeois life, which,
deservedly, won a Design Centre Award in 1964.
Friedland.

198
Pay-on-answer coin box, designed by Douglas Scott
with the GPO, c.1960. British Post Office.

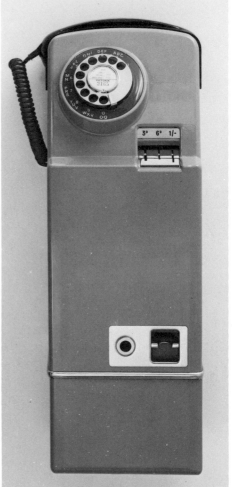

199
'Quartet Major' light fittings designed by Robert Heritage for Rotaflex, 1964. Victoria and Albert Museum.
200
'Merlin' electric alarm-clock, designed by Robert Welch for Westclox, 1964. Robert Welch.

201
'Brownie Vecta' camera designed by Kenneth Grange for Kodak, 1964. The vertical design was based on the premise that most domestic photographs consist of one or two human figures in the standing position. Kenneth Grange.

Director of the Worshipful Company of Goldsmiths. Several dozen new workshops were set up in this period, some – like Gerald Benney's and Louis Osman's – concentrating on special commissions; others – like Robert Welch's and David Mellor's – combining craft silversmithing with industrial design. This was characteristic 1960s thinking. In this period, as well, there were the beginnings of a strong new movement in craft pottery, together with a similar new interest in weaving, developments signalled by the exhibition in the 1960s of weaving by Collingwood and pottery by Coper at the Victoria and Albert Museum, the first time that the Museum showed the work of living craftsmen and the start of a new policy of contemporary exhibitions and commissions. Another memorable exhibition, held at the Design Centre in 1965, was 'Hand and Machine' which emphasised the traditional overlap of craft and mass production within design in Britain.

Seen from the 1980s, these were halcyon days indeed. But maybe the excitement was too frenzied to be lasting. Although the decade had been in many ways so fruitful, as well as so eventful, for the design profession, the 1960s did not end as well as they began. They ended on a note of acrimony and anxiety. 'Will the designer', asked Bruce Archer in an article on design management in *Design* in 1969, 'be fit to face the world of the 70s? Can he adapt himself to the highly professional, multi-disciplinary team: to the vertical integration of industrial innovation? Is he willing and able to provide the link – the calculable link – between the absolute value, marginal value, price, premium and cost without losing control of those intangible, cultural values of which he must remain the guardian?' This was just the kind of question, asked with increasing earnestness, destined to divide designers into sheep and goats, wise and foolish virgins; for though some designers were fit, indeed quite eager, others were noticeably reluctant to face a future full of costs and premiums, not to menion values absolute and marginal. Somehow the prospects seemed a little unalluring, even maybe rather dubious. Questions of designers' professional morality were, by the late 1960s, causing noticeable angst, a situation exacerbated by the student troubles of 1968, and with the approach of the 1970s, a period of remarkable design polarisation, the designers who resisted the whole concept of the vertical integration of industrial innovation (together with those who simply did not understand it), could be detected digging themselves in for the long forthcoming winter of Alternative Design.

The 1970s

The 1970s was a period of extremes within design in Britain. A period of new professionalism for designers, as technological advances in industry demanded corresponding expertise in the design profession, together with a newly-realistic working knowledge of the managerial skills of designing for a market. And also, surprisingly and simultaneously, a time for the renaissance of that amateur approach, that apparently spontaneous, almost off-hand creativity, at which, from time to time, the British are so brilliant. The craft revival movement, which involved the setting up of many dozens of new, individual, often experimental workshops, had been stimulated greatly by the establishment of the government-financed Crafts Advisory Committee (later the Crafts Council); and in this period, the small craft workshops were a source of considerable vitality and optimism. Meanwhile, the mood of intensified awareness of their social responsibilities, a major preoccupation of designers in the conscience-stricken 1960s, continued through the 1970s, the memorable slogans of the period being 'Nearness to Need' and 'Design for the Real World'.

The styles of the time had never seemed such poles apart as they were in the 1970s, so totally divided between the self-effacing and the self-expressive. The Anti-Design tendencies defined by Misha Black back in the mid-1960s had come into their own with the emergent new technology; design, when applied to microprocessor technology, was, it seemed, reduced to a succession of black boxes. Design in the 1970s had, to say the very least, a certain sameness. This was the era for design so unobtrusive it was almost non-existent, the triumph of anonymity. Or so it seemed. For Anti-Design, in the 1970s, was balanced by a concurrent movement of great individuality in which, interestingly enough, some of the themes of the early Arts and Crafts movement were often much in evidence. There was the new mania for perfection of technique, exemplified by John Makepeace's furniture and Gerald Benney's silver. New interest in reworking the vernacular tradition, as in the pottery of Michael Casson, John Leach and Richard Batterham; the rag rugs of John Hinchcliffe. A fresh preoccupation with allusiveness and narrative, as shown by the work of Michael Lloyd in silver: his bowls with trees and moons and grass and corn are right in the tradition of Arts and Crafts symbolic. There has been, in the past decade, a noticeable zest for sheer decorative qualities, the qualities which, in a sense, had been denied to designers in Britain through many long years of the puritan aesthetic. One also finds, in some of the craftwork of the 1970s, a growing sense of double entendre, a subtle wit.

The Crafts Advisory Committee began work in 1971. This was the first time that the importance of the work of British craftsmen, their role in the whole cultural pattern of the country, had really been recognised by central government. The Committee was set up by Lord Eccles, Paymaster General and Minister responsible for the Arts, under the wing of the Council of Industrial Design whose Director, Sir Paul Reilly, had for some years felt the need to coordinate the activities of the different (and often divergent) craft societies by forming a more powerful and far-sighted central body. The Committee's main concern, from its inception, was with the work of 'artist-craftsmen', as its early brief defined them: craftsmen whose work, although often rooted in traditional techniques, has an aim which extends beyond the reproduction of past styles and methods. In other words, its bias was very much towards the creative crafts, and its chief executive, later its Director, was Victor Margrie, himself a well-known potter. Its task was seen as a dual one:

202
Chair in elm designed and made by Richard La Trobe-Bateman, 1977. A version of the traditional smoker's chair, showing the new mood of nostalgic innovation in the craft revival furniture of the 1970s. Richard La Trobe-Bateman.

203
Ebony chair designed by John Makepeace and made by Andrew Whately in Makepeace's workshops at Parnham, 1978. The woven seat and back are nickel silver, and the chair has both the finesse and the touch of eccentricity typical of Makepeace's most recent work. Private collection.

promotional, focusing public attention on the work of modern artist-craftsmen;
and practical, in giving grants to new craft workshops, helping to finance craft-
workshop training, and supporting regional craft activities. Its first major exhibition,
'The Craftsman's Art' held in 1973 at the Victoria and Albert Museum, was an
extraordinary public success; *Crafts* magazine was started that same year; a London
exhibition gallery was opened and an index of craftsmen began to be built up.
Through active, one might almost say intrepid, attempts to bring the public face to
face with artist-craftsmen, culminating in the sponsoring of nationwide tours called
'Meet the Craftsmen', the work of the CAC enormously intensified public awareness
of who craftsmen are and what they can contribute. By 1979, by which time it had
become an independent body, redesignated the Crafts Council, its *raison d'être* was
no longer in question, with a grant which had increased from the £178,000 of its
first year of operation to £1,148,000 for 1978–9.

And yet, for all the success of the Crafts Council in stimulating British craft
activity, it has to be remembered that the seeds were there already. The basic
impulse for the widespread craft revival came not from the Crafts Council but
directly from the craftsmen. The Crafts Council activities to some extent were
simply a reflection of the ideas and the interests which had been steadily
accumulating in the 1960s and which were, in themselves, a development of even
older attitudes towards design and making. These went back, in fact, as far as the
ideas of William Morris and the principle of making things not mainly to make
money but because these are the things which you, quite simply, want to make.

206
Desk from the 'Ash Occasional' range designed by
Dinah Casson for Remploy Furniture, 1979. A design
which demonstrates convincingly a continuity of attitude
to furniture from Gimson to Russell to Heritage and
Carter and on to the RCA designers of the 1970s.
Remploy.

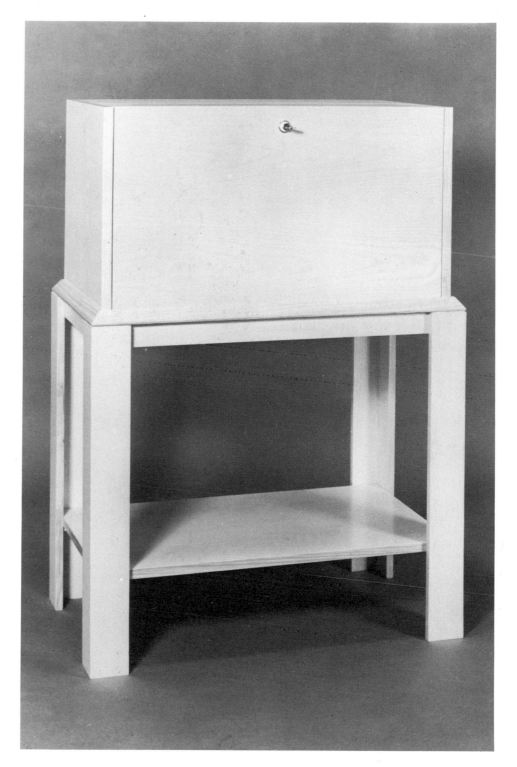

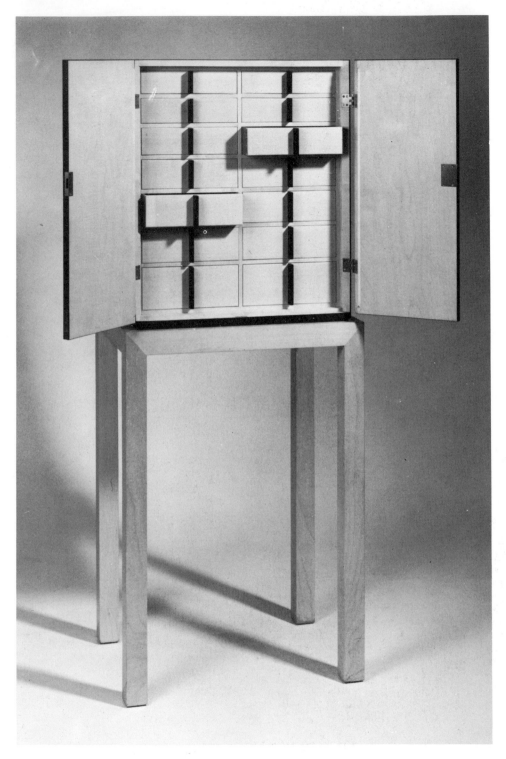

207
Cabinet in sycamore, designed and made by John Coleman, then a final-year student at the Royal College of Art, 1979. John Coleman
208 (*right*)
'Tipster' chair designed by Robert Heritage and Roger Webb for Race Furniture, 1979. The chair both stacks and links and has a tip-up seat. Race Furniture.

The craft revival of the early 1970s was well within the British tradition of idealism. Though it lacked the element of selflessness, the broadly humanistic outlook of the Arts and Crafts movement of the end of the last century, it showed a similar concern with, and distaste for, the materialist structure of contemporary life: it was, in the same way, a very obvious protest movement against the prevailing attitudes to working and standards of environment. It was, once again, a reassertion of individuality, of personal creativity, in a very complex industrial society. It evinced a comparable longing to get back to what were seen as the real and lasting values, which often involved setting up a workshop in the country; for in the 1970s, as in the 1890s, the real lasting values almost always meant rurality. The modern craft revival has been very much in tune with the progressive preoccupations of its time; linked through to the good lifers, natural foods and natural fibres, the drinkers of real ale and the makers of real bread. It can also, perhaps, be seen as the corollary of rather more specific discontents and disenchantments with current tendencies in the design profession, a rejection of the concept of design-for-marketing, the designer as the tool of the materialist society. The craftsmen in a sense set up an opposition faction. This was, of course, the camp which appealed most to many students who embraced the craft revival with a good deal too much fervour. From the design-orientated ideals of the 1950s, when students' main aim was to go out and work in industry, there had now been a total *volte-face* and the dream of the preponderance of students in the 1970s was to set up a craft workshop. In the end the craft revival got a little out of hand.

What it did, which was important, was to redirect attention back to the skills of making. These had partly been forgotten in the early post-war period when emphasis in education was becoming more highly academic: heady days of design-for-industry when the crafts, in most progressive circles, were taboo. In 1977, a sign of the new climate of opinion, the John Makepeace School for Craftsmen in Wood was opened, funded by the non-profit-making Parnham Trust. This school, run alongside John Makepeace's own furniture workshops at Parnham House in Dorset, was set up to train more craftsmen to open more craft workshops: a project unimaginable fifteen years before.

Out of the craft revival, too, came a new interest by designers in involving themselves in actual methods of production. The craft revival, joined with the attractions of the small-is-beautiful philosophy, stimulated the move towards small-unit production. This had many permutations. The small-batch-producing craftsman with one or two assistants, as, for instance, John Leach, making a repeatable standard range of pottery, employing entirely hand-production methods. The craftsman such as Robin Welch, the Suffolk potter, adapting industrial techniques for standardised production in what was still essentially a craft workshop. The designer-manufacturer like David Mellor who in 1973 set up his own cutlery factory in Sheffield, a production unit very highly mechanised yet small enough in scale for freedom of manœuvre, in which the designer would be able to control not only the details of each product but also the layout of the factory and the design of the production machinery. The 1970s were notable for the success of designers, such as Peter Simpson at Bute Fabrics, Frank Thrower at Dartington Glass, in bridging the gap, in small-to-medium size firms, between sales and production. Here, looming

210
'Omstack' chair with pressed steel seat and back, designed by Rodney Kinsman for OMK, 1970. OMK Design.

large, was the missing technician whose absence John Gloag, long ago, had so lamented. The pattern of designer-director, involved in all stages of design, from conception to final production and marketing, could be seen continuing into the 1980s with the small-unit furniture firm Peter Miles Furniture, set up in 1980 at Wirksworth in Derbyshire by Peter Miles and Ronald Carter RDI.

The 1970s became a very specialist decade. Gone were the days of the small all-purpose offices; going, too, was the concept of the versatile designer, central to the

British tradition since the 1930s, the idea of the designer who could turn his hand to
anything, design on any scale, from a machine tool to a teacup. Now, in a way
ironically, since design horizons had widened so immeasurably in the post-war
period, design practice had itself become more narrow, the areas of influence much
tighter, more specific. This change was reflected by a greatly altered emphasis in the
work of the Council of Industrial Design which in 1972 became the Design Council,
having been invited by the government (as its 1972–3 Report explains it) 'to pursue

174

212
Silver bowl, raised by Peter Musgrove, engraved by
Malcolm Appleby, 1975. The craft silver of the 1970s
became much freer in its decoration, showing new
preoccupation with surface patterning and reawakened
interest in symbolic forms. Crafts Council collection.
213
Large stoneware storage jar by Peter Starkey, 1975. The
salt-glaze, the combed decoration, the sheer usefulness
of this jar would place it well within the English country
potters' functional tradition; yet it has a wittiness, a
visual sophistication, which makes it very much a pot of
the mid-1970s, an excellent example of Peter Starkey's
work. W.A.Ismay.
214
Handmade glass, small-batch production, designed and
made by Simon Pearce, 1975. Simon Pearce.
215
Small pots in white bone china with relief decoration, by
Jacqueline Poncelet, 1975. Crafts Council collection.

216
'Concept' tea-set in vitrified earthenware, designed by
Martin Hunt for Hornsea Pottery, 1977, and winner –
with David Mellor's 'Chinese Ivory', no. 211 – of a
Design Award in that same year. Hornsea Pottery.

217
Cast-iron cooking pots with black enamelled finish,
designed by Robert Welch, 1970. Robert Welch.

218
'SM2000' direct-drive record turntable, part of a range of high-performance hi-fi equipment designed by PA Design Unit for Strathearn Audio, 1975. PA Technology and Science Centre.

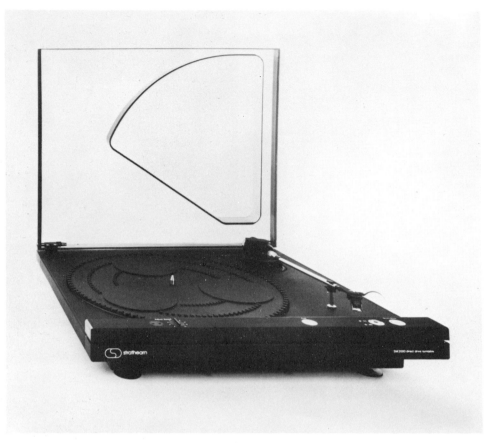

219
Secateurs designed by DCA Design Consultants for Stanley Garden Tools, mid-1970s. Stanley Tools.

its campaigns beyond the boundaries of industrial design and graphic design even more rigorously than before into the vastly more powerful and complex realms of engineering'. In the fifteen years or so since its first tentative campaigns for design within the engineering industries, the Council's own approach had been becoming more sophisticated and professional. Where once the stress had been on the obvious 'design' qualities, aesthetic appearance and ergonomics, the Council had moved on to campaign for what it termed as total excellence: to consider not only ergonomics and appearance but also innovation, function, economy and efficiency in manufacture and use.

The change in general outlook in the 1970s, as well as the expansion in the work of the Design Council, is illustrated nicely by a quick comparison of the first group of Design Centre Awards, given in 1957, with the Design Awards of twenty years later. Both, in their way, are vintage collections. But whereas the early awards are

220
'Executive' calculator designed and manufactured by Sinclair Radionics, 1972. Victoria and Albert Museum.
221
'Powerflood' floodlamp system designed by Robert Heritage for Concord Lighting, 1971. Concord Lighting International.

222
Push-Button Telephone, one of a range designed by DCA Design Consultants for British Telecom, 1979.

223
Fire-engine cab developed by Ogle Design with Dennis Motors, 1978. Dennis Motors.

224
'Boss Mark III' front-loading fork lift truck, designed by London & Upjohn with Lancer Boss design team and manufactured by Lancer Boss; winner of Capital Goods Design Award in 1970. Lancer Boss.

225
Truck-mounted hydraulic telescopic Crane 725 CM, designed by D.Hassall and Cosmos design team for Cosmos Crane Co., 1976. This crane was intended for high-speed lifting and placing of loads, with rapid transit between work sites. The design shows great attention to practical detail, including exceptional provision for the comfort of the driver, minimising the dangers of operator fatigue. Cosmos Crane Co.

179

all domestic, from the Rotaflex lampshades to the Strawberry Hill china, the 1977 Awards are much more varied, many of them much more technical, immensely further reaching, far beyond the ken of the ordinary housewife who so preoccupied those early design panels. The 1977 Awards came in five categories. Consumer and Contract Goods, extending from digital clocks and pocket calculators to the Topper Sailing Dinghy; the pottery tea-set and the stainless steel cutlery seemed almost to be pieces from a long-forgotten era. Awards were given to Engineering Products: spectrophotometers, sidelift trucks and telescopic boom cranes. Awards were also given to Engineering Components, such products as high-performance gear pumps and powered cable reels. The fourth category was the British Motor Vehicle Industry. The fifth for Medical Equipment. Nowhere was the change of emphasis so marked as in this last highly technical, professional and specialist category in which the awards ranged from the Charnley-Howorth Sterile Operating Unit and the Wilj Gamma-Counting system to a set of particularly well-designed false teeth.

'Industrial design is now fifty years on', as Frank Height so truly commented in 1977, in his RCA Professorial Address, 'and has grown out of its heroic period'. By the 1970s, the heroes, the individual stars of the design world, were either dead and buried or else keeping a low profile. In industrial design, the scene was now too complex for old-style atelier-based British designing, and in training designers for the engineering industries the stress was now on teamwork, on specific expertise. New professionalism in attitudes to training of designers in the country as a whole, in the design departments of many Polytechnics, as well as at the RCA, became apparent, and moves were being made to integrate the training of industrial and engineering designers. In 1980, mainly at the instigation of Professor Frank Height, a course in industrial design engineering was introduced, run jointly by the RCA and Imperial College of Science and Technology, for graduate engineers and scientists; at the same time, collaboration had begun between the RCA and Cranfield Institute of Technology, including the establishment of two related Fellowships, one based at the RCA and one at Cranfield, directed to Computer-Aided Design.

Design offices enlarged and equipped themselves to tackle more specialist projects. Bill Moggridge Associates, for instance, a practice founded in 1969, has specialised increasingly in microelectronics, in office technology, telecommunications, scientific and engineering equipment, and by 1980 had set up a second unit in the Silicon Valley area, near San Francisco. Allied Industrial Designers, established by James Pilditch in 1959, now the largest design consultancy in Britain with a staff of 100, has pursued an energetic marketing-directed policy. In 1980, the year in which AID became a public company, the first design consultancy in Britain to go public, they acquired two further companies: Business Decisions Ltd, a market-research company; and DVW Microelectronics Ltd, a firm which designs and develops microprocessor-based products and processes. James Pilditch's reasoning in acquiring DVW was that since the product designers in his office had already been designing the 'outer casing' for a number of electronic products, and since the software firm had designed a lot of interior mechanisms, it made sense to offer a combined service. Besides, he added, AID had a good 'innovations' group, helping firms to develop new products, and it was obviously impossible to be effective in that particular aspect of designing without knowing what microelectronics were about.

226
High-Speed Diesel Train developed by British Rail and
first put into service in 1975. Kenneth Grange of
Pentagram was design consultant for the power cab, and
working to a brief of extraordinary complexity, arrived
at a solution which is admirably British, functional and
elegant, a design of which Frank Pick would surely have
approved. British Railways Board.

227
'Mini-Variset' cloakroom system designed by Kenneth Grange for A.J.Binns, 1978. Extruded aluminium rail with grey nylon hooks and straps. A.J.Binns.

228
Monitor Terminal designed by Kenneth Grange for Reuters, 1980. The system provides information for the money market: the cabinet houses a 9-inch screen data terminal; the alpha-numeric control keyboard is used remotely. Reuters.

182

'Witney' sideboard in stained mahogany, designed by
Ronald Carter for Peter Miles Furniture. An excellent
example of the neo-Arts and Crafts style of the early
1980s, superbly well detailed and immaculately made.
Peter Miles Furniture.

As the 1970s progressed, the design world was becoming a very different place,
more competitive, more thrusting, more obviously allied to the marketing and
advertising agencies than at any previous period in British design history. The
national economic crisis, joined with the problems of a world recession, had the
effect of toughening the design profession, with lip-service being paid rather more
to marketing than art. One effect of the recession in Britain was to propel British
design firms to look for work abroad. In this, they were remarkably successful. By
1980, Pentagram Design had opened an office in New York: thirty to forty per cent
of its design work was being done for clients outside Britain. BIB Design Group, a
specialist product design practice was, again, by 1980, working for a forty per cent
foreign clientele, including four Japanese companies. Conran Associates, with an
office in Paris, were also doing a great deal of work abroad, especially in shop
design. Their policy, as propounded by John Stephenson, Managing Director, in a
statement to *The Times*, was straightforwardly aggressive. The Conran group, he
said, was 'as much run by businessmen as designers'. Its philosophy was 'making
money', a policy so unashamedly materialistic as to bring British design almost
back to where it started.

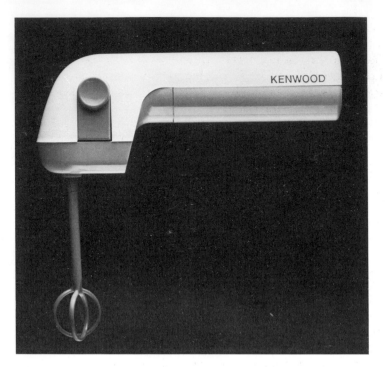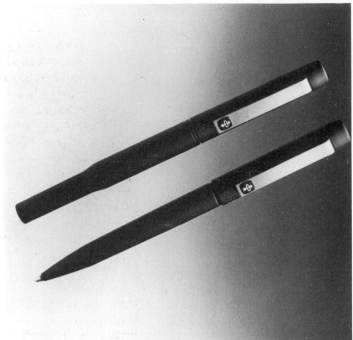

230
Battery whisk, a low-cost hand-held food mixer designed
by Kenneth Grange for Kenwood Manufacturing Co.,
1975. Kenneth Grange.
231
'Parker 25' pen range, designed by Kenneth Grange for
the Parker Pen Co., 1975. Kenneth Grange.

In the 1970s, Conran won commissions for three fairly similar ranges of plastics kitchenware for three different clients, Boots/Timothy Whites, Marks & Spencer and Woolworths: a considerable achievement both in terms of skilful business and in terms of bringing good design to the mass markets. But in terms of human need? Well, that was surely a rather different question, another kind of argument. It was interesting how, as the 1970s developed, attitudes and aims among professional designers became more and more divergent. What were their true objectives? What was good design about? The large businesslike consultancies had one idea: that good design was, simply, commercially effective. But a much more earnest view, the more traditional belief that the best design was socially beneficial, that designers had community responsibilities, had many strong adherents. This was the great age of ecological awareness, and as the Design Council Annual Report for 1976–7 pointed out, in the new and frugal mood of conservationism, the designers' built-in talents were particularly relevant: 'Seldom can the hallowed principles of good design, whether expressed as economy of means or intelligence made visible, have been more in tune with the times than in the mid-nineteen seventies.' It was, after all, the metier of the designer, both by training and by instinct, to search out the simplest, most economical solution to any problem; many designers, the Report suggested, 'may even welcome the new restrictions as a recall to sober, functional, socially valid yardsticks'.

Certainly, through the 1970s, the number of socially valid design activities grew rapidly. The SIAD, for instance, set up an Alternative Design Group; the DIA inaugurated a series of Melchett Awards, annual prizes for research into socially-responsible design. The handbook of the movement was, of course, Victor Papanek's *Design for the Real World*, and its focal event the 'Design for Need' symposium and exhibition held at the RCA in 1976. As a result of this conference, an intense new awareness of the potential social implications of designers' work developed. This was particularly strong in the design schools. The consciousness that the work of the designer had its hazards, in terms of consumption of resources and also possible harmful side-effects, was balanced by the perception that design could be a positive force for the improvement of conditions among the aged, the infirm, the socially disadvantaged, all areas which up till then had suffered from neglect. The needs of the Third World began to be considered, and in 1977 the RCA established a specialised section within its School of Industrial Design for studies in Resources, Environment, Aid and Development (generally known, conveniently, as READ).

It is perhaps significant that, through this pursuit of social validity, design to some extent rediscovered its identity. The repeated emphasis on the moral issues of industrial design had, by the end of the decade, reinstated the designer in the role of reconciler, the link-figure, the agent through whom the enormous possibilities of modern technology took on a comprehensible, humanitarian form. In the late 1970s, the crucial importance of design-awareness in society was being argued very plausibly on many different levels. Dr Patrick Nuttgens was putting the case forward for a new and much more practical approach to higher education, a greater concentration on 'the world of doing and making'. Dr Bruce Archer was theorising cogently about the need to recognise an academic discipline besides the traditional sciences and humanities: the missing discipline was seen to be designing. And, in the persuasive and powerful report on *Design Education at Secondary Level*, published by the Design Council in 1980, Professor David Keith-Lucas, Chairman of the working party, emphasised the gap in national educational policy at a more fundamental stage. 'If education', he wrote, 'is concerned with trying to fit children to play a full part in the adult life of tomorrow, there can be few more important educational experiences for the children than to grapple with the sort of problems they will meet as adults – problems of the environment, of man-made things and how they can be improved, of the quality of living – or, in other words, "design" in all its forms.'

Into the 1980s

Over the past century enormous energy and indeed expertise have been directed towards the improvement of national design standards; or, to put it more accurately, towards bringing national standards into line with what the design cognoscenti recommended. The belief that such a revolution in taste was not only feasible on a national scale but also actually socially beneficial dominated the campaigns of the succession of reform groups: the late nineteenth-century Arts and Crafts societies and the short-lived but vociferous National Association for the Advancement of Art and its Application to Industry; the Design and Industries Association in the period between the Wars; the Pick Council in the 1930s. This was the thinking, optimistic and paternal, behind the stepping up of the campaign for good design in the early post-war period: the expansion of the Council of Industrial Design; the reorganisation of the Royal College of Art; and later, in the 1960s, the considerable enlargement and upgrading of the whole national network for the training of designers, by then mainly within the large-scale Polytechnic system.

The national design establishment is now extensive. By 1980, the Design Council had expanded from its original ten staff in 1945 to around 230; its grant had increased from £550,000 in 1970 to £2,811,000 in 1980. The Crafts Council received a further £1m. Design education had enlarged dramatically: the number of Polytechnics and Colleges approved by the Council for National Academic Awards for degree courses in 3-Dimensional Design had risen from 22 in 1970 to 31 in 1980; the equivalent figures for Fashion and Textiles courses were 16 in 1970, 23 in 1980. In 1980 (the most recent year for which figures are available) CNAA degrees were awarded to 609 3-Dimensional Design students, 581 students of Fashion and Textiles, and 93 students in the relatively new, but fast-growing, area of History of Art and Design. With so many resources directed towards training, the design profession has shown signs of an explosion. Membership of the Society of Industrial Artists and Designers had risen from the ten or so of 1930 to 3,500 in 1970 to 6,500 in 1980; and the total is still multiplying rapidly.

The efforts, the resources, the build-up of activity in British design has been enormously impressive; the idea has been pursued with more energy in Britain than in any other country. But what of the results? Is Britain, as it should be, by now design world leader? If one answers truthfully, one has to answer no. The fact is, and in the 1980s it began to be admitted, that British design, compared with that of other nations such as Italy, Japan and Germany, lacks sophistication. What is more, the gulf between the standards of accepted taste among the pundits and the national aesthetic as one sees it in the High Streets has never seemed so obvious, so totally unbridgeable. Good design is still, just as it appeared at the time of Pevsner's 1937 national survey, an almost wholly middle-class preserve: the upper class ignores it; the working man rejects it. Indeed, perhaps the gap seems even greater than it was, for there were signs in the 'contemporary' era, the period surrounding the Festival of Britain, of a growth of understanding, almost a *rapprochement*, between the purists and the taste of the mass market. But those days of hope are over and the purists now left stranded, the tucket sounding faintly. There is only Habitat.

The early 1980s have proved an anxious period of stock-taking and soul-searching. The death of Gordon Russell, who embodied a whole movement in British design history, from Arts and Crafts to modern; the retirement of the close-knit group of RCA Professors who had been a powerful influence since the days of Robin Darwin; the break-up of the old hierarchies; the erosion of old certainties in British design attitudes: all this has contributed to a vague sense of dislocation in the design profession. There are also the problems and frustrations of the current economic situation, within which there seems so little experimental leeway. A long-drawn-out period of financial retrenchment is inevitably hard for those whose job is innovation. But this is surely only half the explanation: there has been a good deal more to it than that.

Some of the unease of designers in the 1980s has arisen from the feeling, a gradually growing suspicion, that their energies have tended to be misdirected. Has the moral emphasis in British design tradition, a deep-rooted distrust of capitalist practice which goes back as far as Ruskin and Morris, together with a dilettante attitude to marketing, resulted in designers, especially designers in the consumer industries, failing to carry ideas through with clear conviction? 'Many talented designers', said Terence Conran sternly in autumn 1980, 'have not achieved success for themselves, or their clients, because they have not studied the market properly before they conceived their designs, or followed the product through from the manufacturer to the consumer, checking that at every stage the design is properly presented. So many designers still believe that if form follows function and the product is efficiently manufactured, then their job has been well done.' There were few to disagree with him. Design ideals have sharpened since the early 1950s, and by the 1980s it is obvious to designers that the decent job, plain and simple, is not enough. It has become clear that more research is needed into product innovation and marketing, and in 1981 Frank Height, Professor of Industrial Design at the RCA, was strenuously advocating the establishment of an advanced institute of design, sponsored by both government and industry, to determine the directions which new design should take.

Artistic uncertainties have also proved disorientating to the designers of the early 1980s. The immense technological advances of the past decade, the phenomenon described by Frank Height as 'the triumph of invisible technology', has left the designer, whose professionalism is based on an essentially visual interpretation of the physical world, in an understandable state of disarray. The ground, in a sense, has been shifted from beneath him. The old aesthetic theories seem to have lost their relevance. The form-follows-function idea has become redundant when the actual mechanism of the product is in some cases so complex as to be beyond the designer's comprehension in any but the very broadest terms. The designers of microelectronics products have, for instance, in some ways a more demanding task than designers of more traditional artefacts because here the design solution is open-ended. Designers, in this context, can do anything they choose to. They can (the solution most in favour in the 1970s) put the components neatly into little boxes, giving an appearance of functional efficiency, although in fact the form is not particularly relevant to what goes on inside it. Or, an approach now becoming much more fashionable, the designer can by-pass a merely functional appearance and shape the object for the emotional satisfaction, or indeed the sheer amusement, of the customer.

The 1980s show signs of being the decade in which form-follows-function changes very subtly, but in fact quite radically, to form-expresses-function. We are back to the yearning for symbolism; emotional overtones; mystery and myth; all of which is possible, indeed extremely tempting, in designing in relation to the new technology. Here, again, is the designer in the role of the interpreter, designer as the form-giver to human understanding. An exhibit in the 1981 Degree Shows at the RCA was a paramount example of the new poetic tendencies. This was a convector heater encased not, as it would have been in years gone by, in smart grey unobtrusive squared-off metal sheeting, but taking the free form of a convector-heater-sculpture expressing, logically enough, a puff of wind.

British design books and exhibition catalogues

Since the publication of Anthony Coulson's massively informative *Bibliography of Design in Britain 1851–1970* (London, Design Council, 1979), any further attempt to compile a comprehensive book list would be superfluous. For those who need to find it, everything is there.

This list is therefore more of a personal selection of books I have found particularly useful or illuminating. Some are the obvious, essential, major studies of the design and the designers of this period. Others are obscurer, but have some special quality of originality or authenticity which, in my opinion, makes them worthwhile hunting out.

The same is broadly true of the exhibition catalogues. These, I think, can be especially informative. The contemporary catalogues – say, from 'Britain Can Make It', and the Festival of Britain – have an extraordinary immediacy even now. The retrospective catalogues, of whatever period, give a very valuable insight into contemporary ratings: how particular designers or movements in design seemed to the cognoscenti of the time. I have of course included the seminal exhibitions, those – such as 'Victorian and Edwardian Decorative Arts' at the Victoria and Albert Museum in 1952 – which influenced the attitude of its whole generation. But I have also selected from the increasing number of smaller exhibitions of more peripheral design practitioners, or design phenomena, those which seem most useful ventures into unknown territory or which have a particularly interesting slant.

The Early Period, 1880 to 1914

Books, articles and papers

Adburgham, Alison. *Liberty's. A Biography of a Shop* (London, George Allen & Unwin, 1976)

Anscombe, Isabelle, and Gere, Charlotte. *Arts and Crafts in Britain and America* (London, Academy Editions, 1978)

Arts and Crafts Exhibition Society. *Arts and Crafts Essays* (London, Rivington Percival, 1893)

Ashbee, C.R. *Craftsmanship in Competitive Industry* (London, Grant & Co., for Essex House Press, 1908)
An Endeavour towards the Teaching of John Ruskin and William Morris (London, Essex House Press, 1901)

A Few Chapters in Workshop Reconstruction and Citizenship (London, Guild of Handicraft, 1894)

Memoirs (Unpublished typescript in Victoria and Albert Museum MSS Collection, 1938; original journals in King's College Library, Cambridge)

Should We Stop Teaching Art? (London, Batsford, 1912)

Aslin, Elizabeth. *The Aesthetic Movement: Prelude to Art Nouveau* (London, Elek, 1969)

19th Century English Furniture (London, Faber, 1962)

Benson, W.A.S. *Drawing: Its History and Uses*, with memoir by Hon. W.N.Bruce (Oxford University Press, 1925)

Benton, Charlotte, and Benton, Tim. *Form and Function. A Sourcebook for the History of Architecture and Design 1890–1939* (London, Crosby, Lockwood, Staples for Open University, 1975)

Billcliffe, Roger. *Charles Rennie Mackintosh, Furniture and Interiors* (Guildford, Lutterworth Press, 1979)

Blomfield, Sir Reginald. *Memoirs of an Architect* (London, Macmillan, 1932)

Blount, Godfrey. *Arbor Vitae: A Book on the Nature and Development of Imaginative Design for the use of Teachers, Handicraftsmen and Others* (London, Dent, 1899)

The Science of Symbols (London, Arthur C. Fifield, 1905)

Blunt, Wilfred. *Cockerell* (London, Hamish Hamilton, 1942)

'England's Michelangelo': A Biography of Frederic Watts (London, Hamish Hamilton, 1975)

Burne-Jones, Georgiana. *Memorials of Edward Burne-Jones* (London, Macmillan, 1904)

Callen, Anthea. *Angel in the Studio: Women in the Arts and Crafts Movement, 1870–1914* (London, Astragal Books, 1979)

Clark, Fiona. *William Morris: Wallpapers and Chintzes* (London, Academy Editions, 1973)

Cobden-Sanderson, T.J. *The Arts and Crafts Movement* (London, Hammersmith Publishing Society, 1905)

Cosmic Vision (London, Richard Cobden-Sanderson, 1922)

Journals (London, Richard Cobden-Sanderson, 1926)

Comino, Mary. *Gimson and the Barnsleys* (London, Evans Brothers, 1980)

Cooper, John Paul. 'The Work of John Sedding, architect'. Series of articles in *Architectural Review*, vols. 3 and 4, 1898

Crane, Walter. *An Artist's Reminiscences* (London, Methuen, 1907)

William Morris to Whistler (London, G.Bell & Sons, 1911)

Crawford, Alan, and Bury, Shirley, intrs. *C.R.Ashbee: Modern Silverwork* (New edition, London, Weinreb, 1974)

Cross, A.J. *Pilkington's Royal Lancastrian Pottery and Tiles* (London, Richard Dennis, 1980)

Crow, Gerald H. 'William Morris Designer'. Special issue of *The Studio*, Winter 1934

Davey, Peter. *Arts and Crafts Architecture* (London, Architectural Press, 1980)

Davidson, Eleanor. *The Simpsons of Kendal* (Lancaster University Visual Arts Centre, 1978)

192

Day, Lewis F. *Everyday Art: Short Essays on the Arts Not-Fine* (London, Batsford, 1882)

Dresser, Christopher. *Principles of Art* (London, 1881)
   Principles of Decorative Design (London, Cassell, Peter & Galpin 1873)
   Studies in Design for House Decorators, Designers and Manufacturers (London, Cassell, Peter & Galpin, 1876)

Faulkner, Thomas. 'W.R.Lethaby: tradition and innovation', from *Design 1900–1960*, papers given at Newcastle Polytechnic Conference (Newcastle Polytechnic, 1976)

Fitzgerald, Penelope. *Edward Burne-Jones: A Biography* (London, Michael Joseph, 1975)

Floud, Peter. 'The inconsistencies of William Morris'. Article in *The Listener*, October 14, 1954
   'William Morris as an artist: a new view'. Article in *The Listener*, October 7, 1954

Furst, H.E.A. *Decorative Art of Frank Brangwyn* (London, John Lane, 1924)

Girouard, Mark. *Sweetness and Light: The Queen Anne Movement 1860–1900* (Oxford University Press, 1977)

Harrison, Martin, and Walters, Bill. *Burne-Jones* (London, Barrie and Jenkins, 1973)

Haslam, Malcolm. *The Martin Brothers, Potters* (London, Richard Dennis, 1978)

Heal's Catalogues, 1853–1934. (Newton Abbot, David & Charles, 1972)

Henderson, Philip. *William Morris* (London, Thames and Hudson, 1967)

Howarth, Thomas. *Charles Rennie Mackintosh* (London, Routledge & Kegan Paul, 1952; new edition, 1976)

Hughes, Graham. *Modern Silver, 1880–1967* (London, Studio Vista, 1967)

Jewson, Norman. *By Chance I Did Rove* (Kineton, Warwick, Roundwood Press, 1973)

Kornwolf, James D. *M.H.Baillie Scott and the Arts and Crafts Movement* (Baltimore, Johns Hopkins Press, 1972)

Lambourne, Lionel. *Utopian Craftsmen* (London, Astragal Books, 1980)

Larner, Gerald and Celia. *The Glasgow Style* (Edinburgh, Paul Harris, 1979)

Lethaby, W.R. *Architecture. An introduction to the History and Theory of Building* (Williams & Norgate, 1912; new edition, Oxford University Press, 1955)
   Architecture, Mysticism and Myth (Percival & Co., 1892; new edition, London, Architectural Press, 1975)
   Form in Civilisation: Collected Papers in Art and Labour (Oxford University Press, 1922, reprinted 1957)
   Home and Country Arts (London, Home & Country, 1924)
   Philip Webb and his work (London, Oxford University Press, 1935; new edition, introduced by Godfrey Rubens, London, Raven Oak Press, 1979)

Lethaby, W.R. and others. *Ernest Gimson, his Life and Work* (Stratford-upon-Avon, Shakespeare Head Press, 1924)

Mackail, J.W. *The Life of William Morris* (London, Longmans Green, 1899)

Mackmurdo, A.H. History of the Arts and Crafts Movement (Unpublished manuscript in collection of William Morris Gallery, Walthamstow)

Macleod, Robert. *Charles Rennie Mackintosh* (London, Country Life, 1968)

Massé, H.J.L. *The Art Workers' Guild* (Oxford, Shakespeare Head Press, 1935)

Miller, Alec. C.R.Ashbee and the Guild of Handicraft (Unpublished typescript in Victoria and Albert Museum MSS Collection, c.1952)

Morris, May. *Introductions to the Collected Works of William Morris* (Separate edition, New York, Oriole Editions; London, Journeyman Press, 1973)
William Morris: Artist Writer Socialist (Oxford, Shakespeare Head Press, 1936; new edition, New York, Russell & Russell, 1966)

Morris, William. *Architecture, Industry and Wealth. Collected Papers* (London, Longmans Green, 1902)
Collected Works (London, Longmans Green, 1910–15)
Lectures (London, Longmans, 1898–1901)

Morton, Jocelyn. *Three Generations in a Family Textile Firm* (London, Routledge & Kegan Paul, 1971)

Muthesius, Hermann. *Das englische Haus* (Berlin, Wasmuth, 1904–5; English edition, *The English House,* St Albans, Granada/Crosby Lockwood Staples, 1979)

Naylor, Gillian. *The Arts and Crafts Movement* (London, Studio Vista, 1971)

Nuttgens, Patrick. 'A full life and an honest place', chapter on the Arts and Crafts in *Spirit of the Age: Eight Centuries of British Architecture* (London, BBC Publications, 1975)

Okey, Thomas. *A Basketful of Memories* (London, J.M.Dent, 1930)

Pevsner, Nikolaus. *Pioneers of the Modern Movement* (London, Faber, 1936); new edition, *Pioneers of Modern Design* (Harmondsworth, Penguin, 1960)
The Sources of Modern Architecture and Design (London, Thames and Hudson, 1968)
Studies in Art, Architecture and Design, vol. 2, including Morris, Mackmurdo, Mackintosh, Voysey, Walton (London, Thames and Hudson, 1968)
'William Morris, C.R.Ashbee and the Twentieth Century'. Article in *Manchester Review*, vol.7, Winter 1956

Richards, J.M., and Pevsner, Nikolaus, eds. *The Anti-Rationalists*, including Mackintosh, Mackmurdo, Liberty, and Reynolds-Stephens (London, Architectural Press, 1973)

Rothenstein, William. *Men and Memories* (London, Faber, 1931–9; new edition, London, Chatto & Windus, 1978)

Rushton, James H. *Ruskin Pottery* (West Bromwich, Metropolitan Borough of Sandwell, 1975)

Ruskin, John. *Seven Lamps of Architecture* (London, Smith Elder, 1849)
Stones of Venice (London, Smith Elder, 1851–3)
Two Paths: being lectures on Art and its Application to Decoration and Manufacture (London, Smith Elder, 1859)

Savage, Peter. *Lorimer and the Edinburgh Craft Designers* (Edinburgh, Paul Harris, 1980)

Sedding, John D. *Art and Handicraft* (London, Kegan Paul, Trench, Trübner, 1893)

Shaw, Bernard. 'William Morris as I knew him', reprint of 1936 essay (London, William Morris Society, 1966)

Simpson, Duncan. *C.F.A. Voysey: an Architect of Individuality* (London, Lund Humphries, 1979)

Spencer, Isobel. *Walter Crane* (London, Studio Vista, 1975)

Spencer, Robin. *The Aesthetic Movement: Theory and Practice* (London, Studio Vista, 1972)

Stirling, Mrs A.M.W. *William De Morgan and his Wife* (London, Thornton Butterworth, 1922)

Thompson, Paul. *The Work of William Morris* (London, Heinemann, 1967)

Vallance, Aymer. *William Morris, his Art, Writings and Public Life. A Record* (London, Bell, 1897; new edition, 1909)

Voysey, C.F.A *Individuality* (London, Chapman and Hall, 1915)
  Reason as a Basis of Art (London, Elkin Mathews, 1906)

Watkinson, Raymond. *Pre-Raphaelite Art and Design* (London, Studio Vista, 1970)
  William Morris as Designer (London, Studio Vista, 1967)

There is also a great deal of relevant material for this period in the *Architectural Review* (from 1897) and *The Studio* (from 1893); and the current Newsletters, Journals and occasional publications of the Decorative Arts Society, the Charles Rennie Mackintosh Society, the William Morris Society and the Victorian Society.

Catalogues

The Aesthetic Movement 1869–1890. Exhibition at Camden Arts Centre, London. (London, Academy Editions, 1973)

The Aesthetic Movement and the Cult of Japan (London, Fine Art Society, 1972)

Architect-Designers: Pugin to Mackintosh (London, Fine Art Society, 1981)

The Arts and Crafts Movement (London, Fine Art Society, 1973)

C.R.Ashbee and the Guild of Handicraft (Cheltenham Art Gallery and Museum, 1981)

Good Citizens' Furniture: The Works of Ernest and Sidney Barnsley (Cheltenham Art Gallery and Museum, 1976)

Birmingham Gold and Silver: Assay Office Centenary Exhibition (Birmingham City Museum and Art Gallery, 1973)

The Art of Frank Brangwyn (Brighton Polytechnic, 1980)

Frank Brangwyn: Centenary Exhibition (Cardiff, National Museum of Wales, 1967)

British 20th Century Studio Ceramics (London, Christopher Wood Gallery, 1980)

An Exhibition of Cotswold Craftsmanship (Cheltenham, Montpellier Rotunda, 1951)

The Doulton Story. Catalogue of exhibition at Victoria and Albert Museum (Stoke-on-Trent, Royal Doulton Tableware, 1979)

Christopher Dresser: 1834–1904 (London, Camden Arts Centre, 1979)

The Earthly Paradise. Exhibition of work of the Birmingham Group (London, Fine Art Society, 1969)

Ernest Gimson (Leicester Museums and Art Gallery, 1969)

Ernest Gimson and the Cotswold Group of Craftsmen. Catalogue of collection (Leicestershire Museums, 1969)

Homespun To Highspeed: A Century of British Design, 1880–1980 (Sheffield City Art Galleries, 1979)

Liberty's 1875–1975 (London, Victoria and Albert Museum, 1975)

Charles Rennie Mackintosh. Catalogue of exhibition at the Royal Scottish Museum (Edinburgh, Scottish Arts Council, 1968)

The Eccentric A.H.Mackmurdo, 1851–1942 (Colchester, The Minories, 1979)

Morris and Company 1861–1940. Catalogue of exhibition at Victoria and Albert Museum (London, Arts Council, 1961)

Morris and Company (London, Fine Art Society, 1979)

Morris & Company in Cambridge (Cambridge University Press, 1980)

Textiles by William Morris and Morris & Co, 1861–1940 (Birmingham Museums and Art Gallery, 1981)

The Mortons: Three Generations of Textile Creation (London, Victoria and Albert Museum, 1973)

Omar Ramsden, 1873–1939 (Birmingham City Museum and Art Gallery, 1973)

The Silver Studio Collection: A London Design Studio 1880–1963. Middlesex Polytechnic Exhibition (London, Lund Humphries, 1980)

Victorian and Edwardian Decorative Arts (London, Victoria and Albert Museum, 1952)

Victorian and Edwardian Decorative Art. The Handley-Read Collection (London, Royal Academy, 1972)

C.F.A.Voysey: architect and designer. Catalogue of exhibition at Brighton Art Gallery and Museum (London, Lund Humphries, 1978)

A Choice of Design 1850–1980: Fabrics by Warner & Sons Ltd (Braintree, Warner & Sons, 1981)

Partnership in Style: Edgar Wood and J.Henry Sellers (Manchester City Art Gallery, 1975)

The Middle Period, 1915 to 1939

Books, articles and papers

Arts and Crafts Exhibition Society. *Handicrafts and Reconstruction* (London, John Hogg, 1919)

Barman, Christian. *The Man Who Built London Transport: A Biography of Frank Pick* (Newton Abbot, David & Charles, 1979)

Bayley, Stephen. *In Good Shape: Style in Industrial Products, 1900 to 1960* (London, Design Council, 1979)

Baynes, Ken and Kate. *Gordon Russell* (London, Design Council, 1981)

Benton, Charlotte, and Benton, Tim. *Form and Function. A Sourcebook for the History of Architecture and Design 1890–1939* (London, Crosby Lockwood Staples for Open University, 1975)

Bertram, Anthony. *Design in Daily Life* (London, Methuen, 1938)

Bertram, Anthony, and others. 'Design in everyday things'. Series of articles in *The Listener*, 1933

Bliss, Douglas Percy. *Edward Bawden* (Godalming, Pendomer Press, 1979)

Blake, John and Blake, Avril. *The Practical Idealists: A History of Design Research Unit* (London, Lund Humphries, 1969)

196

Cantacuzino, Sherban. *Wells Coates* (London, Gordon Fraser, 1978)

Cardew, Michael, and others. *Michael Cardew: Collected Essays* (London, Crafts Advisory Committee, 1976)

Carrington, Noel. *Design and a Changing Civilisation* (London, John Lane, Bodley Head, 1935)

Industrial Design in Britain (London, George Allen & Unwin, 1976)

The Shape of Things: An Introduction to Design in Everyday Life (London, Nicholson & Watson, 1939)

Clark, Garth. *Michael Cardew* (London, Faber, 1978)

Cole, Barbie Campbell, and Benton. Tim, eds. *Tubular Steel Furniture* (London, Art Book Company, 1979)

Design in Modern Life. Accompanying pamphlet for series of broadcast talks (London, BBC, 1933)

Digby, George Wingfield: *The Work of the Modern Pottery in England* (London, John Murray, 1952)

Dowling, H.G. *A Survey of British Industrial Arts* (Benfleet, F.Lewis, 1935)

Dunn, Geoffrey. 'One hundred years of furniture'. Illustrated survey in *Cabinet Maker* centenary issue, September 1980

Faulkner, Peter. *William Morris and Eric Gill* (London, William Morris Society, 1975)

Fournier, Robert, ed. *David Leach: A Monograph* (Tanyard, Lacock, Fournier Pottery, 1977)

Gill, Eric. *Autobiography* (London, Jonathan Cape, 1940)

Gloag, John. *Design in Modern Life* (London, George Allen & Unwin, 1934)

Industrial Art Explained (London, George Allen & Unwin, 1934)

Green, A. Romney. Autobiographical fragments (Unpublished manuscript in Victoria and Albert Museum MSS Collection, c.1946)

Hanson, Brian. 'Singing the Body Electric with Charles Holden'. Article in *Architectural Review*, December 1975

Haworth-Booth, Mark. *E.McKnight Kauffer: a designer and his public* (London, Gordon Fraser, 1979)

Heal's Catalogues, 1853–1934 (Newton Abbot, David & Charles, 1972)

Heskett, John. *Industrial Design* (London, Thames and Hudson, 1980)

Hogben, Carol. *The Art of Bernard Leach* (London, Faber, 1978)

Holland, James. *Minerva at Fifty: The Jubilee History of the Society of Industrial Artists and Designers 1930–1980* (Westerham, Hurstwood Publications, 1980)

Holme, Geoffrey. 'Frank Brangwyn designs for British industry'. Article in *The Studio*, vol.100, 1930

Industrial Design and the Future (London, Studio, 1934)

Hughes, Graham. *Modern Silver, 1880 to 1967* (London, Studio Vista, 1967)

Johnson, Stewart. *Eileen Gray: Designer, 1879–1976* (London, Debrett, for Victoria and Albert Museum and Museum of Modern Art, New York, 1979)

Leach, Bernard. *A Potter's Book* (London, Evelyn, Adams & Mackay, 1967)

Martin, J.L., and Speight, Sadie. *The Flat Book* (London, Heinemann, 1939)

Meynell, Francis. *My Lives* (London, Bodley Head, 1971)

Mairet, Ethel. Notes, diaries, letters (Unpublished material in collection of Bath Crafts Study Centre)

Morton, Jocelyn. *Three Generations in a Family Textile Firm* (London, Routledge & Kegan Paul, 1971)

Pevsner, Nikolaus. *An Enquiry into Industrial Art in England* (Cambridge University Press, 1937)

'Omega'. Article on the Omega Workshops in *Architectural Review*, vol.90, 1941

Studies in Art, Architecture and Design, vol.2, including Pick, Russell and the DIA (London, Thames and Hudson, 1968)

Plummer, Raymond. 'Fitness for Purpose: the Story of the DIA'. Reprinted in *Design and Industry* conference papers (London, Design Council, 1980)

Read, Herbert. *Art and Industry. The Principles of Industrial Design* (London, Faber, 1934)

Richards, J.M. 'Towards a rational aesthetic'. Article in *Architectural Review*, vol.78, 1935

Rogers, J.C. *Modern English Furniture* (London, Country Life, 1930)

Rose, Muriel. *Artist Pottery in England* (London, Faber, 1955; new edition, 1970)

Russell, Gordon. *Designer's Trade* (London, George Allen & Unwin, 1968)

Looking at Furniture (London, Lund Humphries, 1964)

Sharp, Dennis, ed. *The Rationalists. Theory and Design in the Modern Movement* (London, Architectural Press, 1978)

Simon, Herbert. *Song and Words: A History of the Curwen Press* (London, George Allen & Unwin, 1973)

Smith, Hamilton T. 'The DIA: the Early Years'. Article in *Design for Today*, May 1935; reprinted in *DIA Yearbook*, 1975, Diamond Jubilee Edition

Spalding, Francis. *Roger Fry* (London, Elek/Granada, 1980)

Speaight, Robert. *The Life of Eric Gill* (London, Methuen, 1966)

Ward, Neville, and Ward, Mary. *Home in the Twenties and Thirties* (London, Ian Allan, 1978)

Williams-Ellis, Clough. *Architect Errant* (London, Constable, 1971)

Woodham, Jonathan. 'British Art in Industry in 1935'. Reprinted in *Design and Industry* conference papers (London, Design Council, 1980)

There is a great deal of generally relevant material for this period in the *Architectural Review*; *Commercial Art and Industry*, later *Art and Industry* (from 1926); *Design and Industries Association Journal* and *News Sheet* (from 1918); *Design in Industry*, published by DIA (1932), replaced by *Design for Today* (1933), later superseded by *Trend in Design of Everyday Things* (1936); *The Society of Industrial Artists Newsletter and Journal* (from 1930); *The Studio*. Also in the current publications of The Thirties Society and The Decorative Arts Society.

Catalogues

Phyllis Barron and Dorothy Larcher: Hand-block Printed Textiles (Bath, Crafts Study Centre, 1978)

Frank Brangwyn. Exhibition of Furniture designed for E.Pollard, Oxford Street (London, The Avenue Press, 1930)

The Art of Frank Brangwyn (Brighton Polytechnic, 1980)

British Art in Industry (London, Royal Academy, 1935)

British 20th Century Studio Ceramics (London, Christopher Wood Gallery, 1980)

Classics of Modern Design (London, Camden Arts Centre, 1977)

Wells Coates, Architect and Designer (Oxford Polytechnic, 1979)

Susie Cooper: Elegance and Utility. Catalogue of exhibition at Sanderson's, London (Barlaston, Josiah Wedgwood, 1978)

Claud Lovat Fraser (London, Victoria and Albert Museum, 1969)

The Worshipful Company of Goldsmiths as Patrons of their Craft 1919–53. Catalogue of collection at Goldsmiths' Hall (London, Worshipful Company of Goldsmiths, 1965)

Hampstead in the Thirties: A Committed Decade (London, Camden Arts Centre, 1974)

Sir Ambrose Heal, Centenary Exhibition (London, Heal's, 1972)

Homespun to Highspeed: A Century of British Design, 1880–1980 (Sheffield City Art Galleries, 1979)

Alec B.Hunter. Textile Designer and Craftsman (Braintree, Warner & Sons, 1979)

The Art of Bernard Leach (London, Victoria and Albert Museum, 1977)

The Modernist Rug 1928–1938 (Brighton, Royal Pavilion, Art Gallery and Museums, 1975)

Alastair Morton and Edinburgh Weavers (Scottish National Gallery of Modern Art, 1978)

The Mortons: Three Generations of Textile Creation (London, Victoria and Albert Museum, 1973)

Keith Murray. Catalogue of travelling exhibition (London, Victoria and Albert Museum, 1976)

Omega Workshops: Furniture, Textiles and Pottery 1913–1918. Catalogue of exhibition at Victoria and Albert Museum (London, Arts Council, 1946)

Elizabeth Peacock: Weaving (Bath, Crafts Study Centre, 1978)

Pel and Tubular Steel Furniture of the Thirties (London, Architectural Association, 1977)

Katharine Pleydell-Bouverie (Bath, Crafts Study Centre, 1980)

The Poole Potteries (London, Victoria and Albert Museum, 1978)

Eric Ravilious 1903–1942 (Colchester, The Minories, 1972)

Shelley Pottery (London, Geffrye Museum, 1980)

Thirties: British Art and Design Before the War (London, Hayward Gallery, 1979)

The Thirties. Progressive Design in Ceramics, Glass, Textiles and Wallpapers. Catalogue of travelling exhibition (London, Victoria and Albert Museum, 1975)

A Choice of Design 1850–1980: Fabrics by Warner & Sons Ltd. (Braintree, Warner & Sons, 1981)

The Modern Period, 1940 to 1980

Books, articles and papers

Archer, L. Bruce. *Systematic Method for Designers* (London, Council of Industrial Design, 1965)

Ashford, F.C. *Designing for Industry: Some Aspects of the Product Designer's Work* (London, Pitman, 1955)

Banham, Mary, and Hillier, Bevis, eds. *A Tonic to the Nation: Festival of Britain*

1951. Book accompanying 1976 commemorative exhibition at Victoria and Albert Museum (London, Thames and Hudson, 1976)

Barry, Sir Gerald. 'The Festival of Britain, 1951.' Cantor lectures reprinted in *JRSA*, August 1952

Barty, Ewan. *Management and Engineering Design* (London, Design Council, 1972)

Bayley, Stephen. *In Good Shape: Style in Industrial Products, 1900 to 1960* (London, Design Council, 1979)

Baynes, Ken. *Industrial Design and the Community* (London, Lund Humphries, 1967)

About Design (London, Design Council, 1976)

Baynes, Ken, ed. *Attitudes in Design Education* (London, Lund Humphries, 1969)

Baynes, Ken and Baynes, Kate. *Gordon Russell* (London, Design Council, 1981)

Beresford-Evans, J. *Form in Engineering Design* (Oxford, Clarendon Press, 1954)

Birks, Tony. *The Art of the Modern Potter* (London, Country Life, 1967)

Black, Professor Misha. 'The education of industrial designers'. Cantor lectures reprinted in *JRSA*, vol.113, 1965

'Engineering and Industrial Design'. Paper reprinted in *Transactions of the Institute of Mechanical Engineers*, vol.186, 1972

'The training of industrial designers'. Paper reprinted in report of *Conference on the Teaching of Engineering* (London, Institute of Engineering Designers, 1964)

Bradshaw, A.E. *Handmade Woodwork of the Twentieth Century* (London, John Murray, 1962)

Carrington, Noel. *Design and Decoration in the Home* (London, Batsford, 1952)

Casson, Hugh. 'Dreams and awakenings'. Chapter on post-war architecture and design in *Spirit of the Age: Eight Centuries of British Architecture* (London, BBC Publications, 1975)

Casson, Michael. *Pottery in Britain Today* (London, Alec Tiranti, 1967)

Clark, Garth. *Michael Cardew* (London, Faber, 1978)

Crawford, Alan, intr. *Robert Welch, Design in a Cotswold Workshop* (London, Lund Humphries, 1973)

Darwin, Robin. 'The Dodo and the Phoenix: the Royal College of Art since the war'. Paper reprinted in *JRSA*, vol.102, 1954

'The training of the industrial designer'. Paper reprinted in *JRSA*, vol.97, 1949

Dunn, Geoffrey. 'One hundred years of furniture'. Illustrated survey in *Cabinet Maker* centenary issue, September 1980

Farr, Michael. *The Council of Industrial Design*. Monograph written on occasion of Gran Premio Internazionale Award, La Rinascente, Milan (London, Council of Industrial Design, 1959)

Design in British Industry – A Mid-Century Survey (Cambridge University Press, 1955)

Frayn, Michael. 'The Festival of Britain'. Chapter in *The Age of Austerity*, eds Michael Sisson and Philip French (London, Hodder & Stoughton, 1963)

Gloag, John. *The Missing Technician in Industrial Production* (London, George Allen & Unwin, 1944)

Goldsmiths, The Worshipful Company of. *Modern British Silver* (London, Worshipful Company of Goldsmiths, 1963)

Gorb, Peter, ed. *Living by Design: Pentagram Design Partnership* (London, Lund Humphries, 1978)

Goslett, Dorothy. *Professional Practice for Designers* (London, Batsford, 1961)

Height, Frank. ' . . and cheap tin trays'. RCA professorial inaugural lecture (London, Royal College of Art, 1977)

Hennessey, Elizabeth. 'Terence Conran, International Designer.' Chapter in *The Entrepreneurs* (Newbury, Scope Books, 1980)

Heskett, John. *Industrial Design* (London, Thames and Hudson, 1980)

Hillier, Bevis. *Austerity Binge: the Decorative Arts of the Forties and Fifties* (London, Studio Vista, 1975)

Holland, James. *Minerva at Fifty: The Jubilee History of the Society of Industrial Artists and Designers 1930 to 1980* (Westerham, Hurstwood Publications, 1980)

Hughes, Graham. *Modern Silver, 1880 to 1967* (London, Studio Vista, 1967)

Jones, J.Christopher. *Design Methods: Seeds of Human Futures* (London, Wiley-Interscience, 1970)

Lyall, Sutherland. *Hille: 75 Years of British Furniture.* Book accompanying retrospective exhibition at Victoria and Albert Museum (London, Elron Press, 1981)

Mayall, W.H. *Industrial Design for Engineers* (London, Iliffe, 1967)
Machines and Perception in Industrial Design (London, Studio Vista, 1968)

Middleton, Michael. *Group Practice in Design* (London, Architectural Press, 1967)

Nuttgens, Patrick. 'Learning to some purpose'. Paper given for SIAD/Burton Design Award, reprinted by Society of Industrial Artists and Designers, 1977

Papanek, Victor. *Design for the Real World. Making to Measure* (London, Thames and Hudson, 1972)

Plummer, Raymond. 'Fitness for Purpose: The Story of DIA'. Reprinted in *Design and Industry* conference papers (London, Design Council, 1980)

Rose, Muriel. *Artist Pottery in England* (London, Faber, 1955; new edition, 1970)

Russell, Gordon. *Designer's Trade* (London, George Allen & Unwin, 1968)
'Skill'. Paper reprinted in *JRSA*, November 1978
'What is good design?' Article in *Design*, January 1949
'Work of the Royal Designers for Industry', Paper reprinted in *JRSA*, vol.97, 1948

Russell, Gordon, intr. *Design in the Festival* (London, HMSO, 1951)

Society of Industrial Artists. *Designers in Britain.* Review of work of members (London, Wingate, 1947, 1949, 1951; London, Deutsch, 1953, 1957, 1964, 1971)

Young, Dennis and Barbara. *Furniture in Britain Today* (London, Alec Tiranti, 1964)

There is a great deal of generally relevant material for this period in *Crafts*, published by the Crafts Advisory Committee, later the Crafts Council (from 1973); *Design*, published by the Council of Industrial Design, later Design Council (from 1949); *Design and Industries Association Yearbook*; *House & Garden*; *Society of Industrial Artists Journal*, later *The Designer*.

Catalogues

Britain Can Make It: Design '46. Survey of exhibits in Council of Industrial Design exhibition at Victoria and Albert Museum (London, HMSO, 1946)
British 20th Century Studio Ceramics (London, Christopher Wood Gallery, 1980)
Classics of Modern Design (London, Camden Arts Centre, 1977)
Collingwood/Coper. Rugs and wallhangings by Peter Collingwood, Pots by Hans Coper (London, Victoria and Albert Museum, 1969)
Crafts Council Collection Catalogue of acquisitions (London, Crafts Council, 1980)
The Craftsman's Art. Crafts Advisory Council exhibition (London, Victoria and Albert Museum, 1973)
Design at Work: An Introduction to the Industrial Designer. Catalogue of Royal Designers for Industry exhibition at Royal Academy (London, Royal Society of Arts and Council of Industrial Design, 1948)
The Festival of Britain: Catalogue of exhibits, South Bank Exhibition (London, HMSO, 1951)
Homespun to Highspeed: A Century of British Design, 1880 to 1980 (Sheffield City Art Galleries, 1979)
Enid Marx: A Retrospective Exhibition (London, Camden Arts Centre, 1979)
Masterpiece: A Jubilee Exhibition of Crafts (London, Crafts Advisory Council, 1977)
Lucie Rie (London, Arts Council, 1967)
Utility Furniture and Fashion 1941–1951 (London, Geffrye Museum, 1974)
A Choice of Design 1850–1980: Fabrics by Warner & Sons Ltd (Braintree, Warner & Sons, 1981)
The Way We Live Now: Designs for Interiors 1950 to the Present Day (London, Victoria and Albert Museum, 1978)

British design collections

It is all very well to read the books and see the pictures and sort through the transparencies: but British design history has another vital element. It is, after all, a question of *objects*. There is no substitute for looking at the thing before you. Ten minutes spent examining a Gimson sideboard tells you more about the Arts and Crafts than reading the most conscientious of dissertations. Once you see, face to face, a 1930s Ekco radio set, designed in modern style by Wells Coates or Serge Chermayeff, you begin to realise why, in their time, these designs appeared quite so startling, so exciting. Look at a Race chair and you can understand the Festival of Britain. The sense of immediacy is sometimes quite uncanny. To get the sharpest impression of the work of some of this century's most innovative and influential of designers, the high British design movement this book has been describing, it is worth searching it out in the museums and the galleries, the archives and the salerooms, as well as some of the historic houses of this period, in which British design can be viewed in total context. It is, for instance, revealing and inspiriting to watch the meticulous attention to detail in Lutyens' grand design for Castle Drogo; or to have a vista of Elizabeth Peacock's Dartington Hall banners, one of the great craft commissions of this century, hanging in the big romantic space for which they were intended.

The practical problems entailed in any survey of British design have already been outlined in the introduction, for we still lack a coherent national modern design collection. This list has no claims to be exhaustive; but it may suggest a few good starting-points. I have asterisked some collections I especially recommend.

Where the majority of the collection is usually on show and normally accessible, this has been categorised '*Public collection*'.

Where part of the collection is on show and some in store, this has been labelled '*Public/Study collection*'. Viewing the study collection will entail advance arrangements.

Where the category is '*Study collection only*', this indicates that, while serious researchers are allowed in, by arrangement, the casual visitor will not be welcomed.

In any case, in these days of curtailed grants and cut-down staffing, it is always wise, before embarking on a special journey, to check what opening hours will be, and which exhibits visible.

Bath

Crafts Study Centre, Holburne Museum,
University of Bath, Great Pulteney Street,
Bath, Avon
Public/Study collection*

A relatively new collection, opened in 1977, and still very much evolving, which at present concentrates on the period from 1920 to 1940, giving a unique insight into the development of British crafts between the two World Wars. The idea developed from discussions among craftsmen and crafts enthusiasts from the older generation who felt there should be some focal point where the work of major artist-craftsmen of this century could be seen and studied in depth. The Centre is sponsored by the University of Bath and occupies part of the Holburne Museum, with exhibition and study areas purpose-designed by Neville Ward. The basis of the collection, which has been built up mainly through donations, many by the craftsmen themselves, consists of craft pottery, woven and printed textiles, calligraphy and furniture. Its highlights are the collection of almost 100 pots given by Bernard Leach himself and spanning his whole life's work; the marvellous hand-block prints of Phyllis Barron and Dorothy Larcher from the 1920s and 1930s; a substantial collection of Ethel Mairet's weaving, together with a great deal of useful source material, samples, notebooks, letters, photographs, from Ethel Mairet's workshop. It is the policy of the Centre, consistently and thoughtfully carried out, to focus attention on interesting areas hitherto neglected, such as the lady weavers of the 1920s; and a succession of changing exhibitions both reflects and stimulates research in progress.

Beaminster

Parnham House, Beaminster, Dorset
Historic house open to public

John Makepeace, the furniture designer, moved into Parnham House, a historic Dorset mansion of great interest and beauty, in 1977. Parnham houses (in some style) the John Makepeace School for Craftsmen in Wood, a charitable foundation which trains young craftsmen, and also contains John Makepeace's own workshops, making one-off furniture to special commission. These workshops are on public view, together with changing displays of Makepeace furniture, much of it en route to customers and exhibitions, and frequent displays of work by other craftsmen. A friendly, eventful, very optimistic enterprise.

Bedford

The Cecil Higgins Art Gallery,
Castle Close, Bedford
Public/Study collection

In recent reorganisations at Bedford, the late nineteenth-century collection has, they say, been arranged in room settings 'to evoke the atmosphere of a late Victorian family home'. Some family home: for the main source for this collection was the famous, rich, exotic, highly personal selection of Victorian and Edwardian *objets d'art* amassed with such devotion by Charles and Lavinia Handley-Read, fanatic collectors of that period, and dispersed in 1972, after their tragic deaths. The emphasis is on the strange and the flamboyant: good metalwork; magnificently eccentric pottery, Doulton, Martin Brothers, Minton, Elton, superlative De Morgan. The general idiosyncrasy extends to the supporting collections: even Gimson and Voysey appear at their least straightforward. There are newly-acquired pieces of John Paul Cooper metalwork, and continuing the tradition of flamboyance on into modern pottery, a 'Fish and Tulips' bowl by Alison Britton, purchased in 1980. For me, the *pièce de résistance* of the collection is the delicate and yet spectacular embroidered screen with entwined floral decoration designed by William Morris or perhaps his daughter May.

Bibury

Arlington Mill Museum,
Bibury, Gloucestershire
Public collection

In this country-life museum in a restored mill-building in Bibury, the village William Morris once designated the most beautiful in England, there is a large room full of Arts and Crafts furniture, including, rather touchingly, Ernest Gimson's work-table (just as unpretentious as one might imagine). The extremes of Cotswold furniture are illustrated nicely by the Peter Waals walnut cabinet, smug, grandiose and splendid, and the Sidney Barnsley dresser, ostentatious in its plainness. Which, one might well wonder, was the real Cotswold style?

Birmingham

City Museum and Art Gallery,
Chamberlain Square, Birmingham
Public/Study collection

The Birmingham City collections have two main specialist areas: textiles and metalwork. The full scope of the holdings of Morris & Co. textiles, including not only the large narrative tapestries designed by Burne-Jones but also the vast and glorious variety of printed and woven Morris fabrics, was revealed in the 1981 exhibition 'Textiles by William Morris and Morris & Co.', much the largest exhibition on this subject ever organised. There is normally a good semi-permanent display of metalwork at Birmingham for although the quantity, and quality, of pieces actually owned is disappointing, there has been some judicious borrowing, and it is possible to trace in an interesting way the influence of the Arts and Crafts silversmiths on Birmingham trade metalwork. The local connection is also very evident in the large collection of Ruskin Art Pottery, from the works founded in 1898 in Smethwick. The Martin Brothers and De Morgan are well represented, the latter with a collection of 150 pieces recently acquired. Although, as in most national civic collections, there are few acquisitions from the post-Edwardian period, and furniture has been almost totally ignored, connoisseurs of British crafts c.1980 will be delighted to discover a new gallery of craftwork purchased for Birmingham by West Midlands Arts under the title 'A Certain Style', showing the work of such modern artist-craftsmen as the furniture-maker Fred Baier, the silversmiths Michael Lloyd and Malcolm Appleby, the potters Elizabeth Fritsch and Glenys Barton, the weaver Roger Oates.

Braintree

Warner & Sons Ltd,
2 Anglia Way, Chapel Hill, Braintree,
Essex
Study collection only

Warner & Sons have been energetically cataloguing and rearranging their large archive, which covers Warners' production of woven and printed furnishing fabrics from the mid-nineteenth century to the present day. Warners' is an interesting example of a firm which has always had a dual design policy: a consistently safe traditional bourgeois output as the background to a succession of fabrics commissioned from the avant-garde designers of the period, such as Godwin and Mackmurdo in the late nineteenth century and Marion Dorn in the 1930s. Marianne

Straub has worked regularly for Warners' in the post-World War II period. Alec Hunter, son of Edmund Hunter of the St Edmundsbury Weaving Works, was Warners' design manager from 1932 until his death in 1958. He was the subject of an exemplary small-scale exhibition organised recently by Warners', one of a series of travelling exhibitions based on material from the archive.

Brighton

Art Gallery and Museums and The Royal Pavilion, Brighton
Public collection*

Adjacent as it is to the Brighton Royal Pavilion, the ultimate expression of the whimsical tradition in British design history, one might have predicted the Art Gallery collection would determinedly avoid the dull and deadpan, and it is in fact an inspiringly eclectic gathering-in of the decorative arts, English and Continental, between 1890 and 1960, with the emphasis (so far) on the pre-World War II period. The collection is laid out very stylishly, along with contemporary paintings and sculpture. The qualities of British design – well represented by some fine pieces of Voysey and the dining-room suite designed by Charles Rennie Mackintosh for the Bassett-Lowke country cottage – are pointed up by their proximity to the work of Gallé, Majorelle and Bugatti. The recent, and generous, Robertson Gift of *art nouveau* includes some excellent Arts and Crafts metalwork. But, from the point of view of British designers, the strength of the collection is really in the furniture, and in particular, perhaps, in two exceptional 1920s pieces: the architect's table in oak by Frank Brangwyn which marvellously exemplifies the continuing Arts and Crafts tradition, and the walnut and macassar ebony buffet (see illustration no.110) designed in 1928 by Serge Chermayeff which shows British design taking quite a different turning. It is worth a trip to Brighton to see those alone.

Bristol

City Art Gallery, Queen's Road, Bristol
Public/Study collection

Bristol, the birthplace of E.W.Godwin, is, suitably, the place to go for Anglo-Japanese. The Art Gallery collection includes a group of 13 pieces of furniture designed by Godwin for Ellen Terry, bequeathed by their daughter Edith Craig. There is also some interesting furniture by Marcel Breuer, designed for Crofton Gane's Bristol house in the mid-1930s when Breuer worked in England, and a few examples of Utility. Art and studio pottery is reasonably well represented, with some especially good Staite Murray pieces in the loan collection. The metalwork has recently been greatly boosted by loans from the very perspicacious private collection of *art nouveau* and Arts and Crafts metalwork formed by a local expert, Dr K.C.P.Smith.

Broadway

Gordon Russell Ltd, Broadway, Worcestershire
Study collection only*

The Gordon Russell collection, a small museum section within the Broadway factory, is, in a way, my favourite of all design collections. It says so much about not just the evolution of Gordon Russell furniture but also the whole Gordon Russell design ethos, the tradition of the Cotswolds, the British design story. It has never been a formal, academic kind of collection but a collection which has accumulated very much at random, and this gives it a wonderful sense of authenticity. There are very good examples of all Gordon Russell periods, from the Arts and Crafts phase of the early 1920s to the 1930s' almost-international modernism, including the notorious Gordon Russell boot cupboard which, according to Pevsner, marked the turning-point in style. Later designs are to be seen not in the museum but in the factory showroom; some of the designs we now regard as post-World War II classics are in fact very much still in production. Besides the furniture, there is of course a collection of R.D.Russell's famous Murphy radio cabinets.

Cambridge

Fitzwilliam Museum,
Trumpington Street,
Cambridge
*Public/Study collection**

The Fitzwilliam Museum, for me, comes near perfection: in size, in atmosphere, in its discriminating collecting, it is surely everything a museum ought to be. The Fitzwilliam has particular links with Morris and associates through Sydney Cockerell, its Director from 1908 to 1937. Cockerell had previously been Secretary to the Kelmscott Press and a kind of right-hand man William Morris, and the Morris collection at the Museum is, not surprisingly, remarkable: especially the printing, but also the furniture and textiles which were memorably brought together in the Fitzwilliam exhibition 'Morris & Company in Cambridge' in 1980. Though the collection on the whole is at its strongest in the Arts and Crafts period, including a few pieces of quite interesting metalwork, the small, but discerning, selection of studio pottery – Martin Brothers, Leach, Staite Murray, Coper, Rie, Mary White, Colin Pearson – continues to the present day.

Kettle's Yard,
Northampton Street,
Cambridge
*Public collection**

Kettle's Yard began as a private collection made by Jim Ede, art connoisseur, author of the important book on Gaudier-Brzeska, and his wife Helen. These were the things they lived with. The collection is now administered by the University of Cambridge, but Kettle's Yard retains an intense, indeed an almost ghostly, atmosphere of domesticity in which the paintings, sculptures and works of craft mingle in immaculately casual near-to-real-life room sets. Some excellent pottery: Leach, Staite Murray, Katharine Pleydell-Bouverie, Robin Welch; engraved glass by David Peace; a rug by Roger Oates. A strange and slightly magic place.

Chagford

Castle Drogo, nr Chagford, Devon
National Trust House

Castle Drogo, the last of the Great Houses, was built by Sir Edwin Lutyens for Julius Drewe, Home and Colonial Stores tycoon, between 1910 and 1930. This colossal building, breathtakingly sited high above a gorge on a massive granite outcrop, is amazing not only for the total grandiosity of Lutyens' concept but also for his near-obsessive zest for detail which makes much twentieth-century design look namby-pamby. Even his design for a dish-rack in the kitchen is, in itself, a *tour de force*.

Cheltenham

Art Gallery and Museum,
40 Clarence Street, Cheltenham,
Gloucestershire
*Public collection**

The Cotswolds were the main rural outpost of Arts and Crafts activity at the turn of the century, and this is well reflected in the Cheltenham collection, built up gradually since the 1930s, which now has some magnificent examples of the period. The substantial collection of furniture by Sidney Barnsley and Ernest Gimson covers the whole spectrum from the very basic ash ladderback chairs, much used in simple life, to the grander, more ornate and intricately inlaid display pieces. There is some marvellous metalwork by Gimson, and the collection is backed up by a great many working drawings. A very impressive recent acquisition is the large Ward Higgs collection of furniture by Voysey, including the Swan chair and the Kelmscott Chaucer cabinet: especially interesting in the Cotswold context for it shows what was, in some ways, quite an opposite approach.

The Museum has pursued an enterprising policy in the past few years of important exhibitions of Cotswold-orientated Arts and Crafts: 'Good Citizens' Furniture, The Work of Ernest and Sidney Barnsley' in 1976; 'C.R.Ashbee and the Guild of Handicraft' in 1981.

Dudley

Broadfield House Glass Museum,
Kingswinford, Dudley, West Midlands
Public collection

The top two rooms of this new museum, a suburban department of Dudley Art Gallery, concentrate on the glass of the past century: mainly late nineteenth-century industrial production of the Stourbridge area, but also, increasingly, modern studio glass from the growing number of British craft glass workshops.

East Grinstead

Standen, East Grinstead, Sussex
National Trust House

Standen was built by Philip Webb, the father figure of Arts and Crafts architects, in 1894. It is a picturesque and pleasant building, perhaps a bit more quirky than one might have expected from the man who liked his work to appear absolutely ordinary, but predictably full of the special atmosphere, the peculiar combination of the rich and decorative with the pure and the highminded, which was such a feature of that period in design. It does much for one's understanding of the movement to see the Morris & Co. furniture and carpets in situ, rather worn, and the Morris wallpaper, some of it original, some more recently reprinted by Sanderson's using the old blocks. Around the house, there is much decorative pottery, especially De Morgan; lamps by Benson; furniture designed by Ashbee for the Guild of Handicraft: a coherent, vivid collection gradually being added to by the very knowledgeable National Trust tenant at Standen, Arthur Grogan.

Exeter

Royal Albert Memorial Museum,
Queen Street, Exeter
Public collection

The craft collection – pottery and glass – was begun at Exeter in the early 1940s with a large gift from the Contemporary Art Society. It covers the great modern potters, Leach, Staite Murray, Cardew, Pleydell-Bouverie; and it also has a local bias, with contemporary work from such south-western potters as Marianne de Trey, Peter Starkey and Svend Bayer.

Gateshead

Shipley Art Gallery,
Prince Consort Road, Gateshead,
Tyne and Wear
Public collection

The collection at Gateshead is a very good example of a growing national trend: the gradual building up of modern crafts collections with the help of Regional Arts associations. The Permanent Collection of Contemporary British Craft (as they call it in Shipley), established in 1976, financed partly by the local authority and partly by Northern Arts, is a deliberately general one, including pottery by Lucie Rie, Gordon Baldwin, Alison Britton, Mary Rogers; glass by George Elliott, Pauline Solven, Dillon Clarke; tapestry by Archie Brennan; and a good selection of modern jewellery. Much of the work is being bought direct from craftsmen, and some has been specially commissioned for the collection.

Glasgow

Art Gallery and Museum,
Kelvingrove, Glasgow
Public/Study collection

All C.R.Mackintosh's major buildings are in Glasgow, and so are the main public collections of his work. The Kelvingrove Museum houses the furnishings from the Ingram Street Tea-Rooms, from the tables and chairs, in considerable variety, down to the specially-made silverplated cutlery. The Museum has embarked on an interesting policy of collecting furniture in the form of room-sets, with the intention of eventually displaying the history of modern interior design from the Mackintosh period to the present day. So far, among their acquisitions is furniture designed in the early 1900s for a house in Birmingham by Edward Taylor, a Glasgow designer contemporary with Mackintosh, the husband of the illustrator Jessie King; and also the bedroom and lounge furniture from a house in Southgate designed in the late 1920s. The bedroom is by E.Arthur Brown; the lounge by Gordon Russell, including an excellent Marian Pepler carpet.

Hill House, Helensburgh, Glasgow
*House owned by the Royal
Incorporation of Architects in Scotland,
open to the public**

Hill House, a lovely building in best Mackintosh-suburban, commissioned by the publisher Walter Blackie in 1902, is one of the best places to see Mackintosh's furniture, as an essential part of his interior. Hill House is, in a sense, a building of extremes: the white bedroom, the black drawing room; the quickly-changing spaces of the corridors and stairways; the elongated forms; startling motifs of decoration. It is full of surprises, down to the smallest detail. But the final impression is anything but restless. The house has great coherence, an extraordinary stillness of atmosphere, romantic and evocative. It is nicely cared for, and a joy to wander through.

Glasgow School of Art,
Renfrew Street, Glasgow
Study collection only*

Much the most spectacular example of Charles Rennie Mackintosh in action is this amazing building. It was designed by Mackintosh, in two phases, between 1897 and 1909, and it is still very much a working art school. It shows all Mackintosh's guiding principles of structure and decoration at their most impressive and also their most subtle: it is a building of immense sophistication. Besides the well-known landmarks – the Director's Room, the 'Hen Run', the much-photographed, much-televised tall, galleried School Library – and the many built-in details, ironwork and clocks and furniture, which give the School of Art its extraordinary character, a separate collection of furniture by Mackintosh has gradually accumulated, through a sequence of gifts from Mackintosh aficionados, and a few perceptive purchases by the School itself. The furniture is kept, in pleasantly informal setting, in the Mackintosh Room within the Art School, and it is an especially rewarding collection, with some marvellous pieces of early Mackintosh in the 'Spooky School' style so much derided by contemporary mainstream English Arts and Crafts designers.

Hunterian Art Gallery,
The University, Glasgow
*Public collection**

The largest and most highly representative collection of Charles Rennie Mackintosh's work is owned by the University of Glasgow. The basis of the collection was acquired in the mid-1940s and, with the addition of later gifts and purchases, it now amounts to over 600 drawings, watercolours and designs as well as more than 60 pieces of furniture. But it is only recently, with the opening of the University's new Hunterian Art Gallery, that this major collection has been put on show. The purpose-designed Mackintosh wing at the Hunterian, opened in 1981, is in effect a curious kind of reparation for the destruction by the University of 78 Southpark Avenue in Glasgow, which had been the Mackintoshes' house from 1906 to 1913: the University had kept and stored much of the interior, and the original panelling and fitted furniture has been used to make a facsimile reconstruction of 78 Southpark Avenue at the Hunterian. Reinstated in the room in which he used to sit at it is Charles Rennie Mackintosh's own writing cabinet, sold at Sotheby's for the record sum of £89,200, in 1979, and later bought back by Glasgow University after a public appeal. Besides the important Southpark Avenue material, there is the well-known white bedroom furniture from Mains Street, and Mackintosh furniture exhibited, and much acclaimed, in turn-of-the-century Vienna and Turin. The complete suite of rather later bedroom furniture, designed in 1919 for the Bassett-Lowke house, 78 Derngate, Northampton, shows Mackintosh's style in what might have been a striking stage of evolution, half way to modernism. But alas this was to be his last sizeable commission.

Guildford

The Watts Gallery,
Compton, near Guildford, Surrey
Public collection

G.F.Watts, alias 'England's Michelangelo', was one of the most highly-revered Victorian painters, and his wife Mary, also an artist, was very much embroiled in the Home Arts and Industries activities of the late nineteenth century. Shortly before Watts' death in 1904, she started her own local rural industry, the Potters' Art Guild, and the wares of the Guild were sold commercially, notably through Liberty's. Their Celtic-motif garden pots won prizes in their day. In and around the Watts Gallery at Compton there are examples of Potters' Art Guild work, but the best display of all is at the nearby Compton Mortuary Chapel, designed by Mary Watts, with terracotta decorations carried out by the villagers under her direction. The interior of the Chapel is ornate and very complex, Art and Crafts at its most vivid and symbolic. Mary Watts herself described it as 'glorified wallpaper'. She greatly underestimated its effect.

210

Hove

Museum of Art,
19 New Church Road, Hove,
Sussex
Public collection

Augmenting their major collections of eighteenth- and nineteenth-century ceramics,
Hove Museum has a small but steadily growing group of modern studio pottery –
by Lucie Rie, Quentin Bell, Joanna Constantinides, Derek Davies, Jacqueline
Poncelet and other practitioners, some local – and a few good pieces of
contemporary glass.

Kendal

Abbot Hall Art Gallery,
Kendal, Cumbria
Study collection only

In twentieth-century handmade woodwork, there have been two main lines of
descent: the Gimson/Barnsley line which descends to Edward Barnsley and the
craftsmen who trained with him, including Alan Peters; and the Romney Green
tradition which goes down to Stanley Davies (of the two, the Romney Green is the
most strongly intellectual). The Abbot Hall Art Gallery has been most fortunate in
recently acquiring a collection of choice pieces of Stanley Davies furniture. Davies
worked for many years in Windermere, and made the bequest, which includes many
working drawings and photographs, shortly before he died in 1977. The Museum
also owns a few examples of furniture by Simpson's of Kendal, local craft
workshops who made furniture for C.F.A.Voysey (among others); and it is hoped
that these two complementary collections will eventually be seen on permanent
display together.

Lechlade

Kelmscott Manor,
Kelmscott, nr Lechlade, Oxfordshire
*House owned by the Society of
Antiquaries of London, regularly, but
infrequently, open to the public**

Kelmscott Manor was Morris's ideal style of building: unpretentious yet dignified
Cotswold vernacular with stone roofs and wide gables and great yew trees in the
garden. Although in the beginning his tenancy there was ill-fated and unhappy, for
he shared the building with Rossetti, a most uneasy ménage, he grew to love it more
and more as he got older, and his daughter May lived on there until she died in
1938. Kelmscott, in recent years, has been extremely well restored by the Society of
Antiquaries. It is full of atmosphere. It is also full of treasures: paintings by
Rossetti; furniture by Philip Webb and the box-like green-painted bedroom furniture
designed by Ford Madox Brown at his most workmanlike. The chief glory of the
collection at Kelmscott is the superb embroidery, the best assembly anywhere of
hangings, covers, curtains, designed and (mostly) carried out within the Morris
family: from the famous 'Daisy' hanging worked by William and Jane Morris not
long after their marriage to the magnificent bed curtains designed by May Morris
for her father a few years before he died.

Leeds

Lotherton Hall,
Aberford, near Leeds, West Yorkshire
Public collection*

The most interesting modern craft collection in the north, indeed I think the best in
any civic gallery, is centred at Lotherton Hall, a not, in itself, especially distinguished
Edwardian country mansion given to Leeds by Sir Alvery and Lady Gascoigne in
1968. With the house came a generous endowment, which has allowed Leeds City

211

Art Gallery, which administers the house, to build up a considerable collection not only of pieces from the late Victorian and Edwardian periods – a fine Gimson corner cupboard was an early acquisition – but also contemporary crafts and modern fashion, assembled with great expertise and sense of style. The ceramics are especially impressive: some very good examples of Fritsch, Britton, Rie, Coper, Glenys Barton; and a charming series of 'Lotherton Hall' tiles in porcelain, incised and painted by Kate Wickham. The modern collection has a few exceptional textiles – a particularly beautiful Eng Tow quilted hanging – and a sensitive selection of modern furniture from Fred Baier, Eric de Graaf and David Colwell. The excellent Museum Shop furniture, and furnishings and showcases for the new Oriental Gallery, were specially commissioned from Jack Hardy, whose workshops are in Penistone, nearby.

Leicester

Leicestershire Museum and Art Gallery,
New Walk, Leicester
*Public/Study collection**

Ernest Gimson, the most influential furniture designer of this century, was born in Leicester, and the very large collection of his work at the Leicestershire Museum began in the year of his death, 1919, when Gimson's widow presented his drawings for the new federal capital of Australia (not built: or, anyway, not built as Gimson planned it). The nucleus of Gimson relatives and patrons around Leicester have been generous in giving examples of his work and the work of Gimson's colleagues, with the result that Leicester now has one of the two major national collections of the furniture of Gimson, Sidney and Ernest Barnsley and Peter Waals. (The other major collection is at Cheltenham, *q.v.*) Leicester owns a number of prize pieces, several of which are illustrated in this book: for instance Gimson's superb macassar ebony cabinet inlaid with mother-of-pearl (on page 69); the massive three-sided plain oak cupboard with brass handles which belonged to Harry Peach (page 73); Ernest Barnsley's mediaevalist oak chest with light oak floral inlay (page 64). Besides, you will find many smaller, less obtrusive pieces, still impeccable in detail, which tell you a great deal about the Gimson way of doing things. There is some of Gimson's plasterwork, embroidery and metalwork; and the whole collection is described and illustrated in Annette Carruthers' very good and careful catalogue.

Liverpool

Merseyside County Museums,
William Brown Street,
Liverpool
Public/Study collection

Merseyside is becoming a serious centre for the study of twentieth-century studio ceramics. The Museum for some years has had a reasonable coverage of the early period (Ruskin, Doulton, Della Robbia) and the 1920s and 1930s (Charles Vyse, Reginald Wells, Bernard Leach, Katharine Pleydell-Bouverie). More recently, with the help of the Crafts Council, the Museum has begun buying steadily from modern potters (Batterham, Fritsch, Caiger-Smith, Ewen Henderson, Michael Cardew, Mary Rogers), and expanding their ceramics-orientated study services. A changing selection of twentieth-century studio and workshop pottery is always on display.

Williamson Art Gallery and Museum,
Slatey Road, Birkenhead
Public collection

The Della Robbia pottery company, founded in Birkenhead in 1894 by Harold Rathbone, was one of those poignantly short-lived enterprises of the Arts and Crafts period, age of high ideals. It was probably hoping for too much to start reworking the aesthetic principles of Italian Renaissance pottery in turn-of-the-century Birkenhead. The pottery closed down again in 1906, in financial trouble. But not without producing some memorable pottery, Italianate but also very English, strong, flamboyant, a good collection of which is at the Williamson, a suitable tribute to a unique local venture.

London

Crafts Council,
12 Waterloo Place, London SW1
Study collection, a large proportion of which is frequently on exhibition around the country*

One of the original ideas when the Crafts Advisory Committee (which became the Crafts Council) was founded in 1971 was to earmark a proportion of its funds for actually purchasing work from modern craftsmen. The resulting collection, which is rapidly expanding, with a total at present of around 600 objects, is intended to be a working collection, for use for loans to museums and arts centres and for special exhibitions. It is (unlike the collection at the Bath Crafts Study Centre, which tends to concentrate on the between-wars period) emphatically a contemporary collection: its earliest objects are two bowls by Lucie Rie which date from the mid-1950s, and most of the collection in fact consists of pieces from the 1970s and 1980s, selected – and, needless to say, severely argued over – by a changing committee of these same modern craftsmen. The committee's main guide-line is that of quality, to buy the best they can, and on the whole this works effectively. Almost all the major names in contempory crafts are represented by some quite distinguished pieces: which is surely as much as one can hope for (maybe more). The collection's shortcomings in fact are mainly technical. Furniture, one feels, is rather under-represented, presumably because of storage and transport problems. Metalwork, as in so many modern collections, is meagre; though the Crafts Council jewellery collection is a strong one. It is perhaps, however, an accurate reflection of the state of British crafts that the silversmiths and glassmakers are poorly represented compared with the producers of textiles and ceramics. Good weavers and good potters are much thicker on the ground.

Geffrye Museum,
Kingsland Road, London E2
Public/Study collection

This original and intriguing museum, housed in the now vacated eighteenth-century almshouses of the Ironmongers' Company, has a permanent display of period rooms showing the development of the middle-class British home from about 1600 onwards. The sequence of the styles includes a room of furniture by Voysey, genteel Arts and Crafts in ambience. (Whistler once denounced an interior by Ashbee as an example of the disastrous effect of art upon the middle classes: he might well have done the same for Voysey.) Another bourgeois room has furniture by Gordon Russell, in the played-down modern style of Broadway, Worcs., in the 1930s. It is to be hoped that the powers at the Geffrye soon decide to disinter Utility, of which they have an excellent collection in the basement, to make a room which shows the English style in wartime. It was at the Geffrye that the first retrospective exhibition of Utility was held in 1974.

Goldsmiths' Hall,
Foster Lane, London EC2
Study collection, some of it on show to
the public during exhibitions*

The Worshipful Company of Goldsmiths has much the largest and by far the most remarkable collection of modern British silver in the country, built up assiduously from the 1920s onwards first by George Hughes, Art Secretary and later Clerk to the Company, and then by his son Graham, who was Art Director from 1953 to 1981. Though the Goldsmiths' Hall collection is relatively thin on the late Victorian and Edwardian periods, apart from some good Dresser and a lovely double-handled silver sugar bowl by Ashbee, it comes into its own in the mid-1920s, with superb pieces by Gleadowe, H.G.Murphy, Harold Stabler and, a classic of its period, the Goldsmiths' Hall cigar box in grey shagreen designed by John Paul Cooper (this is illustrated on page 93). The post-war collection is equally impressive. The Goldsmiths' Company carried on its policy of commissioning pieces from the leading modern craftsmen, and 1960s silversmiths – Gerald Benney, David Mellor, Robert Welch – are well represented not only by their specially commissioned one-off pieces, some of them spectacular, but also by their metalwork designs for mass production. This means that, as well as being a main source for modern silverwork, the Goldsmiths' Company has an interesting collection of early British modern stainless steel.

Heal & Son Ltd,
196 Tottenham Court Road,
London W1
Study collection only

In a rooftop storeroom, high above its sales floors of modern furniture, Heal's keep a small collection of historic furniture, which is occasionally brought out on exhibition. It contains good examples of all the main Heal periods: Heal Arts and Crafts style of the 1890s/1900s (see the plain and simple washstand on page 67, part of the Heal collection); Heal DIA-functional of the post-World War I era; the fumed oak furniture of the later 1920s, when Heal designs were turning a bit more neo-Georgian; the Heal modernist phase; a few 'contemporary' pieces. An important little collection, unique and very personal.

Kingston upon Thames Museum
and Art Gallery,
Fairfield West, Kingston upon Thames
Public/Study collection

Kingston acquired the prestigious Ernest Marsh ceramics collection in 1945. Ernest Marsh was a great expert in this area, and he had collected some wonderful examples of English studio pottery, from Fishley of Fremington and Cox of Mortlake to Wells of Chelsea, Bernard Leach, William Staite Murray. The greatest part of the collection is the Martinware: almost 80 pieces, not so much grotesques as jugs and vases, jars and teapots, chosen with a connoisseur's discrimination. It seems, to say the least, a pity that 35 years after the acquisition of a collection of this stature only a small proportion is on public exhibition.

Leighton House Art Gallery and
Museum,
12 Holland Park Road, Kensington,
London W14
Public collection

The house where Lord Leighton used to live is one of the most fantastical, romantic buildings in London. The authentically reconstructed Arab Hall, designed as an integral part of the building by the architect George Aitchison, is an amazing spectacle, in which the genuinely oriental tiles shipped in by Lord Leighton and his friends from Rhodes, Damascus, Cairo and so on, are mingled with the quasi-Oriental work of the Arts and Crafts designers Walter Crane and William De Morgan. Besides his tiles (in situ), there is a very large (and more free-standing) collection of De Morgan's highly decorative pottery, presented to Leighton House by Mrs Perrin, a long-term De Morgan admirer and supporter, and now owned by the Borough of Kensington and Chelsea. This is always on show at Leighton

House, together with the work of Leighton himself and other artists of the period, and good late Victorian furniture: a High Victorian shrine of great resplendence. As well as the Leighton House holding of De Morgan, there is a substantial collection in the keeping of the London Borough of Hammersmith and Fulham, at Fulham District Library; but this is a study collection, and access is very limited. The large and particularly splendid De Morgan Trust collection, covering the whole Chelsea – Merton Abbey-Fulham cycle, which used to be on show at Old Battersea House but which was dispersed when the London Borough of Wandsworth sold the building, is at present, sad to say, in packing cases, and plans for its future are apparently still vague.

Middlesex Polytechnic, Bounds Green Road, London N11
Study collection only

Almost by chance, in 1967, as a result of an article in *The Guardian*, Middlesex Polytechnic acquired a gargantuan collection of the work and records of the Silver Studio, one of the earliest and most prolific commercial design studios. Between 1880 and 1963, the Studio produced nearly 30,000 designs, mostly for furnishing textiles and wallpapers, but also for plasterwork, dress fabrics, metalwork, furniture, even complete interiors, some under its own name, some incognito. They could turn their hand to anything. As John Brandon-Jones commented in the foreword to the excellent (and, mercifully, quite selective) centenary exhibition organised in 1980 by the Polytechnic: 'In the Silver Studio Exhibition we can, at last, see the work of one of the greatest Ghost organisations ever to work in the field of applied art'.

Victoria and Albert Museum, Cromwell Road, South Kensington, London SW7
Public/Study collection*

For those with the stamina to seek them out through the maze of Primary Galleries, Study Collections and subterranean storerooms, the Victoria and Albert Museum has some prime examples of the work of almost all the major designers in this area in the last hundred years. The British modern collections at the V & A have, so far, had a somewhat chequered history. Though the early modern designers, the designers of the Aesthetic Movement and first phase of Arts and Crafts, have been relatively secure, in the safe keeping of a departmental network responsible for all collections up to 1900, the twentieth century has been rather an anomaly, the fief of the Circulation Department, which organised the Museum's travelling exhibitions; the modern collections only recently reverted to the individual departments, when the Circulation Department was closed down.

Because of its past history, especially the fact that collecting has tended to be focused on the special needs and pressures of current exhibitions, the collection has particular strengths in some directions – its coverage, for instance, of the work of Keith Murray, subject of an exhibition in the 1970s, is peculiarly intensive – but in other areas it can be relatively patchy. There are many signs, however, of new energy and interest in overhauling totally the modern collections at South Kensington, both the representation of industrial design and crafts from individual workshops. One useful move has been the assembly of a 20th Century Study Collection which, although displayed in a rather disconcertingly uncompromising manner, Anti-Display at its most blatant, at least helps identify the collection's strengths and weaknesses: at long last one can see what it, more or less, consists of. Plans for the imminent opening of a large new 20th Century Primary Gallery, an international design collection, 1903 to 1950, in a prestige position near the Museum entrance, together with the stimulus of activities at the Conran Foundation Boilerhouse (*q.v.*) should, within the next few years, make the V & A the obvious major centre for contemporary design: which was, after all, how Sir Henry Cole intended it. Indeed it could have important influence on how design develops in Britain from now on.

In detail, in spite of sundry oddnesses and weakness, the collections are of an extraordinary quality.

The Furniture and Woodwork Department, in the 19th Century Primary Galleries, has some wonderful pieces of Arts and Crafts, with more in the 20th Century Study Collection where the bulk of modern furniture is shown. From the early period, there are excellent examples of Godwin, Mackmurdo, Voysey, George Walton, C.R.Ashbee and a stunning Ballie Scott piano which the Museum has quite recently acquired. The Cotswold School is rather weakly represented, but there is good Heal and a positive profusion of Omega Workshops furniture. A strong collection from the late 1920s/1930s: good Isokon; an interesting dining set for mass production by the Bath Cabinet Co.; the best piece of 1930s Gordon Russell to be seen in any public collection; quite a lot from the Festival of Britain period and onwards, though so far the assortment seems to be a little random. The new craft revival furniture is represented with, for instance, a fine eccentric cabinet by Makepeace and a bench especially commissioned (to be sat on) by the V & A from Richard La Trobe-Bateman.

The Metalwork Department works to rather the same pattern, with its prize exhibits of the Victorian period on show in the 19th Century Primary Galleries; with somewhat lesser pieces and with modern metalwork in the specialised Metalwork Galleries; and, of course, with a great deal more in store. One can normally expect to find a very complete collection of late nineteenth/early twentieth-century metalwork: Dresser, Liberty, Ramsden, Benson, John Paul Cooper, C.R.Mackintosh, George Walton Cutlery (page 81). Ashbee's Guild of Handicraft is a Museum speciality, and the Birmingham Guild is well represented too. The collection has fine pieces from the Arts and Crafts enamellers; e.g. an especially superb Nelson Dawson enamelled cup and cover. In the 1920s/1930s period, although the Museum has good pieces here and there, including a fascinating Harold Stabler tea-set, the coverage on the whole is less convincing; here, the Goldsmiths' Hall collection leaves it standing. But it gathers strength once again in the post-war period, with examples of the silver of the 1950s/1960s (Robert Goodden's Festival of Britain tea-set, David Mellor's Embassy, for instance) alongside mass-produced metalwork of that same era; and some magnificent very recent pieces, an enamelled silver jug by Gerald Benney, silver candelabra by Robert Welch, specially commissioned for the Museum collection.

The Ceramics Department is, like the other collections at the V & A, extremely well endowed with designs from the late Victorian period, some of which are on show in the 19th Century Primary Galleries and some of which are displayed in the departmental collections. The Ceramics Galleries, even more than most, suffer from an *embarras de richesses*, and the juxtapositions in the overcrowded showcases can, almost by accident, prove tremendously illuminating: you find handwork cheek by jowl with industrial production, and the examples from the 1920s/1930s are, in this respect, particularly interesting. The V & A has a massive, though uneven, collection of British studio pottery, from the Martin Brothers onwards, and it is still buying. Work by very modern potters – Elizabeth Fritsch, Alison Britton and Jill Crowley, for example – have recently been added. Though the 20th century industrial glass collection is sketchy, really hardly worth the detour, there has been a steady policy of purchases in the more idiosyncratic studio glass areas, mainly from the Glasshouse group – Taylor, Solven, Tookey, Meech, Clarke, Newell – over the last few years.

The modern collection of the Textile Department at the V & A is, predictably enough, one of the strongest in the country. (The only textiles collection comparable in range and quality is at the Whitworth in Manchester, *q.v.*) At any one time, around 200 designs are on view in the Textile Study Room of the Museum, with an immense backing stock to draw on. The Aesthetic Movement, the Arts and Crafts, the modernists are all superbly well represented; the extent and the high quality of 1930s coverage was indicated in 'The Thirties' exhibition at the Hayward in 1979. (The span of the collections up to the end of the 1930s has been summarised in the weighty volume *British Textile Design in the Victoria and Albert Museum*, Vol.III, Victorian to Modern, by Linda Parry and Valerie Mendes, Tokyo, Gakka Co., 1980, with English and Japanese texts.) As at the Whitworth, the collection of post-war industrially-produced domestic textiles has been built up systematically by purchases and gifts from the progressive manufacturers, Heal's, Hull Traders, Liberty's and so on, and it can claim to be extremely comprehensive. The policy of acquisitions has been followed through right to the present day, with Designers' Guild co-ordinated textiles and the weaving and embroidery of the current crafts revival, work by Archie Brennan, John Hinchcliffe, Verina Warren, Kaffe Fassett. The most recent acquisition is a rug from Roger Oates.

Industrial Design is a bit more problematic. At the time of writing, it appears to be in a curious state of limbo. The Museum has a few key pieces of industrial design of the pioneering pre-war period, and some of these are on show (spasmodically) in the 20th Century Study Collections. But the main collection of British industrial design from the late 1950s onwards, an immensely interesting and potentially valuable hoard of past Design Centre Awards, is at present still in store, in a kind of basement no man's land, apparently unclaimed by any V & A department. One hopes that with the reorganisation entailed in opening the 20th Century Primary Gallery this unique design collection will resurface.

Meanwhile, the Prints and Drawings Department, as part of its normal policy of acquisition, has been building up an ever-growing collection of twentieth-century designers' working drawings.

Victoria and Albert Museum:
The Boilerhouse
Public/Study collection of industrial design funded and administered by the Conran Foundation

'The idea for the project arose' (as Terence Conran, its progenitor and chief financier, and Stephen Bayley, its Director, announced in 1980 in *The Designer*) 'because there didn't seem to be anywhere in the world where designers and those people who are interested in industrial design in its true sense could study a collection of products, and their related documents and back-up material.' All too true. This very admirable Conran Foundation enterprise has grandiose and optimistic plans ahead for a whole self-contained purpose-built design complex, including a museum and exhibition area, conference accommodation, a library and archives for the serious study of the design process. For the moment, the project is quite cosily ensconced at the Victoria and Albert Museum, in what used to be a genuine boilerhouse, beneath the buildings along Exhibition Road. As well as organising an exhilarating programme of public exhibitions on industrial design, the Boilerhouse sees its role as that of a collection centre for key pieces in the international history of design for mass production: intending to amass the ultimate collection of design for consumer goods, high style for the mass market. Because of its emphasis not just on finished products but on the whole process of designing, the Boilerhouse acquisitions policy is covering an immense amount of detailed back-up information: sketches, drawings, models (even models unaccepted); information on promotion and advertising; sales graphs. The whole gamut. Perhaps this brings a danger, which could well be self-defeating, of documentation obliterating product; as far as working drawings go, there is a boredom threshold which curators should be wary of. But these are early days.

**William Morris Gallery,
Water House, Lloyd Park,
Forest Road, Walthamstow,
London E17**
Public/Study collection*

Water House was the home of William Morris as a boy, and the William Morris Gallery is certainly the best place to start looking at Morris's life and work. As well as some endearing memorabilia – the steel helmet Morris used as model costume armour for the Oxford Union murals, the chair that Morris actually sat upon while weaving – the Gallery contains a large coherent display of Morris's designs for textiles and for wallpapers, arranged informatively with biographical material on Morris and his circle, together with Morris & Co. furniture and carpets, and a multitude of drawings and decorative design work. An extensive and deeply interesting collection, only a fraction of which can be shown at any one time. The William Morris Gallery also houses major British collections both of the work of that very enigmatic Arts and Crafts designer A.H.Mackmurdo – with some rare examples of Century Guild furniture and fabrics – and of Mackmurdo's life-long friend, Frank Brangwyn. Alongside the many paintings and prints by Brangwyn, there are two very impressive pieces of his furniture (one illustrated on page 109), and a whole dinner service in the 'Harvest' pattern he designed for Doulton in 1930 (see page 97).

218

Besides the well-established public collections it is often worth investigating the (by their nature) more changeable displays of modern design in London galleries and auction rooms. A growing number have begun to specialise in the design of the past hundred years. For the Aesthetic Movement and Arts and Crafts, there are almost always interesting pieces to be seen at the Fine Art Society, New Bond Street; Haslam and Whiteway, Phillips and Harris and Richard Dennis, all in Kensington Church Street (Richard Dennis is an expert in Arts and Crafts ceramics).

For the period between the two World Wars, there are now several specialist galleries which have sprung up around Motcomb Street, in the shadow of Sotheby's, Belgravia; the Chenil Galleries along King's Road is also a good hunting-place for 1920s/1930s pieces. Jeremy Cooper, Galen Place, WC1, covers design 1830 to 1940. Post-war design is, in dealer's terms, still a fairly unknown quantity, though Sotheby's, Belgravia has recently tried hard with it. Design in current production is most easily investigated at (obviously) the Design Centre in the Haymarket, and the design-orientated stores: Heal's, Liberty's and Conran.

The Crafts Council Gallery in Waterloo Place; the British Crafts Centre in Earlham Street; the Craftsmen Potters' Shop in Marshall Street; and Liberty's One-off Department are the best places to start at for contemporary crafts. See also the directory of craft galleries in *Crafts*.

Manchester

City Art Gallery,
Mosley Street, Manchester M2
Public/Study collection

The main City Art Gallery, with its very famous collection of High Victorian and Pre-Raphaelite painting, has eagerly begun to buy the objects of this period. The Gallery now shows signs of becoming a total experience in Victorian design. Its many acquisitions of the past three years, Continental and British – including a superb Liberty 'Cymric' clock, a terrific Benson kettle – have been chosen with considerable flair. The collection of Late Victorian and Edwardian art pottery, especially the Royal Lancastrian by Pilkington's, with its strong Mancunian connections, has always been impressive and appreciated; the studio pottery of later periods – Cardew and Pleydell-Bouverie from the 1930s, Waistel Cooper and Geoffrey Whiting purchased from the Red Rose Guild in the 1950s, some good Rutherston collection 1970s additions – can be seen from time to time amongst the modern paintings in the Athenaeum galleries. Also, unknown to many, Manchester possesses a remarkable Industrial Art Collection of pottery and glass produced in the 1930s, amassed devotedly and with great discrimination, year by year, from 1929 until the War. Sadly, this, the most coherent collection of its period in the country, including fine examples of Keith Murray, Susie Cooper, Truda Carter, Harold Stabler, Eric Ravilious and many others, is so far, hardly ever put on show.

Whitworth Art Gallery,
University of Manchester,
Whitworth Park, Manchester M15
Public/Study collection*

This is, on the whole, an admirable collection, in some ways a unique one, most intelligently organised. It covers the Arts and Crafts period with distinction, with some stupendous Morris tapestries and hangings, and a very good selection of Voysey, Day and Crane and lesser luminaries such as Lindsay Butterfield. There is something of a lull in the 1920s and 1930s: Ethel Mairet and Barron and Larcher are included, but machine-produced fabrics are poorly represented. The collection springs to life again in the post-war period, with a massive holding of modern printed textiles, gathered in, year by year, from the contemporary ranges of Heal Fabrics, Hull Traders, Edinburgh Weavers, Warner's, Cepea and so on; a collection of enormous future value to historians. The acquisitions seem to stop in the mid-1970s, but one hopes that this is just a minor aberration: a collection built up with such expertise and diligence must surely be continued and expanded.

Norwich

Sainsbury Centre for the Visual Arts,
University of East Anglia, Norwich,
Norfolk
Study collection, occasionally on
exhibition

The Sainsbury Centre, avant-garde symbol of the 1970s, has an extremely interesting small collection of an avant-garde symbol of the 1930s: the Isokon furniture produced by Jack Pritchard to the designs of Marcel Breuer and Walter Gropius during their brief working life in England. Part of this collection was presented by Jack Pritchard; some has been purchased by the University of East Anglia. The collection includes (how could it not do?) an original Isokon Long Chair with laminated frame in birchwood (see page 105). Now slightly battered, this is terribly evocative. The modern versions, although relatively faithful reproductions, somehow never look the same.

Poole

Poole Pottery Ltd,
Poole, Dorset
Study collection only

The potteries at Poole were at their most creative in the period between the two World Wars. In 1921, the designers Harold Stabler and John Adams joined Charles Carter and his son Cyril, owners of Poole potteries, to form a new subsidiary, Carter Stabler Adams. The designs which they produced, under the name Poole Pottery, quickly won approval in the DIA circles, and sold well at Heal's and Liberty's. Most of the shapes were the work of John Adams, most of the patterns were supplied by Truda Carter (first the wife of Adams, then the wife of Cyril Carter: the personal relationships at Poole were rather tortuous). In the public collections, Poole Pottery of this important period is quite well represented, especially at the V & A which in 1978 held an exhibition showing Poole right through the century; the exhibition catalogue is a particularly useful one. The pottery itself has now begun a collection, with a few superb examples of Truda Carter Primitive, as well as interesting pieces from the 1930s, by which time Poole was becoming much more stylish and commercial.

Portsmouth

City of Portsmouth Museums and
Art Gallery,
Museum Road, Old Portsmouth,
Hampshire
Public collection

The Portsmouth collection aims to show the development of British taste from the seventeenth century to today. No mean ambition; and, inevitably, so far, the collection is much stronger in some respects than others. But the acquisitions policy is conscientious, and where gaps are most apparent – as, for instance, in the studio pottery of the early twentieth century – the Museum is endeavouring to fill them. It also has a serious commitment to the buying of contemporary crafts. As it stands at present, the collection is at its best in its ceramics: a very generous coverage of the late nineteenth/early twentieth centuries (De Morgan, Martin Brothers, Ruskin,

Doulton, Della Robbia) and a substantial collection of modern craft pottery (not just the fairly usual Fritsch, Rie, Poncelet and so on, but more esoteric choices like Pepper, Lord and Mellon). The collection includes some interesting modern textiles (a rug by John Hinchcliffe on loan from Southern Arts, a specially-commissioned Margaret Smitten hanging depicting the Museum in its gardens), and the furniture on show illustrates with great effectiveness the U-turn in taste from the work of Ernest Gimson, represented by a staid and beautiful inlaid dining suite, to that of Nigel Shelley, a new craftsman, whose bright-red glass-topped table, which must seem very startling to some of the more solid of the citizens of Portsmouth, was added recently, with a fifty per cent purchase grant from the V & A.

Rothbury

Cragside, Rothbury, Northumberland
National Trust House

Between 1870 and 1884, Norman Shaw built this house; or, rather, he expanded an existing weekend villa to make a stately home fit for Lord Armstrong, the great armaments tycoon. In such a grand and eclectic kind of building, self-assured yet volatile, brilliant Norman Shaw baronial, there are bound to be echoes, and many premonitions, of national traditions. Cragside, of course, is full of them: in its intrepid, and successful, combination of the Anglo-Japanese with the Old English; its overtones of High Aestheticism; its hints of coming Arts and Crafts. There is even a vast fireplace, a ten-ton marble chimney-piece exquisitely carved in florid Renaissance manner, designed by – of all people – W.R.Lethaby, Shaw's chief assistant at the time of Cragside. Strange to reflect that 35 years later Lethaby was the great prophet of 'efficiency style', founder-father of the DIA.

Sheffield

City Museums,
Weston Park, Sheffield
Public/Study collection

The main expertise in Sheffield is in Old Sheffield Plate, of which the Museum has a renowned collection. The bias of this collection is, of course, traditionalist, and seen in this context, some good pieces of Dresser, who designed for several Sheffield firms, seem all the more remarkable for their innovation. Sheffield also owns some impressive Omar Ramsden – including the great covered cup we show on page 92 – and a small collection of Sheffield modern cutlery, some from the 1930s, some from the post-war period, which could, one feels, be usefully expanded.

Silsden

Morton Sundour Museum Collection,
C.H.Fletcher (Silsden),
Airedale Shed, Silsden, Keighley,
West Yorkshire
Study collection only*

The Morton textiles firm has been the most consistently progressive in Britain in this century, through from its Arts and Crafts period – a fruitful one, with a whole succession of designs by C.F.A.Voysey – to the immensely influential Edinburgh Weavers' abstract collections of the 1930s and the large-scale printed textiles of the Festival of Britain period. The Morton Sundour archive, one of the very richest and most comprehensive modern design collections in the country, was maintained at Morton Sundour's headquarters in Carlisle (in large oak storage cupboards purpose-built by Gordon Russell) until, in the reorganisation following the takeover of the firm by Courtauld's, it was rehoused in the factory of

221

C.H.Fletcher, a Courtauld's subsidiary in Silsden. Here, perhaps indefinitely, it still is. Although the collection is in no immediate danger – it is kept in quite good order, there is no problem of access – this does, perhaps, raise fairly crucial questions about the right locations for important design collections. One sees the point about decentralisation: no one wants all major collections to be kept in London. But is there any sense, and any future, in siting a collection in a location with which it has no particular connection? The effect of this, in fact, in time could well be deadening. And, for practical purposes, for the convenience of the researchers and design students who would benefit from fairly frequent visits to the collection, isn't Silsden, in West Yorkshire, rather off the beaten track?

Southampton

Southampton Art Gallery,
Civic Centre, Southampton,
Hampshire
Public collection

Southampton has a marvellous, though not enormous, collection of the work of British studio potters of the 1920s/1930s, assembled in its period by the Very Rev. Eric Milner-White, late Dean of York, and given to Southampton, home of his father. (The other, larger half of the Milner-White collection was presented to York Art Gallery, *q.v.*). Southampton has a very good representation of Sam Haile, Bernard Leach, Charles Vyse, and especially Staite Murray, with some pots of extreme size and of great quality. More recently, to complement the Milner-White collection, the Gallery has bought some contemporary pottery.

With modern pottery at Southampton, Hove and Portsmouth, the South Coast is now a prime place for ceramicists' excursions.

Stoke-on-Trent

City Museum and Art Gallery,
Broad Street, Hanley,
Stoke-on-Trent
Public/Study collection*

The pottery collection in the new museum complex in Stoke-on-Trent is, understandably, a huge one, very catholic in feeling, not at all a purists' collection, but containing some remarkable material in each period. It has, to begin with, an exceptional selection of late nineteenth/early twentieth-century art pottery: some exquisite Pilkington, Bernard Moore and Ruskin, a definitive group of work by Edmund Elton, and many more examples, acquired early on in the Museum's history. It has the largest collection anywhere of pots by Michael Cardew, some superb ones, and work by other potters in the 1920s/1930s, in all around 500 pieces, bequeathed in 1949 by Dr Henry Bergen, friend of Bernard Leach. The Museum has also been active in buying modern craft pottery, mainly figurative, and has recently been concentrating on acquiring good examples of industrial production from the 1930s onwards, to balance its fine representation of crafts. Stoke-on-Trent is not afraid of the ephemeral and fashionable, and some mid-1950s 'Midwinter' designs by Terence Conran and Hugh Casson certainly have considerable nostalgia value. Among current acquisitions has been a useful collection of Susie Cooper pottery, both her pre-war and her post-war production, filling a small gap in British middlebrow design.

The Wedgwood Museum,
Barlaston, Stoke-on-Trent
Public collection

The Wedgwood Museum collection is historic, but in recent years it has been dawning on the Barlaston curators that the twentieth-century is part of history too, and the Museum now has some good examples of the work of Keith Murray and Eric Ravilious for Wedgwood in the 1930s, and the Coronation Mug designed by Richard Guyatt, in the idiom of Ravilious, fanciful and very British, in 1951 (p. 135).

Sudbury

Sudbury Hall, Sudbury, Derbyshire
Public collection

This collection of modern ceramics, only started in 1978, is located in the somewhat unlikely setting of Sudbury Hall, one of the richest and most lavish seventeenth-century houses in the country. It takes quite a lot to compete with Grinling Gibbons; but the ceramics collection is, at first sight, a convincing one, with pots by Coper, Rie, Ray Finch and Michael Casson, Gwyn Hanssen and Val Barry, and others, knowledgeably chosen. A collection to watch.

Swindon

Museum and Art Gallery,
Swindon, Wiltshire
Public collection

In 1974, Swindon began a collection of modern British pottery from individual workshops. Before the gentle reader exclaims 'goodness, not another', let me explain quickly that the collection was started for the perfectly good reason that the area around Swindon has a long tradition of pottery; the relationship between the Gallery and the Department of Ceramics is a close one, and potentially profitable; the collection itself, with pots by Richard Batterham, Alan Caiger-Smith, Hans Coper, Lucie Rie, Katharine Pleydell-Bouverie and others of such stature, shows all the signs of being a sound one. And yet, though Swindon, it appears, has every reason for embarking on its collection of ceramics, and pottery of course is eminently collectable (being relatively cheap, quite easily available, convenient to store and fairly simple to display), it is possible to wonder, when faced with just so many collections of ceramics up and down the country, whether modern potters are being too much boosted, perhaps at the expense of other British crafts.

Totnes

Dartington Hall, near Totnes, Devon
*Hall owned by Dartington Hall Trust,
open to the public*

Between 1930 and 1938, the weaver Elizabeth Peacock was at work on her largest and most complex commission, indeed one of the most ambitious individual craft commissions of this century. This was the weaving of ten large heraldic-abstract banners for the great fourteenth-century hall at Dartington. The banners had a functional purpose, to improve the acoustics of the Hall, to make it suitable for the many musical activities of the Dartington Foundation. The banners also had a grand symbolic aim, to glorify the purpose of the Dartington community by representing the work of the various departments of the estate. Miss Peacock took the commission very seriously. She came from her home in Sussex to visit Dartington. 'She came several times', as Dorothy Elmhirst, co-founder of Dartington, recounted later: 'She spent long quiet hours sitting alone in the Great Hall absorbing the qualities and atmosphere of the building and soon afterwards began working on the first banner.' It is very moving to see those finished banners in the Hall at Dartington, in which they still hang now.

Wolverhampton

Wightwick Manor,
Wolverhampton, West Midlands
National Trust House*

Wightwick is a house very much worth seeing as the best example of a Morris and Co. interior which is still extant. The house used to belong to the Mander family – Theodore Mander, a local magnate, began building it in 1887 – and the present Lady Mander, a devotee of Morris and his circle, lives at Wightwick, as National Trust tenant, surrounded with what is still a quite extraordinarily vivid collection of Pre-Raphaelite paintings, Morris textiles, Morris wallpapers, embroideries and tapestries mingled, in the manner of the period, with antiques and Oriental *objets d'art*.

York

Art Gallery,
Exhibition Square, York
Public collection

At York the main claim to fame is the collection of ceramics given to the City by the late Dean of York, the Very Rev. Eric Milner-White, between 1951 and 1963 (the remainder of the collection is at Southampton, *q.v.*). It is a large and also a fastidious collection, totalling about 150 pieces, dating from the 1920s/1930s, when Milner-White first began buying pots from Bernard Leach, Staite Murray, Michael Cardew, together with some very good examples of Hamada; and extending to the Dean's later purchases, examples of the work of Leach and Cardew in the 1950s. York also keeps a small group of pots by William De Morgan, and, unusual in this area, the Anglo-Japanese not being much seen north of Watford, an E.W.Godwin ebonised occasional table and a second table Godwin obviously inspired.

Index of designers

Roman figures refer to book pages, italic figures to illustration numbers

Adams, John 220; *121*
Adams, Katharine 70
Allied Industrial Designers (AID) 142, 180
Appleby, Malcolm 205; *212*
Ashbee, C. R. 22–3, 24, 26, 28, 42, 50, 62–3, 65, 69, 71–2, 84, 99–101, 208, 216; *65, 67*
Ashley, Laura 55
Aufseer (later Tisdall), Hans 112

BIB Design Consultants 151, 183
Bacon, Clive *182*
Barman, Christian *131*
Barnsley, Edward 98–9, 211
Barnsley, Ernest 8, 24, 41, 71, 103, 208, 211, 212; *48*
Barnsley, Grace *9*
Barnsley, Sidney 8, 24, 26, 41, 71, 103, 205, 208, 211, 212; *54*
Barron, Phyllis 101, 204; *11*
Bassett Gray 117
Batterham, Richard 163
Bawden, Edward 30; *158*
Bell, Vanessa 42
Benney, Prof. Gerald 30, 162, 163, 214, 216; *154, 188*
Benson, W. A. S. 74; *66*
Bernard, Oliver 50
Best, Robert *135*
Black, Prof. Sir Misha 23, 45, 46, 115, 117–20, 129, 141, 143–4, 156, 163
Blomfield, Sir Reginald 41
Blount, Godfrey 24, 71, 82
Blow, Detmar 32
Booth, David *148*
Braden, Norah 97
Brangwyn, Sir Frank 65–6, 206, 218; *99, 102, 112*
Brannam, C. H. 61
Breuer, Marcel 44, 108, 121, 206, 220; *104, 108*
Brewer, Cecil 82, 86
Brown, Barbara *21*
Brown, F. Gregory 85
Brown, Ford Madox 32, 55, 211
Burne-Jones, Sir Edward 32, 55

Capey, Reco 44
Cardew, Michael 11, 97, 101, 222
Carr, Alwyn *87*
Carter, David 28
Carter, Ronald 167, 172; *149, 209, 229*

Carter, Truda 85, 220; *10, 121*
Carwardine, G. *134*
Casson, Dinah *206*
Casson, Sir Hugh 45, 222
Casson, Michael 163
Chadwick, Hulme *174, 195*
Chamberlin, Powell & Bon *196*
Chermayeff, Serge 43, 50, 103, 115, 203, 206; *105, 110, 130*
Coates, Wells 43, 44, 50, 115, 203; *129, 133, 137*
Cobden-Sanderson, T. J. 66
Cockerell, Douglas 72, 104
Coleman, John *207*
Collingwood, Peter 162
Collins, Jesse 119
Conran Associates 142, 183–4; *28*
Conran, Terence 11, 143, 156–9, 188, 217–8, 222; *179*
Cooper, John Paul 41, 101, 204, 214; *89, 90*
Cooper, Susie 44, 101, 114, 222; *96, 136, 138, 139*
Coper, Hans 136, 162
Craig, E. Gordon 44
Crane, Walter 24, 28, 47, 53, 56, 58, 63, 66, 214–5, 219; *39*
Craven, Shirley *19, 20*
Crowley, Jill 30
Curwen, Harold 42, 91
Cuzner, Bernard *117*

DCA Design Consultants (see also Carter, David) *219, 222*
Davies, Stanley 99, 211; *85*
Dawson, Nelson 216
Day, Lewis F. 48, 55, 58, 219
Day, Lucienne 11, 58; *17, 165*
Day, Robin 131; *146, 147, 169, 178, 183*
Design Research Unit (see also, Black, Prof. Sir Misha and Gray, Milner) 45–6, 120, 141, 145, 149
Dixon, Arthur *64*
Dobson, Frank 43
Dorn, Marion 112, 205; *13*
Dresser, Christopher 50, 53, 56, 58, 221; *2, 41–5, 47*
Dunn, Geoffrey 79, 121–2
Dutton, Norbert 46

Elton, Sir Edmund 61, 204, 222
Exton, R. V. *176*

Fisher, Alexander 66
Fletcher, Benjamin 91–2; *82, 84*
Frampton, George 41
Fraser, Claud Lovat 29, 58, 85
French, Neal *157*
Frewing, Nicholas *177*
Friend, George *93, 97*
Fritsch, Elizabeth 205, 212, 217
Fry, Roger 42, 85; *100*

Gardner, James 44, 129
Gibberd, Sir Frederick 46
Gill, Eric 24, 27, 44, 50, 73, 96–7, 104
Gimson, Ernest 8, 22, 24–5, 29, 32, 41, 42, 50, 65, 71, 103, 167, 203, 205, 208, 211, 212, 221; *52, 53, 58, 75*
Gleadowe, R. M. Y. 101, 214; *93, 97, 115*
Godwin, E. W. 47, 50, 53, 54, 205, 206, 216; *29, 30, 31*
Goodden, Prof. Robert 30, 43, 44, 45, 115, 129, 159, 216; *152*
Grange, Kenneth 28, 143; *192, 201, 226, 227, 228, 230, 231*
Grant, Duncan 27, 42, 44
Gray, Eileen 49
Gray, Milner 44, 45, 46, 117, 141; *122*
Green, A. Romney 31, 99, 211; *85*
Gropius, Walter 44, 108, 220
Gurney, Michael 27
Guyatt, Prof. Richard *159*

Harvey, A. E. *118*
Hassall, D. *225*
Havilland, Sir Geoffrey de 44
Havinden, Ashley 44, 112
Heal, Sir Ambrose 25, 42, 44, 79–82, 86, 91–2, 214; *50, 78, 83, 103*
Heal, Christopher *170*
Heaton, Clement 62
Height, Prof. Frank 156, 180, 188
Henderson, Ian 107
Hepworth, Barbara 112
Heritage, Prof. Robert 11, 141, 143, 167; *184, 199, 208, 221*
Hewitt, Graily 73
Hinchcliffe, John 163, 217; *23*
Hogan, James 44, 104
Holden, Charles 88, 91
Holland, James 43

Horne, Herbert 62
Howe, Jack 43; *173*
Hunt, Martin *216*
Hunter, Alec 101, 112, 206
Hunter, Edmund 71, 206

Image, Selwyn 62
Industrial Design Partnership 117–20
Irving, Laurence 44
Issigonis, Sir Alec *175*

Jackson, Ernest 86
Joel, Betty 107
Johnston, Edward 73, 88

Kauffer, E. McKnight 104
Kinsman, Rodney 156; *181, 210*
Knox, Archibald 76; *76*

Larcher, Dorothy 101, 204; *11*
Leach, Bernard 50, 97–8, 101, 204, 222; *16*
Leach, John 163, 170
Leischner, Margaret 27, 112
Lethaby, W. R. 12, 21, 22, 24, 26, 30–1, 32, 41,
    42, 49, 65, 72–3, 86, 87–8, 221
Levy, Audrey *164*
Lloyd, Michael 163, 205
London, Noel *224*
Lutyens, Sir Edwin 49, 207

Macartney, Mervyn 41
Macdonald, Margaret *61*
Mackintosh, Charles Rennie 50, 65, 206, 209–10;
    51, 59, 60, 61, 70
Mackmurdo, Arthur Heygate 62, 100, 205, 216,
    218; *32, 35, 40*
McLeish, Minnie 85; *101*
Mairet, Ethel 27, 44, 101, 112, 204
Mairet, Philippe 101
Makepeace, John 30, 163, 170, 204; *203*
Mansfield, Leslie 91
Martin Brothers 61, 205, 214; *46*
Marx, Enid 27, 29, 101, 117, 121; *125, 127*
Mason, J. H. 44, 104
Mellor, David 27, 141, 162, 170, 214, 216; *153,
    166, 185, 186, 193, 211*
Meynell, Sir Francis 44
Moggridge, Bill, Associates 180
Moholy-Nagy, Laszlo 108
Moorcroft, William *98*
Moore, Bernard 222; *7*
Moorman, Theo 112
Morgan, Fay *25, 26*
Morgan, William De 28, 50, 53, 61–2, 204, 205,
    214–5; *1*
Morris, May 31, 32, 48, 211; *6*
Morris, William 11, 12, 22, 23, 26, 28, 32, 47, 49,
    50, 53, 55–6, 58, 61, 62, 65, 66–9, 73, 74, 76, 83,
    84, 86, 156, 166, 205, 207, 208, 211, 218, 224; *3,
    4, 34, 36, 38*
Morrison, Bryan 156

Morton, Alastair 23, 112, 120, 131
Moulton, Sir Alex *194*
Murphy, H. G. 101, 104, 214; *93, 97, 114, 115*
Murray, Keith 29, 43, 104, 114–5, 215, 223; *120,
    123, 124*
Murray, William Staite 97–8, 222

Nash, Paul 43; *126*
Nicholson, Ben 112
Nicholson, Charles 44

Oates, Roger 217; *25, 26*
Ogle, David *172*
Ogle Design 141–2; *223*
Osman, Louis 30, 162
Olejnik, Jurek 156

P A Design Unit *218*
Paterson, K. H. *167*
Peacock, Elizabeth 203, 223
Pearce, Simon *214*
Pentagram (see also Grange, Kenneth) 46, 50, 183
Pepler, Marian 209
Peters, Alan 211
Pinder, John *205*
Pleydell-Bouverie, Katharine 97, 207
Poncelet, Jacqueline *215*
Pond, Eddie *162*
Powell, Alfred 41
Prior, Edward 41, 65
Punnett, E. G. *62*
Purvis, Tom 104

Quant, Mary 156

Race, Ernest 11, 131, 203; *143, 144, 145*
Ramsden, Omar 221; *87, 88, 92*
Rathbone, Harold 69, 213; *77*
Ravilious, Eric 11, 30, 115, 121, 135, 223; *15*
Read, A. B. 44, 91, 117
Reich, Tibor *18*
Ricardo, Halsey 72
Richter, Charles 107
Rie, Lucie *160*
Riss, Egon *107*
Rooke, Noel 73
Rossetti, Dante Gabriel 32, 55
Russell, Sir Gordon 11, 12, 21, 24–5, 27, 44–5,
    49, 88–91, 92, 101, 108, 115–7, 121–2, 123–4,
    125–9, 131, 134–5, 142, 145, 151, 188, 206–7;
    79, 80, 81
Russell, Prof. R. D. 26, 30, 43, 44, 45, 106, 108,
    115–7, 167, 207; *132*
Russell, W. H. *109, 150*

Scott, Douglas *198*
Scott, M. H. Baillie 28, 216
Schultz, Robert Weir (later Robert Schultz Weir)
    31, 41
Sedding, J. D. 25, 27, 31, 41
Shaw, Norman 41, 55, 221

Sheringham, George 104
Shiner, Cyril *116*
Silver, Arthur 58, 215
Silver, Rex 76, 215
Simpson, Peter 170; *22*
Skellern, Victor 114–5
Smith, Percy Delf 44
Smith, R. Catterson 72–3
Speight, Sadie 46
Spence, Sir Basil 129
Spence, T. R. 41
Spencer, Edward *95*
Stabler, Harold 25, 27, 44, 86, 91–2, 101, 104,
    214, 216, 220; *86, 91, 113*
Starkey, Peter *213*
Stevens, Richard *168*
Stevenson, Norman *197*
Straub, Marianne 27, 112, 205–6; *12*
Street, G. E. 65
Summers, Gerald *106*
Sumner, Heywood 62
Sutherland, Graham 43

Tandy, John 112; *14*
Taylor, Edward 209
Taylor, Fred 104
Taylor, W. Howson 69
Thrower, Frank 170; *191*
Tisdall, Hans (see also Aufseer) *24*
Trobe-Bateman, Richard La *202*
Turner, Hugh Thackeray *8*

Upjohn, Howard *224*

Voysey, C. F. A. 28, 50, 62, 65, 74–6, 104, 206,
    208, 213, 216, 219, 221; *5, 49, 63, 71*

Waals, Peter 205, 212
Walker, Sir Emery *32*
Wallis, Sir Barnes 44
Walton, Allan 27, 43, 44, 112
Walton, George 76, 216; *56, 57, 72*
Ward, Mary *163*
Ward, Neville 204; *163*
Warren, E. P. 41
Waterer, John *128, 171*
Watts, Mary 78, 210
Webb, Philip 25–6, 32, 55, 65, 86, 208, 211
Webb, Roger *208*
Welch, Robert 27, 141, 162, 214, 216; *151, 155,
    156, 187, 190, 200, 217*
Welch, Robin 170, 207; *189*
White, David *157*
Wigglesworth, Peter *176*
Williams-Ellis, Clough 30, 93
Williamson, Rupert *204*
Wilson, Henry 28, 41, 65
Wyburd, Leonard F. 53–4; *55*

Zinkeisen, Anna 44

General index

Abacus *166*
Adamsez 143
Adie Brothers *113*
Aesthetic Movement 53–62, 204, 221, 224
Allied Ironfounders *172*
Alternative Design Movement 162, 163, 170,
  184–5
Anarchic Design Movement 42, 49
Anderson, Sir Colin 121
Anglepoise Lighting 117; *134*
Anti-feminism in British design tradition 48
Archer, Bruce 145, 156, 162, 185
Architectural Association 108
Architectural Review 82
Architecture, links of design with 44, 66, 103, 112
Art Furnishers' Alliance 56, 58
Art Pottery Movement 58, 61–2, 69, 76, 78, 204,
  205, 208, 210, 213, 214–5, 220–1
Art Workers' Guild 32, 41, 42–3, 47, 48, 63, 65,
  70, 72, 74
Artificers' Guild 95
Arts and Crafts Exhibition Society 32, 42–3, 63, 84
Arts and Crafts Movement 7, 11, 12, 21–2, 23–4,
  26, 28, 30 1, 32, 41–2, 47, 48, 49, 50, 53, 62–3,
  64–84, 85–6, 91, 92, 93, 100, 123, 141, 163, 170,
  183, 187, 204–224
Ashbee, Janet 24
Atlas Lighting *168*

Back-to-the-land movement 24
'Barum Ware' 61
Bauhaus 43, 44, 73, 112
Bazaar, Knightsbridge 156
Beddington, Jack 43
Bedford Park, London 55
Benham & Froud *41*
Bergen, Dr Henry 222
Best & Lloyd *135*
Binns, A. J. *227*
Birch, William *56, 62*
Birmingham Guild of Handicraft 69, 216; *64, 74*
Birmingham School of Art 155
Blake, John 145
Board of Trade 87, 107, 123–4, 126
Boilerhouse, The 9, 217–8
Boots/Timothy Whites 184
Brain, E. *122*: see also Foley China
'Britain Can Make It' exhibition, 1946 23, 125,
  126–9, 141

British Broadcasting Corporation 122; *105*
British Institute of Industrial Art 93–6
British Motor Corporation (BMC) *175*
British Rail 141; *226*
British Telecom *222*
Bucknell, Alfred *69, 75*
Burmantofts Faïence 61
Bute Fabrics 170

Camberwell School of Arts and Crafts 155
Capital goods design 151–2, 155–6, 177–80
Carpenter, Edward 24, 26
Carpet Manufacturing Co. *161*
Carrington, Noel 88, 91–2
Carter Stabler Adams 30, 85, 101, 134, 220: see
  also Poole Pottery
Celtic design influence on British tradition 65,
  82, 210
Central School of Arts and Crafts, London 72–3
Century Guild 62, 218; *32, 35, 37, 40*
Ceramic design 58–9, 69, 76, 78, 114–5, 175,
  216–7, 219, 220, 222
Chance Glass 115
Chipping Campden, Gloucestershire 26, 71–2,
  99–101
Clarke, S. *128*
Clissett, Philip 70
Cockerell, Sydney 32, 207
Coldstream Report 143, 155
Cole, E. K. 115; *129, 130, 133*
Cole, Sir Henry 216
Collins & Hayes 143; *209*
Computer-Aided Design Centre, Cambridge 152
Comyns, W. *72*
Concord Lighting *221*: see also Rotaflex
Conran Foundation 9, 217–8
Conran Furniture 143, 149; *179*
'Constructivist' fabrics 112
Cooper, Susie, Pottery 101, 114; *96, 136, 138, 139*
Cosmos Crane Co. *225*
Council for Art and Industry (Pick Council) 11,
  27, 107, 125, 187
Council of Industrial Design (COID), later Design
  Council 7, 12, 21, 23, 26, 45, 46, 107, 123,
  124–3, 131, 134–42, 145, 151–2, 164, 173, 187:
  see also Design Centre; Design Centre Awards;
  Duke's Prize for Elegant Design
Council for National Academic Awards (CNAA)
  187

Country traditions, place of in British design
  24–5, 28–9, 47, 56, 64, 70, 170, 175
Craft Revival Movement 163–70, 205, 208, 209,
  211, 212, 213, 216, 220–1, 223
Crafts Advisory Committee (later Crafts
  Council) 163–6
Crafts Council 30, 163–70, 187, 213
Crafts magazine 166
'Craftsman's Art' exhibition, 1973 166
Cranfield Institute of Technology 180
Crawford's Agency 44
Crayonne Plastics *28*
Cresta Shops 43
Cripps, Sir Stafford 126–9
'Cymric' silver 76

Dartington Glass 170; *191*
Dartington Hall, Devon 97, 203, 223
Darwin, Sir Robin 30, 45, 123, 129–31, 188
Della Robbia Pottery 69, 213; *77*
Dennis Motors *223*
Department of the Environment *193*
Department of Overseas Trade 124
Design Centre 135
Design Centre Awards (later Design Awards) 8,
  21, 123, 131, 135–41, 143, 150, 152, 156, 160,
  175, 177–80, 217
Design Council 107, 173–7, 184: see also Council
  of Industrial Design
Design education 43, 46, 72–3, 107, 129–31, 143,
  155–6, 162, 170, 180, 185, 187
Design Furnishing Contracts *182*
Design groups, corporate 117–8, 141–2
Design and Industries Association (DIA) 7, 11, 23,
  25, 42–3, 44, 46, 47, 49–50, 82, 85–93, 101, 117,
  123, 124, 131, 184–5, 187
Design magazine 135, 141, 145, 156, 162
Design management 131, 145–9, 162
Design profession, development of 43, 58, 74–6,
  103–4, 117–20, 129–31, 141–2, 149–51, 162,
  172–3, 180–4, 185, 187
Design reform movements 7, 12, 21–3, 25, 42, 45,
  74, 85–6, 92–6, 124–9, 156–9, 173–7, 187–8
Designers' Guild 217
Deutscher Werkbund 46, 47, 85
Ditchling, Sussex 24, 96–7, 99–101, 112
Dixon, James 58; *45*
Donald Brothers *22*
Dorland Hall exhibition, 1933 122

Doulton & Co. 54, 58; *99*
Doulton, Henry 58
Dresser & Holme 56
Dryad Cane Furniture Works 11, 25, 85; *82, 84*
Duke of Edinburgh's Prize for Elegant Design 133, 156
Dunbar Hay 121
Dunn's of Bromley 79, 121–2, 156

Eccles, Lord 164
Edinburgh Weavers 23, 43, 101, 112, 120, 131, 220, 221–2
Elmhirst, Dorothy 223
Engineering Design Centre, Loughborough 152
Engineering industries, design for 115–20, 139, 141, 144–5, 151–2, 155–6, 157, 177–80, 181
English landscape, place of in British design tradition 24, 30, 80
Ergonomic factors in design, recognition of 141, 144–5

Federation of British Industries (FBI) 96, 151
Feilden Reports 151
Festival of Britain, 1951 23, 30, 45, 123, 126, 129, 131, 134, 141, 188
Festival Pattern Group 131
Fine art, links of design with 32, 42, 44, 98, 103–4, 112
'Fitness for purpose' theories in British design 11–12, 21, 86–8, 93, 115–7, 143–4, 163, 185, 188
Fletcher, C. W. *71*
'Florian' pottery 76–8
Foley China 43; *122*
Folk art, cult of in British tradition 23–4, 29, 85
Foreign influence on British design 46, 47–8, 75, 89, 103, 107, 131, 141
Foxton, W. 85; *101*
Friedland 143; *197*
Furniture design 41, 76, 79–83, 98–9, 108, 123–4, 131, 151, 156, 164, 165, 167, 170, 172, 183, 204–14, 216, 218, 220

Gane, Crofton 91, 121–2, 206
General Post Office (GPO) 43; *198*
Gent & Co. *173*
Gilbey 149
Glasgow School 49, 209–10
Glass design 114, 115, 155, 170, 175, 208, 217
Glasshouse, The 217
Gloag, John 42, 48, 172
Goldsmiths, The Worshipful Company of 101, 159–62, 214
Good Furniture Group 121–2
Gorell, Lord 107
Goslett, Dorothy 149
Gray, A. E. 101; *96*
Gregynog, Powys 97
Guild movement in Arts and Crafts 22–3, 24, 69
Guild of Handicraft 22–3, 62–3, 71–2, 84, 216; *65*
Guild of St Joseph and St Dominic 96–7

HMV *131*
Habitat 53, 83, 134, 156–9, 188
Hand-and-machine bias in British design tradition 9, 24–5, 26–8, 72–3, 85, 101, 112, 131, 162
Handley-Read, Charles and Lavinia 204
Handweaving Movement 71, 101, 112, 162, 204, 223
Haseler, W. H. 76
Haslemere Peasant Industries 71, 82
Haslemere, Sussex 24, 71, 82
Hay, Athole 121
Heal Fabrics 143, 217, 220; *17, 21 165*
Heal & Son 79–83, 85, 92, 149, 156, 214, 217, 220; *50, 78, 83, 103, 170*
Helios *12*
Heron, Tom 43
Hille 112, 131, 143, 149; *146, 147, 178, 183*
Hobby Horse, The 62
Home Arts and Industries Association 210
Hornsea Pottery *216*
Howell & James 54, 61
Hughes, George 101
Hughes, Graham 101, 159–62
Hukin & Heath 58; *42, 43, 44, 47, 118*
Hull Traders 217, 220; *19, 20*

Imperial College of Science and Technology, London 180
Isokon 103, 108–12, 120, 216, 220; *104, 107, 108*

Jaeger 149
Jeffrey & Co. 55; *36*
John, Augustus 29
Jones, A. E. *94*
Jones, J. Christopher 145

Keith-Lucas Report 185
Kelmscott Press 69, 207
Kenton & Co. 41–2, 71
Kenwood Manufacturing Company *230*
Kilburn, Cecilia Dunbar (later Lady Sempill) 121
Kodak *201*

Lambeth School of Art 58
Lancer Boss *224*
Lawn Road Flats, Hampstead 44; *137*
Leicester College of Art 155
Leighton, Lord 41, 214–5
Leslie, S. C. 125
Liberty, Arthur Lasenby 48–9
Liberty & Co. 53–4, 61, 76, 78–9, 210, 216, 217; *55, 56, 68, 73, 76*
Linthorpe Art Pottery 58; *2*
Little Gallery, The 101
London County Council (LCC) Technical Education Board 72
London Decorating Co. 58
London Transport 11, 29, 43, 44, 46, 88, 101, 120, 141, 149; *125, 127*

Makepeace, School for Craftsmen in Wood, The 170, 204
Makers of Simple Furniture 106
Mappin & Webb 114
Margrie, Victor 164
Marks & Spencer 184
MARS Group 44
Marsh, Ernest 214
Melchett Awards 184–5
Merton Abbey, Surrey 53, 61
Metalwork design 76, 101, 152–3, 159–62, 170, 173, 175, 205, 206, 214, 216, 221
Microelectronics industries, design for 163, 180, 182, 188–9
Miles, Peter, Furniture 172; *229*
Milner-White, The Very Rev. Eric 222, 224
Milward *192*
Ministry of Public Building and Works 141; *185, 186*
Ministry of Reconstruction 93
Ministry of Transport 141; *193*
Minton Art Pottery 54, 58
Modern Movement, British 44, 48, 103, 108–12, 220
Monotype Corporation 27
Moorcroft Pottery 76; *98*
Morris, Marshall, Faulkner & Co. (later Morris & Company) 24, 32, 42, 45, 55–6, 62, 83, 205, 207, 208, 211, 218, 219, 224; *6, 33, 34, 36, 38*
Morton, Alexander, & Co. 74–6, 221–2; *5, 63*
Morton, James 74, 101, 112
Morton Sundour Fabrics 101, 112, 221–2
Moulton Bicycles 143; *194*
Murphy, Frank 120
Murphy Radio 115–7, 120, 207; *132*

National Association for the Advancement of Art and its Application to Industry 74, 187
National Council for Diplomas in Art and Design (NCDAD) 155
National Diploma in Design (NDD) 155
National Register of Art Designers 107
Neumann, Professor 47
New Handworkers' Gallery, The 101
Norris, S. E. *167*
Nuttgens, Dr Patrick 31, 185

Old Hall 141; *151, 155, 156, 187*
Omega Workshops 42, 85; *100*
OMK Design 156; *182, 210*
Orient Line 121; *151, 158*
Osborne-Little Wallpapers 156

Papanek, Victor 185
Parker Pen Co. *231*
Peach, Harry 25, 42, 91–2
Peasant Art tradition 24, 28–9, 71, 82–3, 86, 149, 156
Peasant Arts Society 71
Pel 112; *105, 111*
Pepler, Hilary 96

Pevsner, Sir Nikolaus 25, 46, 121, 188
Pick Council: see Council for Art and Industry
Pick, Frank 11–12, 21, 25, 27, 28, 29–30, 42, 43, 44, 46, 47, 49, 88, 91–2, 97, 107, 120, 141, 181
Pilditch, James 180
Pilkington's 222
Plush Kicker 143; *176*
Pollard, E. *112*
Polycell *180*
Poole Pottery 29, 85, 114, 220; *10, 121*: see also Carter Stabler Adams
Potters' Art Guild, The Compton 210
Primavera 134
Pritchard, Jack 44, 108–12, 120, 121, 220
Pritchard, Molly 44, 121
Pye *169*

Race Furniture 123, 131; *143, 144, 145, 177, 208*
Read, Sir Herbert 46, 122
Red Rose Guild 219
Reilly, Paul (later Lord Reilly) 151, 164
Remploy Furniture *206*
Retailing, role of in British design 53–8, 76–83, 92, 101, 121–2, 134, 156–9, 184
Reuters *228*
Roberts & Belk *119*
Rogers, John C. 103
Rose, Muriel 101
Rotaflex 180; *199*
Rothschild, Henry 134
Royal College of Art, London 26, 27, 30, 45, 72, 73, 112, 117, 121, 123, 129–31, 143, 155–6, 159, 167, 168, 180, 185, 187, 188–9
Royal Designers for Industry 27, 44–5, 104
Royal Lancastrian Pottery: see Pilkington's
Royal Society of Arts 44, 104, 149
Ruskin, John 21–2, 23, 31, 49, 62, 63, 69, 73, 91, 97
Ruskin Pottery 69, 205, 222
Russell, Gordon Furniture 9, 25, 88–91, 101, 108, 115–7, 121–2, 149, 206–7, 209, 213; *79, 80, 109, 132, 148, 150*

St Edmundsbury Weaving Works 71, 206
Samuely, Felix 46
Shand, Philip Morton 48
Sheffield City Polytechnic 155
Shell-Mex and BP 43
Shelley Potteries 114
Shine, Archie 141; *184*
Silversmithing design 76, 101, 153, 159–62, 175, 214, 216, 221
Simmonds, William 71
Simon, Herbert 91
Simple Life movement 24
Simpson, W. B. 55
Simpson's of Kendal 211
Sinclair Radionics *220*
Smith, Hamilton Temple 25, 91
Society of Industrial Artists (SIA), later Society of Industrial Artists and Designers (SIAD) 43, 44, 45, 48, 103–4, 107, 149, 184, 187

Society for the Preservation of Ancient Buildings (SPAB) 32–41, 48
Sottsass, Ettore 49
Sparkes, John 58
Spode *157*
Stanley Tools *219*
Stenning, J. W. *102*
Stephenson, John 183
Stevens & Williams 114; *124*
Strathearn Audio *218*
'Street furniture' design 139, 157, 160
Studio Pottery Movement 61–2, 97–8, 136, 162, 163, 170, 175, 204, 207, 208, 211, 212–3, 214, 217, 219, 220–1, 222, 223, 224
Studio, The 66, 76
Symbolism in British design tradition 30–1, 163, 175
Systematic methods in design, development of 145–9

Tallents, Sir Stephen 43
Tamesa Fabrics *24*
Tecton 44
Terry, Herbert *134*
Textile design 71, 101, 112, 131, 170, 205–6, 211, 215, 217, 219–20, 221–2, 223
Tomkinson's Carpets *163*
Troughton & Young 44, 117
'Tudric' pewter 76
Turnbull & Stockdale 58
Twyfords *196*

Utility Furniture 44, 101, 123–4, 206, 213; *140, 141, 142, 170*

Victoria and Albert Museum 9, 55, 129, 162, 215–8

Wakely & Wheeler *86*
Walker & Hall 141; *153*
Wallpaper Manufacturers, The *164*
Wardle, Bernard *162*
Wardle, Thomas *34*
Waring & Gillow 103; *110*
Warner & Sons 9, 112, 205–6, 220
Watt, William 53; *29, 30, 31*
Weaver, Sir Lawrence 47
Wedgwood, Josiah & Sons 11, 30, 103, 114, 223; *15, 120, 158, 159*
Weir Report 124
Westclox *200*
Wilcock & Co. 61
Wilde, Oscar 47
Wilkinson Sword *174, 195*
Wilton Royal Carpet Manufacturing Company *13*
Woollands, Knightsbridge 156
Woolworths 184
Worboys Report 157

Yardley & Co 44